The Village London Atlas

THE GROWTH OF VICTORIAN
LONDON 1822–1903

The Village London Atlas

THE GROWTH OF VICTORIAN
LONDON 1822–1903

The Alderman Press

Published by The Village Press Limited
7d Keats Parade, Church Street, Edmonton, N9 9DP.

November 1986.

First published November 1986
First reprint January 1987
Second reprint September 1988
Third reprint June 1989

British Library Cataloguing in Publication Data

The Village London atlas: the changing face of Greater London 1822-1903

1. London (England) ____________ Maps
912'.412 G1819.L7

ISBN 0-946619-26-3

Typesetting by Stone Associates, Winchmore Hill.
Printed and Bound in Gt Britain by
Staples Printers (Rochester) Limited,
Love Lane, Rochester, Kent.

Acknowledgements.

The publishers would like to thank the following for their great help during the preparation of this Atlas.

The staff of the Map Library and Photographic Department of The British Library.

Graham Dalling. Archivist for the London Borough of Enfield.

All maps reproduced by kind permission of The British Library.

Chapter I

A Victorian's view of changing London. by Percy Fitzgerald

One only has to read a few lines of Percy Fitzgerald's book – 'Victoria's London – The Suburbs' – to realise what a tremendous feeling, as well as knowledge, he had for old London. There was at that time, the 1880's and 1890's, a great welling up of nostalgia for London's past which equals that of today. Perhaps it is the almost unconcious feeling that the century is drawing to a close which brings this about, certainly there is parallel with our own time. At any rate when an introductory chapter was required for The Village London Atlas we needed to look no further than the opening chapter of Victoria's London.

The Publishers.

For the true Londoner nothing can be so pleasing as to note the affectionate interest that is now shown in the history of his much-loved city. Within a few years there has been a general revival of interest in this fascinating subject. Artists and writers have explored unfrequented quarters and forgotten lanes, in search of all that is picturesque; thus lending attraction to the magazine or to some imposing tome, such as was the predecessor of the present. It would seem as if these ardent labourers were hurrying to be in time to secure some record at least of the older monuments; indeed, it is now necessary to use all convenient speed; for every day and hour almost is bringing with it its note of coming destruction, and the paragraph "Disappearing London" recurs with alarming frequency. Every old house or old church or college may be said to be under sentence; for it "cumbereth" valuable ground. It is almost pathetic to note the fine old house in the suburbs standing in its fair gardens and lawns looking on the highroad; for it is already marked by the spoiler. Some forty or fifty years hence this rapacious greed will have wrought incalculable havoc. Business men and practical-minded persons seem to have a positive dislike to any old memorials of the kind. They would have them carted away: among the symmetrical modern structures they seem an eyesore. Soon or late, and more likely soon, there is certain to be a combined onslaught on the City churches, whose sites are coveted for palatial City warehouses, and such pressure it will be difficult to resist. When a substantial morsel of the old Roman wall is laid open to view in digging foundations, the utmost grace accorded is a day or two's delay to allow the antiquaries to come and see it.

One of the most interesting things in the study of London is the variety, the marked distinction, between the component parts that make up the great whole. We are told of the "growth of London," of the yearly absorption of outlying districts; but London has never become one homogeneous mass. Yet, in spite of all, it still remains "London City," with London Suburbs attached to it; and a continued familiarity prevents us observing how all these annexed districts retain marked characteristics of their own. A stranger taken for the first time through the various quarters could hardly fail to note their distinctive character. Thus Westminster, "Belgravia," Mayfair, Islington, Knightsbridge, St. John's Wood, the Regent's Park, The Boltons, the new Queen Anne district ("Cadogan Land," as we might style it) the "Borough", Paddington, Pimlico, and many more such quarters, all offer "notes" and peculiarities of their own. The more "official" suburbs, such as Chelsea and Kensington, or St. John's Wood, still retain, in spite of the efforts of the builder, a kind of rural air: in Buckingham Palace Road, close to Victoria Station, there is still to be seen the survival of gardens in front of the houses; while in a street within view of Sloane Square only a year or two ago were to be found the green roadside wooden palings, stunted trees, with public-house signs suspended from posts. This individuality has been not a little fostered by the erection of Town Halls, which suggest an idea of municipal independence, and which tend to concentrate all the local energies. A concert—say at the Westminster Town Hall—has quite an air of local festivity; we seem to be in a provincial town where some rare gala has roused the natives into some excitement. A walk through the High Street of Southwark or Bishopsgate Street suggests a prosperous country town. There is a snug, old-fashioned air, with framed and gabled houses here and there hedged in between more pretentious neighbours; while the shops have a provincial glitter. The waggons and carriers' carts are moving slowly out countrywards. The ponderous church has a rural look. Or, as we pass out of Harley Street into the Marylebone Road, what an abrupt change! We are in a suburb at once: here are villas walled round, such as Dickens's house, presenting large gardens, and a sort of "high-road," with trees, and other rural accompaniments. With this we may contrast the little "shabby-genteel" streets of Mayfair, which have their psychological meaning; for a poor district promoted into fashion signifies houses on valuable sites. Dickens and Thackeray, who understood their London psychology well, have interpreted these odd concatenations. And who will say that there is not a distinct physiognomy in the dreary, chilling lines of Wimpole Street, Harley Street, and their neighbours, where the houses have, as it were, been "run" in the one mould? There seems some fitness in the one perpetual succession of gloomy doctors' parlours and patients' rooms, where sentences of life and death are being waited for all the day long. So with the region of the great squares – Grosvenor, Berkeley, and Portman – there is a tone of solid, old-fashioned state, and every second house seems a mansion. How curious too are the feelings aroused by the Bayswater region! Here we find wastes of "compo" mansions, terraces and squares in abundance, and trees also. There is a general pretentiousness—from the uniform, stuccoed balustrades, the languid trees, and dusty foliage. "Middle-class" folk live in these would-be palaces and terraces. Mixed up invariably with this affected state, we find streets, rows of flashy shops, and all the vulgar incidents of traffic, omnibuses, carts, etc. Then, turning to "Queen Anne's land" by Knightsbridge, we seem to find ourselves transported to some Dutch city: every house ruby red, each competing with its neighbour in fantastic shapes and outlines. Or we take a flight to Westminster, to that street of monstrous, beetling houses,—Victoria Street,—all chambers and offices and hotels signifying but a temporary occupation and a flitting to the country or suburbs when the day's work is done. Or we may hurry to the modern district of South Kensington, with its palatial mansions, somewhat out of fashion and deserted, but which sprang up at a season of "inflation", when every one was, or fancied he was, growing rich. Now it is found that small but roomy houses are "your only wear." Or we may flit to that forlorn district beyond Islington where there are rows upon rows of yellow villas, stuccoed, well smirched, stained, and decayed, and with a spurious air of country—villas that had seen better days, but now inexpressibly forlorn and decayed, patched and stained.

It adds a piquancy to our London promenades to note the many survivals of the old suburban character, which are to be encountered in even the most urban districts. Habit soon helps to detect readily these marks and tokens. The familiar Primrose Hill, that breezy playground, is now encompassed by streets and houses, though it commands a pleasant view of the northern heights. It is difficult to realise that in this very public place, once so secluded and free from interruptions, what was the last duel in England was fought, on a post then known as Chalk Farm. Again, in the rather rustic-looking street Davies Street, close to Berkeley Square, we may note a gloomy, well-grimed mansion, set at an angle to the street, with a court or scrap of garden in front, Bourdon House, as it is called; it was once a part of the Old Manor House, a country seat of the opulent Davies, the lord of the soil. It therefore once stood on the country road; and here are Farm Street and Hill Street close by. The Jesuit church has for forty years and more stood in what is literally a stable lane, or mews, rudely paved.

A quaintly-minded Londoner seeking to appreciate better his loved city once conceived the idea, old established resident as he was, of *travelling* through London, and of sojourning in the different quarters so as to participate in their tone and flavour. With this view he first put up at the vast foreign-looking hotel on the Embankment, from whose window as he rose in the morning he could see the whole river life: the barges moving languidly by, the flitting steamers. Thence he moved on to the huge Midland Hotel at St. Pancras, a little city in itself, full of animation and life, situated high in the air, in a sort of Islington bustle; and whence he saw London, through the eyes, as it were, of innumerable northerners who had come to town. What a bustle from converging tram lines! what a fine air, and splendid views of the heights of Hampstead and Highgate and the country generally! hence he passed to the Great Western Hotel at Paddington, where he found a world of another complexion; the tame yellow houses of Westbourne and other terraces being close by, with a curious general stagnation: these side by side with a "huckstering" neighbourhood, streets and shops of a poorish sort. Later he sat him down at one of the curious hostelries in Charterhouse Square, where he seemed to be in an ancient country town, or in one of those inns of fiction where say Mr. Squeers might have alighted. There were other houses of which he made trial, such as the Arundel, the resort of country sight-seers, and where he lived, as it were, close to the roar of the Strand. He may have found the most original experience of all at the Covent Garden Hotel, situated in the market, and finally at the great "Metropole" hard by Trafalgar Square. No one who had not enjoyed these experiences, he protested, could have any idea of what the great city really was. Yet the unobservant resident who has known his London for a life will take little note of these dramatic differences.

The growth and absorption of territory has been as sudden as it is rapid. There is many an "old inhabitant" whose father must have "minded the time" when London was a huge detached city, the country coming up to its gates; it is only within average living memory that almost every rural outlet has been closed up by buildings. Towards the end of last century the Duke of Bedford's great mansion, which filled the northern side of Bloomsbury Square, had a clear uninterrupted view of Hampstead and Highgate. The open country too came up close by Portland Road and all the district round. "The Foundling" hard by, when built lay really in the country. It is more astonishing to think that there must be people now alive who recall the time when the Regent's Park was a waste of pasture land, and its terraces were not.

A significant proof of the gradual absorption by London City of all adjoining suburbs is found in the number of "High Streets" which we find in all quarters of the city: such for instance as High Street, Marylebone. This was, of course, the main and chief street in each suburb. There are, indeed, over a score of streets so named. But, as has been often said, a sort of history of London could be roughly evolved from the very names of its streets.

An idea of how tremendous is this ever-growing, ever-absorbing London may be conceived from some figures which are of a startling kind. It contains some five millions of inhabitants, increased every year by over fifty thousand souls. The value of its houses, property, etc., is rated at some thirty millions of pounds annually, and its trade, import and export, at two hundred millions. Nearly seven hundred thousand houses and buildings are spread over some seven hundred square miles, and there are—and this is truly astonishing—three thousand miles of streets. Four millions of sheep and nine millions of poultry and game are consumed in the year!

A casual glance at the map issued "'tis sixty years since" – not a very great stretch backwards – shows us how this great London has expanded with leaps and bounds, as it were. Then, Brompton, Chelsea, Pimlico, and Knightsbridge, were comparatively uncovered by streets; Kennington, Vauxhall, and Southwark, were open to Deptford. Poplar or the Isle of Dogs, was a comparative blank; so were Bethnal Green, Hackney, Islington, Camden and Kentish Towns. Islington, Pentonville, Hackney, Bethnal Green, were each crossed by a road or street, while Paddington and Bayswater offered stretches of territory with but few houses and fewer streets.

London City, like British rule in India, has drawn all. But it is the southern side of the river that offers the most extraordinary contrast to what it presents in our time. In 1833 the only portion that was laid out in streets and houses and might be considered "town" was the portion comprised within the curve of the river, and bounded by a line drawn from Lambeth Palace by Newington, and ending at Bermondsey. Outside this "pale," as we might call it, all lay open. Beginning where Battersea Park now is, we find a great waste, formerly known as Battersea Fields, where "the Duke" fought a political duel without being interrupted, and whither he rode out as to the country. We pass by "Nine Elms," leaving the Vauxhall gardens on our left. Between the gardens and Lambeth Palace was an open tract, which spread away to Newington Butts and Kennnington, whose "common" was then unenclosed. Another tract, comprising Walworth and Rotherhithe, led on to Deptford and Greenwich, It is extraordinary to contrast with this the densely populated streets that in a short space of time have since spread over these regions. Again, the abolition or destruction of Brompton, its fair grounds, villas, and market gardens, with the creation of the new Kensingtons, dates only from the Exhibition year, 1851. To the Crystal Palace we owe the creation of the great Norwood and Sydenham districts; while "Belgravia," with its streets and fine squares, was laid out within living memory, as well as the newer and less aristocratic district that stretches from Buckingham Palace Road down to the river. Russell Square, once sacred to lawyers, was laid out so recently as 1804, which shows how rapid has been the growth of the great city. The picturesque little Queen Square in Bloomsbury, which has its side to the north uncovered by houses, testifies significantly to this vicinity of the country; for the space was purposely left vacant so that, as an old writer says, the denizens of the square might command a full view of the "beautiful landscape" and the northern heights. And Mr. Wheatley tells us that in certain streets of this district the northern side is a story or two lower, so as not to interrupt their opposite neighbour's view.

We could imagine nothing more interesting than a series of these comparative maps on the same scale, showing the gradual increase of London territory. One of only thirty or forty years ago set beside one of the present day would excite almost as much astonishment as the old one of Aggas put beside a great railway map of to-day. One of the best topographical pictures of London suburbs over one hundred years ago is Dodsley's account, which is welcome for its natural, unaffected style, and the tone of admiring awe with which the wonders of the town are depicted.

Were we to impress a stranger with an idea of the grandeur and splendour of this London of ours, we should lead him—not to the heart of the City, or to the Bank, Charing Cross, Fleet Street, or to Rotten Row, or to the "Church Parade" in Hyde Park of a Sunday morning – we should place him at the middle of Westminster Bridge with his face to St. Paul's. There we would see the long line of gigantic buildings stretching away on the left like palaces; the new red police office; the Whitehall Terrace, with Somerset House beyond; the huge hotels; the great

Embankment below, with its richly verdant belt of plane trees; the light and not unpleasing railway bridge; the noble Waterloo Bridge, worthy of old Rome; the other bridges beyond; St.Paul's and the City spires in the distance; while below are the ever-flitting steamboats, the barges, following the majestic bends of the great river. Then we turn and see just behind us the luxuriantly Gothic pile of the Houses of Parliament, with the terraces and pinnacles; the scattered, cheerful-looking buildings of the great hospital on the other side of the river; while to our right are the converging streets at Palace Yard, – one of the busiest quarters of London, – with the fine Clock Tower, and a glimpse of the Park beyond. All this combination suggests an idea of power, traffic, and magnificence that no other city can furnish. This dramatic scene is likely to escape many who are too engrossed to pause on their way, and who hurry across the bridge in pursuit of their business. And all has been but the growth of the last twenty or thirty years. It is curious to contrast with this bustling picture the reflections of the great poet who stood on the older bridge years ago, and expressed his feelings in a famous sonnet:

Earth hath not anything to show more fair.
The city now doth like a garment wear
The beauty of the morning: silent, bare,
Ships, towers, domes, theatres, and temples lie
Open unto the fields, and to the sky;
All bright and glittering in the smokeless air.

A tranquil, almost rural scene. At that time–well-nigh a century ago–the busiest portion of the river was beyond London Bridge, where, in the once proverbial phrase, "the forest of masts" was to be seen. "Forest of funnels" is now more appropriate; the masts have retreated to the innumerable docks. Wordsworth then saw but a sedgy foreshore, lined with shanties, sheds, and small warehouses: there too stood Inigo Jones's Water Gate at the edge of the water, washed by the stream; and the terrace or "mall" which then touched the river. No suspension or railway bridge was at Hungerford Stairs. The Adelphi Terrace, then new and conspicuous, was admired as a sort of monumental structure, and there was no fringe of vast buildings between the river and the shadowy outlines of St. Paul's.

Percy Fitzgerald, c.1890

Chapter II

A brief outline of the pattern of change in Victorian London

by

B.R. Bruff

On today's maps, London appears as an unbroken sprawl of bricks and mortar from Enfield in the north to Purley in the south, from Uxbridge in the West to Hornchurch and Upminster in the east. Yet only a century-and-a-half ago, the city's limits extended barely beyond Shoreditch and Westminster, Finsbury and Southwark. Outside these limits was a landscape of farmland, heath, wood and marsh, hamlets, villages and small market towns. Today's inner city areas, Hackney for example, were pleasant semi-rural suburbs, populated by wealthy city gentry.

The rapidity of London's expansion is remarkable. Between 1816 and 1880 the city spread outwards, with the two main booms in building occurring between 1816 and 1826 and 1868 and 1880; a third took place in the first decade of the present century. When they were over, the rural hinterland had ceased to exist, and London had taken on more or less its modern shape.

The first areas to be affected by the sudden growth of London were Paddington and Bayswater, Stoke Newington, Hackney, Clapham and Camberwell, but like a creeping tide development moved on and village after village found itself part of the 'Great Wen' and the 'cockney' had to go farther afield for his day in the country.

To Victorian historians like Edward Walford, Walter Thornbury and Percy Fitzgerald, it seemed that the London that they knew and loved so well was disappearing before their eyes, and they made it their mission in life to describe it for future generations before it vanished entirely. Londoners owe them a debt of gratitude.

Thornbury and Walford, particularly in their momumental works, London Recollected and Village London, recorded every old street and building inn and palace. Village and hamlet, manor and farm, all were described. Every person of note, whether they were prince or peasant has their own niche in this history. They wrote against a backcloth of tremendous change; social, political, financial, and, while they railed against the disappearance of the lovely countryside that lay around London, they knew nothing was going to stop it.

Fitzgerald, writing in the 1890's, says of villages like Greenford, Wembley and Dollis Hill: 'These places can scarcely be considered within the range of 'suburban London'. But they are clearly marked down for absorption as much as Hampstead and Norwood were. The process is prompt and speedy. One day the fair smiling place is found out and speedily covered with terraces and buildings, and from that moment it begins to stretch its hand to the Metropolis, eager to join it'.

And so it proved. The Capital's ever-increasing population created an insatiable demand for new housing. In the century between 1811 and 1911, the population of the County of London as a whole quadrupled, rising from 1,139,355 to 4,521,685, and in some areas the increase was almost two hundred-fold: Hampstead, for example, saw the number of its inhabitants grow from 3,483 to 85,945 (Census of England and Wales.)

When one drives across London today, it is next to impossible to imagine the landscape of wooded hills and winding narrow lanes that existed a bare century ago. By change – or, in some fortunate cases, foresight–vestiges remain: Epping Forest, Hampstead Heath and Wimbledon Common are major examples, Highgate Woods another. The hawthorns that line the North Circular Road at Finchley are the last remnants of Finchley Common, where once highwaymen like Dick Turpin lay in wait for coaches climbing up out of London, and where, in 1724, Jack Shephard was finally captured after his escape from Newgate Prison. For many years the northern boundary of London was the great New Road, the city's first bypass. Begun in

1836, it eventually become the Marylebone Road, Euston Road and Pentonville Road of today. Beyond, from the flat fields of Greenford round to the Northern Heights of Hampstead and Highgate was farmland, devoted mostly to the production of hay for the thousands of horses working in London, and worked by gangs of men moving from field to field and farm to farm in rotation. But during the early 1800's, like floodwaters released from behind a bursting dam, the tide of houses surged northwards.

Much of the initial development took place along the line of the turnpike roads which radiated out from the city to the rim of the London Basin, where towns like Romford, Barnet, Epping, Watford, Uxbridge, Kingston, Croydon and Dartford stand. These turnpikes were for the most part based on the network of Roman Roads – Watling Street, for example, the modern Edgware Road, leading to Chester, and Ermine Street, running through Shoreditch, Dalston, Stamford Hill and Tottenham on its way to Lincoln. Between these arterial roads meandered the old medieval field ways.

The turnpike roads were built for the swifter and smoother progress of the stage coaches, which for some two centuries provided the sole means of long-distance passenger transport. At the height of the coaching age, over 150 a day passed through High Barnet (known then as Chipping Barnet) on the Great North Road alone. There they would mingle with the great herds of livestock being driven southwards to feed London's growing population. To the people of those days, modern traffic would probably seem calm and orderly in comparison.

As road surfaces improved and commuting into London became easier, ribbon development took place along the line of the turnpikes. Comfortable suburbs such as Clapham, Hampstead, Hackney, St. John's Wood grew up as the middle classes took their new wealth out of the overcrowded city. The Georgian houses that front Camden Road, Clapton Road, Mildmay Park and other areas which have escaped Hitler's bombers and modern-day property developers bear witness to this early expansion. Very probably to the consternation of their owners, industry too moved out of the city, and workers' dwellings rapidly filled in the spaces between the mansions.

The real acceleration of London's outward growth began with the coming of the railways in the 1830's, which sounded the death knell of both the turnpike roads and the stagecoaches. Today one can see at Seven Sisters the result of this, for here the Eastern Counties Turnpike, begun in the 1820's to provide a most necessary good road between London and East Anglia, was abandoned in 1834. Those generations of travellers who have since arrived at Manor House to face a crawl through the narrow streets of Harringay, Tottenham, Edmonton and Clapton now know who to blame.

Nevertheless, it was to be some years before the railway companies realised the profit that might be made from commuter traffic and began to open suburban stations – their principal objective was to reach London from the provinces. Once the local stations began to open, though, the days of rural London were numbered. Wood Green, for instance, described by Walford as 'a retired country spot, hemmed in by green lanes and sturdy hedgegrows, where the ruralising cockney might betake himself in the summertime'. The building of Alexandra Palace Station by the Great Northern Railway soon changed all that; in the space of twenty years Wood Green was a thriving industrial area and 'ruralising' only a distant memory. North and East London along the lines of the Great Northern and Great Eastern Railways were, indeed, among the first areas to feel the effects, Stamford Hill, Tottenham and Edmonton soon joining hands, and Bromley, Bow, West Ham, Stratford and Ilford doing likewise. Wherever a station was opened, the speculators moved in, buying up the large houses, the farms and the nurseries and erecting row upon row of workmen's cottages, doubtless to the chagrin of the local gentry, and doubtless to their profit also.

Certainly the aristocrats who owned by far the major proportion of the land in and around London – the Dukes of Portland and Bedford, Marquis Camden, Lord Southampton and others whose names are commemorated in the districts they once owned – substantially increased their fortunes by the sale of their lands, though they allowed the railways to have as little effect as possible on their estates, driving them underground and into culverts wherever they could. Elsewhere, with powers given by Parliament, the railway companies drove in roughshod, displacing thousands of people in the process, with no obligation, it seems, to rehouse them. In inner London, where vast areas were needed for the great termini, for sidings and junctions, engine sheds and repair depots, hundreds of houses were demolished. One whole area, Agar Town, was erased from the map entirely. The railways built imposing hotels, many still to be seen, though very few now serve their original purpose, and shopping parades followed soon after.

In East London, the population of Stratford, Canning Town, Barking, Leyton, Leytonstone, Walthamstow, Wanstead and Woodford, doubled from 112,000 to 224,000 in the decade between 1871 and 1881. Many of the new inhabitants of these districts were forced to move into them from the City because of the loss of their homes to railway and road-building. In East Ham and West Ham, where the land had previously been used for market gardening, there was a similar rise. The greatest increase in this area was around Plaistow, which by 1881 had grown from a small village, lacking even a church, to an industrial suburb with a population of 67,000. This spectacular growth was due to the effect of the railways and the Victoria

Dock, later to become the Victoria and Albert Docks. These alone employed some 12,000 men. New industries were springing up in the area now called Silvertown, named for Mr. Silver's India-Rubber Clothing Factory.

The West London areas of Hammersmith, Kensington, Fulham, Acton and Chiswick were all swallowed up. In 1861 Willesden had a population of less than 4,000; in ten years this had quadrupled, and by 1881 almost doubled again. Willesden Green, once one of the most rustic spots near London, with its 'Spotted Dog' tavern and tea-garden, was covered with homes in a generation. Here, the railway had almost as much impact as at Clapham, with five lines meeting at Willesden Junction, and huge new yards being built. With the stations at Brondesbury, Kensal Green, Harrow Road and Neasden a completely new district developed, Stonebridge Park, where previously had stood a handful of villas occupied by City gentlemen who had retired there to enjoy life in the country. Five hundred men were employed at the railway works at Neasden, an indication of the new industry brought to the area. A few areas held out a little longer; even as late as 1882, the parish of Perivale had only some twenty inhabitants, but it lay only seven miles from Marble Arch, and its days were numbered.

South of the river, development was initially much slower, but here the railways eventually had perhaps an even greater impact, with the intricate network of surburban lines developed by the South-Eastern and Chatham, London, Brighton and South Coast and London and South Western Railways and their predecessors. Vast tracts of land, mostly unpopulated, were taken over for the two great junctions at Clapham and Bricklayers Arms. Croydon, served by two lines and no fewer than eleven stations at one time, increased its population from 6,000 in 1801 to 78,947 in 1881, becoming the largest suburban town in the neighbourhood of London. It was in Croydon that another new feature of suburban transport, the horse tramway, made its first appearance, running to Wandsworth. The later electric tramways, with their greater flexibility, gave the railways serious competition until the latter were themselves electrified after the Great War. Woolwich, always a busy town owing to its Army and Navy establishments, grew more steadily, but Plumstead, further down the line of the old North Kent Railway, increased rapidly to rival its neighbour in size. In 1800 there were only 200 houses in the whole parish; by 1851, however, the population was 8,000, and had risen to 33,000 thirty years later. The North Kent Railway was also the cause of the growth of the old village of Bexley: here, the new town, in contrast to others, had grown up on the coach road to Dover. The building of a station on the North Kent's loop line soon accelarated the growth of the old village, which saw its population quadruple in just a few years.

Bromley, because it was an old, well-established town, did not feel the impact of the railway as immediately as did its neighbours Beckenham and Penge. The latter of these in particular, with the wide open spaces of its common to be used, became an important junction for the lines running east-west and north-south. With three stations, it grew from almost nothing in 1850 (Walford describes it as 'an unimportant country village with but one inn 'The Crooked Billet' the oldest house in Penge') to a town with a population of 180,000 in 1881, with several hotels, its own newspaper and, in a few years, several theatres. One town that resisted the coming of the railway for a while was Kingston-Upon-Thames. The nearest that its councillors would allow the line to approach was Surbiton, then a hamlet on the outskirts of the town. Almost instantly, Surbiton was transformed into a dormitory suburb: hardly had the station been completed than speculators had surrounded it with the geometric layout of streets that today's map shows. The building of a line to Kingston itself could not long be delayed, and a branch line, running through New Malden, was duly constructed. Houses mushroomed around the new station, which became known as New Kingston.

Sutton, Cheam and Ewell all had similar populations in 1851. The railway soon brought an influx of commuters, attracted by the pleasant countryside. Sutton showed the sharpest increase, from 1,100 in 1835 to around 9,000 in 1881. Cheam and Ewell roughly doubled in size. Their turn was to come in the twentieth century. Surrey was to escape the speculators' clutches for a few years yet; it is a remarkable fact that at the beginning of the nineteenth century one sixth of Surrey consisted of wild uncultivated heath and scrub.

The feelings of the old inhabitants of London's villages who lived through Victoria's reign must have been duplicated in this century by those of the old population's of towns like Harlow, Stevenage or Hemel Hempstead, or perhaps even more so by those engulfed by the growth of post-war Birmingham or Manchester. The decision to create the Green Belt came in the nick of time for Londoners, and luckily they can still get a breath of country air in the Surrey hills or Epping Forest.

Writing in 'Village London', Edward Walford, whose words were to be echoed by Percy Fitzgerald fifteen years later, had this to say of the Caterham Valley, for which he held a particular admiration, but the words apply to all the lost villages of London.

"Caterham Valley, which abuts upon Warlingham, and runs east and west about four miles to the south of Croydon, is, so far as it has escaped building operations, very rural and pretty. It is, however, as stated above, traversed by a branch line of railway; and it may be safely inferred, therefore, that it is only a question of time before green and smiling meadows will give place to rows of streets or villas with trim gardens. It has been truly remarked that London is almost daily growing. First come the long monotonous lines of streets and houses, extending on every side, and pushing out arms and feelers in the direction of the country. But far beyond these the builder is busy at his work. He has to meet the wants and wishes of men who seek to combine the advantages of London and of country life. There is a large and increasing class who are not content to be Londoners in the old sense of the word. They must have more space and elbow-room than the close neighbourhood of London can afford. They are impatient of life in a street, and they are driven every year farther and farther afield in search of open and unoccupied ground. In these days of rapid railway communication there is hardly any spot safe from them within reasonable distance of town. They will fix themselves anywhere, so only that there is a railway-station not too far off; and there are very few of the outlying suburbs of London which are not thus suitable for them. But where they settle the charms of the country disappear. What was lately a field is enclosed, and becomes a garden or a private park, from which the public are shut out. Forests are cut down to make room for the new occupants, or are left standing only as far as they are ornamental appendages to the property. This is the sort of process which has been going on for many years past on all sides of London. We may like or dislike it, but we can raise no objection to it. We must take it as part of the general growth of London, and, so viewed, it rises almost to the dignity of a natural law. All that we can ask is that some limits may be assigned to it—that some spots of ground here and there may be kept sacred from intrusion, and may be protected from the flood which is overwhelming all around them."

Every city dweller will, we are sure, say Amen to Walford's words of a century ago.

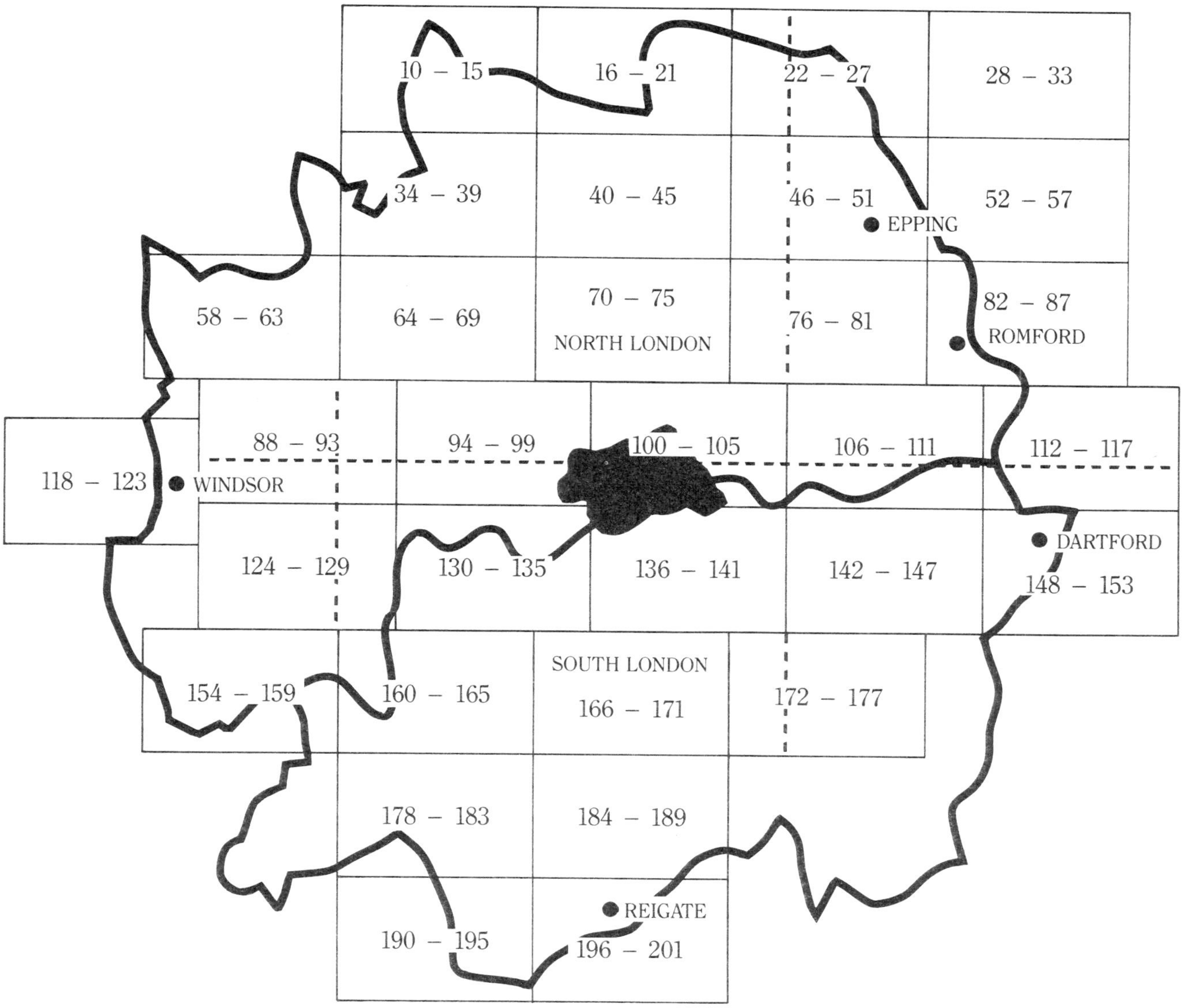
10 – 15
16 – 21
22 – 27
28 – 33
34 – 39
40 – 45
46 – 51
52 – 57
EPPING
58 – 63
64 – 69
70 – 75
NORTH LONDON
76 – 81
82 – 87
ROMFORD
118 – 123
WINDSOR
88 – 93
94 – 99
100 – 105
106 – 111
112 – 117
DARTFORD
124 – 129
130 – 135
136 – 141
142 – 147
148 – 153
154 – 159
160 – 165
SOUTH LONDON
166 – 171
172 – 177
178 – 183
184 – 189
REIGATE
190 – 195
196 – 201

The Maps

Publisher's Note

The maps in this Atlas are based on a scale of two inches to the mile. However, because of the number of different maps involved and the reproduction thereof there may be some minor variations in scale. The age of the maps and the fact that there could be as much as fifteen years difference between the dates of survey of adjoining maps, plus the handling and folding which has taken place over the years, have also meant that there are small differences here and there which are impossible to eradicate.

The publishers have made every effort to minimise these faults and trust the reader will make allowances for any slight imperfections.

Jeroms
Butlers
Kettlewell
Long
Spring
Pre
Mill
Beech
Mains
Cherry
Tree
Bernard
Heath
3 Chimnies
Gorham
Bury
Ruin
Doltons
St. Peter
St. Michaels
St. ALBANS
Bottom
Ho.
Pre Wood
F.
Silk Mill
Pre Wood
Hill
End
Toll
Gate
Sopwell
Ruins
Beech
Tree
St.
Stephens
Windridge
Sopwell
Mill
Maiden
Crouch
Birch
Wood
Apes Pond
West Fields
St.
Julians
Park
Wood
New Barn
Potters
Crouch
Cuckmans
F.
Plasters
Chiswell
Green
Bone
Hill
Serge Hill
White Ho.
The Noke
Burstons
F.
Searchers
F.
Park
Street
Ninning
The Holt
Tenements
Plowmans
F.
Lye Lane
Black
Green
The Red
New
Park
Winch
Hill
Cecil Lodge
Waterdell
F.
Bricket Wood
Moor Mill
Snug Oak
Trolley
Bottom
Fortunes
Park
Bury
High
Elms
Bricket
Thrift
Hansteads
Waterside
F.
Wood
Bricket
Poor Dell
Wood
Wild
F.

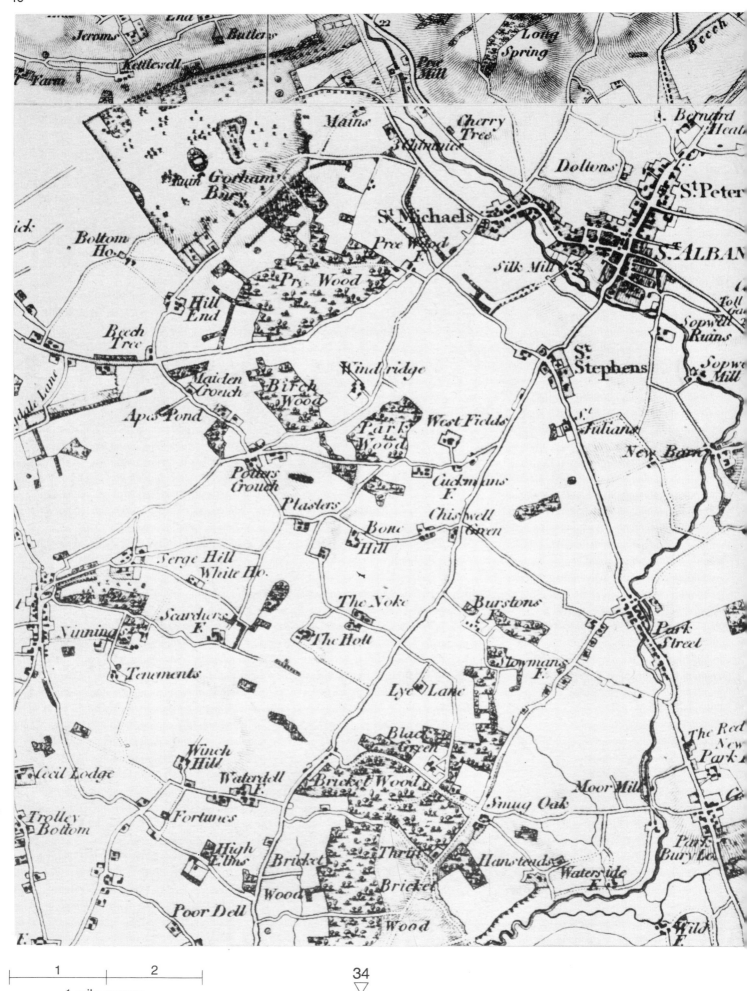

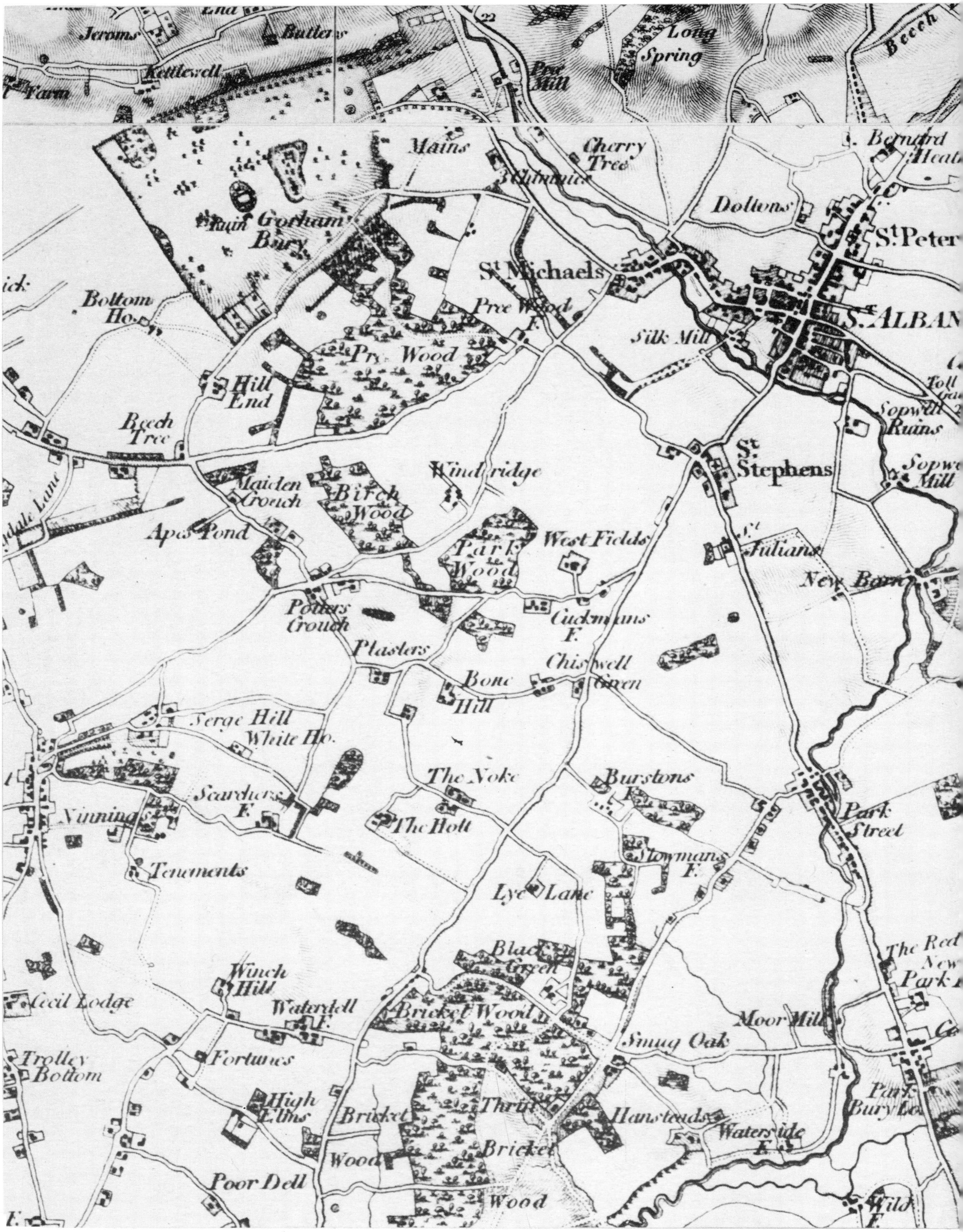

1 2
1 mile approx.

34
▽

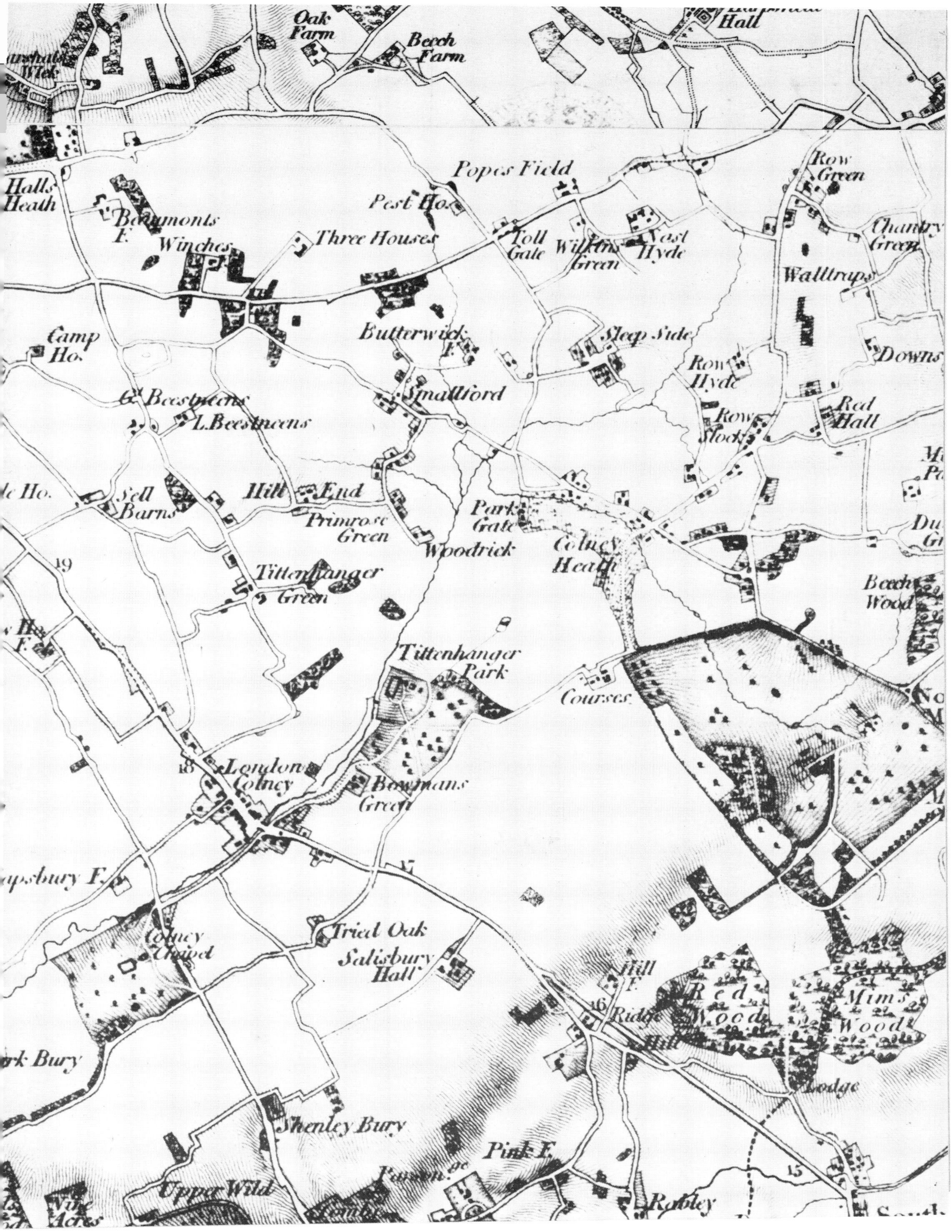
Oak Farm
Beech Farm
Hall
Halls Heath
Popes Field
Pest Ho.
Row Green
Chantry Green
Beaumonts F.
Winches
Three Houses
Toll Gate
Wilkins Green
Nast Hyde
Walltrups
Camp Ho.
Butterwick F.
Sleep Side
Downs
Row Hyde
Gt. Beestneens
L. Beestneens
Smallford
Red Hall
Row Stock
Sell Barns
Hill End
Primrose Green
Park Gate
Colney Heath
Woodrick
19
Tittenhanger Green
Beech Wood
Tittenhanger Park
Courses
18
London Colney
Bowmans Green
Colney Chapel
Trial Oak
Salisbury Hall
Hill F.
Red Wood
Mims Wood
16
Ridge Hill
Lodge
Shenley Bury
Pink F.
Upper Wild
15
Rabley

16 ▷

35 ▽

Published 1822.

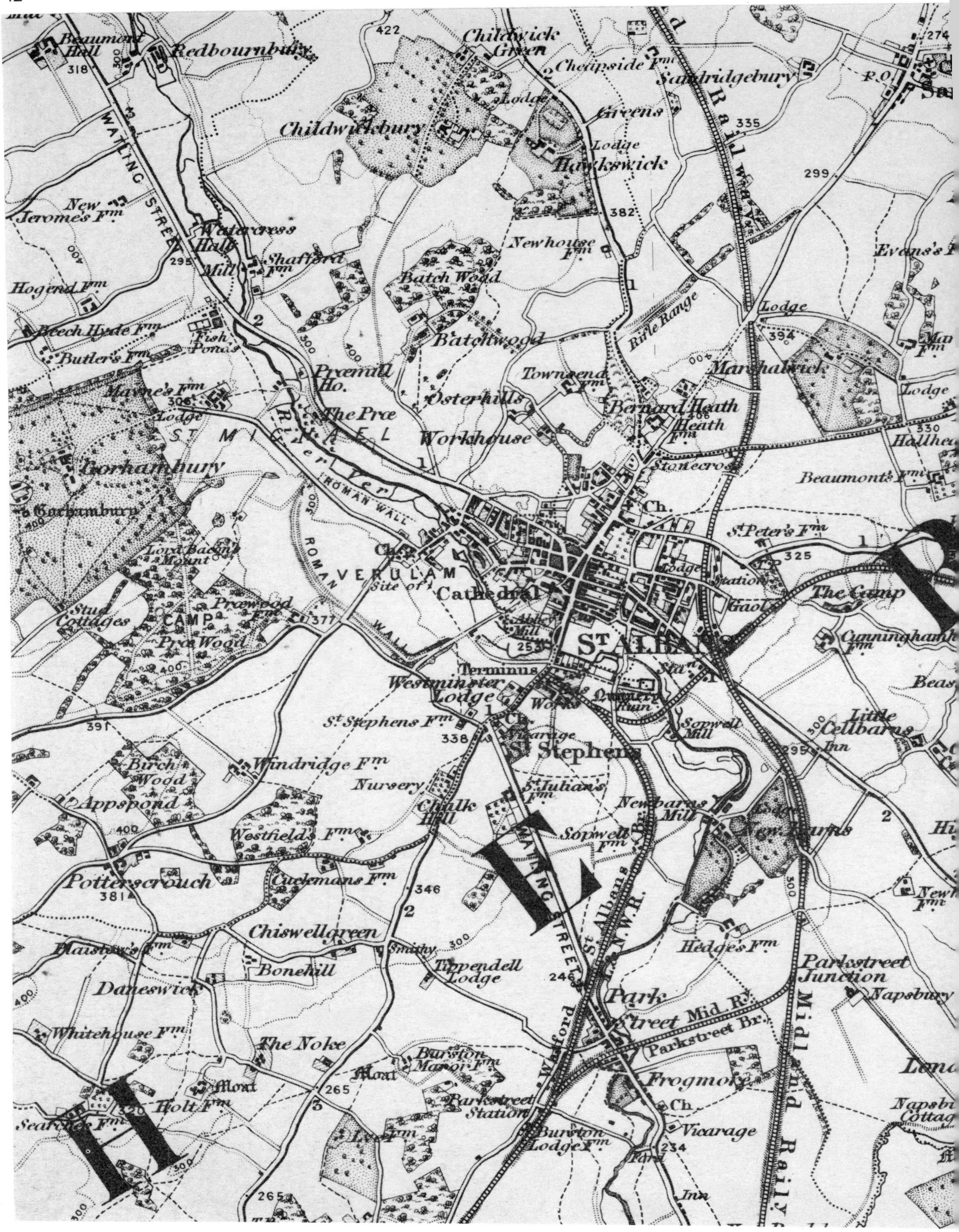

Beaumont Hall
Redbournbury
Childwick Green
Cheapside Fm.
Sandridgebury
Childwickbury
Lodge
Greens
Hawkswick
WATLING STREET
New Jeromes Fm.
Watercress Hall
Mill
Shafford Fm.
Newhouse Fm.
Batch Wood
Batchwood
Hogend Fm.
Beech Hyde Fm.
Butler's Fm.
Fish Ponds
Rifle Range
Marshalwick
Evans's
Lodge
Praemill Ho.
The Pre
Townsend Fm.
Osterhills
Bernard Heath
Heath Fm.
Mayne's Fm.
Lodge
ST MICHAEL
River Ver
Workhouse
Stonecross
Hallheath
Gorhambury
ROMAN WALL
Beaumont's Fm.
Lord Bacon's Mount
Ch.
VERULAM
Site of
Cathedral
St. Peter's Fm.
Lodge
Station
Gaol
The Camp
Stud Cottages
CAMP
Prawood Fm.
Pre Wood
Abbey Mill
ST ALBANS
Cunningham Fm.
Terminus
Westminster Lodge
Works
Sta.
St. Stephens Fm.
Ch.
Vicarage
St Stephens
Sopwell Mill
Little Cellbarns
Inn
Birch Wood
Windridge Fm.
Nursery
St. Julian's Fm.
Appspond
Chalk Hill
Newbarns Mill
New Barns
Westfield's Fm.
Sopwell Fm.
Potterscrouch
Cuckmans Fm.
Chiswellgreen
Smithy
Hedge's Fm.
Bonehill
Tippendell Lodge
Parkstreet Junction
Daneswick
Park Street Mid. R.
Napsbury
Whitehouse Fm.
The Noke
Parkstreet Br.
Burston Manor Fm.
Moat
Frogmore
Holt Fm.
Parkstreet Station
Ch.
Vicarage
Burston Lodge Fm.
Ford
Inn
Midland Railway
L. & N.W.R.
Watford
St. Albans

1 2

1 mile approx.

36
▽

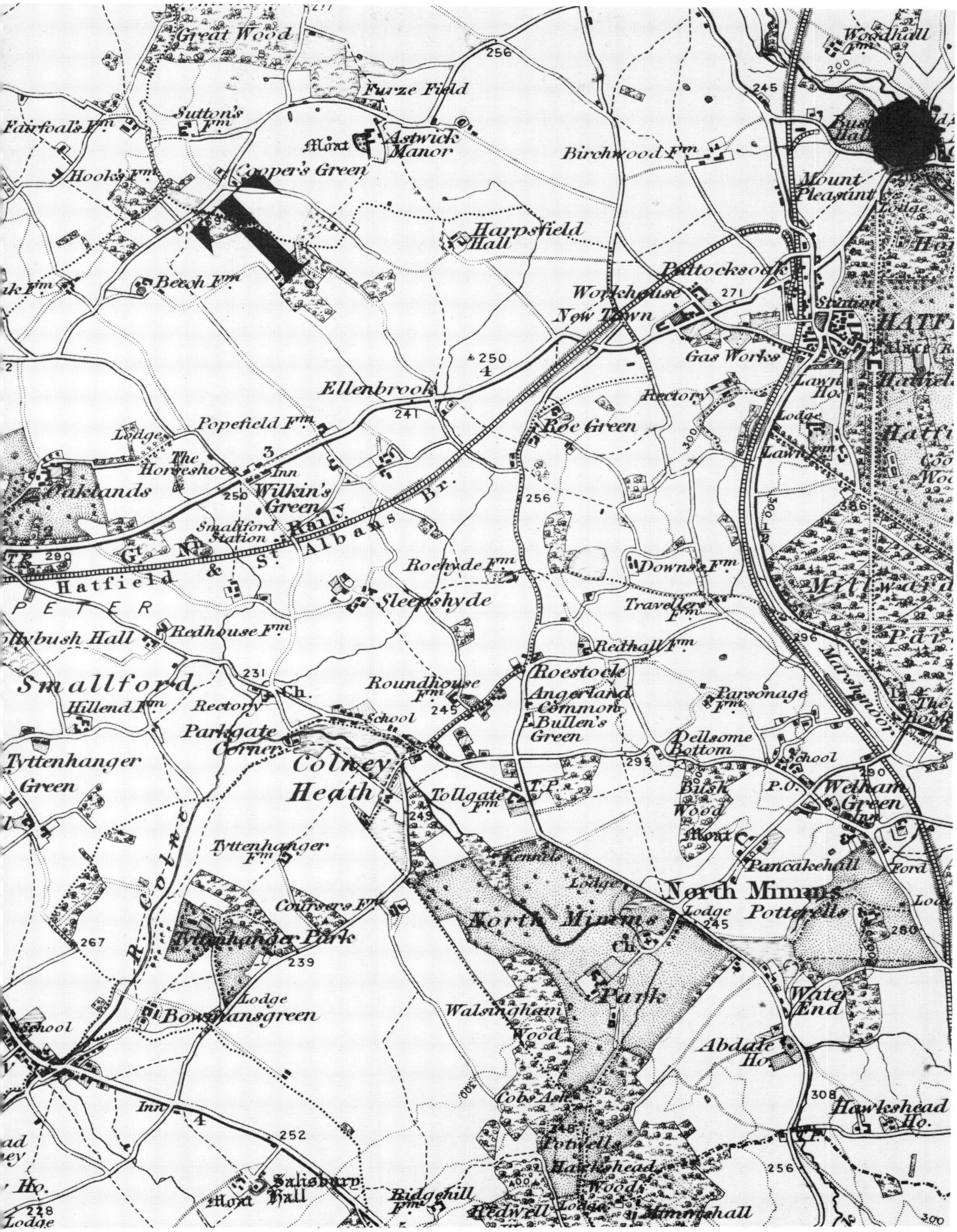

Great Wood
Furze Field
Sutton's Fm
Fairfoal's Fm
Moat
Astwick Manor
Hooks Fm
Cooper's Green
Birchwood Fm
Woodhall Fm
Mount Pleasant
Harpsfield Hall
Beech Fm
Workhouse
New Town
Station
Gas Works
Ellenbrook
Popefield Fm
Rectory
Roe Green
Lodge
The Horseshoes Inn
Wilkin's Green
Oaklands
Smallford Station
Gt Nn & St Albans Raily Br.
Hatfield
Roehyde Fm
Downs Fm
Sleapshyde
Travellers Fm
Redhouse Fm
Redhall Fm
Smallford
Roundhouse Fm
Roestock
Angerland Common
Bullen's Green
Parsonage Fm
Hillend Fm
Rectory
Ch.
School
Parkgate Corner
Dellsome Bottom
School
Tyttenhanger Green
Colney Heath
Tollgate Fm
T.P.
Bush Wood
Moat
P.O.
Welham Green
Inn
Tyttenhanger Fm
Kennels
Pancakehall
Coursers Fm
North Mimms
Lodge
Potterells
North Mimms
Ch.
Tyttenhanger Park
R. Colne
Lodge
Park
Water End
Bowmansgreen
School
Walsingham Wood
Abdale Ho.
Cobs Ash
Hawkshead Ho.
Inn
Potwells
Hawkshead Wood
Salisbury Hall
Moat
Ridgehill Fm
Redwell
Lodge
Mimmshall
Marshmoor
Millward Park

18▷

37
▽

Surveyed 1865-1880. Published 1887.

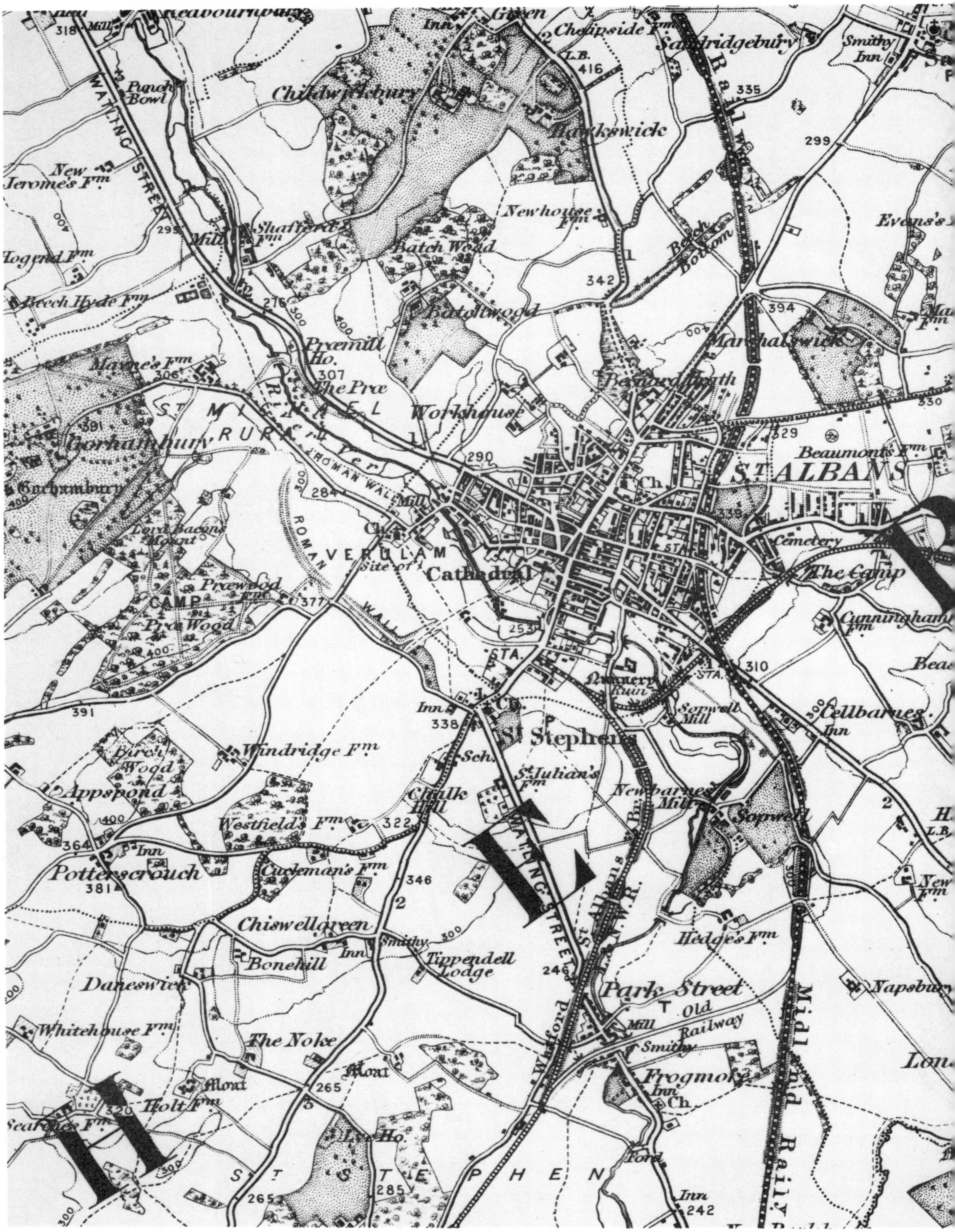
Punch Bowl
New Jerome's Fm
WATLING STREET
Shafford Fm
Mill
Beech Hyde Fm
Batch Wood
Batchwood
Newhouse Fm
Beech Bottom
Cheapside Fm
Sandridgebury
Smithy Inn
Railway
Marshalswick
Praemill Ho.
The Pre
Mayne's Fm
Workhouse
ST MICHAEL RURAL
Gorhambury
Roman Wall
Mill
ST. ALBANS
Beaumonts Fm
Ch.
Cemetery
The Camp
VERULAM
Site of
Cathedral
Lord Bacon's Mount
Prewood Fm
CAMP
Pre Wood
STA.
Nunnery Ruin
Sopwell Mill
Cellbarnes
Inn
St Stephens
Sch.
St Julian's Fm
Windridge Fm
Birch Wood
Appspond
Chalk Hill
Westfield's Fm
Newbarnes Mill
Sopwell
Potterscrouch
Cuckman's Fm
St Albans Br.
L.N.W.R.
Chiswellgreen
Smithy
Inn
Bonehill
Tippendell Lodge
Hedge's Fm
Daneswick
Park Street
Old Railway
Whitehouse Fm
Napsbury
Midland Railway
The Noke
Moat
Holt Fm
Frogmore
Inn
Ch.
Ford
ST STEPHEN

1 2

1 mile approx.

38 ▽

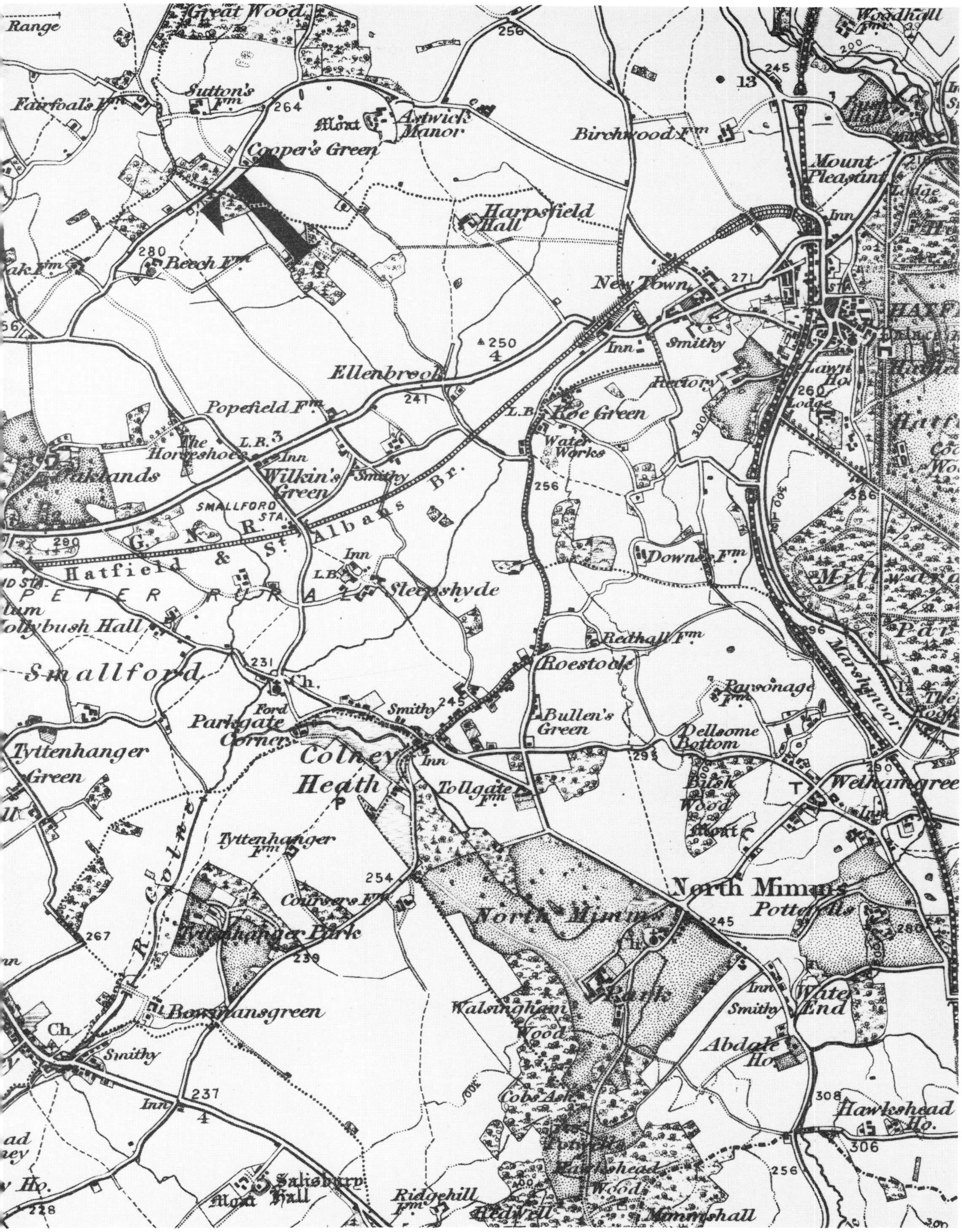
Great Wood
Range
Sutton's Fm
Fairfoal's Fm
264
256
13
245
Woodhall Fm
200
Astwick Manor
Moat
Cooper's Green
Birchwood Fm
Mount Pleasant
Lodge
Harpsfield Hall
Inn
280
Beech Fm
New Town
271
250
4
Inn
Smithy
Ellenbrook
Rectory
Lawn Ho
241
260
Lodge
Popefield Fm
L.B.
Roe Green
The Horseshoes
L.B. 3
Inn
Water Works
300
Oaklands
Wilkin's Green
Smithy
Br.
256
SMALLFORD STA.
Albans
386
G. N. R.
St
290
Hatfield
&
Inn
Downes Fm
L.B.
P E T E R
R U R A L
Sleepshyde
296
Redhall Fm
Smallford
231
Ch.
Roestock
Parsonage Fm
Marshmoor
Ford
Parkgate Corner
Smithy
245
Bullen's Green
Tyttenhanger Green
Colney Heath
Inn
Dellsome Bottom
293
290
Birch Wood
T
Welhamgree
Tollgate Fm
P
Moat
Tyttenhanger Fm
R. Colne
254
Colliers Fm
North Mimms
Potterells
North Mimms
245
267
Tyttenhanger Park
239
280
Ch.
Park
Inn
Smithy
Water End
Bowmansgreen
Walsingham Wood
Ch.
Abdale Ho
Smithy
Cobs Ash
300
308
Hawkshead Ho.
237
Inn
4
306
Potterells
Hawkshead Wood
256
Salisbury Hall
Moat
Ridgehill Fm
Redwell
Mimmshall
228
Ho.
300

20▷

39
▽

Surveyed 1865-1880. Revised 1902. Published 1904.

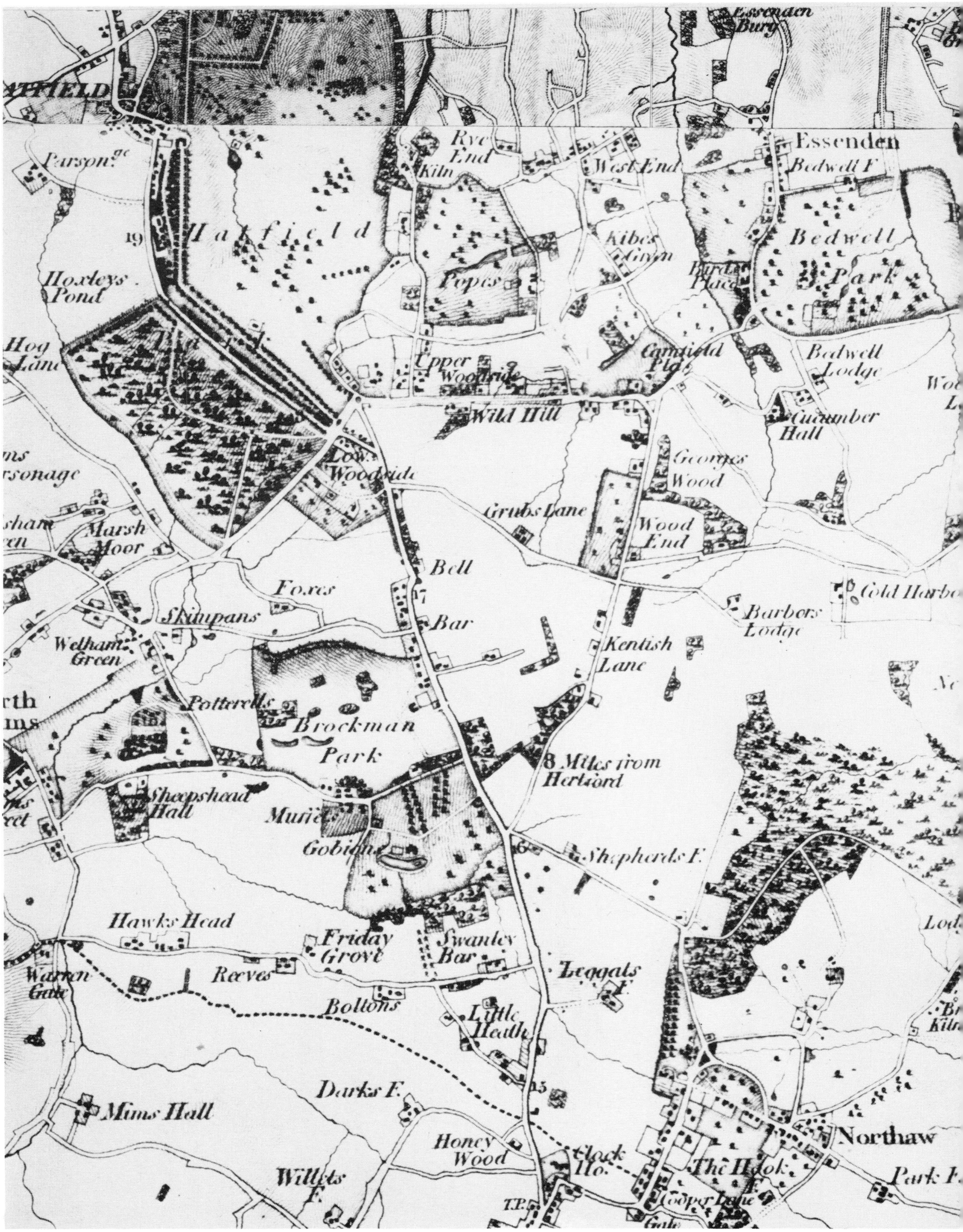
Essenden Bury
Parson.ge
Rye End
Kiln
West End
Essenden
Bedwell F.
Hatfield
Kibes Green
Bedwell Park
Hoxleys Pond
Popes
Hog Lane
Upper Woodside
Camfield Place
Bedwell Lodge
Wild Hill
Cucumber Hall
Low Woodside
Georges Wood
Parsonage
Marsh Moor
Grubs Lane
Wood End
Bell
Foxes
Cold Harbo
Skimpans
Bar
Barbers Lodge
Welham Green
Kentish Lane
Potterells
Brockman Park
8 Miles from Hertford
Sheepshead Hall
Muriels
Gobions
Shepherds F.
Hawks Head
Friday Grove
Swanley Bar
Warren Gate
Reeves
Leggats F.
Boltons
Little Heath
Darks F.
Mims Hall
Northaw
Honey Wood
Clock Ho.
The Hook
Willets F.
Park F.
Cooper Lane
T.P.

◁11

40 ▽

1 2

1 mile approx.

Bayford Hall
Bayford
Wades Fm
Box Wood
Goose Gr.
Hoddesdon Park Wood
Observatory
Bayford Green
Broxbourn Wood
Brickingdon Green
Broxbourn Park
Epping Green
Ishing Grove
Outer Claypits
Little Wood
Gate
Etridge Cross
Wormley Wood
Wormley West End
Wormley Bury
Punsborn Park
Lodge
Punsborn F.
St Lawrence F.
Beaumont Gr.
Dorry's Wood
Newgate Street
Tallamores
Long Grove
Limekiln
Cheshunt Com
Applebury Street
Flamsted End
Hanyards
Goughs Oak
Hammonds Street
Canna Hill
Cheshunt
Cottleys
Sopers F.
Love Grove
Love Grove
Turners Hill

22▷

41
▽

Published 1822.

◁13

River Lea
Cecil Mill
Holwell Fm.
Mill
Essendonbury
Woolmers Park
Roxford
Water Hall
How Green
Kennel Ho.
Bunkers Hill
Bayford Hall
Smithy
Essendon
Lower Westend Fm.
West End
Bedwellpark Fm.
Little Berkhampstead
Little Berkhampstead Ho.
Essendon Place
Bedwell Park
Pope's Fm.
Bush Fm.
Buck's Fm.
Bedwell Lodge Fm.
Cucumber Hall
Woodside Place
Woodcock Fm.
Epping House
Woodside
Wildhill
Warrenwood
Lower Woodside
Woodhill
Woodfield
Coldharbour Fm.
Tyler's Causeway
School
Kentishlane Fm.
Barberslodge Fm.
Fox's
Newpark Fm.
Vicarage
P.O. Newgate Street
Georges Wood
Justice Hill
Great Wood
Grims Brook
Brookmans
Mimwood Ho.
Woodlands
The Ridgeway
Home Wood
Hanyards Fm.
Manor Fm.
Leggatts Fm.
Leggatts
Nyn Park
Brickkiln Fm.
Cuffley Hills
Reeves Fm.
Bolton's Fm.
Hemps Hill
Site of Kings Well

42
▽

1 2

1 mile approx.

Bayfordbury
Brickendon Bury
Ducketts Wood
Blakefield
Clements
Elbowlane Fm
Light Wood
Dalmonds
Jepps
Sewards
Monk's Green
Highfield Wood
Haileybury College
Woollensbrook
Box Wood
Westfield
Highleigh Fm
HODDESDON
High Leigh
Hoddesdonpark Wood
Spital Brook
Hoddesdon Bury
Warren Ho.
Bayfordplace Fm
Fanshaws
Ford
Hacketts
Brickendon Green
Cowheath Wood
Brickendon Grange
Broxbourne Wood
Broxbourne Bury
Broxbourne
Claypits
Cold Hall
Bads Hill
Calais Wood
Emanuel Pollards
Carneles Green
Wormleyhill Fm
West Lea
Manor Fm
West End
Wormleybury
Wormley
Lodge
Beaumont Manor
Thunderfield Grove
Factory Fm
Moat
Tanfield Fm
St Lawrence Fm
Appleby Street
Cheshunt Park
Turnford
Nunsbury
Hammond Street
Roundcroft
Brookfield Fm
Burton Grange
Park Fm
Reservoir
Lucas End
Windmill
Flamstead End
Reynoldsgreen
Mill Lane Fm
Goffs Oak
Cheshunt Street
Site of CAMP
Cheshunt Great Ho.
Gews Corner
Pantilehall
Poundon Pits
Coles Grove
Moat
River Lea
Lea Navigation
New River
Cambridge Line G.E.Ry
Ford
Lodge
Ch.
School
Inn
P.O.
243
191
316
129
229
262
257
252
203
302
341
200
218
112
16
368
268
170
312
151
113
354
300
78
357
79
14
239
119
324
258
85
18

24 ▷

Surveyed 1865-1880. Published 1887.

River Lea
Essendonbury
Essendon
West End
Essendon Place
Bedwell Park
Little Berkhampstead
Hoy Green
Kennel Ho
Woolmer's Park
Roxford
Water Hall
Bush Fm
Cucumber Hall
Woodcock Lodge Fm
Woodside Place
Woodside
Wildhill
Warrenwood
Lower Woodside
Woodhill
Woodfield
Tyler's Causeway
Bruberslodge Fm
Kentishlane Fm
Fox's
Bell Bar
Newpark Fm
Newgate Street
Justice Hill
Great Wood
Brookmans
Mimwood Ho.
Woodlands
The Ridgeway
Home Wood
Hanvards
Nyn Park
Reeves Cottg
Bolton's Fm
Cuffley Hills
Hemps Hill
Site of Kings Well

◁15

44 ▽

1 2
1 mile approx.

26▷

45
▽

Surveyed 1865-1880. Revised 1902. Published 1904.

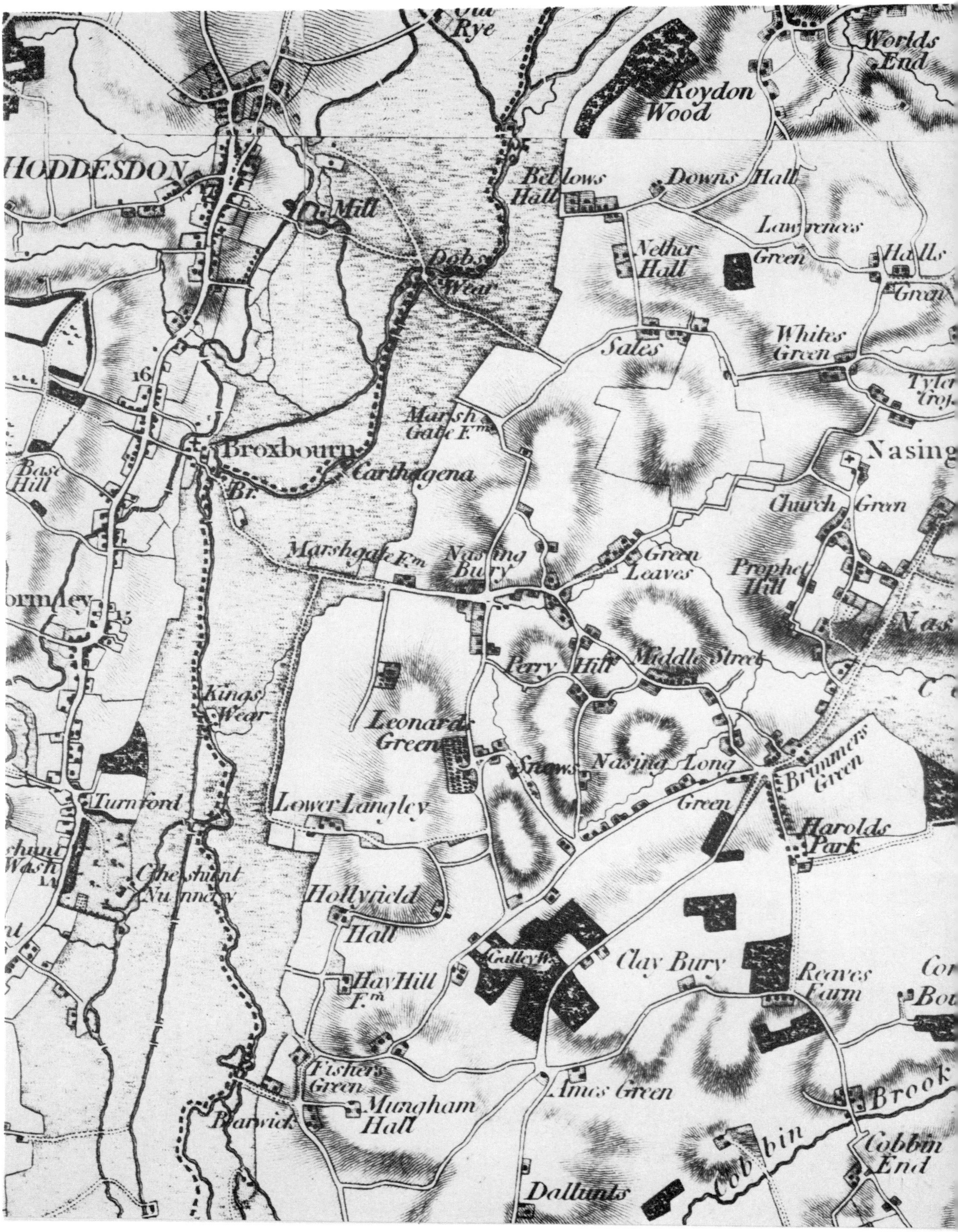
Rye
Roydon
Wood
Worlds
End
HODDESDON
Bellows
Hall
Downs Hall
Mill
Lawrences
Nether
Hall
Green
Halls
Green
Dobs
Wear
Sales
Whites
Green
16
Marsh
Gate F.m
Broxbourn
Nasing
Base
Hill
Carthagena
Br.
Church Green
Marshgate F.m
Nasing
Bury
Green
Leaves
Prophet
Hill
Perry Hill
Middle Street
Kings
Wear
Leonard
Green
Snows
Nasing Long
Green
Brimmers
Green
Turnford
Lower Langley
Harolds
Park
Cheshunt
Nunnery
Hollyfield
Hall
Galley H.
Clay Bury
Hay Hill
F.m
Reaves
Farm
Fishers
Green
Ames Green
Brook
Mungham
Hall
Cobbin
Cobbin
End
Dallunts

◁17

46 ▽

1 2
1 mile approx.

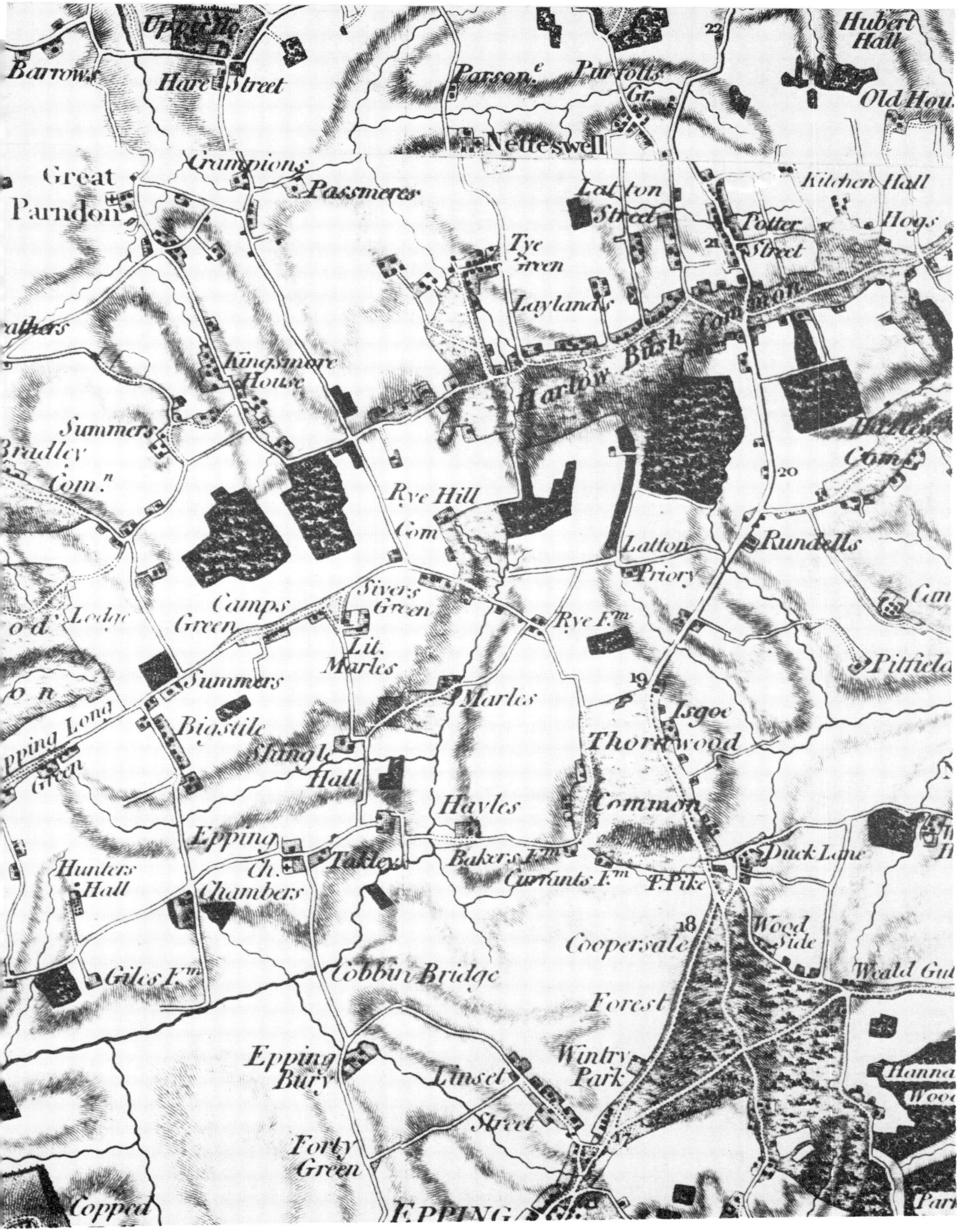
Upper Ho.
Barrows
Hare Street
Parson.e
Purfolls
Gr.
Netteswell
Hubert Hall
Old Hou
Great Parndon
Crampions
Passmeres
Latton Street
Kitchen Hall
Potter Street
Hogs
Tye Green
Laylands
Harlow Bush Common
Kingsmore House
Summers
Bradley Com.n
Rye Hill Com
Latton Priory
Rundells
Camps Green
Sivers Green
Rye F.m
Lit. Marles
Ledge
Summers
Marles
Isgoe
Pitfield
Epping Long Green
Bigstile
Shingle Hall
Thornwood Common
Hayles
Epping Ch.
Takeley
Bakers F.m
Currants F.m
T. Pike
Duck Lane
Hunters Hall
Chambers
Coopersale
Wood Side
Giles F.m
Cobbin Bridge
Forest
Weald Gu
Epping Bury
Linset Street
Wintry Park
Forty Green
Copped
EPPING
Hanna Woo
Par
22
21
20
19
18
17

28 ▷

47 ▽

Published 1805.

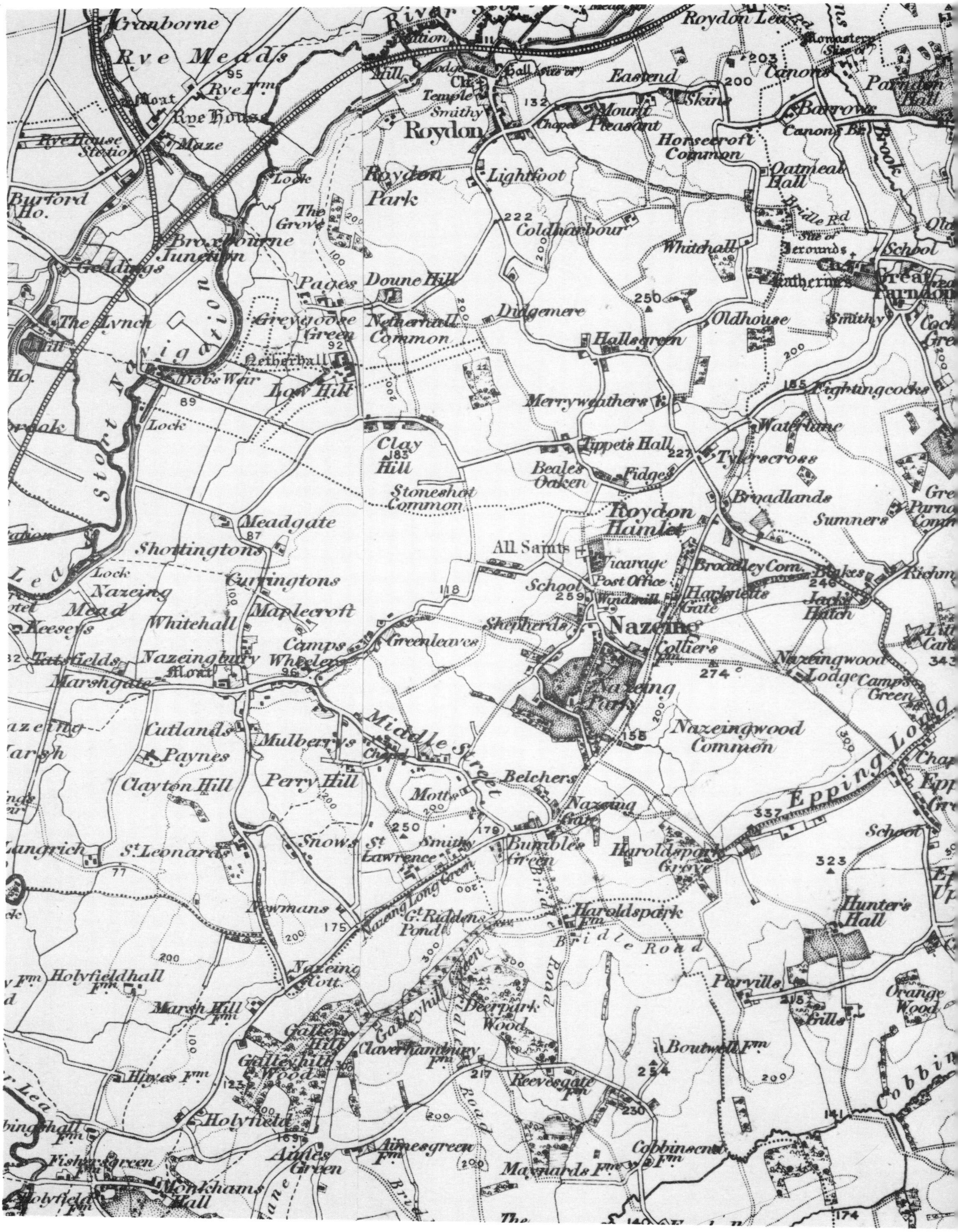

Cranborne
Rye Meads
Rye Fm.
Moat
Rye House
Maze
Rye House Station
Burford Ho.
Broxbourne Junction
Geldings
The Lynch
Stort Navigation
Dobs Weir
Lock
Meadgate
Shottingtons
Nazeing Mead
Curringtons
Maplecroft
Whitehall
Tatsfields
Nazeingbury
Moat
Marshgate
Camps
Wheelers
Greenleaves
Cutlands
Mulberrys
Paynes
Clayton Hill
Perry Hill
Middle Street
Chapel
Motts
St. Leonards
Snows
St. Lawrence
Smithy
Bumbles Green
Belchers
Nazeing Gate
Newmans
Nazeing Long Green
Gt. Riddens Pond
Holyfieldhall Fm.
Marsh Hill Fm.
Nazeing Gate
Galleyhill Green
Galley Hill
Galleyhill Wood
Deerpark Wood
Claverhambury Fm.
Hayes Fm.
Holyfield
Fishers Green
Aimes Green
Aimesgreen Fm.
Monkhams Hall
Reevesgate Fm.
Maynards Fm.
Cobbinsend Fm.
Boutwell Fm.
Haroldspark Fm.
Bridle Road
Haroldspark Grove
Parvills
Frills
Hunter's Hall
Orange Wood
School
Epping Long Green
Nazeingwood Common
Nazeingwood Lodge
Camps Green
Nazeing Park
Colliers Fm.
Nazeing
Shepherds
Windmill
Post Office
Vicarage
School
All Saints
Harknetts Gate
Broadley Com.
Blakes
Jacks Hatch
Roydon Hamlet
Broadlands
Sumners
Tylerscross
Waterlane
Fightingcocks
Fidges
Beales Oaken
Tippets Hall
Merryweathers
Stoneshot Common
Clay Hill
Low Hill
Netherhall
Greygoose Green
Netherhall Common
Pages
Doune Hill
Didgemere
Hallsgreen
Oldhouse
Smithy
Great Parndon
St. Katherines
Jerounds (Site of)
School
Whitehall
Coldharbour
Lightfoot
Roydon Park
The Grove
Roydon
Smithy
Temple
Hall
Chapel
Mount Pleasant
Eastend
Skins
Horsecroft Common
Canons
Canons Br.
Barrows
Parndon Hall
Oatmeal Hall
Bridle Rd
Monastery (Site of)
Roydon Lea
River Stort
Station
Lodge

1 2
1 mile approx.

◁19

48 ▽

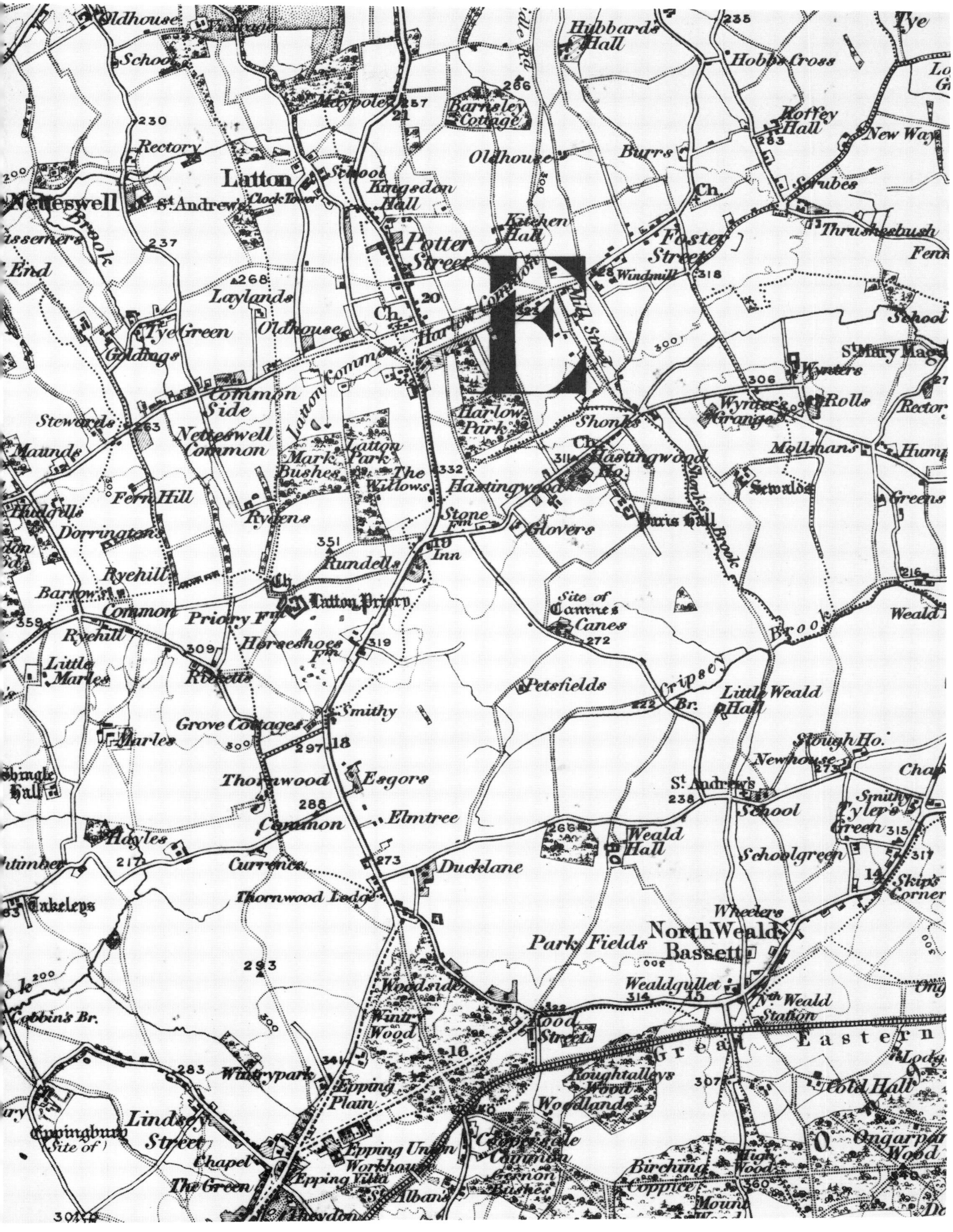
Oldhouse
Vicarage
School
Maypole
Barnsley Cottage
Hubbards Hall
Hobbs Cross
Tye
Roffey Hall
New Way
Burrs
Oldhouse
Rectory
Latton
School
Kingsden Hall
Netteswell
St. Andrews
Clock Tower
Brook
Ch.
Scrubes
Kitchen Hall
Potter Street
Foster Street
Thrushesbush
End
E
Windmill
Laylands
Harlow Common
Milk Street
Tye Green
Oldhouse
Ch.
School
Goldings
Latton Common
St. Mary Magd
Wynters
Common Side
Shonks
Wynter's Grange
Rolls
Rectory
Stewards
Netteswell Common
Harlow Park
Maunds
Latton Park
Ch.
Hastingwood Ho.
Mollmans
Mark Bushes
The Willows
Hastingwood
Sewalds
Fern Hill
Greens
Rydens
Stone Fm.
Glovers
Paris Hall
Dorringtons
Rundells
Inn
Ryehill
Ch.
Site of Cammes Canes
Barrow's
Latton Priory
Weald
Common
Priory Fm.
Brook
Ryehill
Horseshoes Fm.
Little Marles
Rickets
Petsfields
Cripsey Br.
Little Weald Hall
Smithy
Grove Cottages
Marles
Slough Ho.
Newhouse
Shingle Hall
Thornwood
Egors
St. Andrew's
School
Chapel
Smithy
Tyler's Green
Common
Elmtree
Weald Hall
Hayles
Schoolgreen
Currence
Ducklane
Skips Corner
Thornwood Lodge
Takeleys
Wheelers
North Weald Bassett
Park Fields
Woodside
Wealdgullet
Nth. Weald Station
Cobbin's Br.
Wintry Wood
Rood Street
Great Eastern
Lodge
Wintrypark
Epping Plain
Roughtalleys Wood
Woodlands
Cold Hall
Lindsey Street
Eppingbury (Site of)
Ongar Park Wood
Chapel
Epping Union Workhouse
Coopersale Common
High Wood
The Green
Epping Villa
Birching Coppice
St. Albans
Gernon Bushes
Mount Wood

30 ▷

49
▽

Surveyed 1869-1878. Published 1886.

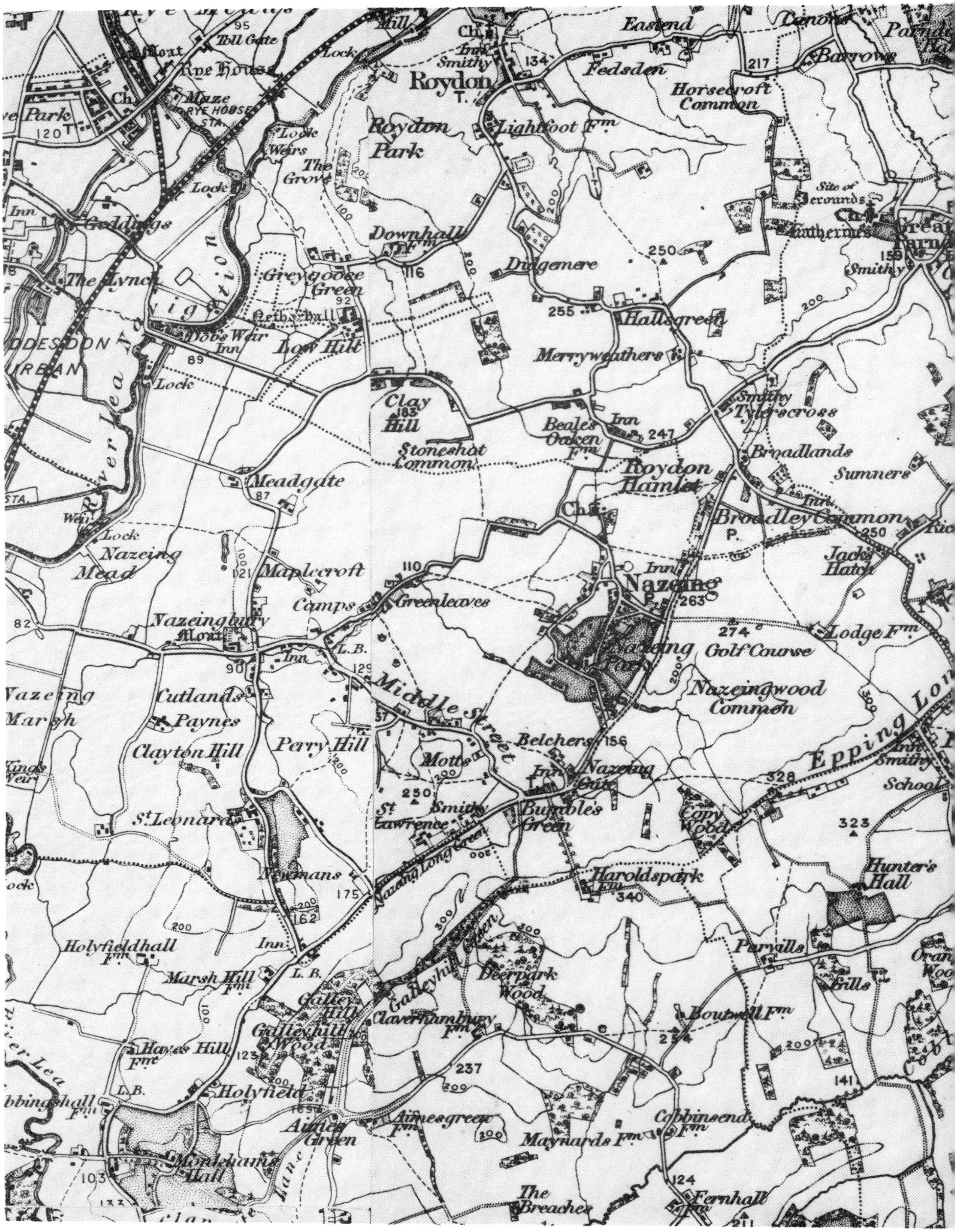
Toll Gate
Moat
Rye House
Lock
Ch.
Maze
RYE HOUSE STA.
Mill
Ch.
Inn
Smithy
Roydon
Eastend
Fedsden
Horsecroft Common
Barrows
Lock
Weirs
The Grove
Roydon Park
Lightfoot Fm.
Site of Grounds
Inn
Geddings
The Lynch
Downhall Fm.
Greygoose Green
Netherhall
Dobs Weir Inn
Low Hill
Dudgemere
Hallsgreen
Merryweathers
Smithy
Catherines
Smithy
Lock
Clay Hill
Stoneshot Common
Beales Oaken Fm.
Inn
Smithy
Tylerscross
Broadlands
Sumners
Meadgate
Roydon Hamlet
Ch.
Broadley Common
Weir
Lock
Nazeing Mead
Maplecroft
Greenleaves
Camps
Nazeing
Jacks Hatch
Nazeingbury
Moat
Inn
L. B.
Golf Course
Lodge Fm.
Nazeing Marsh
Cutlands
Paynes
Middle Street
Nazeingwood Common
Clayton Hill
Perry Hill
Motts
Belchers
Nazeing Gate
Epping Long
Inn
Smithy
School
Kings Weir
St. Leonards
St. Lawrence
Smithy
Bumbles Green
Copy Wood
Nazeing Long Green
Newmans
Haroldspark Fm.
Hunter's Hall
Holyfieldhall Fm.
Inn
Marsh Hill Fm.
L. B.
Galley Hill
Galleyhill Wood
Deerpark Wood
Claverhambury Fm.
Parvills
Gills
Boutwell Fm.
Hayes Hill Fm.
River Lea
L. B.
Holyfield
Aimes Green
Aimesgreen Fm.
Maynards Fm.
Cobbinsend Fm.
Monkhams Hall
Lane
The Breaches
Fernhall

◁ 21

50 ▽

1 2

1 mile approx.

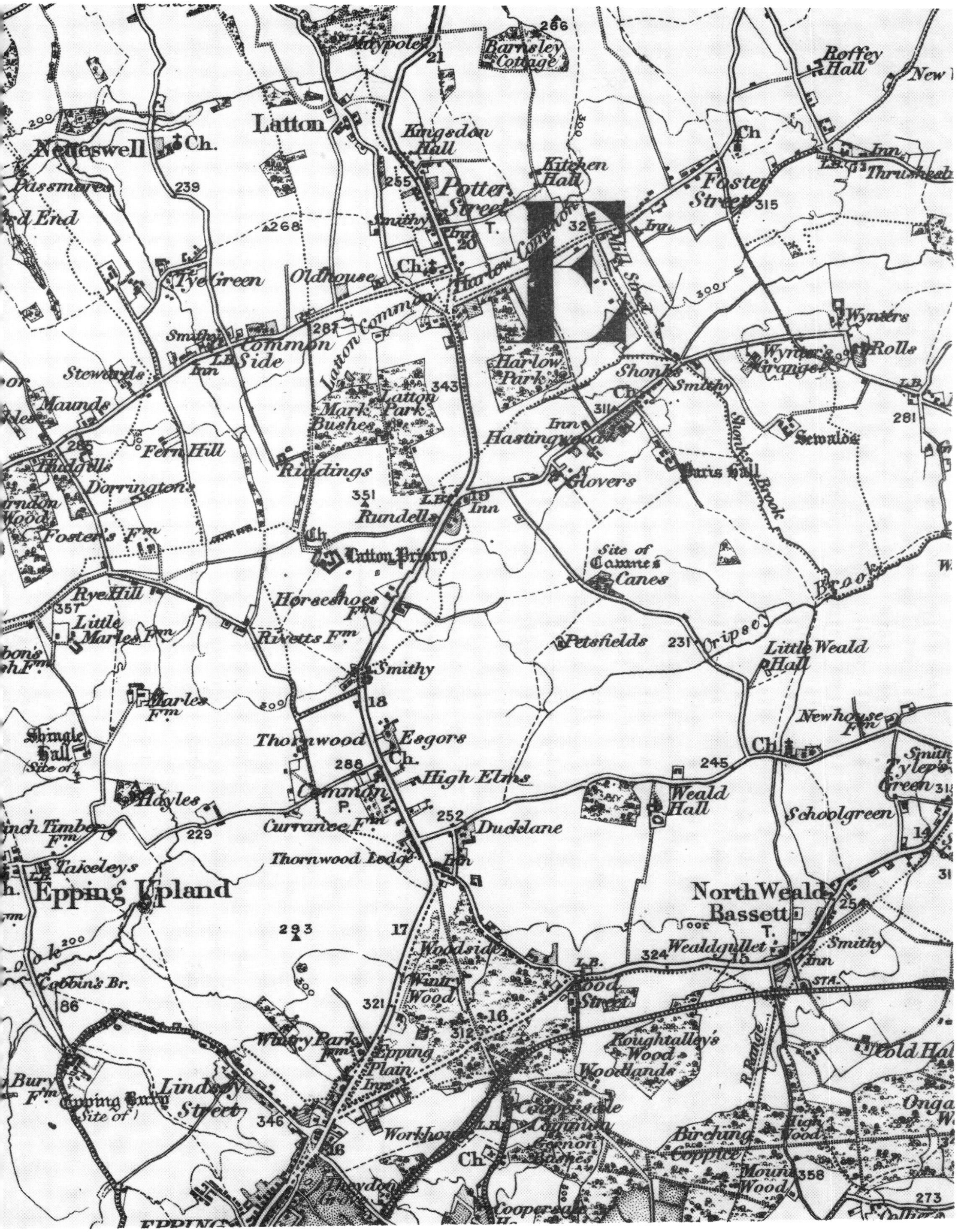

32 ▷

51 ▽

Surveyed 1869-1878. Revised 1902-1903. Published 1905.

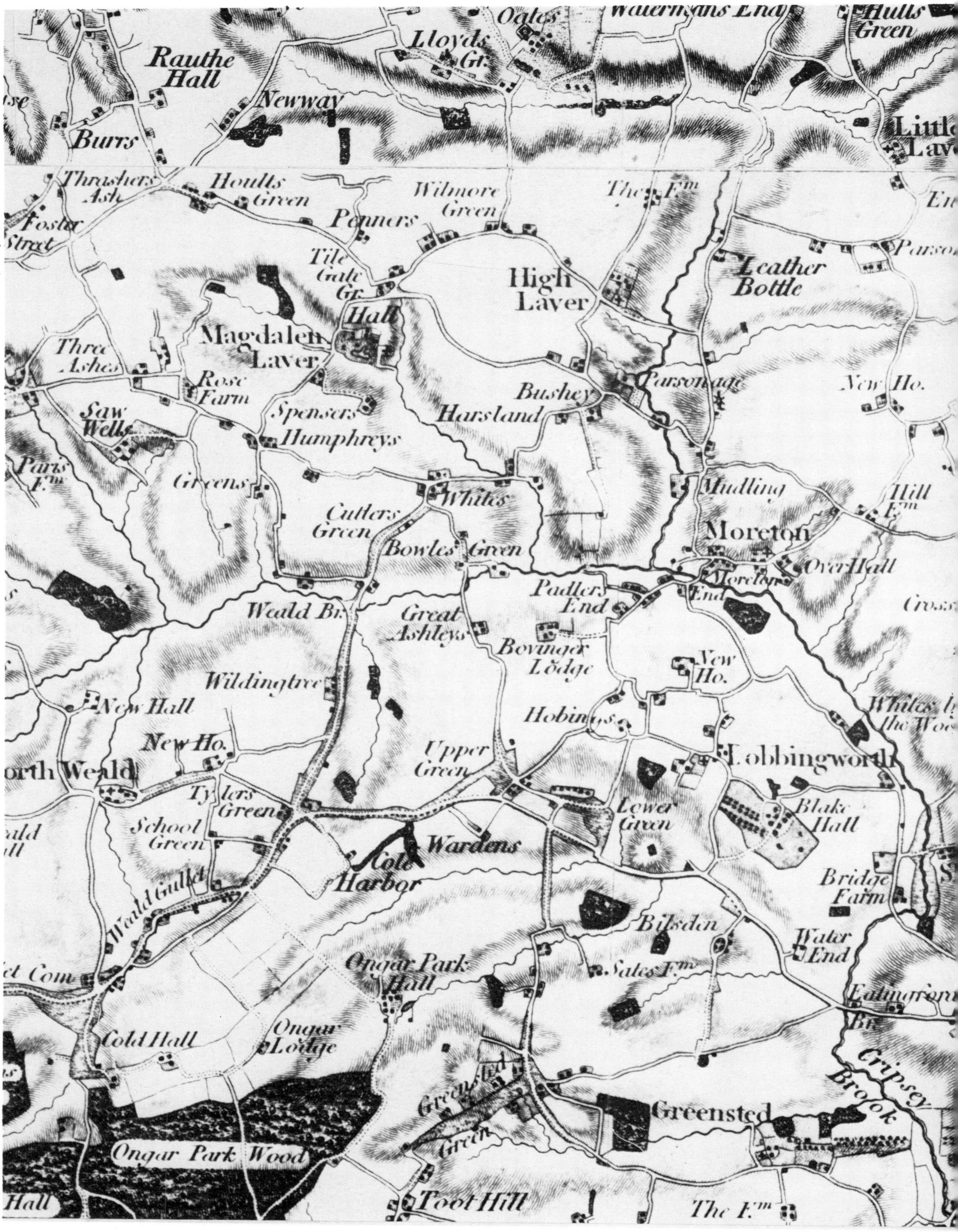
Oates
Watermans End
Hulls Green
Rauthe Hall
Lloyds Gr.
Newway
Burrs
Little Laver
Thrashers Ash
Hoults Green
Wilmore Green
The Fm
Foster Street
Penners
Tile Gate Gr.
High Laver
Leather Bottle
Hall
Magdalen Laver
Three Ashes
Rose Farm
Spensers
Bushey
Parsonage
Harsland
New Ho.
Saw Wells
Humphreys
Paris Fm
Greens
Whites
Mudling
Hill Fm
Cutlers Green
Bowles Green
Moreton
Over Hall
Moreton End
Padlers End
Weald Br.
Great Ashleys
Bovinger Lodge
New Ho.
Wildingtree
New Hall
Hobings
New Ho.
Upper Green
Lobbingworth
North Weald
Tylers Green
School Green
Wardens
Lower Green
Blake Hall
Cole Harbor
Bridge Farm
Weald Gulld
Bilsden
Water End
Ongar Park Hall
Sales Fm
Cold Hall
Ongar Lodge
Greensted Green
Greensted
Cripsey Brook
Ongar Park Wood
Toot Hill
The Fm
Hall

◁ 23

1 2

1 mile approx.

52 ▽

Wicks
Waples Mill
Pepper Green
Parkers
Woodend
Gilberts
Beauchamp Roding
Berners Roding
Larners
Old Hides
Govish
Elms
Horsell down
Dame Ann
Hornish
Buthatch Green
Birds Green
North End
wood
Shellow Br.
Rouse
Willingale Lodge
Diggings
Torrells Hall
Birlings Green
Golds
Pickerells
Millers Green
Dukes
Gardeners
Shellow
Shellow Bowells
Lampets
Willingale Spain
Willingale Doe
Sims
Fyfield
Whitney Green
Wardens Hall
Willingale End
Silvers Lane
Green
Spains Hall
Marvil Green
End
Bury Green
Bockwood
Pigstye Green
Herons
Newarks Hall
Hulks
River
Sprigs Hall
Boarded Barns
Forest Hall
Bassets
New Barns
Hoastly Hatch
Roding
Reddings
Norton Mandeville
Norton Heath
Hoastly Park
High Ongar
Chevers Hall
Spear F.m
Finarith Hall
Withers
Parslow Hall
Pawns
King Street
Clarks
Nine

Published 1805.

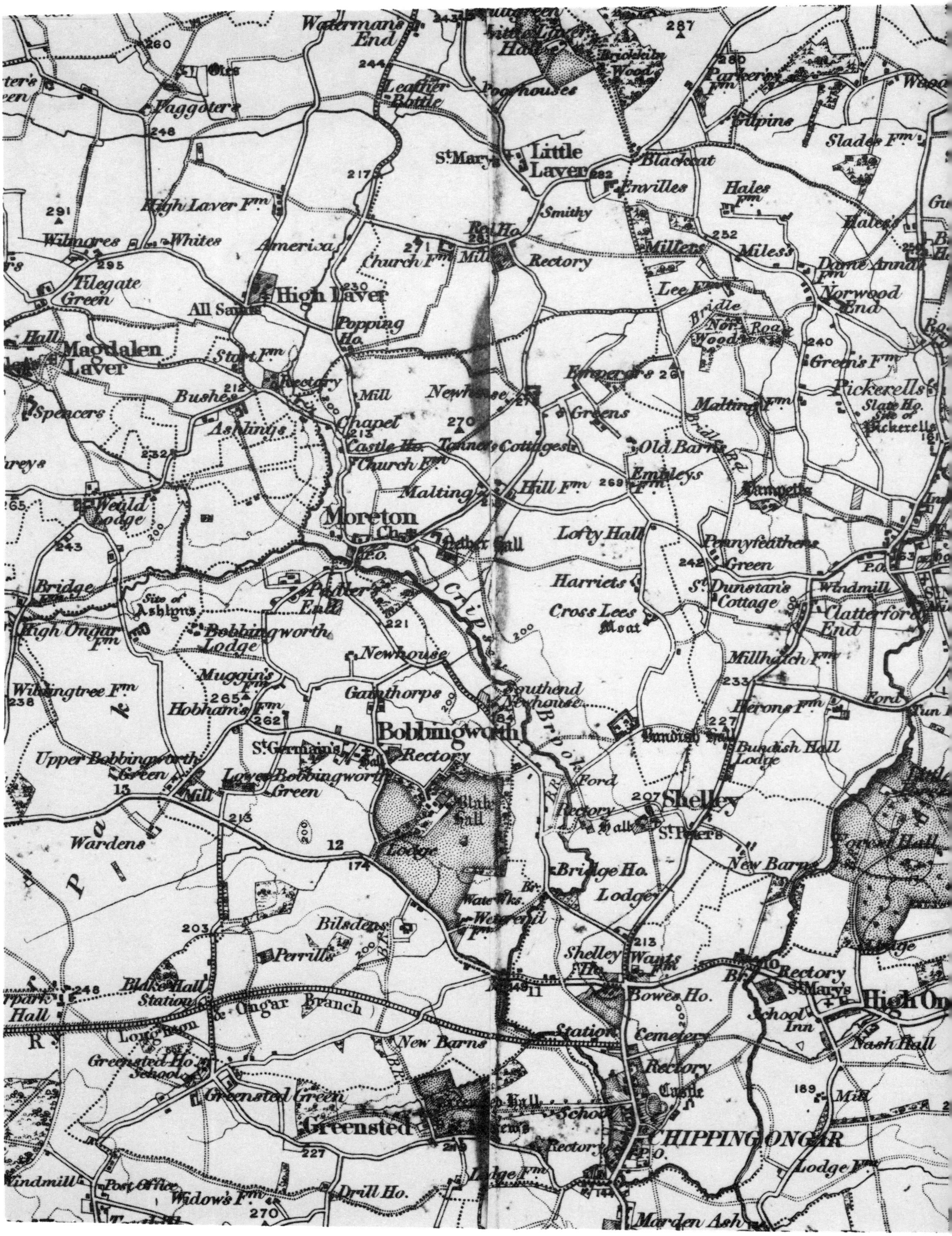
Watermans End
Leather Bottle
Poorhouses
Faggoters
Little Laver
St. Mary's
Blackcat
Envilles
Slades Fm.
Hales Fm.
High Laver Fm.
Whites
Wilmares
Tilegate Green
Amerixa
Church Fm.
Red Ho.
Mill
Smithy
Rectory
Millers
Miless
Dame Annals Fm.
Norwood End
Lee Fm.
High Laver
All Saints
Popping Ho.
Magdalen Laver
Start Fm.
Rectory
Bushes
Spencers
Ashlins
Mill
Chapel
Castle Ho.
Church Fm.
Newhouse
Tanners Cottages
Emperors
Greens
Malting Fm.
Old Barns
Pickerells
Slate Ho.
Malting
Hill Fm.
Emileys Fm.
Weald Lodge
Moreton
Lofty Hall
Pennyfeathers Green
Harriets
St. Dunstan's Cottage
Windmill
Clatterford End
Bridge Fm.
Site of Ashlyns
High Ongar Fm.
Bobbingworth Lodge
Cross Lees
Moat
Newhouse
Millhatch Fm.
Muggin's Fm.
Hobham's Fm.
Wilingtree Fm.
Gainthorps
Southend Newhouse
Herons Fm.
Ford
Bobbingworth
Rectory
Bundish Hall Lodge
Upper Bobbingworth Green
Lower Bobbingworth Green
Mill
Blake Hall
Ford
Rectory
Shelley
Hall
St. Peters
Wardens
Lodge
New Barns
Bridge Ho.
Lodge
Forest Hall
Water Wks.
Bilsdens
Perrills
Shelley Ho.
Wants Fm.
Rectory
St. Mary's
High Ongar
Blake Hall Station
Ongar Branch
Bowes Ho.
School
Inn
Nash Hall
Longhouse
Greensted Ho.
School
New Barns
Station
Cemetery
Rectory
Castle
Mill
Greensted Green
Greensted
Greensted Hall
School
CHIPPING ONGAR
Rectory
Lodge Fm.
Windmill
Post Office
Widow's Fm.
Drill Ho.
Lodge Fm.
Marden Ash

◁ 25

54 ▽

1 2

1 mile approx.

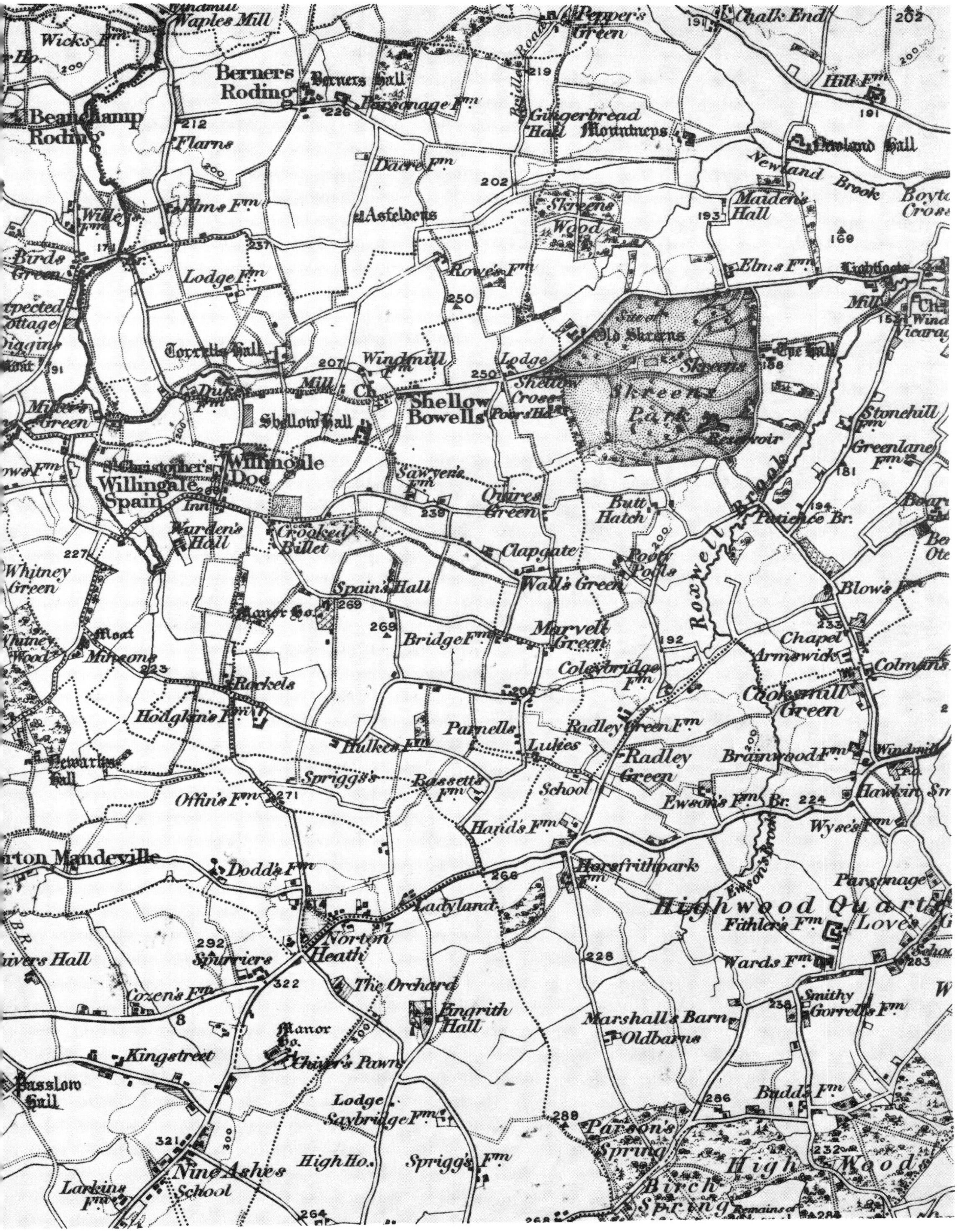
Waples Mill
Wicks Fm.
Berners Roding
Berners Hall
Parsonage Fm.
Pepper's Green
Chalk End
Hill Fm.
Beauchamp Roding
Flarns
Gingerbread Hall
Mountneys
Newland Hall
Newland Brook
Dacre Fm.
Asfeldens
Skreens Wood
Maiden's Hall
Boyton Cross
Elms Fm.
Birds Green
Lodge Fm.
Rowe's Fm.
Old Skreens
Skreens Park
Skreens
Reservoir
Torrells Hall
Windmill Fm.
Mill
Lodge
Shellow Cross
Shellow Bowells
Shellow Hall
Millers Green
Duke Fm.
Willingale Doe
Willingale Spain
St. Christopher's
Inn
Stonehill Fm.
Greenlane Fm.
Sawyer's Fm.
Quires Green
Butt Hatch
Patience Br.
Warden's Hall
Crooked Billet
Clapgate
Pools
Roxwell Brook
Whitney Green
Spain's Hall
Wall's Green
Blow's Fm.
Manor Ho.
Bridge Fm.
Marvell Green
Chapel
Armswick
Colmans
Moat
Mimeons
Coleybridge Fm.
Rockels
Cooksmill Green
Hodgkin's Fm.
Parnells
Radley Green Fm.
Hulkes Fm.
Lukies
Radley Green
Brainwood Fm.
Windmill
Spriggs's
Bassetts Fm.
School
Offin's Fm.
Ewson's Fm.
Br.
Hawkin
Wyses Fm.
Hand's Fm.
Norton Mandeville
Dodd's Fm.
Horsfrithpark Fm.
Parsonage
Ewson's Brook
Ladyland
Highwood Quarter
Fithler's Fm.
Norton Heath
Spurriers
Wards Fm.
The Orchard
Cozen's Fm.
Smithy
Gorrell's Fm.
Fingrith Hall
Marshall's Barn
Oldbarns
Manor Ho.
Kingstreet
Chiver's Pawn
Basslow Hall
Budds Fm.
Lodge
Saybridge Fm.
Parson's Spring
High Wood
Nine Ashes
School
High Ho.
Spriggs Fm.
Larkins Fm.
Birch Spring
Remains of

Surveyed 1869-1878. Published 1886.

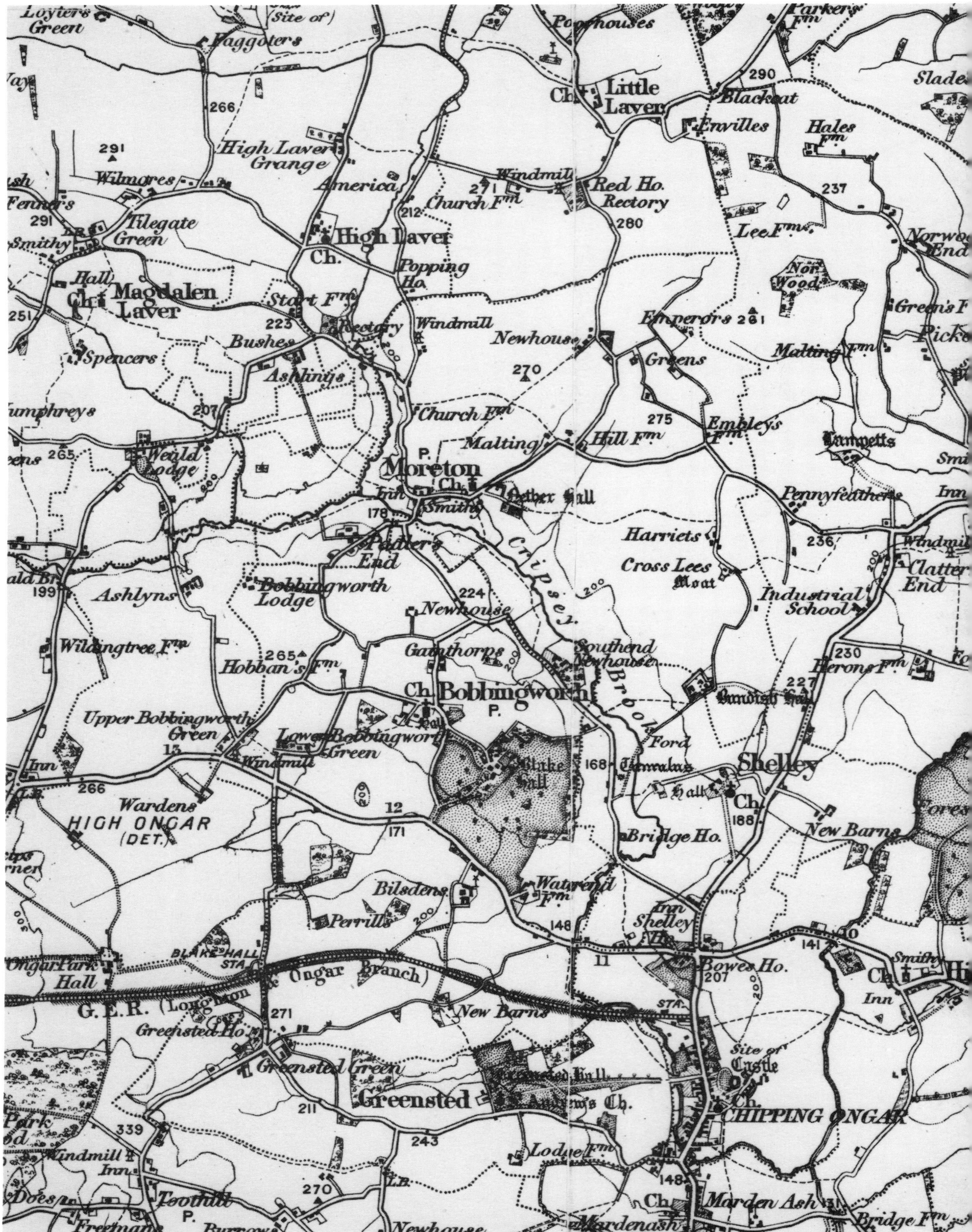
Loyters Green
Faggoters
Poorhouses
Little Laver
Ch.
Blackcat
290
Slades
Parkers Fm
Envilles
Hales Fm
266
High Laver Grange
291
Wilmores
America
Windmill
271
Church Fm
Red Ho.
Rectory
237
Fenners
291
Tilegate Green
Smithy
212
High Laver
Ch.
280
Lee Fm.
Norwood End
Popping Ho.
Nor Wood
Hall
Ch.
Magdalen Laver
Start Fm
Emperors
261
Green's F
251
223
Rectory
Windmill
Newhouse
Bushes
Malting Fm
Spencers
Ashlings
270
Greens
Humphreys
207
Church Fm
275
Embleys Fm
Hill Fm
Malting
Lampetts
265
Weald Lodge
P.
Moreton
Ch.
Inn
Nether Hall
Pennyfeathers
Inn
178
Smithy
Fiddlers End
Harriets
236
Windmill
Cripsey
Cross Lees
Moat
Clatter End
Bobbingworth Lodge
199
Ashlyns
224
Newhouse
Industrial School
Wildingtree Fm
265
Hobban's Fm
Gainthorps
Southend Newhouse
230
Herons Fm
Brook
227
Ch.
Bobbingworth
P.
Upper Bobbingworth Green
Lower Bobbingworth Green
Ford
Windmill
Blake Hall
168
Shelley
13
Inn
266
Hall
Ch.
Wardens
HIGH ONGAR (DET.)
12
171
188
New Barns
Bridge Ho.
Bilsdens
Waterend Fm
Perrills
Inn
Shelley Ho.
148
141
BLAKE HALL STA.
Ongar Park Hall
11
Bowes Ho.
207
Smithy
Ch.
Inn
G.E.R. (Loughton & Ongar Branch)
271
New Barns
STA.
Greensted Ho.
Greensted Green
Site of Castle
Greensted Hall
Greensted
St Andrew's Ch.
211
Ch.
CHIPPING ONGAR
Park
339
243
Windmill
Inn
Lodge Fm
148
270
Toothill
Ch.
Marden Ash
Does
Freemans
P.
Burrows
Newhouse
Mardenash
Bridge Fm

◁ 27

56 ▽

1 2

1 mile approx.

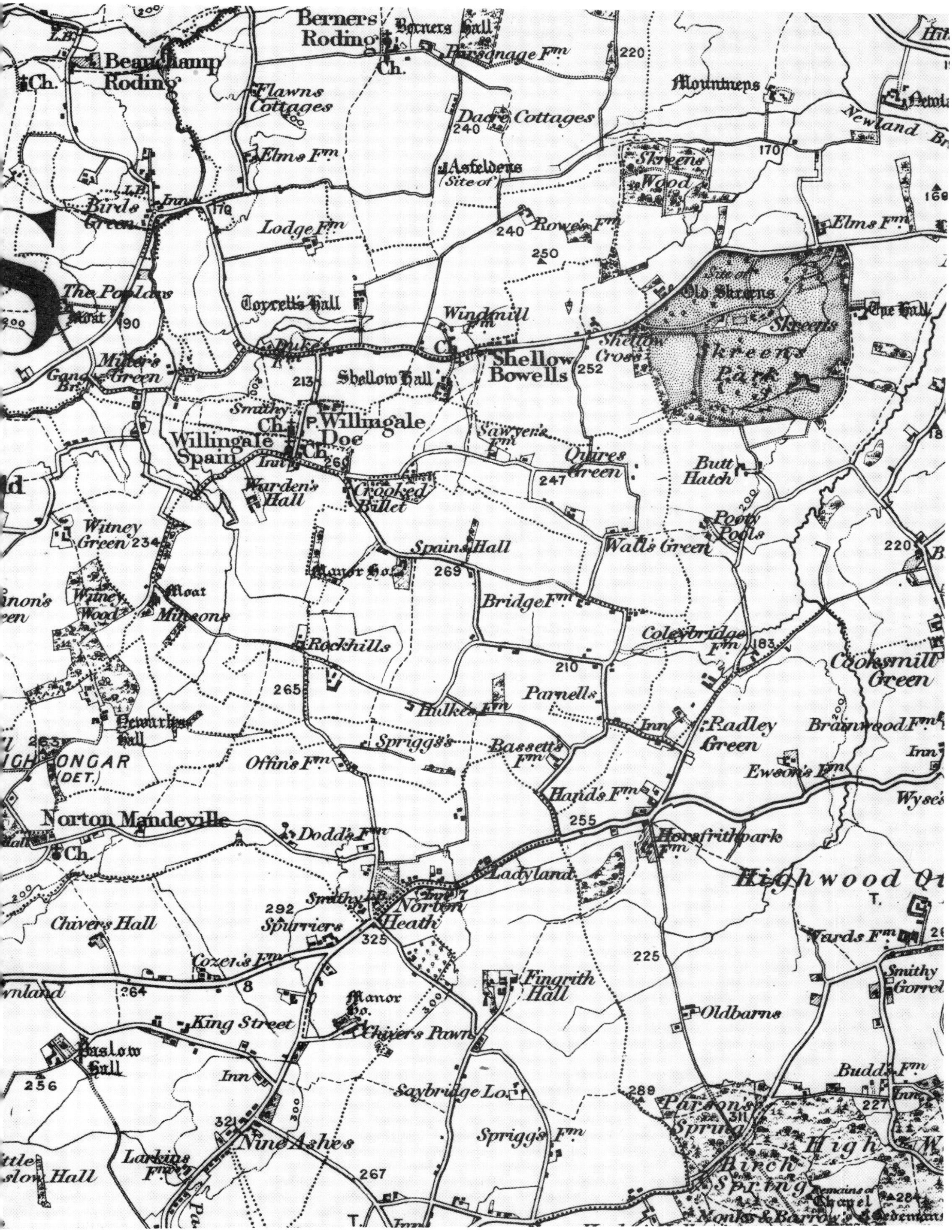

Surveyed 1869-1878. Revised 1902-1903. Published 1905.

△
10

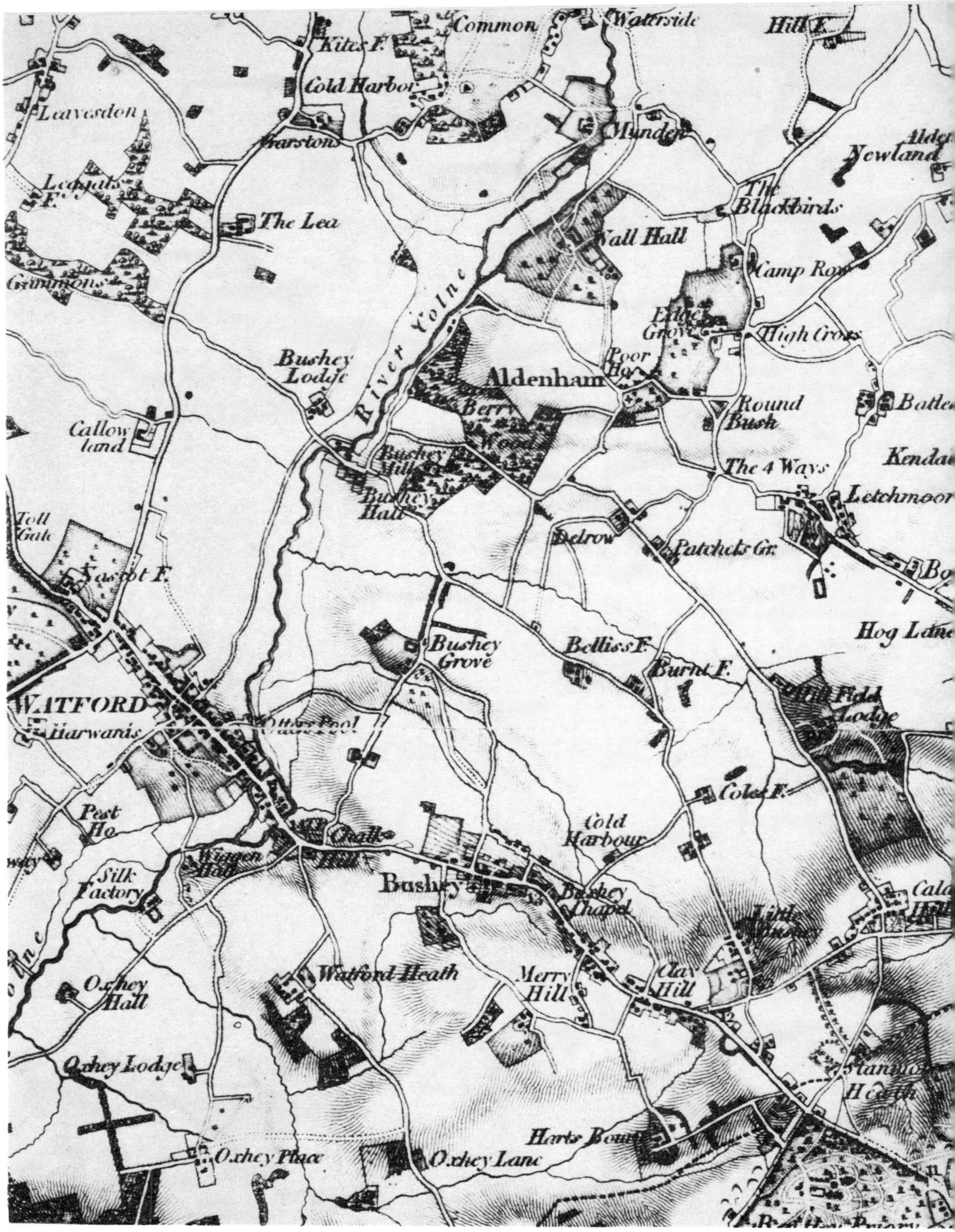
Common
Waterside
Hill F.
Kites F.
Cold Harbor
Leavesdon
Munden
Newland
The Lea
The Blackbirds
Wall Hall
Camp Row
Gammons
River Colne
Edge Grove
High Cross
Bushey Lodge
Aldenham
Poor Ho.
Berry Wood
Round Bush
Callow land
Bushey Mill
Bushey Hall
The 4 Ways
Letchmoor
Toll Gate
Delrow
Patchets Gr.
Nascot F.
Hog Lane
Bushey Grove
Bellis's F.
Burnt F.
WATFORD
Otter Pool
Post Ho.
Coles F.
Cold Harbour
Chalk Hill
Wiggen Hall
Silk Factory
Bushey
Bushey Chapel
Watford Heath
Merry Hill
Clay Hill
Oxhey Hall
Oxhey Lodge
Harts Bourne
Oxhey Place
Oxhey Lane

64
▽

1 2

1 mile approx.

11

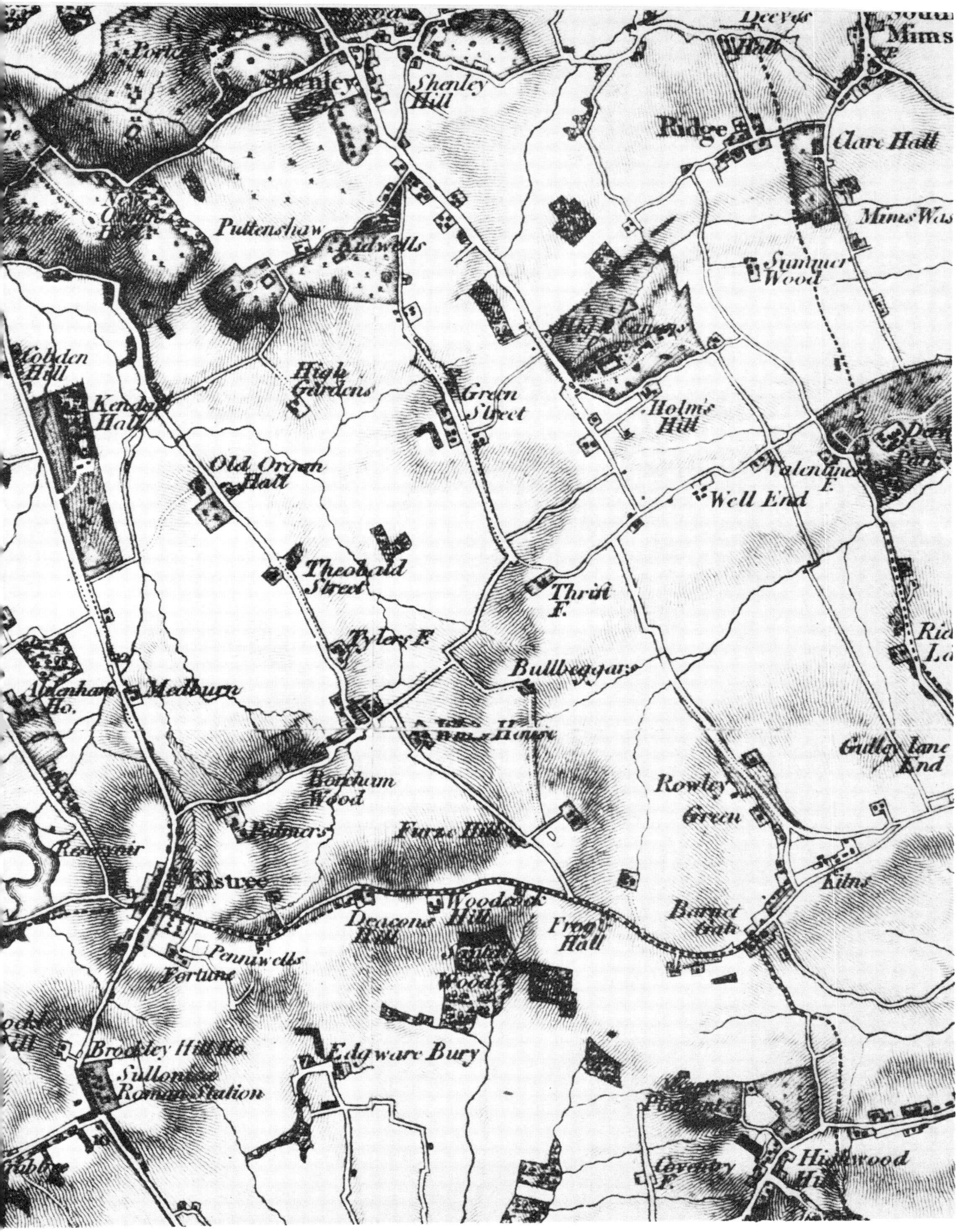
Shenley
Shenley Hill
Ridge
Clare Hall
Summer Wood
Puttenshaw
Bidwells
High Gardens
Green Street
Holm's Hill
Old Organ Hall
Well End
Theobald Street
Thrift F.
Tylers F.
Bullbeggars
Medburn
Boreham Wood
Rowley Green
Gulley lane End
Palmers
Furze Hill
Elstree
Kilns
Deacons Hill
Frog Hall
Barnet Gate
Penniwells
Fortune
Brockley Hill Ho.
Roman Station
Edgware Bury
Highwood

40

65

Published 1822.

12

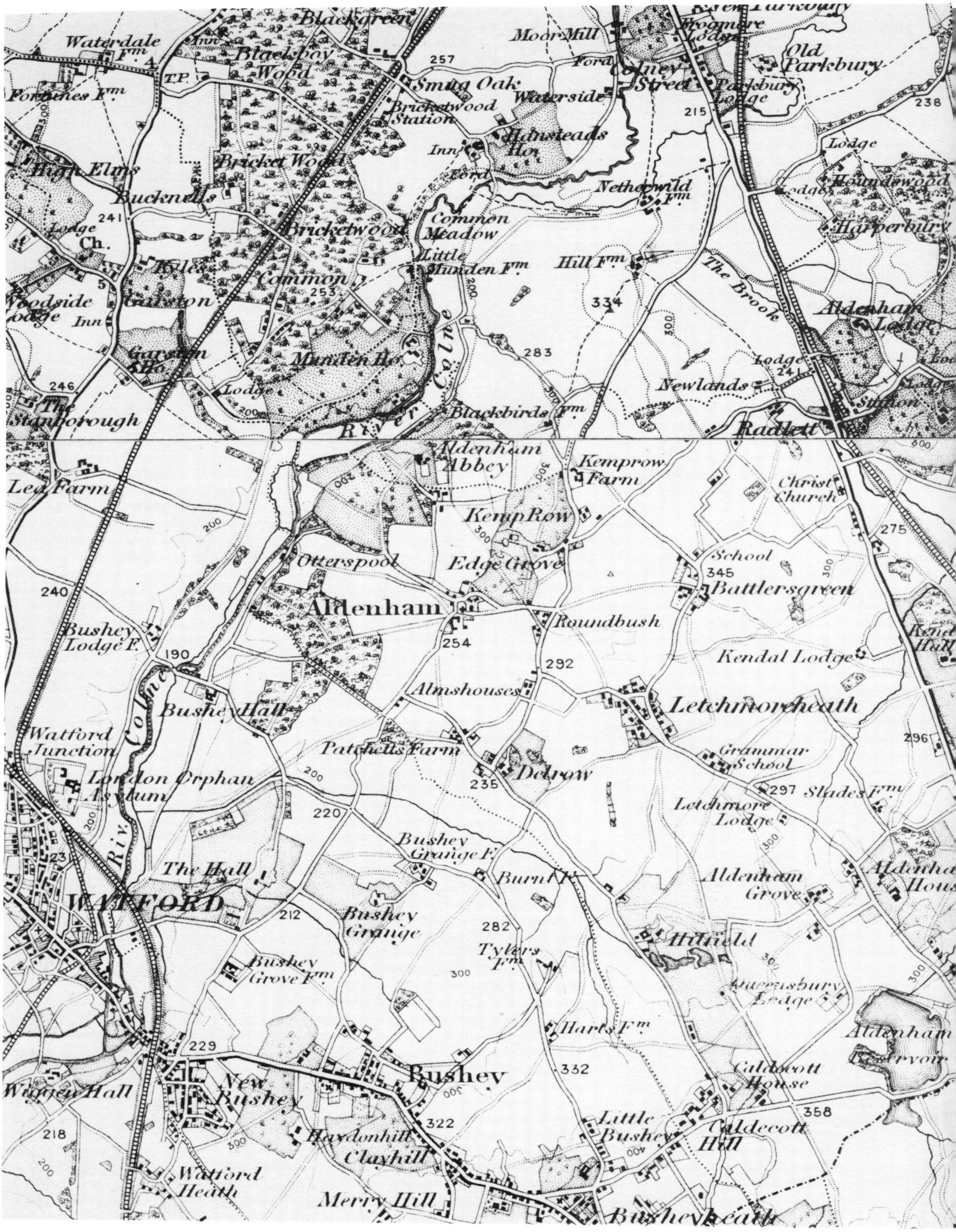
Blackgreen
Waterdale Fm.
Black boy Wood
Smug Oak
Bricketwood Station
Moor Mill
Ford
Colney Street
Old Parkbury
Parkbury Lodge
Waterside
Hansteads Ho.
Inn
High Elms
Bucknells
Bricket Wood
Netherwild Fm.
Lodge
Ch.
Bricketwood
Common Meadow
Houndswood
Harperbury
Little Munden Fm.
Hill Fm.
Kyles
Common
Garston
The Brook
Aldenham Lodge
Garston Ho.
Munden Ho.
Newlands
The Stanborough
River Colne
Blackbirds Fm.
Radlett
Aldenham Abbey
Kemprow Farm
Christ Church
Lea Farm
Kemp Row
Otterspool
Edge Grove
School
Battlersgreen
Aldenham
Roundbush
Bushey Lodge F.
Kendal Lodge
Almshouses
Letchmoreheath
Bushey Hall
Watford Junction
Patchetts Farm
Grammar School
London Orphan Asylum
Delrow
Slades Fm.
Letchmore Lodge
Riv. Colne
Bushey Grange F.
The Hall
Burnt F.
Aldenham Grove
WATFORD
Bushey Grange
Bushey Grove Fm.
Tylers Fm.
Hilfield
Harts Fm.
Aldenham Reservoir
Caldecott House
New Bushey
Bushey
Wiggen Hall
Little Bushey
Caldecott Hill
Haydonhill
Clayhill
Watford Heath
Merry Hill
Bushey heath

1 2

1 mile approx.

66

13

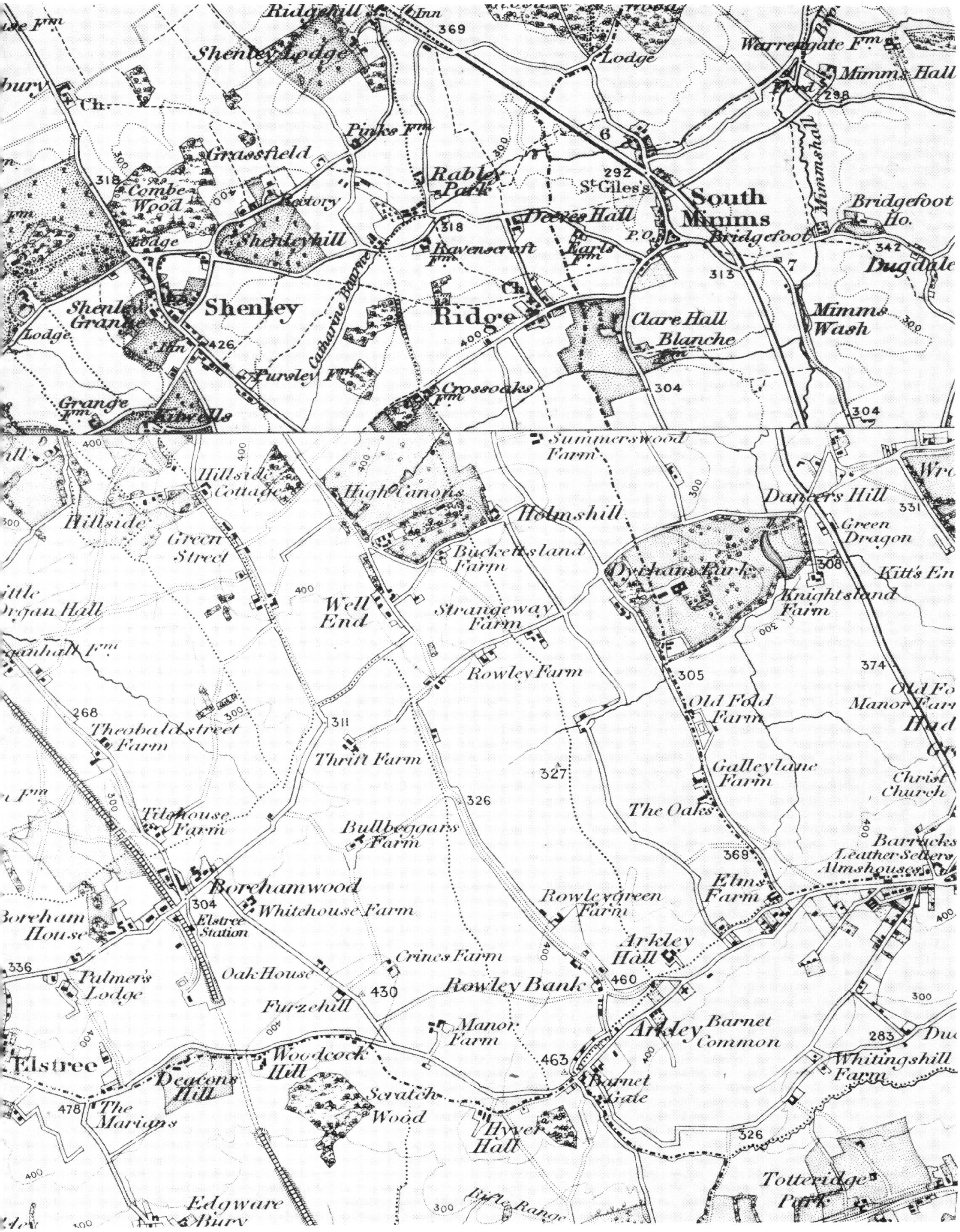
Ridgehill
Inn
369
Shenley Lodge
Lodge
Warrengate Fm.
Mimms Hall
Ch.
Pinks Fm.
Grassfield
Combe Wood
Rectory
Rabley Park
318
St. Giles's
292
South Mimms
Bridgefoot Ho.
Shenleyhill
Lodge
Ravenscroft Fm.
Earls Fm.
P.O.
Bridgefoot
Dugdale
313
342
Shenley Grange
Lodge
Shenley
Inn
426
Catharine Bourne
Ridge
Ch.
400
Clare Hall
Blanche Fm.
Mimms Wash
Mimmshall
Pursley Fm.
Crossoaks Fm.
304
Grange Fm.
Kitwells
Summerswood Farm
Hillside Cottage
High Canons
Holmshill
Dancers Hill
331
Green Dragon
Hillside
Green Street
Bucketsland Farm
Dyrham Park
308
Kitt's En
Knightsland Farm
Organ Hall
Well End
Strangeway Farm
Rowley Farm
305
374
268
Theobaldstreet Farm
311
Old Fold Farm
Old Fold Manor Farm
Thrift Farm
327
Galleylane Farm
Christ Church
326
Tilehouse Farm
The Oaks
Bullbeggars Farm
369
Barracks
Leather Sellers Almshouses
Borehamwood
Elms Farm
304
Elstree Station
Whitehouse Farm
Rowleygreen Farm
Boreham House
Arkley Hall
Crines Farm
336
Palmer's Lodge
Oak House
Rowley Bank
460
430
Furzehill
300
Manor Farm
Arkley
Barnet Common
283
Whitingshill Farm
Elstree
Woodcock Hill
463
Deacons Hill
Barnet Gate
478
The Marians
Scratch Wood
Hyver Hall
326
Totteridge Park
Edgware Bury
Rifle Range

42

67

Surveyed 1862-1880. Published 1887.

14

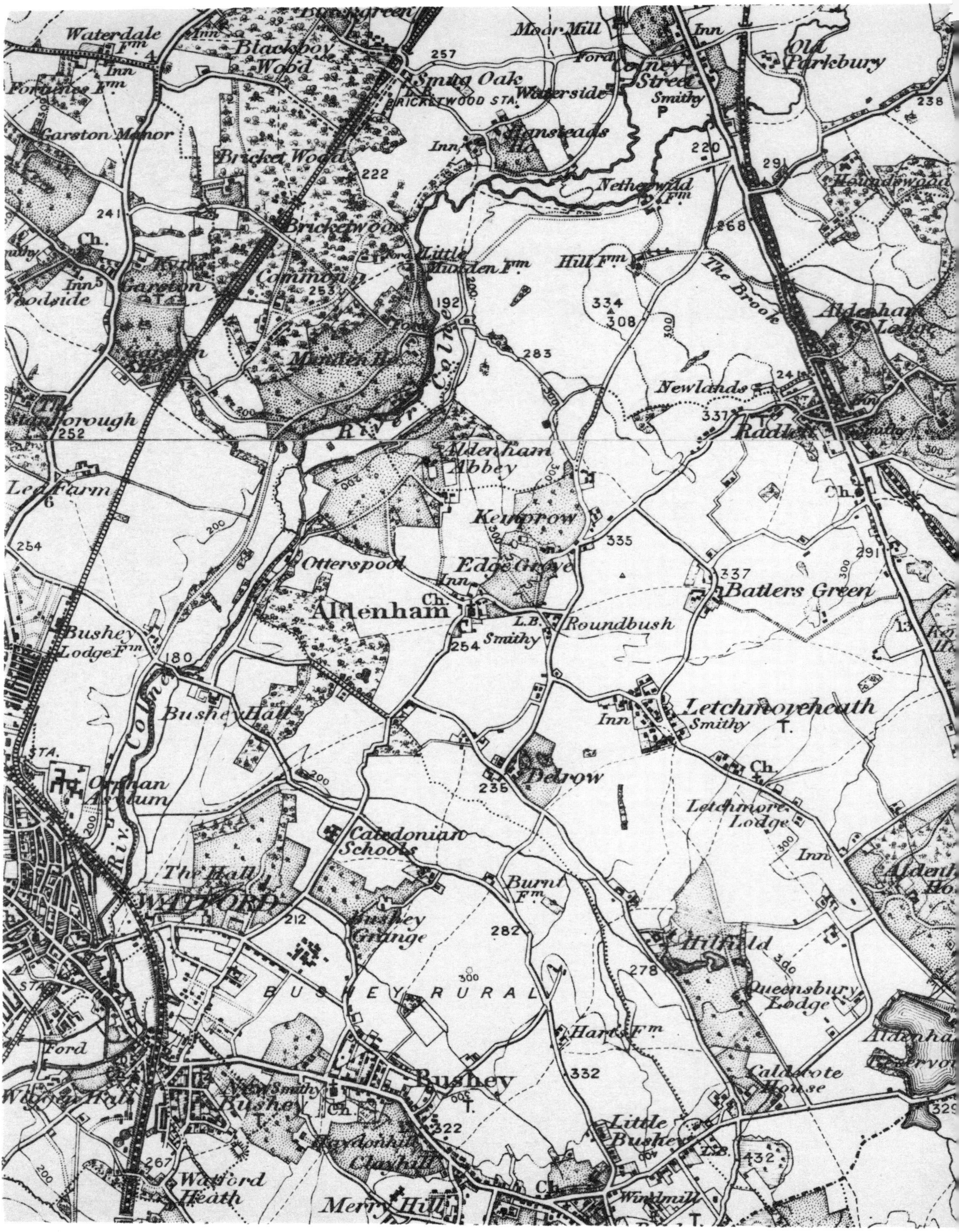
Waterdale Fm.
Blackboy Wood
Smug Oak
BRICKETWOOD STA.
Moor Mill
Waterside
Colney Street
Smithy
Old Parkbury
Garston Manor
Bricket Wood
Hansteads Ho.
Netherwild Fm.
Brickewood Common
Garston
Woodside
Little Munden Fm.
Hill Fm.
The Brook
Munden Ho.
River Colne
Aldenham Lodge
Newlands
Radlett
The Stanborough
Aldenham Abbey
Lea Farm
Kemprow
Edge Grove
Otterspool
Aldenham
Ch.
Roundbush
Smithy
Batlers Green
Bushey Lodge Fm.
Bushey Hall
Letchmoreheath
Smithy
Delrow
Orphan Asylum
Letchmore Lodge
Caledonian Schools
The Hall
WATFORD
Burnt Fm.
Bushey Grange
Hilfield
Queensbury Lodge
BUSHEY RURAL
Harts Fm.
Bushey
New Bushey
Caldecote House
Little Bushey
Watford Heath
Merry Hill
Windmill

68

1 2

1 mile approx.

△
15

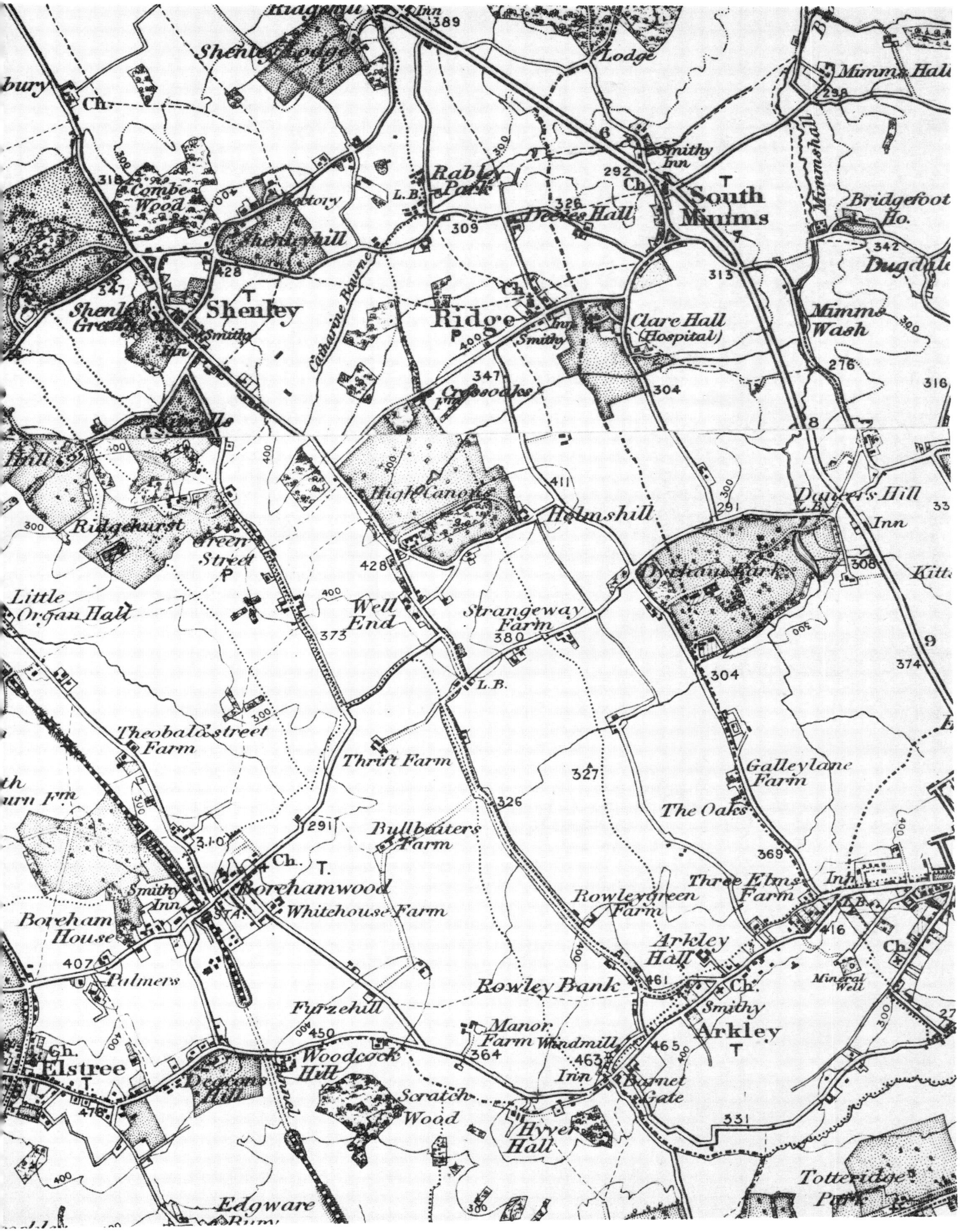

44 ▷

69
▽

Surveyed 1862-1880. Revised 1902. Published 1904.

16

35

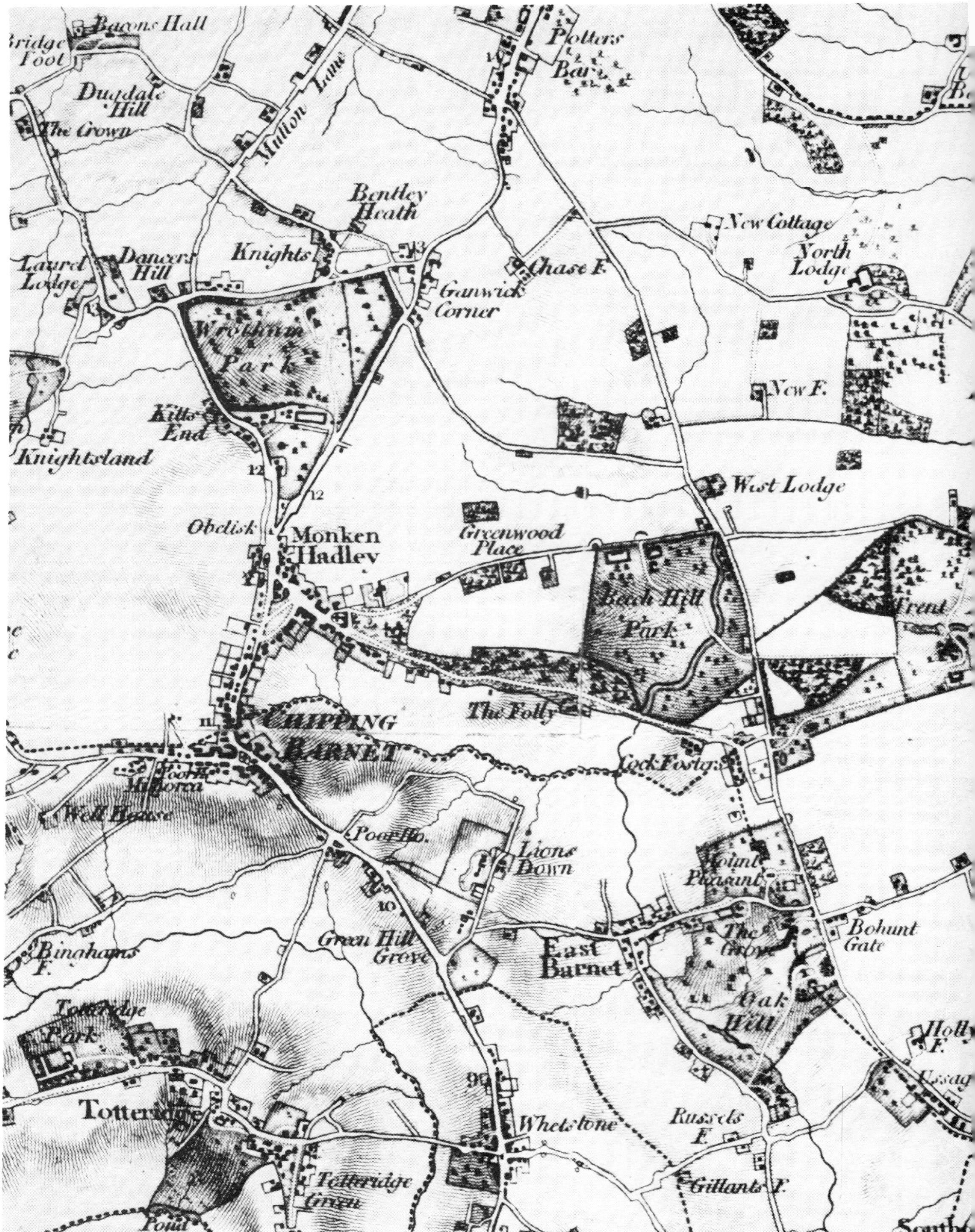
Bacons Hall
Bridge Foot
Dugdale Hill
The Crown
Mutton Lane
Potters Bar
Bentley Heath
Knights
Laurel Lodge
Dancers Hill
Wrotham Park
Ganwick Corner
Chase F.
New Cottage
North Lodge
New F.
Kitts End
Knightsland
West Lodge
Obelisk
Monken Hadley
Greenwood Place
Beech Hill Park
Trent
The Folly
CHIPPING BARNET
Cock Fosters
Well House
Poor Ho.
Lions Down
Mount Pleasant
Binghams F.
Green Hill Grove
East Barnet
The Grove
Bohunt Gate
Oak Hill
Totteridge Park
Holly F.
Totteridge
Whetstone
Russels F.
Totteridge Green
Gillants F.
Pond

70

1 2

1 mile approx.

17

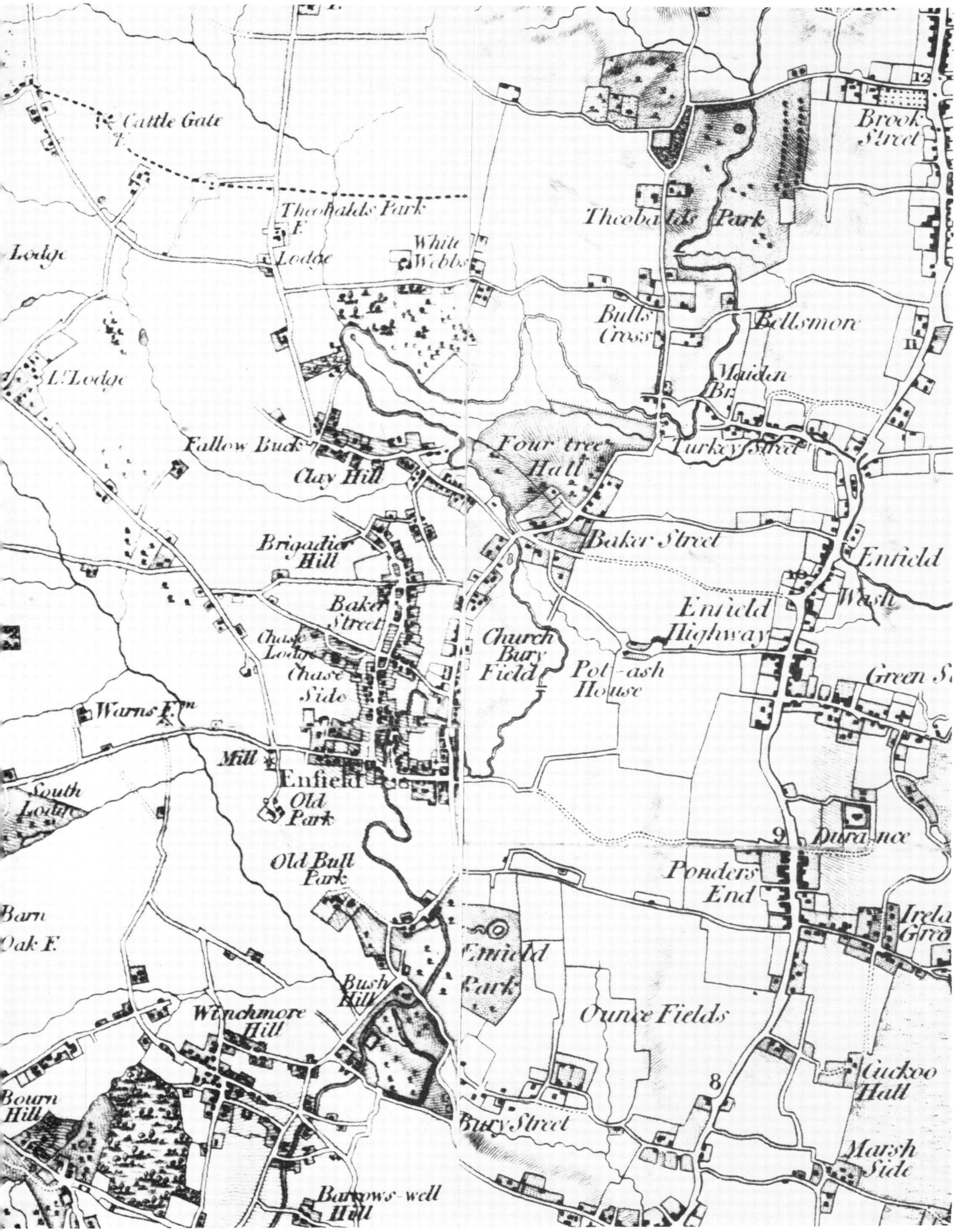
Cattle Gate
Theobalds Park F.
Lodge
Lodge
White Webbs
Lt. Lodge
Theobalds Park
Brook Street
Bulls Cross
Bellsmore
Maiden Br.
Turkey Street
Fallow Buck
Clay Hill
Four tree Hall
Baker Street
Enfield
Brigadier Hill
Wash
Baker Street
Enfield Highway
Chase Lodge
Church Bury Field
Chase Side
Pot-ash House
Green S
Warns F.m
Mill
Enfield
South Lodge
Old Park
Durance
Old Bull Park
Ponders End
Barn
Oak F.
Enfield Park
Irela Gre
Bush Hill
Winchmore Hill
Ounce Fields
Cuckoo Hall
Bourn Hill
Bury Street
Marsh Side
Barrows-well Hill

46

71

Published 1822.

18

37

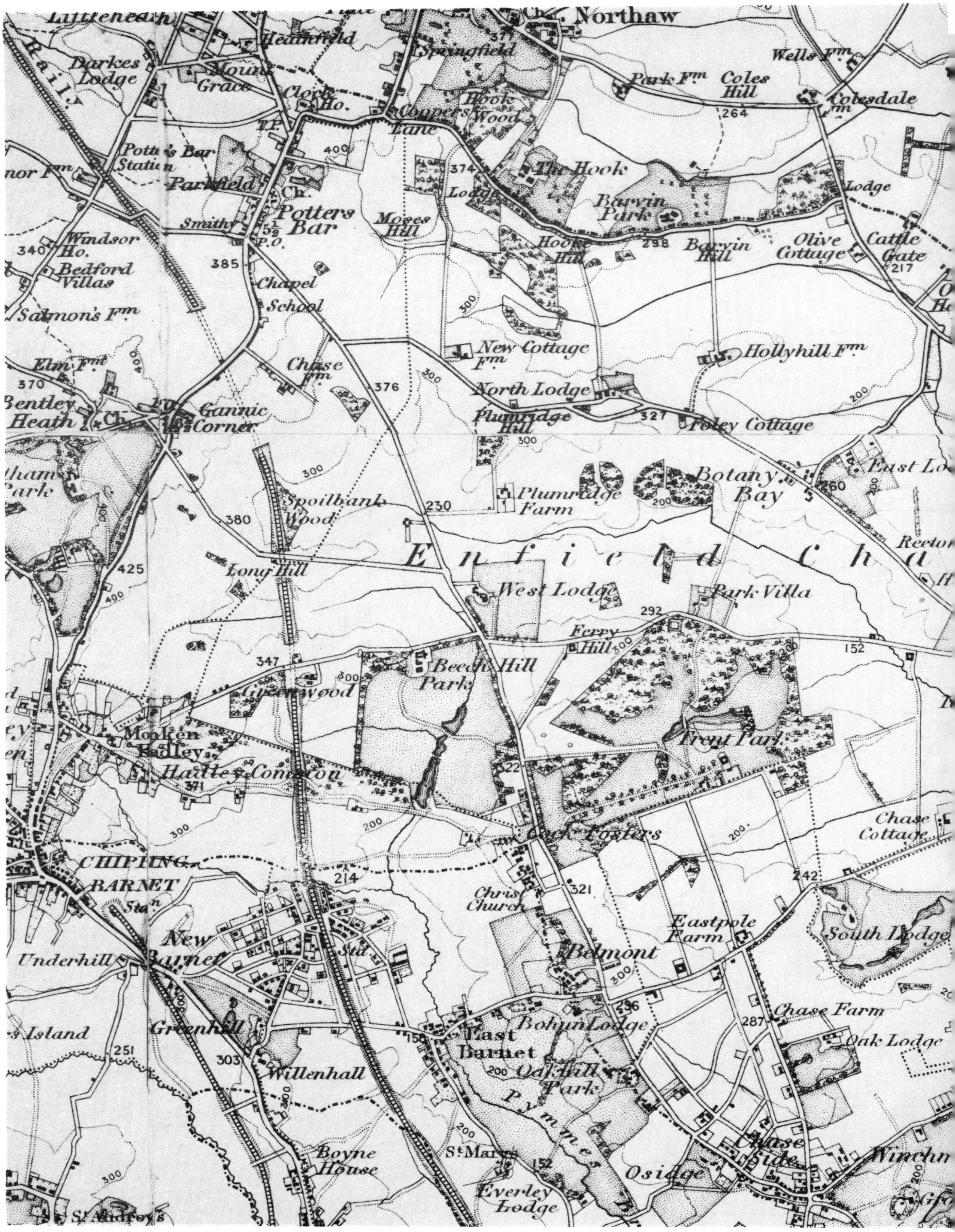
Northaw
Heathfield
Springfield
Darkes Lodge
Mount Grace
Clock Ho.
Wells Fm.
Park Fm.
Coles Hill
Colesdale Fm.
Hook Wood
Coopers Lane
Potters Bar Station
Parkfield
Ch.
Potters Bar
Smithy
P.O.
Moses Hill
The Hook
Lodge
Barvin Park
Hook Hill
Barvin Hill
Olive Cottage
Cattle Gate
Windsor Ho.
Bedford Villas
Chapel
School
Salmon's Fm.
New Cottage Fm.
Hollyhill Fm.
Elm Fm.
Chase Fm.
North Lodge
Bentley Heath
Ch.
Gannic Corner
Plumridge Hill
Foley Cottage
East Lodge
Botany Bay
Spoilbank Wood
Plumridge Farm
Enfield Cha
Long Hill
West Lodge
Park Villa
Ferry Hill
Beech Hill Park
Greenwood
Monken Hadley
Hadley Common
Trent Park
Cock Fosters
Chase Cottage
CHIPPING BARNET
Christ Church
Eastpole Farm
New Barnet
Stn.
Underhill
Belmont
South Lodge
Bohun Lodge
Chase Farm
Island
Greenhill
East Barnet
Oak Lodge
Willenhall
Oakhill Park
Pymmes
Chase Side
Boyne House
St. Marys
Osidge
Everley Lodge
St. Andrews

72

1 2

1 mile approx.

△ 19

Churchgate
Cemetery
Lodge
Woodgreen Park
Burnt Fm
Broadfield Fm
Bury Green
Cheshunt
Windmill Street
Albury Fm
Schools
The Cedars
Theobalds Fm
Oldpark Fm
Theobald's Park
Waltham Cross
Bullscross Fm
Lodges
Cross
Sloman's Fm
Lodge
Boundary Ho.
Capel Ho.
Whitewebbs Park
Wood
White Webbs
White Webbs Park
Freezy Water
Cheshunt Marsh
Waltham Marsh
Rammey Marsh
Myddleton House
Turkey Street
Ordnance Fact. Station
Claysmore
Clayhill
Forty Hall
Jesus Church
Forty hill
Enfield Wash
Enfield Lock
Brooklands
Enfield Highway
New River
Chase Side
Green Street
St. James
ENFIELD
Duranty
Durant's Harbour
Station
The Moat
Chase Park
Park Farm
Old Park Grange
Old Park
Bush Hill
Ponders End
Gt. Ey. Ry.
Enfield Branch
Lock
Spencers Fm
Yardley
Cuckoohall Farm
Causeyware Hall
Bury Street
Rowantree
Laurel Ho.
River Lea
Royal Arms

48▷

73 ▽

Surveyed 1862-1880. Published 1887.

20

39

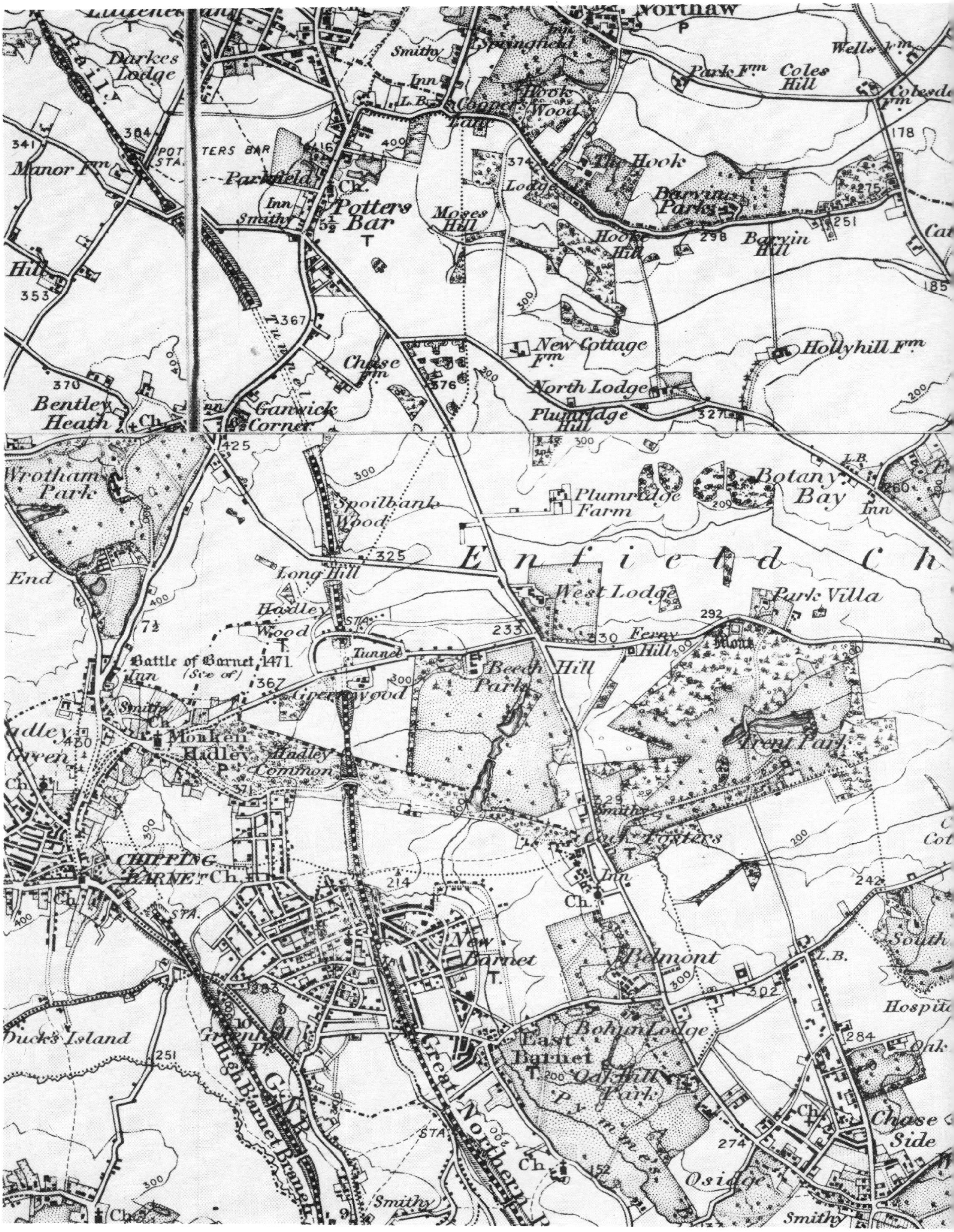

Northaw
Darkes Lodge
Smithy
Springfield
Inn
L.B.
Coopers Lane
Hook Wood
Park Fm
Coles Hill
Wells Fm
Colesdene Fm
178
341
304
POTTERS BAR STA.
416
400
374
Manor Fm
Parkfield
Ch.
Lodge
The Hook
Barvin Park
275
Inn
Smithy
Potters Bar
T
Moses Hill
Hook Hill
298
Barvin Hill
251
Hill
353
185
367
300
New Cottage Fm
Hollyhill Fm
Chase Fm
376
300
North Lodge
Plumridge Hill
327
200
370
Bentley Heath
Ch.
Ganwick Corner
400
425
300
Wrotham Park
Spoilbank Wood
Plumridge Farm
Botany Bay
Inn
L.B.
260
200
300
325
Enfield Ch
End
Long Hill
West Lodge
Park Villa
400
Hadley Wood
STA.
233
230
Ferny Hill
292
Mount
300
200
Battle of Barnet 1471 (Site of)
Inn
Tunnel
Beech Hill Park
367
Greenwood
300
Smithy
Ch.
Monken Hadley
Hadley Common
P
430
Hadley Green
Trent Park
Ch.
371
329
Smithy
300
Cock Fosters
T
200
CHIPPING BARNET
Ch.
Inn
214
242
Ch.
STA.
400
New Barnet
T.
Belmont
300
L.B.
302
Hospital
283
Greenhill Pk
East Barnet
T.
Bohun Lodge
Oak Hill Park
200
284
Duck's Island
251
High Barnet Branch G.N.R.
Great Northern Railway
Pymmes Park
Ch.
Chase Side
300
STA.
274
Ch.
152
Osidge
300
Ch.
Smithy
Smithy

74

1 2

1 mile approx.

△
21

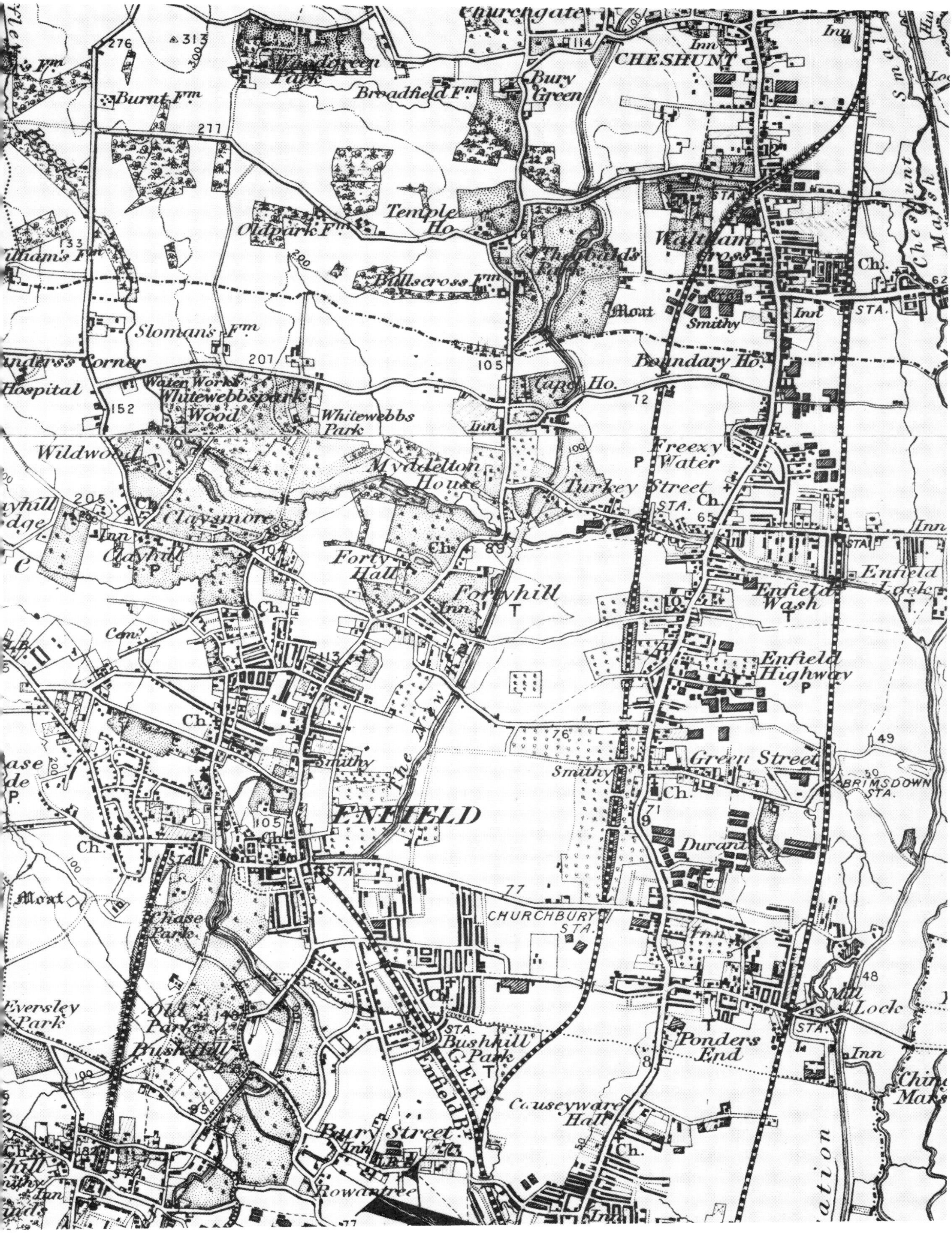
Churchgate
CHESHUNT
Inn
Windgreen Park
Bury Green
Broadfield Fm
Burnt Fm
Temple Ho
Oldpark Fm
Theobald's Park
Waltham Cross
STA.
Ch.
Bullscross Fm
Moat
Smithy
Inn
Sloman's Fm
Boundary Ho.
Hospital
Water Works
Whitewebbspark Wood
Whitewebbs Park
Capel Ho.
Inn
Wildwood
Myddelton House
Freezy Water
Turkey Street
STA.
Ch.
Claysmore
Inn
Clayhill
Forty Hall
Ch.
Forty hill
Inn
Enfield Wash
Enfield Lock
STA.
Inn
Ch.
Cemy
Enfield Highway
The New River
Green Street
Smithy
BRIMSDOWN STA.
Smithy
Ch.
ENFIELD
Ch.
Durants
STA.
Moat
Chase Park
CHURCHBURY STA.
Inn
Eversley Park
Old Park
Bush Hill
Ch.
Mill
Lock
STA.
Bush Hill Park
Ponders End
Inn
G.E.R.
Enfield Br.
Causeyware Hall
Bury Street
Inn
Ch.
Rowantree
Inn

50▷

75
▽

Surveyed 1862-1880. Published 1887.

△ 22

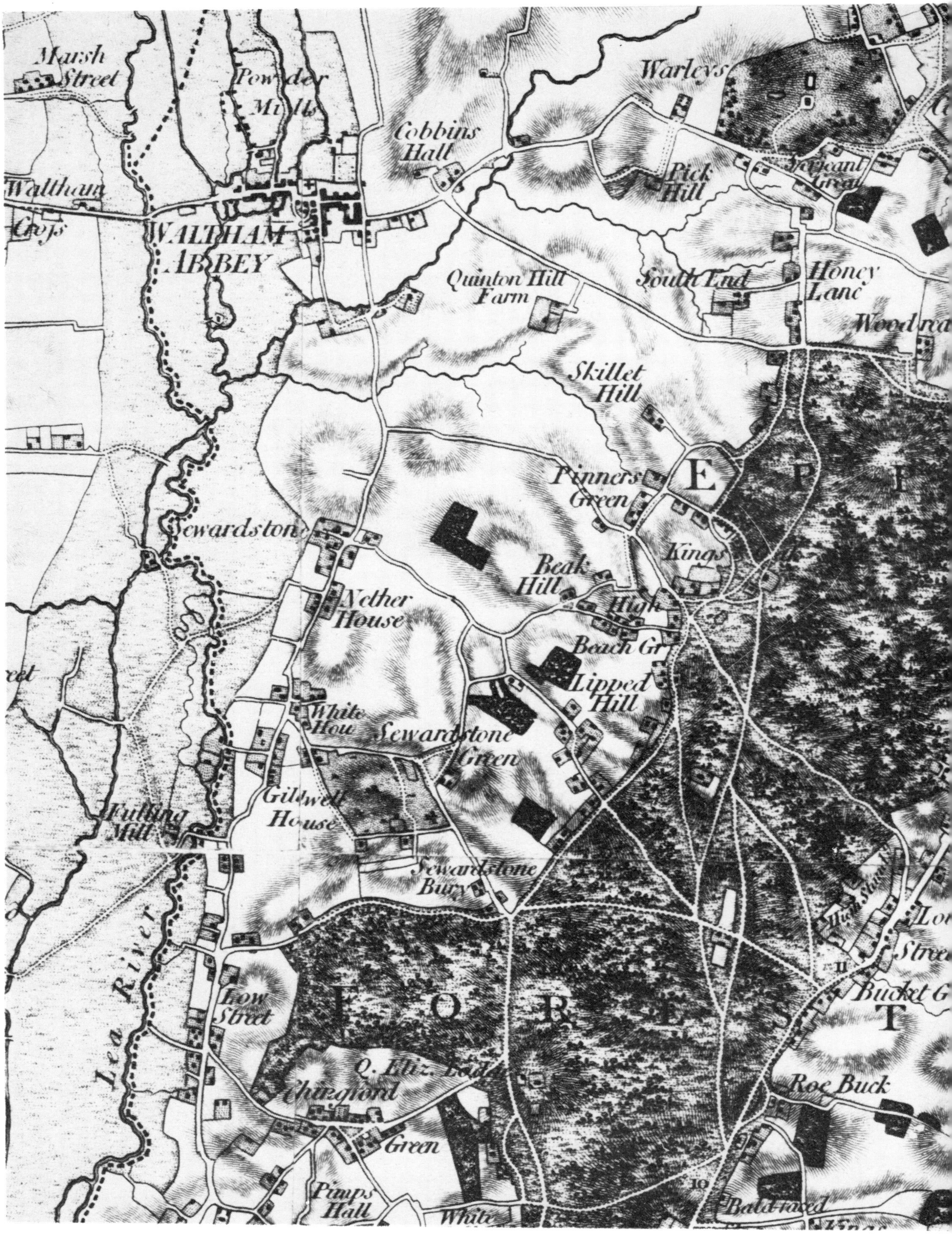
Marsh Street
Powder Mills
Waltham Cross
WALTHAM ABBEY
Cobbins Hall
Warleys
Pick Hill
Quinton Hill Farm
South End
Honey Lane
Skillet Hill
Pinners Green
E
Sewardstone
Kings
Beak Hill
Nether House
High
Beach Gr
Lipped Hill
White Hou
Sewardstone
Green
Gilwell House
Fulling Mill
Sewardstone Bury
Low Street
Lea River
O
R
Bucket G
T
Q. Eliz.
Roe Buck
Green
Pimps Hall
White

◁ 41

76 ▽

1 2
1 mile approx.

23

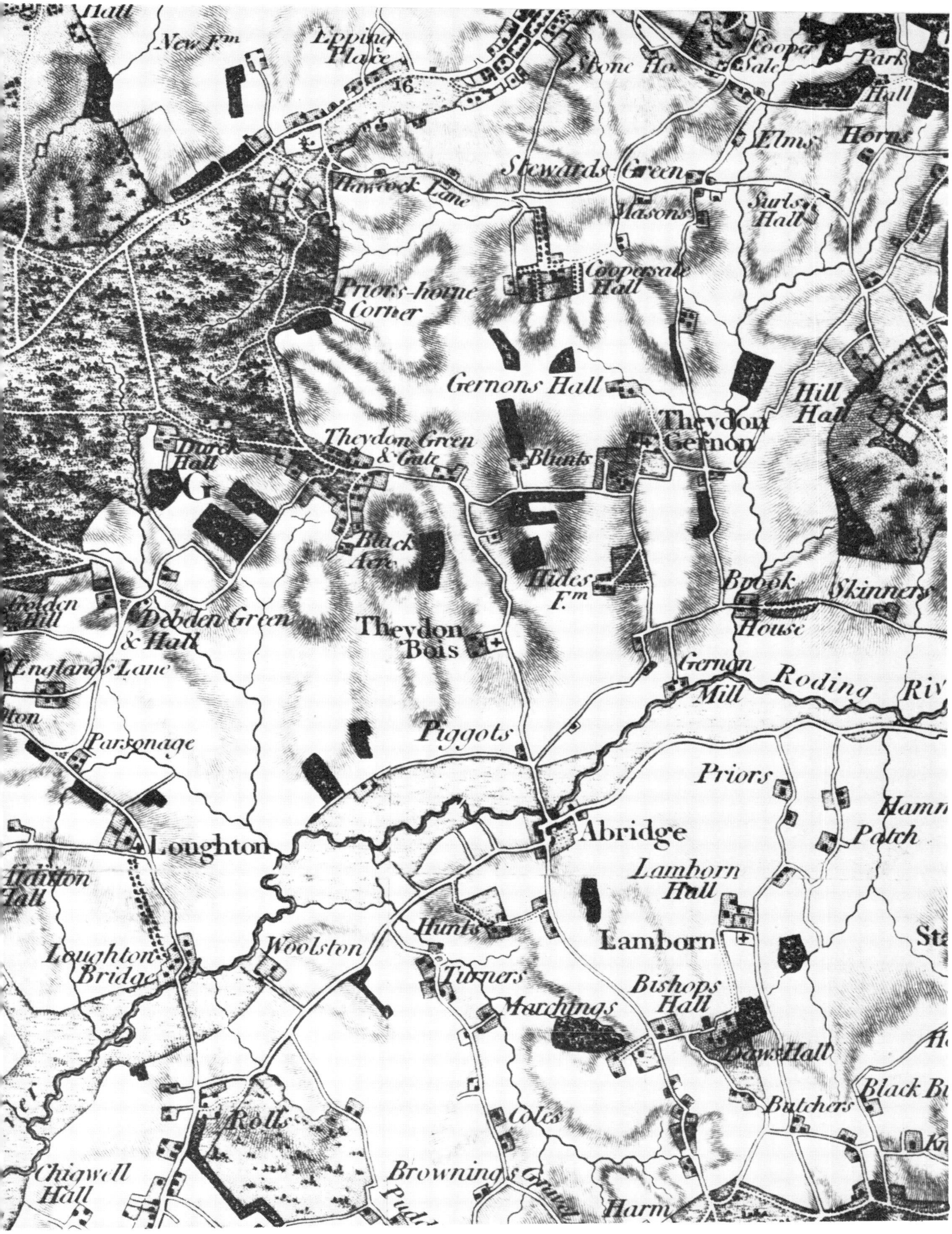

Hall
New Fm
Epping Place
16
Stone Ho
Cooper Sale
Park Hall
Elms
Horns
Stewards Green
Hawock Lane
15
Masons
Surls Hall
Cooparsale Hall
Priors-horne Corner
Gernons Hall
Hill Hall
Theydon Gernon
Duck Hall
Theydon Green & Gate
Blunts
Black Acre
Hides Fm
Brook House
Skinners
Debden Green & Hall
Theydon Bois
Englands Lane
Gernon Mill
Roding
Parsonage
Piggots
Priors
Patch
Loughton
Abridge
Lamborn Hall
Loughton Bridge
Woolston
Hunts
Lamborn
Turners
Bishops Hall
Marchings
Daws Hall
Rolls
Coles
Butchers
Chigwell Hall
Brownings Ground
Harm

52

77

Published 1805.

24

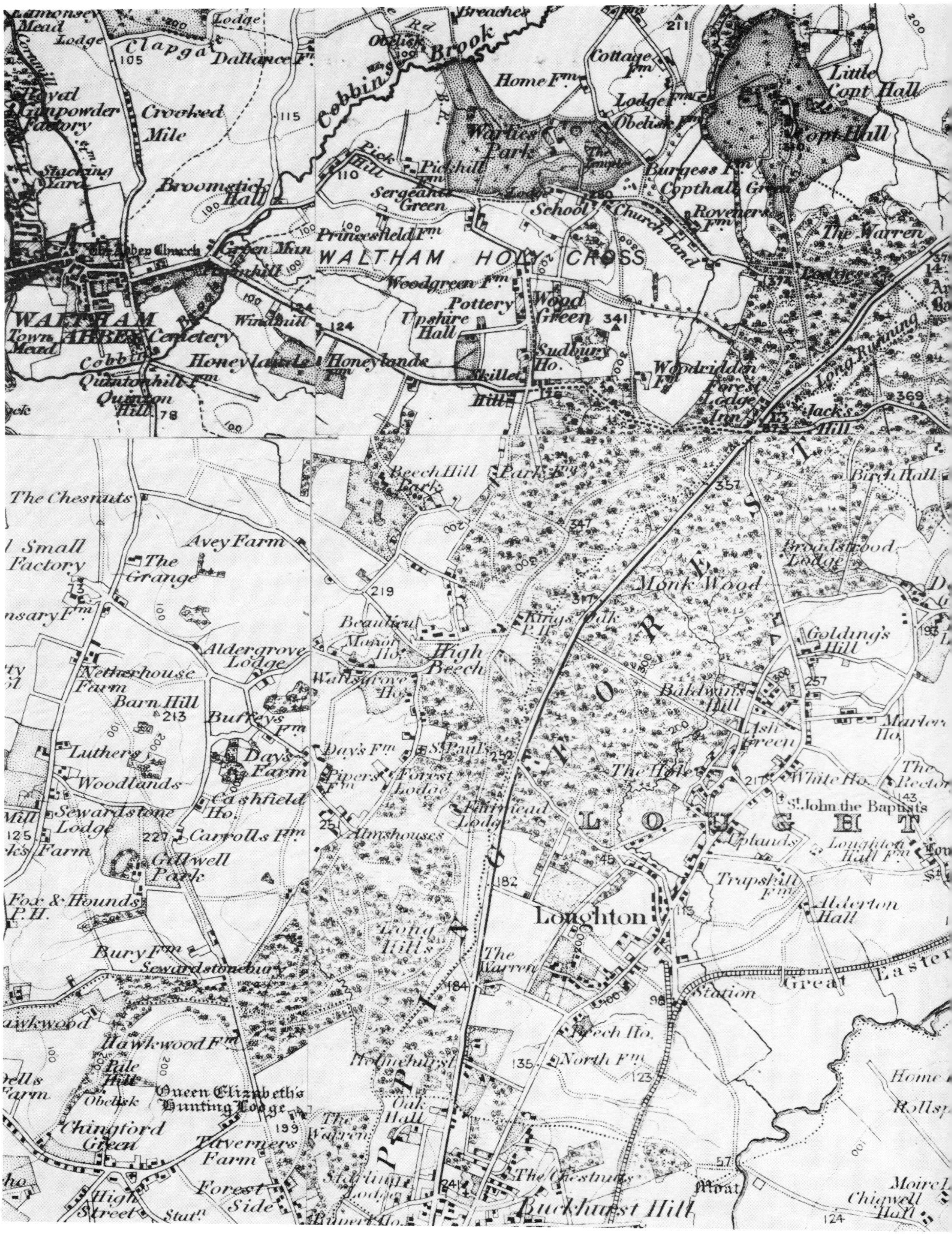

Clapgate
Dallance Fm
Cobbins Brook
Obelisk
Home Fm
Cottage Fm
Lodge Fm
Little Copt Hall
Copt Hall
Royal Gunpowder Factory
Crooked Mile
Warlies Park
Pick Hill
Pickhill
Burgess Fm
Copthall Green
Broomstick Hall
Sergeants Green
School
Church Land
Roveners Fm
The Warren
Princesfield Fm
Green Man
WALTHAM HOLY CROSS
Woodgreen Fm
Pottery
Wood Green
Upshire Hall
WALTHAM ABBEY
Town Mead
Cemetery
Windmill
Honeylands
Honeylands Fm
Sudbury Ho.
Skillet Hill
Woodridden Fm
Forest Lodge Inn
Long Running
Jack's Hill
Quinton Hill
Beech Hill Park
Park Fm
Birch Hall
The Chesnuts
Small Factory
Avey Farm
The Grange
Broadstrood Lodge
Monk Wood
Kings Oak P.H.
Beaulieu
Manor Ho.
High Beech
Aldergrove Lodge
Golding's Hill
Netherhouse Farm
Barn Hill
Waltsgrove Ho.
Baldwins Hill
Buffeys Fm
Ash Green
Marles Ho.
Luthers
Days Farm
Day's Fm
St. Paul's
Pipers Fm
Forest Lodge
The Hole
White Ho.
The Rectory
Woodlands
Cashfield Ho.
St. John the Baptist's
Sewardstone Lodge
Carrolls Fm
Fairmead Lodge
Almshouses
LOUGHTON
Uplands
Loughton Hall Fm
Gilwell Park
Trapshill Fm
Fox & Hounds P.H.
Alderton Hall
Loughton
Long Hills
Bury Fm
Sewardstonebury
The Warren
Station
Great Eastern
Hawkwood
Hawkwood Fm
Beech Ho.
North Fm
Pole Hill
Obelisk
Queen Elizabeth's Hunting Lodge
Chingford Green
Taverners Farm
Oak Hall
The Chestnuts
Moat
Forest Side
High Street
Statn
Buckhurst Hill
Chigwell Hall
EPPING FOREST

43

78

1 2

1 mile approx.

25

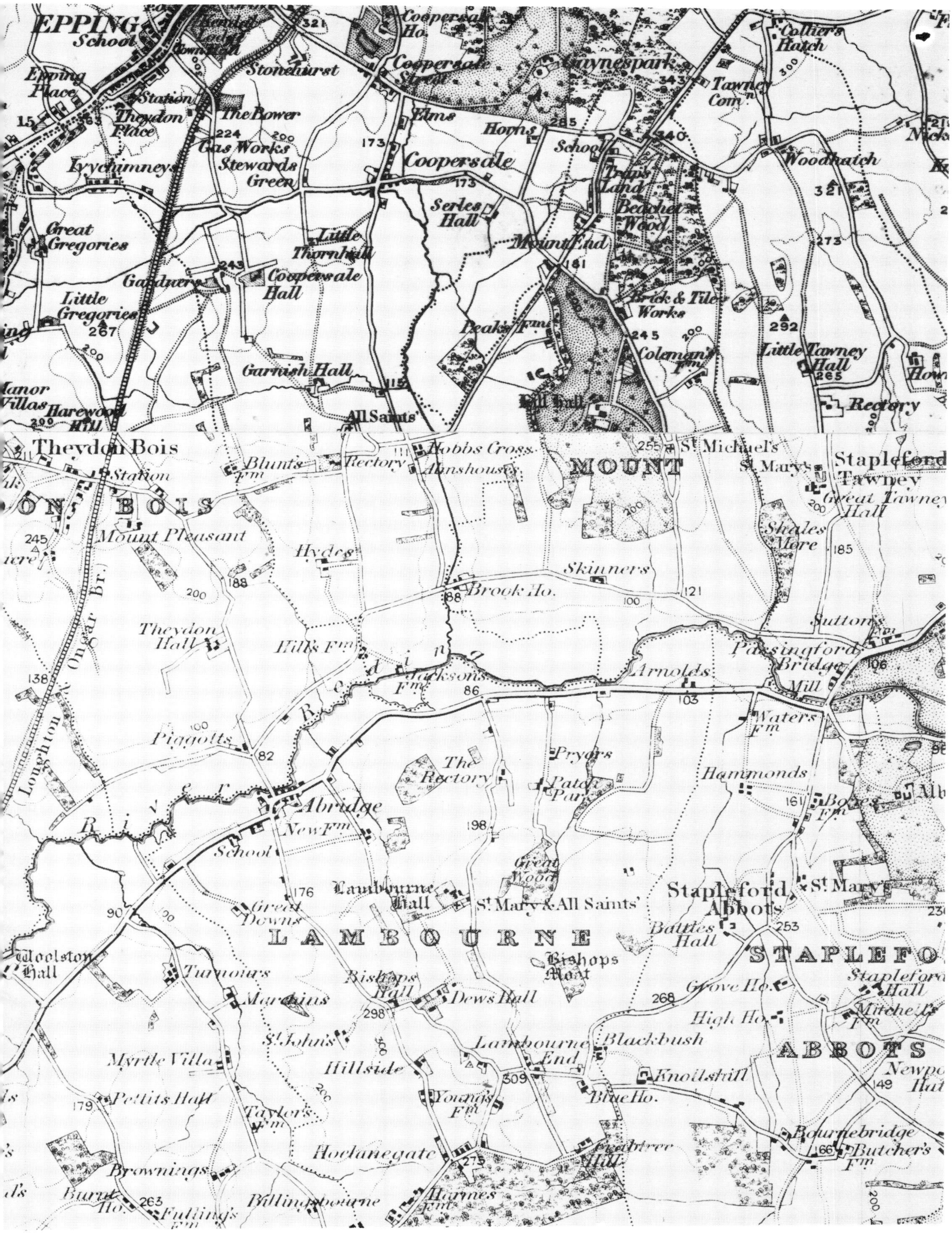
EPPING
School
Stonehurst
Epping Place
Station
Theydon Place
The Bower
Gas Works
Stewards Green
Ivychimneys
Coopersale Ho
Coopersale Street
Gaynespark
Elms
Horns
School
Coopersale
Serles Hall
Collier's Hatch
Tawney Comn
Woodhatch
Trap's Land
Beachet Wood
Mount End
Great Gregories
Little Thornhill
Gardners
Coopersale Hall
Little Gregories
Brick & Tile Works
Peaks Fm
Coleman's Fm
Little Tawney Hall
Garnish Hall
Rectory
Manor Villas
Harewood Hill
All Saints'
Theydon Bois
Station
Blunts Fm
Rectory
Hobbs Cross
Almshouses
St Michael's
MOUNT
St Mary's
Stapleford Tawney
Great Tawney Hall
ON BOIS
Mount Pleasant
Hydes
Shales More
Skinners
Brook Ho.
Theydon Hall
Hills Fm
Suttons
Passingford Bridge
Mill
Arnolds
Jacksons Fm
Loughton & Ongar Br.
River Roding
Waters Fm
Piggotts
The Rectory
Pryors
Patch Park
Hammonds
Abridge
New Fm
Boxes Fm
School
Great Wood
Lambourne Hall
St Mary & All Saints'
Stapleford Abbots
St Mary's
Great Downs
Battles Hall
LAMBOURNE
STAPLEFO
Woolston Hall
Turnours
Bishops Moat
Stapleford Hall
Marchins
Bishops Hall
Dews Hall
Grove Ho.
High Ho.
Mitchells Fm
St Johns
Lambourne End
Blackbush
ABBOTS
Myrtle Villa
Hillside
Knollshill
Newpo Hal
Pettits Hall
Youngs Fm
Blue Ho.
Taylor's Fm
Bournebridge
Butcher's Fm
Hoelanegate
Brownings
Burnt Ho.
Fulling's Fm
Billingbourne
Harnes Fm

Surveyed 1862-1873. Published 1883.

54

79

26

45

Clapgate
Dallance Fm
174
Royal Gunpowder Factory
Crooked Mile
Cobbin Brook
Home Fm
Warlies Park
Obelisk Fm
Pickhill Fm
177
Sergeants Green
271
Copthall Green
Ravens Fm
Ch.
Upshire
Princesfield Fm
100
Smithy
66
72
The Abbey Church
WALTHAM HOLY CROSS
Inn
Lock
WALTHAM ABBEY
Windmill
Upshire Hall
Wood Green
Honeylands
115
Woodridden Fm
L.B.
Cobbin's
84
Royal Gunpowder Factory
Beech Hill Park
The Chesnuts
Rifle Ranges
Royal Small Arms Factory
The Grange
Smithy
347
Monk Wood
Beaulieu
Manor Ho
High Beech
362
313
Aldergrove Lodge
Inn
Patty Pool
71
Barn Hill
243
135
Sewardstone
Baldwins Hill
Ash Green
187
The Hole
Pipers Fm
Inn
Woodlands
Cashfield Ho
Fairmead Lodge
Ch.
Smithy
110
231
Almshouses
Gilwell Park
River Lea
Fox & Hounds
Loughton
Ch.
Alder Hall
176
Long Hills
47
The Warren
Sewardstonebury
96
Hawkwood
211
Beech Ho
119
Dells Farm
Pole Hill
300
Obelisk
Queen Elizabeth's Hunting Lodge
Holmehurst
Oak Hall
Chingford Green
Inn
Ch.
Forest Side
Mount Echo
Fairlands
Moat
Buckhurst Hill

80

1 2

1 mile approx.

27

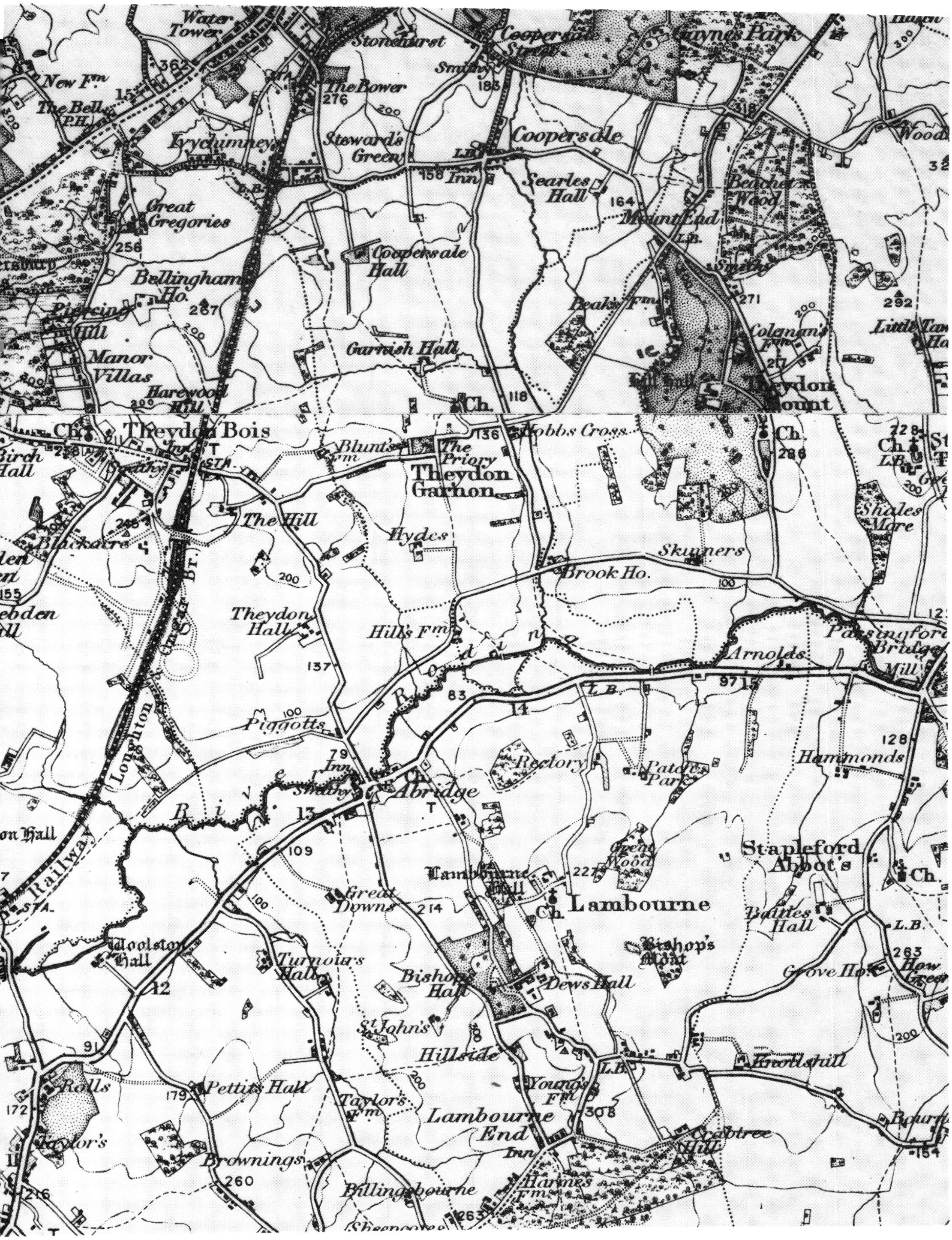

56

81

Surveyed 1862-1873. Revised 1903. Published 1904.

△ 28

◁47

Burrows
Colliers Hatch
Rolles
Blacks
New Ho.
Clarks
Horsnels
Stewards
Nickurlands
Theydon Mount Tom
Wood Hatch
Beachet Wood
Stanford Rivers
Littlebury
Little End
Berwick Farm
Bell Ho.
Bells
Highfield House
Traces
Hare Street
Cotes
Parsonage
Theydon Mount
Stapleford Tawny
Hall
Lane Fm
Navestock Hall
Bennets
Shanks Mill
Suttons
Arnolds
Passingford Br.
Howlets Hall
Navestock
Navestock Heath
Curtmill Green
Savage Green
Stapleford Abbots
Bookham
Horseman Side
Water Hale
How Green
Olives
Dycoats
Walons Green
Weald Side Common
Newport Hatch
Crooked Billet
Bourne Br.
Pergo
Havering

82 ▽

1 2

1 mile approx.

29

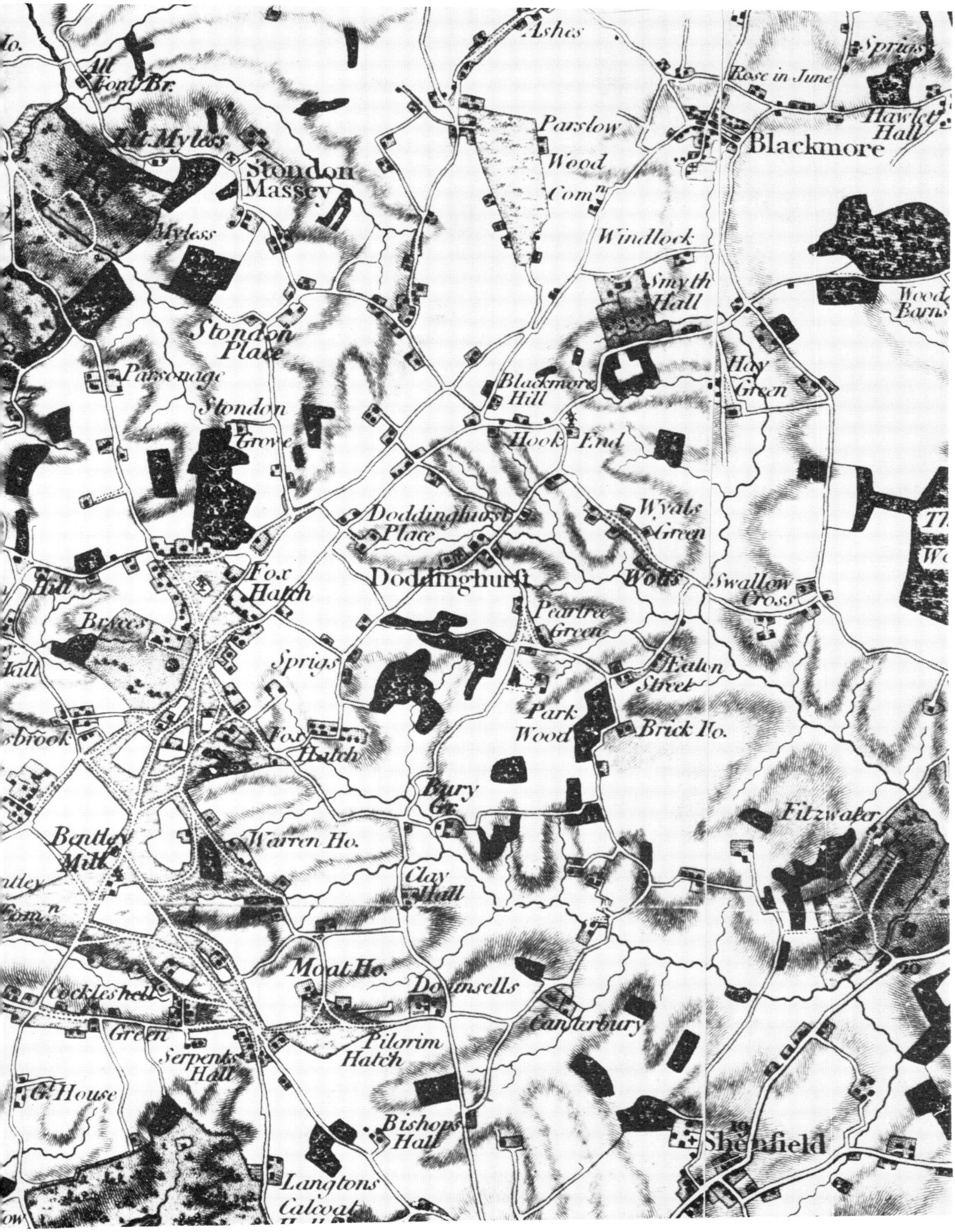
Ashes
Rose in June
Sprigs
All Font Br.
Lit. Myless
Stondon Massey
Parslow Wood Comn
Blackmore
Hawlet Hall
Myless
Windlock
Smyth Hall
Wood Barns
Stondon Place
Parsonage
Blackmore Hill
Hay Green
Stondon Grove
Hook End
Doddinghurst Place
Wyals Green
Doddinghurst
Fox Hatch
Wolls
Swallow Cross
Hill
Brices
Peartree Green
Sprigs
Eaton Street
Park Wood
Brick Ho.
Fox Hatch
Bury Gr.
Fitzwalter
Bentley Mill
Warren Ho.
Clay Hall
Moat Ho.
Cockleshell
Dounsells
Green
Canterbury
Pilgrim Hatch
Serpents Hall
Gt. House
Bishops Hall
Shenfield
Langtons
Calcoat

83

Published 1805.

△
30

◁49

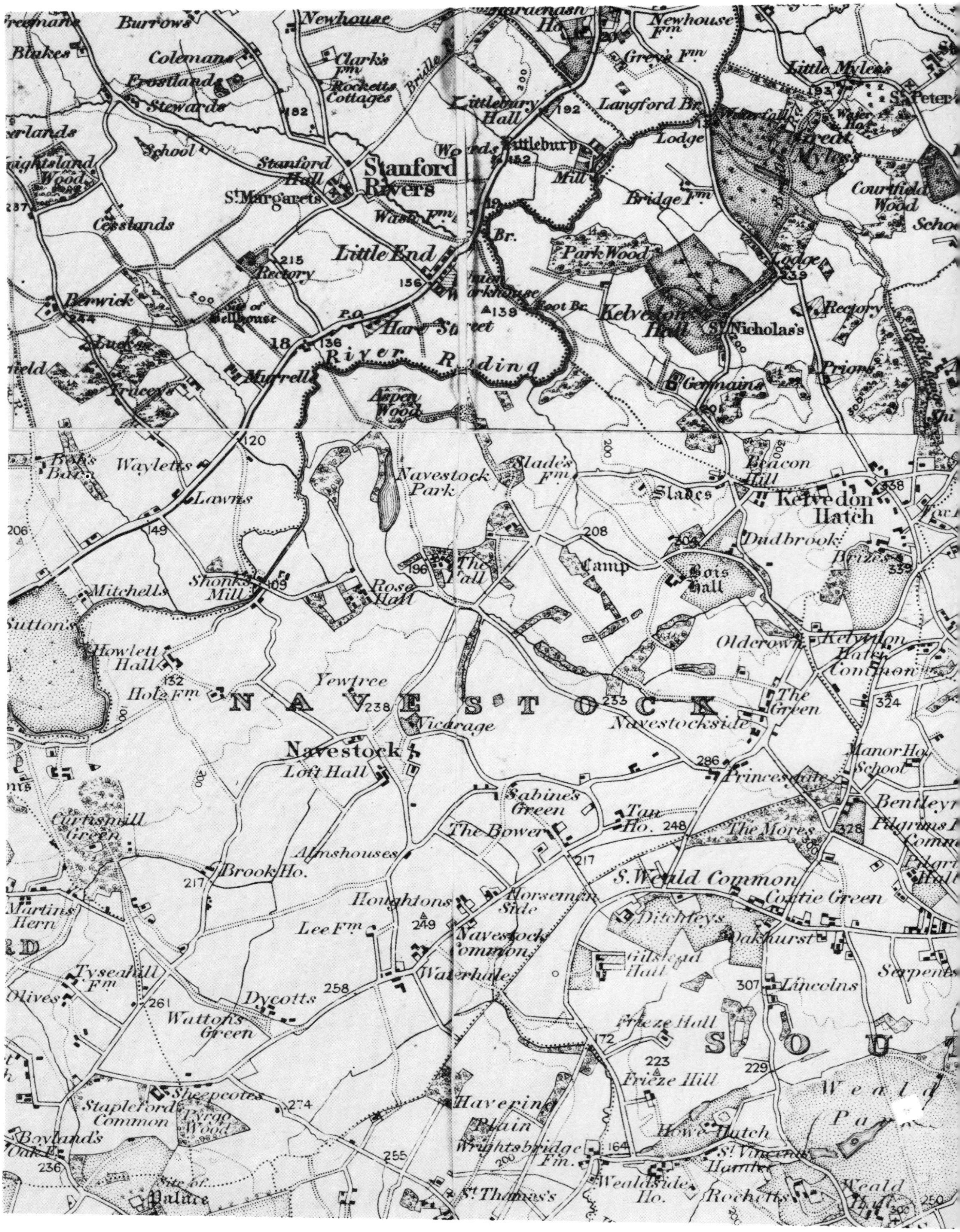

Burrows
Blakes
Colemans
Frostlands
Stewards
Newhouse
Clark's Fm.
Rocketts Cottages
Bridle
182
School
Stanford Hall
Stanford Rivers
St. Margarets
Wash Fm.
Little End
Cesslands
215
Rectory
156
Berwick
244
200
18
136
P.O.
Hare Street
River Roding
Murrells
Aspen Wood
Littlebury Hall
192
Langford Br.
Littlebury
Mill
Lodge
Bridge Fm.
Br.
Park Wood
139
Kelvedon Hall
St. Nicholas's
Rectory
Germains
Priors
Newhouse Fm.
Grey's Fm.
Little Myles's
193
Waterfalls
Great Myles's
Courtfield Wood
Lodge
287
120
Waylettts
Lawns
206
149
Mitchells
Shonks Mill
109
Sutton's
Howlett Hall
132
Holz Fm.
Navestock Park
Slade's Fm.
Slades
Beacon Hill
Kelvedon Hatch
208
304
Dudbrook
Brizes
338
339
196
The Hall
Rose Hall
Camp
Bois Hall
Oldcrown
Kelvedon Hatch Common
Yewtree
238
N A V E S T O C K
233
Vicarage
Navestockside
The Green
324
Navestock
Loft Hall
286
Princesgate
Manor Ho.
School
Sabines Green
Tan Ho.
248
The Mores
328
Curtismill Green
The Bower
217
Almshouses
Brook Ho.
217
S. Weald Common
Coxtie Green
Martins Hern
Houghtons
Horseman Side
Ditchleys
Oakhurst
Lee Fm.
249
Navestock Common
Gilstead Hall
Tysehill Fm.
Olives
261
Dycotts
258
Waterhale
307
Lincolns
Wattons Green
Frieze Hall
172
S O U
223
Frieze Hill
229
Weald Park
Sheepcotes
Staplefords Common
Pyrgo Wood
274
Havering Plain
Howe Hatch
Boyland's Oak F.
236
255
Wrightsbridge Fm.
164
St. Vincents Hamlet
Site of Palace
St. Thomas's
Wealdside Ho.
Rochetts
Weald Hall
250

84
▽

1 2
1 mile approx.

31

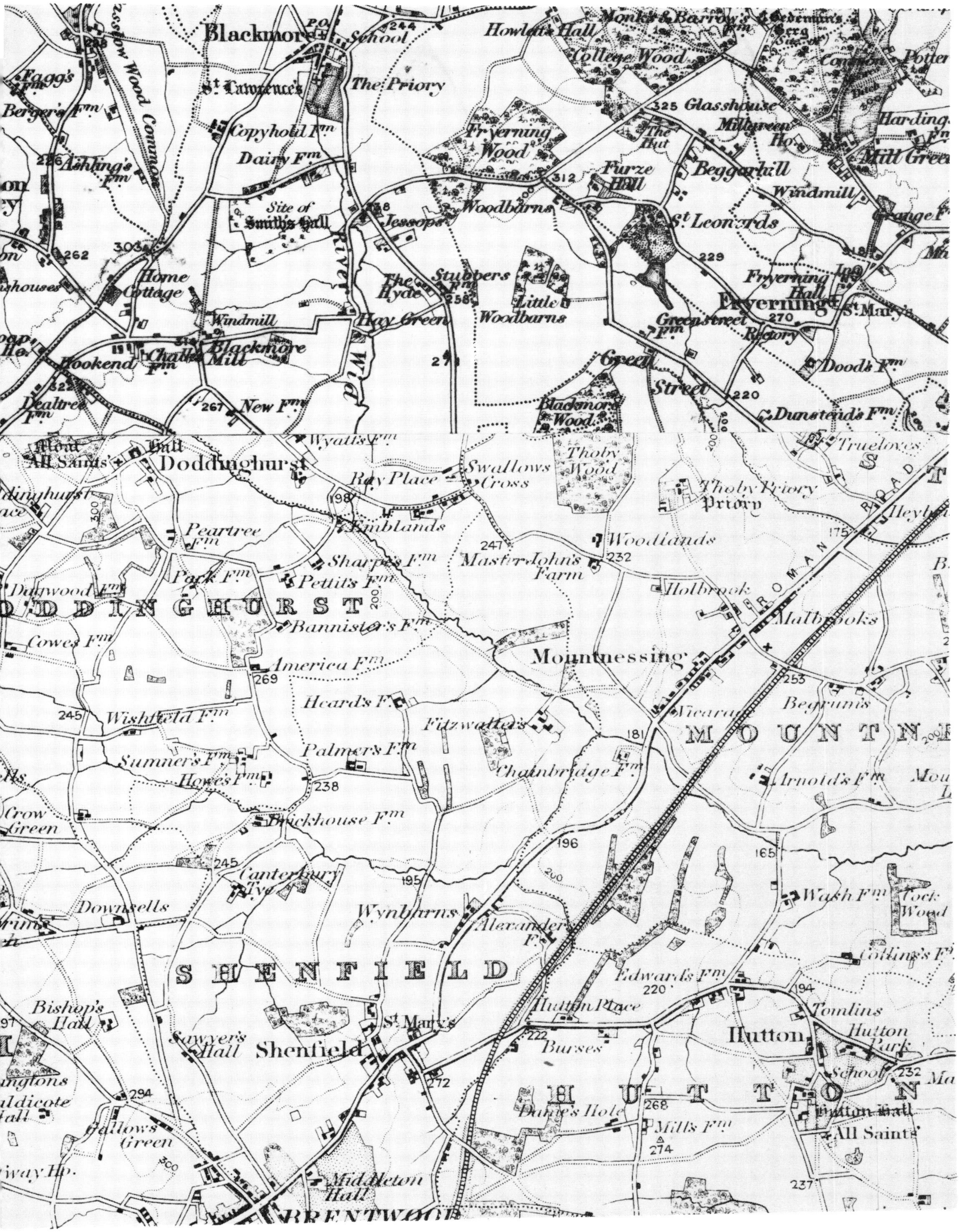
Blackmore
School
Howlett's Hall
College Wood
Fagg's Fm
St. Lawrence's
The Priory
Berger's Fm
Copyhold Fm
Fryerning Wood
Glasshouse
Millgreen Ho.
Mill Green
Dairy Fm
Ashling's Fm
Furze Hall
Beggarhill
Windmill
Site of Smith's Hall
Jessops
Woodbarns
St. Leonards
262
303
229
Home Cottage
The Hyde
Stubbers Fm
Little Woodbarns
Fryerning Hall
Inn
Fryerning
St. Mary's
270
Windmill
Hay Green
Greenstreet Fm
Rectory
Blackmore Mill
Hookend
Dood's Fm
Green Street
Dealtree Fm
267
New Fm
Blackmore Wood
220
Dunstend's Fm
Wyatt's Fm
All Saints
Hall
Doddinghurst
Swallows Cross
Ray Place
Thoby Wood
Thoby Priory
Priory
Truelove's
Peartree Fm
247
Woodlands
175
Sharpe's Fm
Master John's Farm
232
Pack Fm
Pettit's Fm
Holbrook
ROMAN ROAD
DODDINGHURST
Bannister's Fm
Malbrooks
Cowes Fm
America Fm
Mountnessing
269
253
Heard's Fm
Begrums
245
Wishfield Fm
Fitzwalter's
MOUNTN
Palmer's Fm
181
Sumner's Fm
Chainbridge Fm
Arnold's Fm
Howe's Fm
238
Crow Green
Brickhouse Fm
196
165
245
Canterbury Tye
195
Wash Fm
Downsells
Wynbarns
Alexander F.
SHENFIELD
Edward's Fm
220
194
Bishop's Hall
Hutton Place
Tomlins
Sawyer's Hall
St. Mary's
222
Hutton
Hutton Park
Shenfield
Burses
School
232
272
294
HUTTON
268
Dane's Hole
Hutton Hall
Mills Fm
All Saints
Gallows Green
274
Middleton Hall
237
BRENTWOOD

Surveyed 1862-1873. Published 1883.

85

△ 32

◁ 51

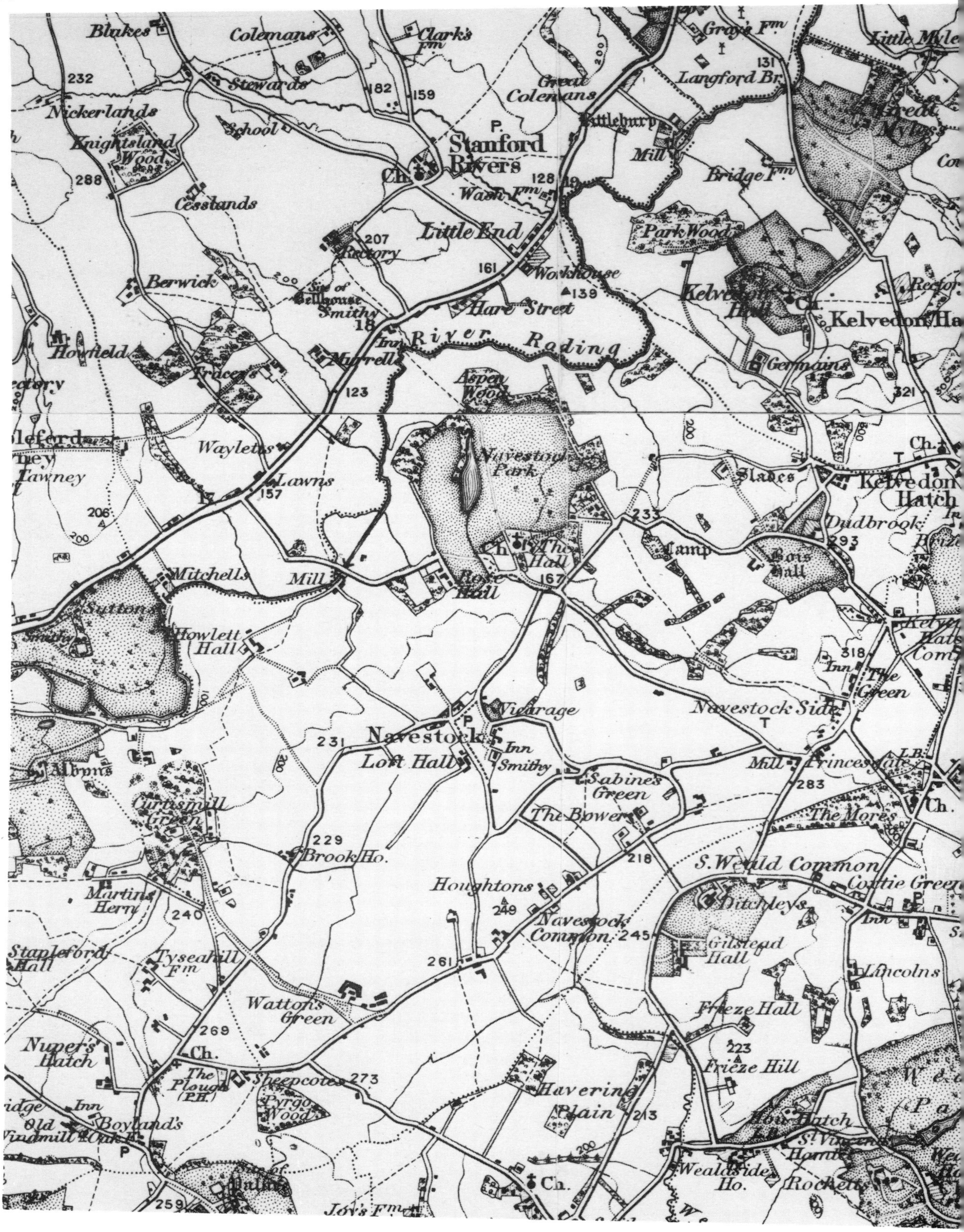
Blakes
Colemans
Clark's Fm
232
Stewards
182
159
Great Colemans
200
Gray's Fm
131
Langford Br.
Little Myle
Nickerlands
School
P.
Stanford Rivers
Littlebury
Knightsland Wood
Ch.
Mill
Great Myles
288
Cesslands
128
Wash Fm
Bridge Fm
Little End
Park Wood
207
Rectory
161
Workhouse
Berwick
Site of Bellhouse
Smithy
139
Hare Street
Kelvedon Hall
Ch.
Kelvedon Ha
Rectory
Howfield
Inn
River Roding
Tracey's
Murrells
Germains
123
Aspen Wood
321
Waylettes
Navestock Park
Ch.
Kelvedon Hatch
Tawney
Lawns
157
Slades
206
233
Dudbrook
200
Camp
293
Ch.
The Hall
Bois Hall
Mitchells
Mill
Rose Hall
167
Suttons
Howlett Hall
318
Inn
The Green
Vicarage
Navestock Side
T
Navestock
231
Loft Hall
Inn
Smithy
Albyns
Sabines Green
Mill
Princesgate
L.B.
283
Curtismill Green
The Bower
The Mores
Ch.
229
Brook Ho.
218
S. Weald Common
Martins Herin
Houghtons
249
Ditchleys
Coxtie Green
240
Navestock Common
245
Inn
Gilstead Hall
Stapleford Hall
Tyseahill Fm
261
Lincolns
Wattons Green
Frieze Hall
269
Nupers Hatch
223
Ch.
Frieze Hill
The Plough (P.H.)
Sheepcotes
273
Havering Plain
Pyrgo Wood
Inn
Old Windmill
Boyland's Oak
213
Hoo Hatch
St. Vincent's Hamlet
P
Wealdside Ho.
Rocketts
Ch.
259
Joy's Fm

86 ▽

1 2
1 mile approx.

△ 33

87 ▽

Surveyed 1862-1873. Revised 1903. Published 1904.

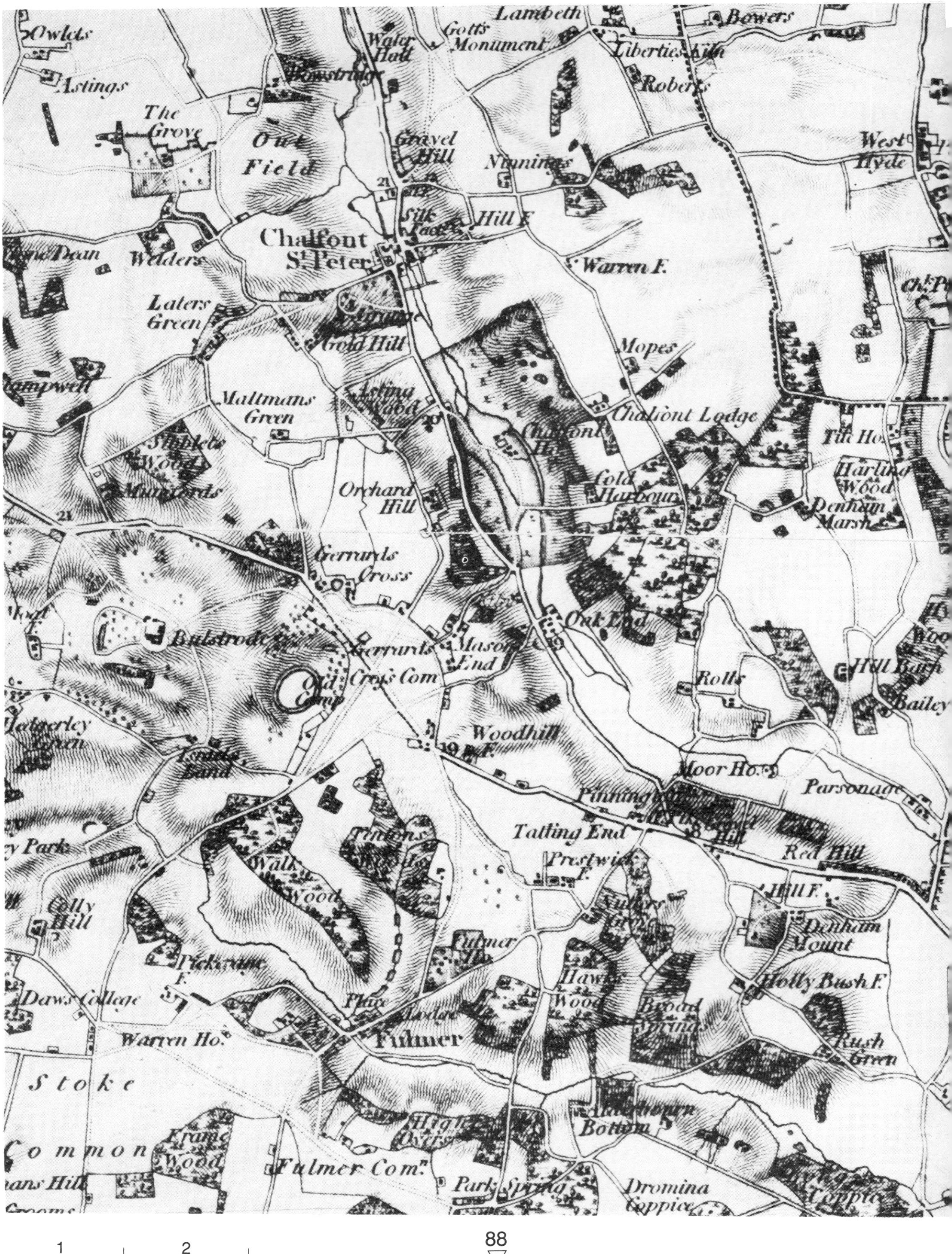
Owlets
Astings
The Grove
Out Field
Lambeth
Water Hall
Gott's Monument
Bowers
Liberties hill
Roberts
Gravel Hill
Ninnings
West Hyde
Silk Factory
Hill F.
Chalfont St. Peter
Welders
Warren F.
Laters Green
Gold Hill
Mopes
Maltmans Green
Chalfont Lodge
Chalfont Ho.
Tile Ho.
Harling Wood
Denham Marsh
Cold Harbour
Orchard Hill
Gerrards Cross
Oak End
Bulstrode
Gerrards Cross Com
Mason End
Old Camp
Rolls
Hill Bush
Bailey
Woodhill F.
Moor Ho.
Parsonage
Tatling End
Red Hill
Prestwick F.
Hill F.
Denham Mount
Colly Hill
Walk Wood
Fulmer Ho.
Holly Bush F.
Daws College
Place
Lodge
Warren Ho.
Fulmer
Rush Green
Stoke Common
Frame Wood
Fulmer Com.
Bottom
Park Spring
Dromina Coppice

88

1 2

1 mile approx.

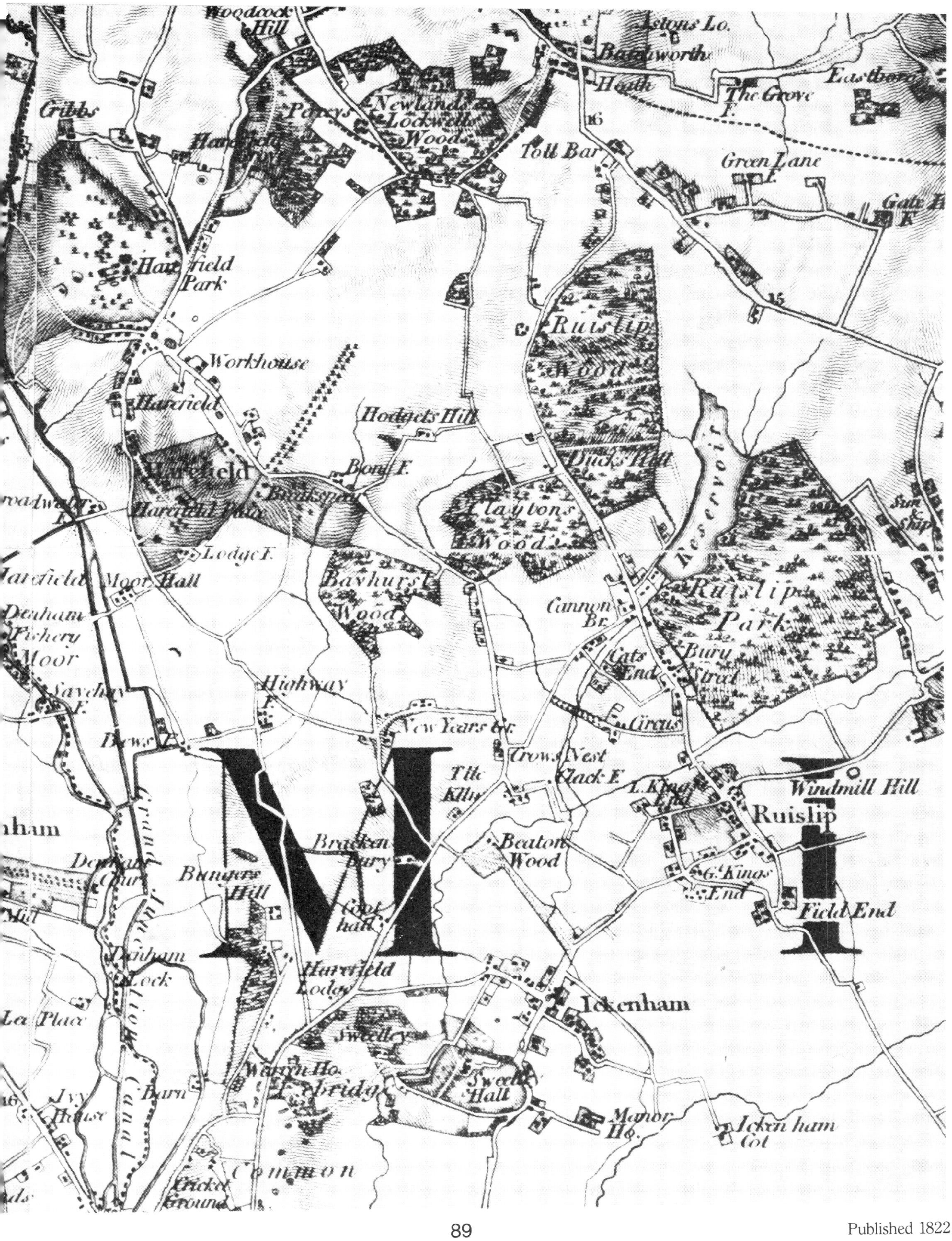
Woodcock Hill
Astons Lo.
Batchworth
Heath
Eastbury
The Grove F.
Gribbs
Parrys
Newlands
Lockwell Woods
16
Toll Bar
Green Lane F.
Gate F.
Harefield Park
15
Ruislip Wood
Workhouse
Harefield
Hodgets Hill
Ducks Hill
Reservoir
Harefield
Brackspear
Bons F.
Claytons Wood
Sun & Ship
Harefield Place
Lodge F.
Harefield Moor Hall
Bayhurst Wood
Ruislip Park
Denham Fishery
Moor
Cannon Br.
Cats End
Bury Street
Highway F.
Circus
New Years Gt.
Dews F.
Crows Nest
Clack F.
Tile Kiln
L. Kings End
Windmill Hill
Ruislip
Bracken Bury
Beaton Wood
Grand Junction Canal
Denham Court
Bungers Hill
Gt. Kings End
Field End
Mill
Cot hall
Denham Lock
Harefield Lodge
Ickenham
Lea Place
Swelley
Warren Ho.
Uxbridge
Swell Hall
Ivy House
Barn
Manor Ho.
Icken ham Cot
Common
Cricket Ground
M
I

64 ▷

89 ▽

Published 1822.

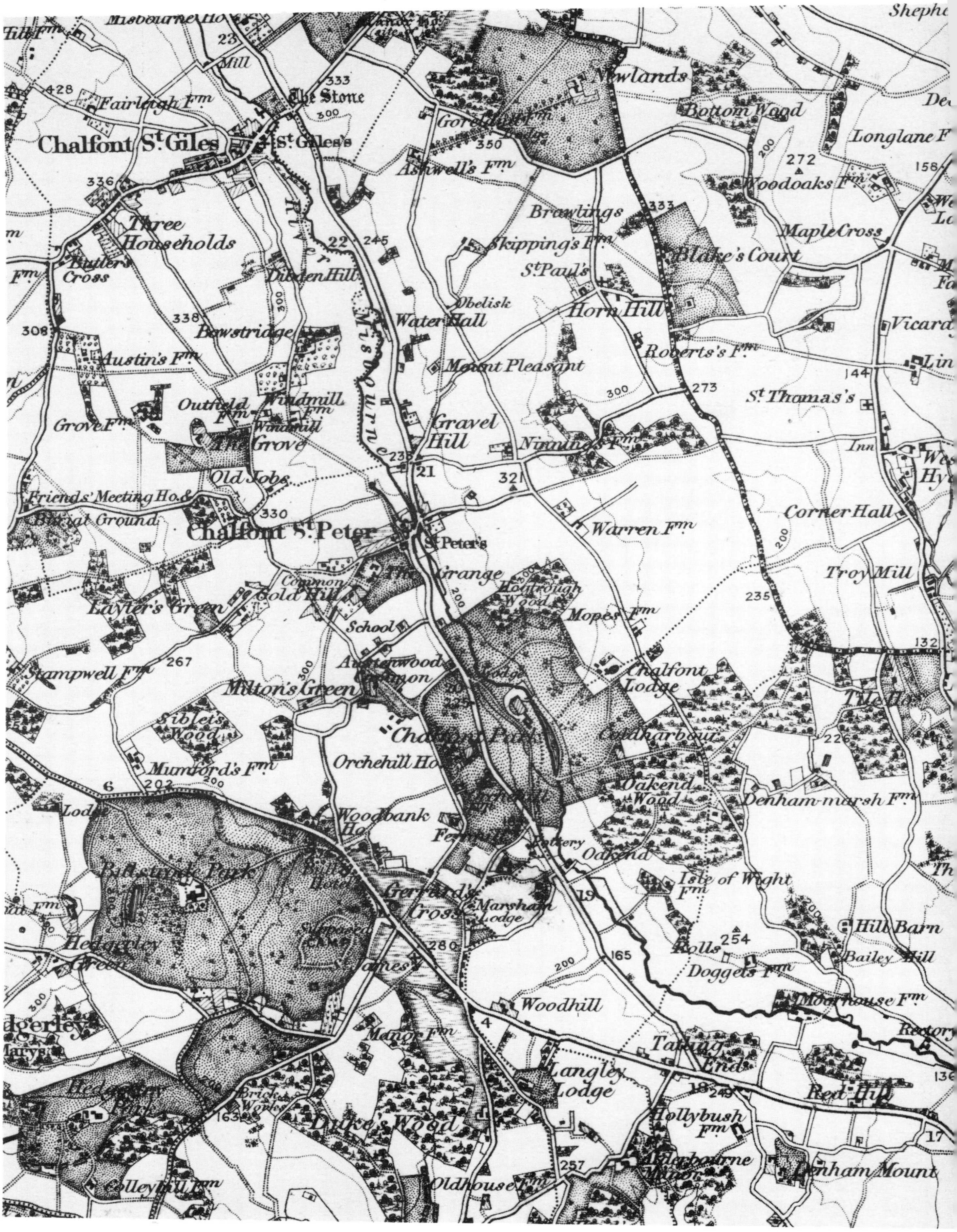
Misbourne Ho.
Mill
The Stone
Newlands
Fairleigh Fm.
Bottom Wood
Chalfont St. Giles
St. Giles's
Longlane F
Ashwell's Fm.
Woodoaks Fm.
Three Households
Brawlings
Skipping's Fm.
Maple Cross
Butler's Cross
Blake's Court
St. Paul's
Dibden Hill
Obelisk
Horn Hill
Water Hall
Bowstridge
River Misbourne
Austin's Fm.
Roberts's Fm.
Mount Pleasant
St. Thomas's
Outfield Fm.
Windmill Fm.
Grove Fm.
Gravel Hill
Windmill
The Grove
Ninnings Fm.
Inn
Old Jobs
Friends' Meeting Ho. & Burial Ground
Corner Hall
Warren Fm.
Chalfont St. Peter
St. Peter's
The Grange
Troy Mill
Common
Gold Hill
Layter's Green
Mopes Fm.
School
Stampwell Fm.
Austenwood Common
Chalfont Lodge
Milton's Green
Siblets Wood
Chalfont Park
Coldharbour
Mumford's Fm.
Orchehill Ho.
Lodge
Oakend Wood
Denham-marsh Fm.
Woodbank Ho.
Bulstrode Park
Pottery
Oakend
Isle of Wight Fm.
Gerrard's Cross
Marsham Lodge
Hill Barn
Hedgerley Green
Bailey Hill
Doggets Fm.
Woodhill
Moorhouse Fm.
Manor Fm.
Tatling End
Langley Lodge
Red Hill
Brick Works
Duke's Wood
Hollybush Fm.
Denham Mount
Oldhouse Fm.
Colleyhill Fm.

1 2

1 mile approx.

90 ▽

Moneyhill
Bury Fm.
R. Colne
Batchworth
Frogmoor
Drive
Moorpark Farm
Moor Park
Moor Farm
Lodge
Hamper Mills
Sandylodge Farm
Stocker's Fm.
Springwell Farm
Pipers Fm.
Astons Lodge
Oxhey Woods
Eastbury Fm.
Woodcock Inn
Hall
Batchworth Heath P.O.
Grove Fm.
Lodges
Eastbury
Lodge
Cripp's Fm.
White Hill
Bishop's Wood
Trinity
Greenhill Fm.
Hillend
Harefield Grove
North Wood
Greenlane Fm.
Gateshill Fm.
Whiteheath
Lodge
Northwood Hall
Rifle Range
Harefield Park
Sydenham Lodge
Shepherdshill Farm
Kiln Farm
Kirby Hall
Lodge Farm
The Green
The Hundred Acres Fm.
Duckshill Farm
Copse
Ducks Wood
Northwood Fm.
T.P.
P.O.
Harefield
Knightscote Farm
Hill
Langley Fm.
Inn
Poors' Field
Haste Hill
Joel Street Farm
Bourne Farm
Poors Field
St. Mary's
Breakspear
Ruislip Reservoir
Hillend
Inn
Grand
Lodge Farm
Park
Haydon Hall
Bayhurst Wood
Moorhall Farm
Chapel
Moor
Eastcote
Wood
Harefieldmoor Wharf
Junction
Bury Street
M
I
Weir Cott.
Highway Fm.
Southcote Fm.
High Grove
Colne
Newyears Green
Ford
Clack Fm.
Ruislip
Hill Fm.
Windmill Hill
Dews Farm
St. Martin's Park Ho.
Denham
Brackenbury Farm
Beetonswood Farm
Wilkin's Farm
Kingsend
Ickenham Green
St. Mary's
Denham Court
Copthall Fm.
Fieldend Farm
Rectory
Harefield Place
Newpond Farm
St. Giles's
Ickenham

66 ▷

91 ▽

Surveyed 1863-1876. Published 1880.

Chalfont St. Giles
Smithy
Inn
Three Households
Butler's Cross
Dibdin Hill
Bowstridge
Austin's Fm.
Windmill Fm.
Grove Fm.
The Grove
Jordan's Fm.
Chalfont St. Peter
Gold Hill
Common
Schools
Inn
Austenwood Common
Stampwell Fm.
Gibbets Wood
Mumford's Fm.
Bulstrode Park
Camp
Gerrards Cross
Ch.
Woodbank Ho.
Smithy
Orchehill Ho.
Duke's Wood
Colleyhill Fm.
Oldhouse Fm.
Manor Fm.
L.B.
Woodhill
St. Huberts
Tatling End
Hollybush Fm.
Alderbourne Manor
Denham Mount
Red Hill
Inn
Moorhouse Fm.
Rectory
Smithy
Doggets Fm.
Hill Barn
Isle of Wight Fm.
Oakend
Oakend Wood
Denham-marsh Fm.
Chalfont Lodge
Oldharbour
Mopes Fm.
Hogtrough Wood
Grange
Chalfont Park
Warren Fm.
Corner Hall
Troy Mill
Smithy
Ford
Gravel Hill
Nunnings Fm.
Mount Pleasant
Water Hall
Obelisk
The Colony
Ch.
Brawlings
Horn Hill
Inn
L.B.
Roberts's Fm.
Hornhill Court
Maple Cross
Smithy
Inn
Ch.
Smithy
Inn
Ashwell's Fm.
Shrubs Wood
Newlands
Bottom Wood
Rickmansworth Rural (Dist.)
Lonylane Fm.
Woodoaks Fm.
Stone
Inn
Misbourne River
362
300
238
349
338
272
200
346
150
300
248
21
321
327
188
234
135
200
235
314
267
188
129
199
200
6
235
259
163
19
254
200
4
256
18
244
17
258
257

1 2

1 mile approx.

92
▽

68 ▷

93 ▽

Surveyed 1863-1876. Revised 1902. Published 1904.

△ 34

◁59

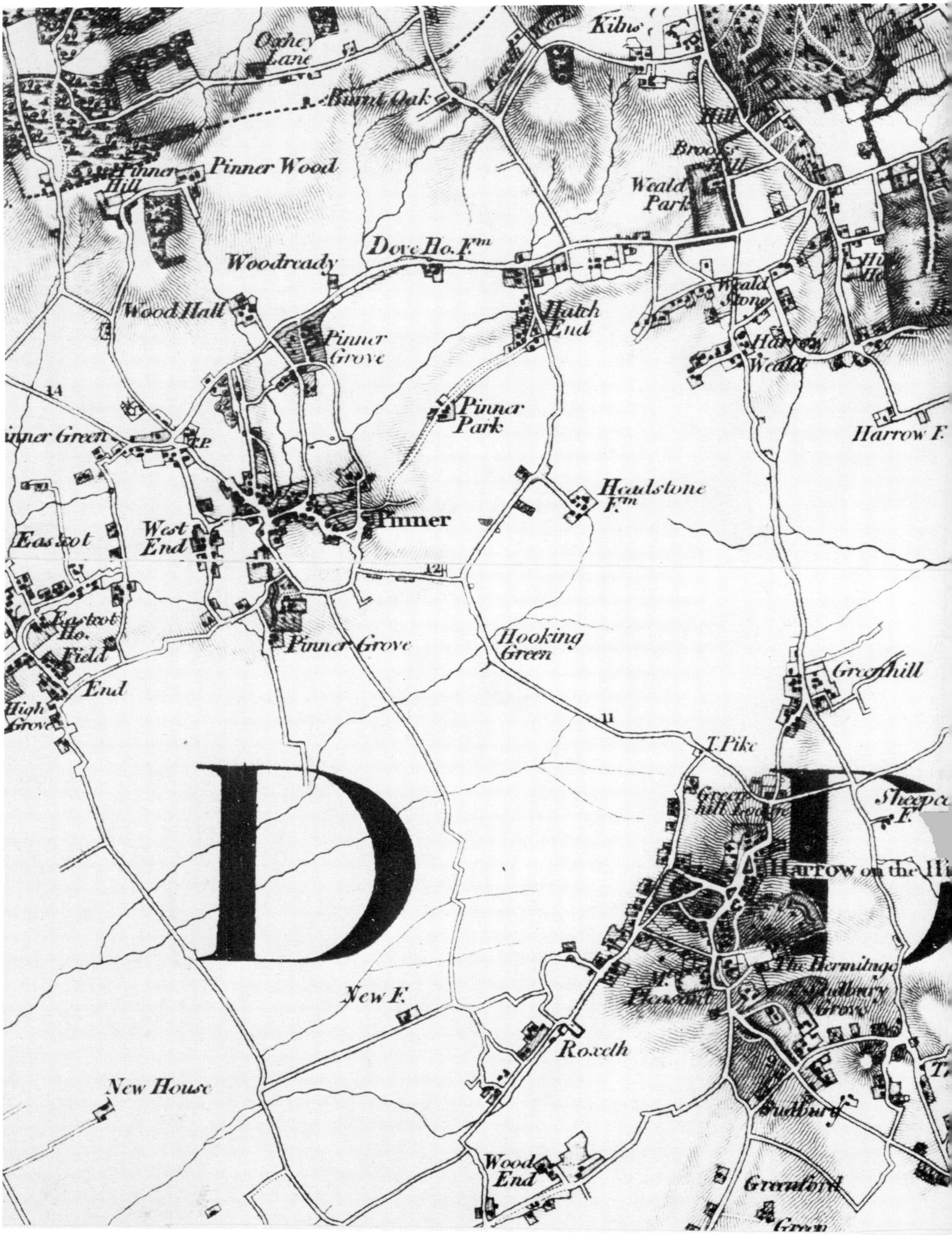
Oxhey Lane
Burnt Oak
Kilns
Hill
Weald Park
Pinner Hill
Pinner Wood
Dove Ho. Fm
Woodready
Wood Hall
Pinner Grove
Hatch End
Weald Stone
Harrow Weald
Pinner Park
Harrow F.
14
Pinner Green
T.P.
Headstone Fm
Pinner
West End
Easkot
12
Eastcot Ho.
Field End
Pinner Grove
Hooking Green
Greenhill
High Grove
11
T. Pike
Greenhill Lodge
D
Harrow on the Hi
The Hermitage
Mt. Pleasant
Sudbury Grove
New F.
Roxeth
New House
Sudbury
Wood End
Greenford

1 2

1 mile approx.

94 ▽

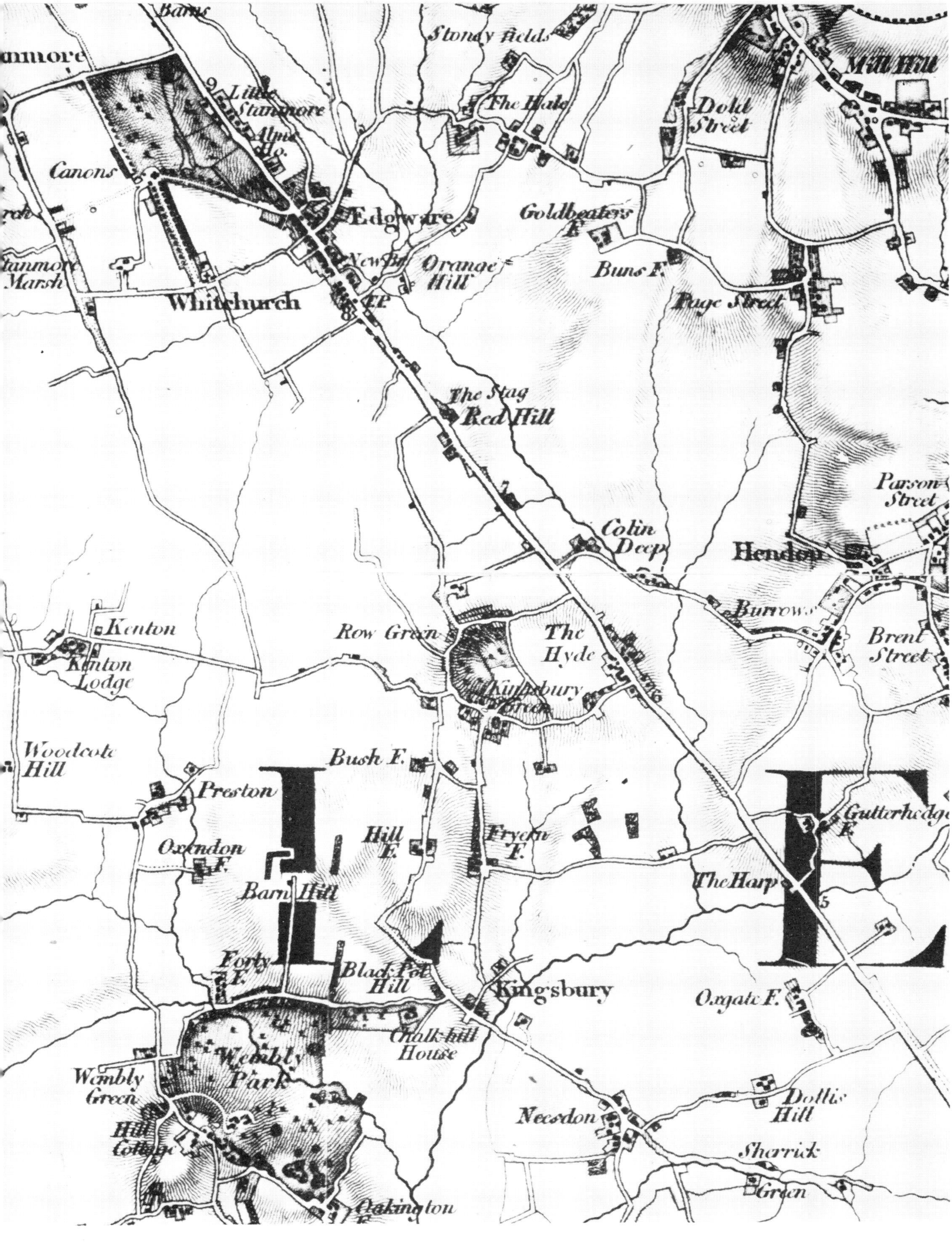
Stanmore
Little Stanmore
Alms Ho.
Canons
Stony Fields
The Hale
Mill Hill
Dold Street
Edgware
Goldbeaters F.
Buns F.
Page Street
Stanmore Marsh
Whitchurch
New Pit
Orange Hill
The Stag
Red Hill
Parson Street
Colin Deep
Hendon
Burrows
Brent Street
Kenton
Kenton Lodge
Row Green
The Hyde
Kingsbury Green
Woodcote Hill
Bush F.
Preston
Gutterhedge F.
Hill F.
Fryern F.
Oxendon F.
Barn Hill
The Harp
Forty F.
Black Pot Hill
Kingsbury
Oxgate F.
Chalk-hill House
Wembly Park
Wembly Green
Neasdon
Dollis Hill
Hill Cottage
Sherrick Green
Oakington

70▷

Published 1822.

△
36

◁ 61

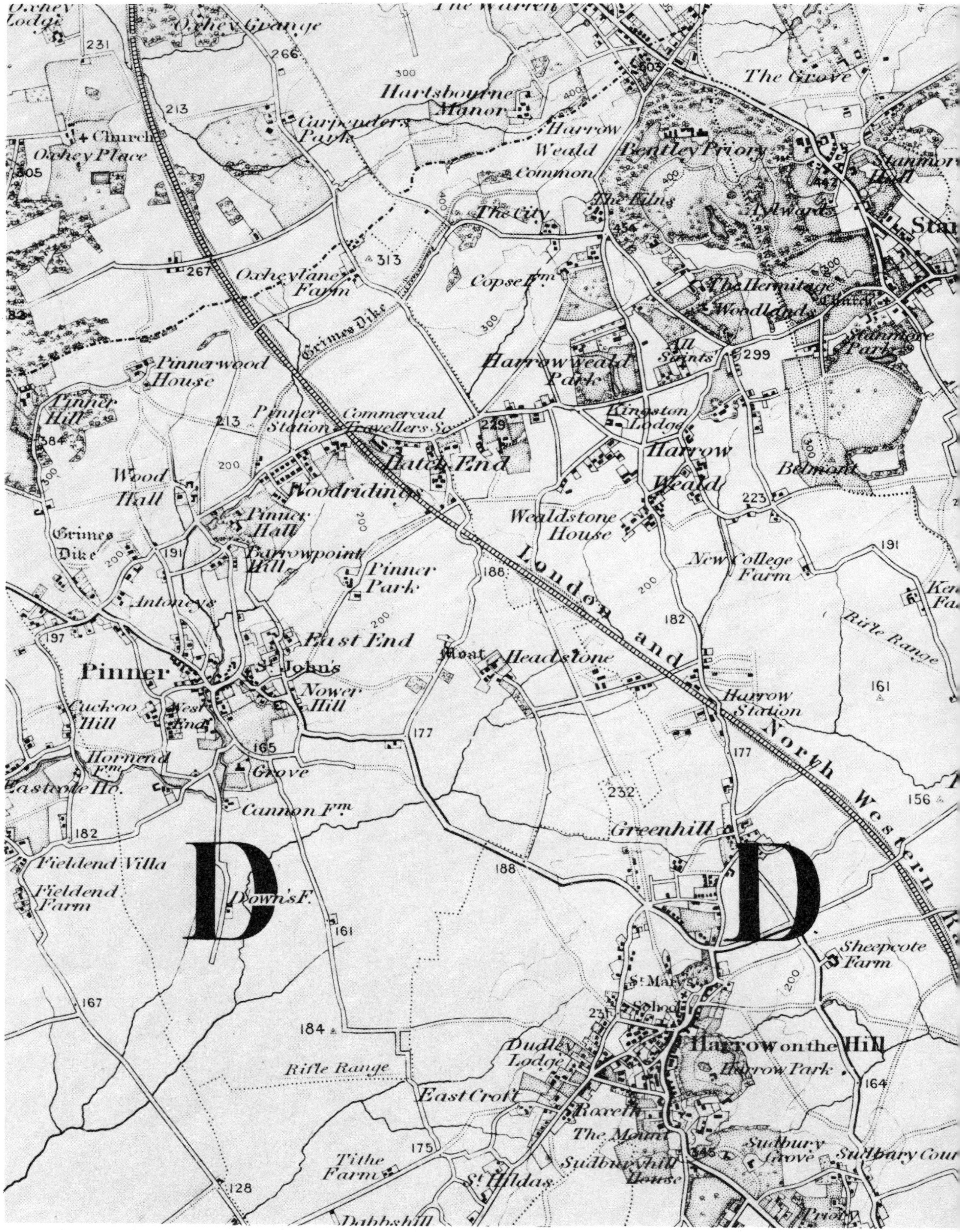
Oxhey Grange
The Warren
Hartsbourne Manor
Carpenders Park
Church
Oxhey Place
The Grove
Harrow Weald Common
Bentley Priory
Stanmore Hall
Aylwards
The Kilns
The City
Oxheylane Farm
Copse Fm
The Hermitage
Woodlands
Church
Stanmore Park
Grimes Dike
Pinnerwood House
Harrow Weald Park
All Saints
Pinner Hill
Pinner Station
Commercial Travellers Sc
Kingston Lodge
Hatch End
Harrow Weald
Belmont
Wood Hall
Woodridings
Wealdstone House
Pinner Hall
Grimes Dike
Barrowpoint Hill
Pinner Park
London and North Western
New College Farm
Antoneys
East End
Rifle Range
Pinner
St. John's
Moat
Headstone
Nower Hill
Harrow Station
Cuckoo Hill
West End
Hornend Fm.
Grove
Eastcote Ho.
Cannon Fm.
Greenhill
Fieldend Villa
Fieldend Farm
D
Down's F.
D
Sheepcote Farm
St. Mary's
School
Harrow on the Hill
Harrow Park
Dudley Lodge
Rifle Range
East Croft
Roxeth
The Mount
Sudbury Grove
Sudbury Court
Sudburyhill House
Tithe Farm
St. Hildas
Dabbshill
231
266
300
213
305
400
313
267
300
299
213
229
384
200
223
300
191
188
200
191
182
197
200
161
177
165
177
232
156
182
188
161
167
184
164
175
128

1
2
1 mile approx.

96
▽

37

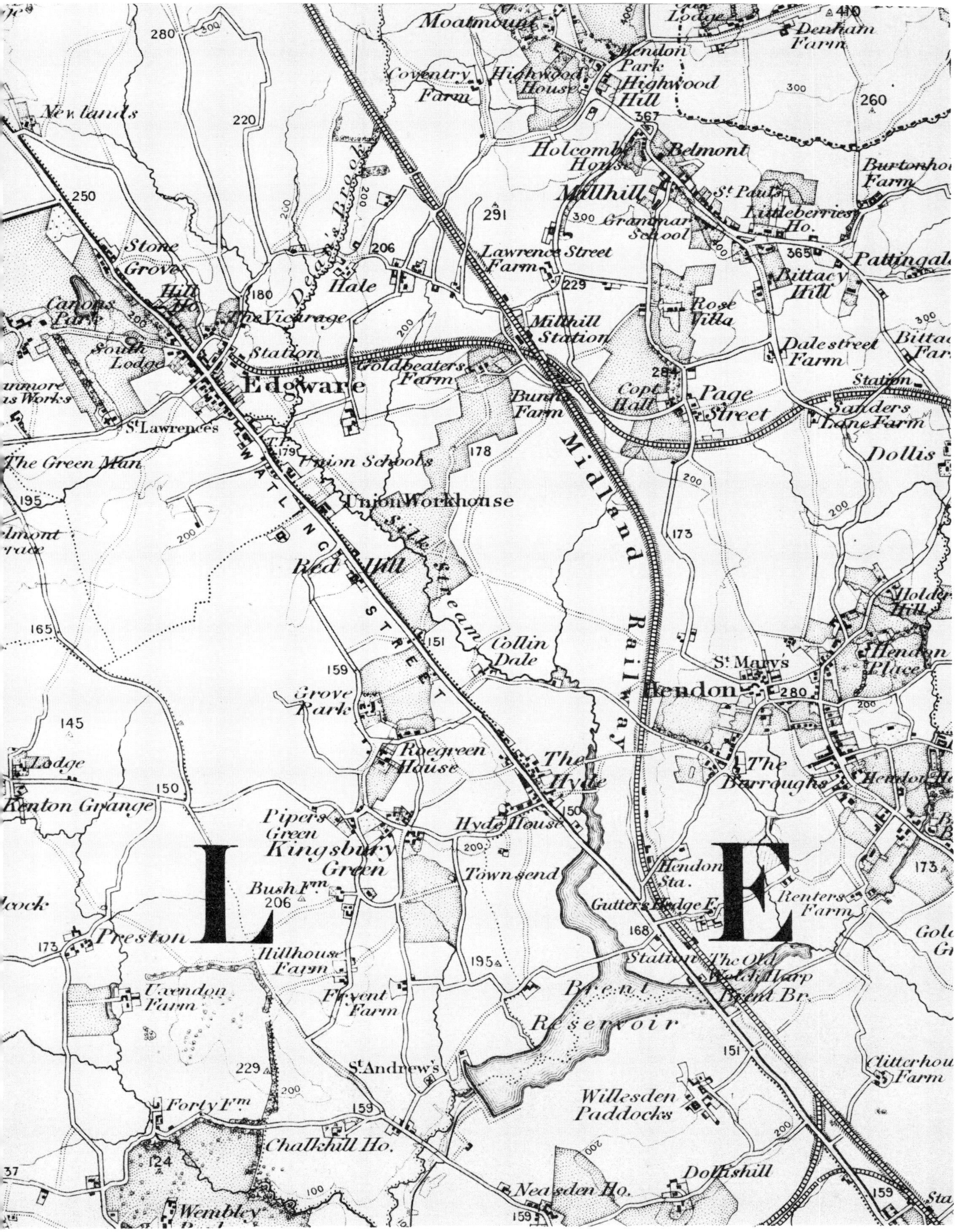

Moatmount
Coventry Farm
Highwood House
Hendon Park
Highwood Hill
Denham Farm
300
260
Newlands
280
220
367
Holcombe House
Belmont
Burtonhole Farm
Millhill
St. Pauls
Grammar School
Littleberries Ho.
291
250
Stone Grove
Hill Ho.
Deans Brook
206
Hale
Lawrence Street Farm
229
365
Pattingale
Bittacy Hill
Rose Villa
Canons Park
The Vicarage
180
Millhill Station
South Lodge
Station
Goldbeaters Farm
Dale street Farm
Edgware
Copt Hall
Page Street
Bunns Farm
Station
Sanders Lane Farm
St. Lawrences
The Green Man
179
Union Schools
178
Dollis
195
Union Workhouse
WATLING STREET
Midland Railway
Silk stream
200
173
Red Hill
165
151
Collin Dale
Holders Hill
159
St. Mary's
Hendon Place
Grove Park
Hendon
280
145
Lodge
Roegreen House
The Hyde
The Burroughs
Kenton Grange
150
Pipers Green
Kingsbury Green
Hyde House
Townsend
Bush Fm.
206
Hendon Sta.
173
Renters Farm
Gutters Hedge F.
Preston
L
E
168
Hillhouse Farm
195
Station
The Old Welch Harp
Brent Br.
Uxendon Farm
Freyent Farm
Brent Reservoir
151
229
St. Andrew's
Clitterhouse Farm
Forty Fm.
Willesden Paddocks
159
Chalkhill Ho.
124
Dollishill
37
100
Neasden Ho.
Wembley
159

72

97

Surveyed 1862-1871. Published 1877.

△ 38

◁ 63

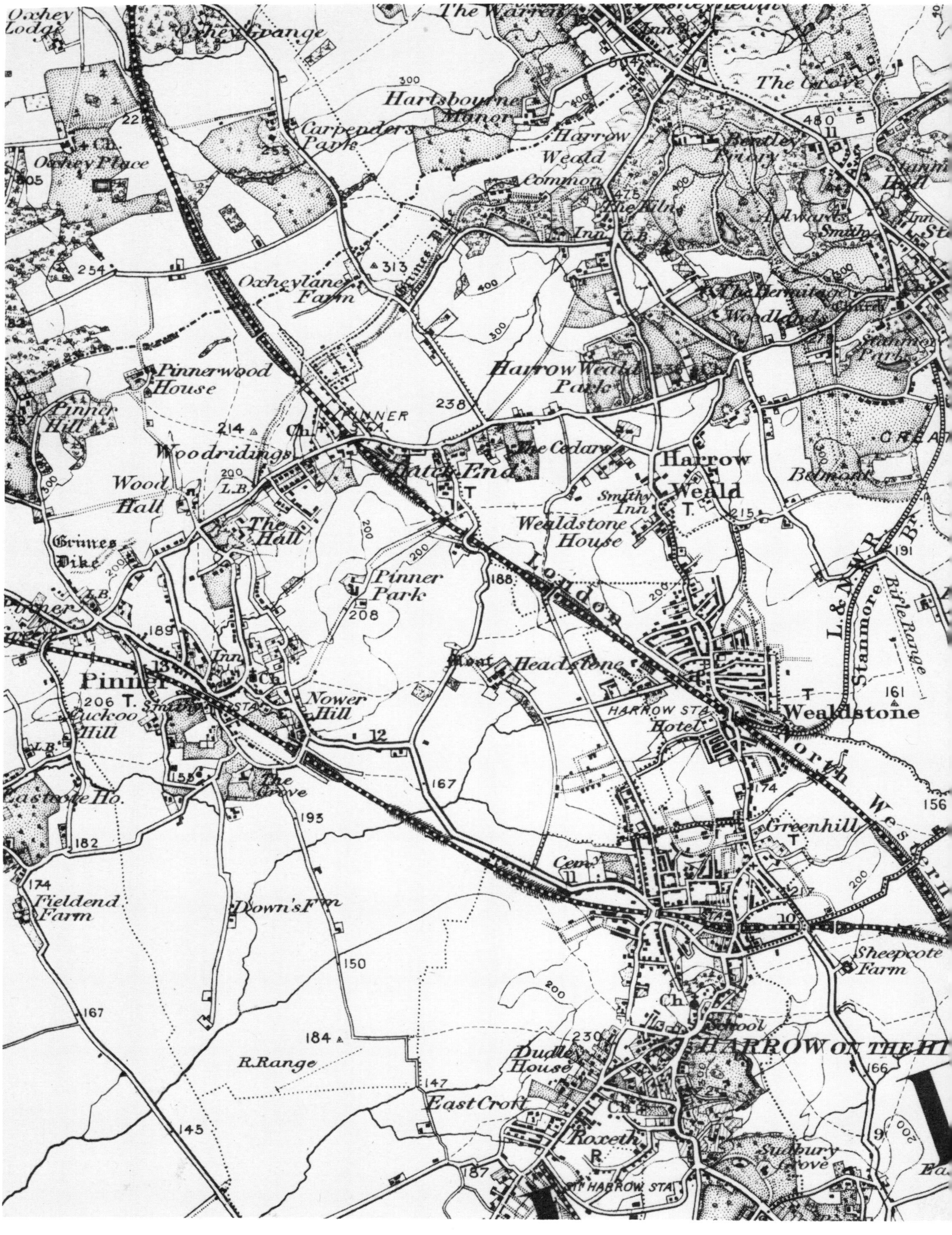

Oxhey Lodge
The Warren
Oxhey Grange
Hartsbourne Manor
Carpenders Park
Harrow Weald Common
The Grove
Bentley Priory
Oxhey Place
Oxheylane Farm
Grimes Dike
The Hermitage
Woodland
Pinnerwood House
Harrow Weald Park
Pinner Hill
PINNER STA.
Woodridings
Pinner End
The Cedars
Harrow Weald
Wood Hall
The Hall
Smithy Inn
Wealdstone House
Belmont
Grimes Dike
London
Pinner Park
L. & N.W.R. Br.
Stanmore
Rifle Range
Pinner
Headstone
Moat
Nower Hill
HARROW STA.
Hotel
Wealdstone
Cuckoo Hill
North Western
Eastcote Ho.
The Grove
Greenhill
Fieldend Farm
Down's Fm
Cemy
Sheepcote Farm
School
HARROW ON THE HILL
R. Range
Dudley House
East Croft
Roxeth
Sudbury Grove
SOUTH HARROW STA.

1 2

1 mile approx.

98 ▽

△ 39

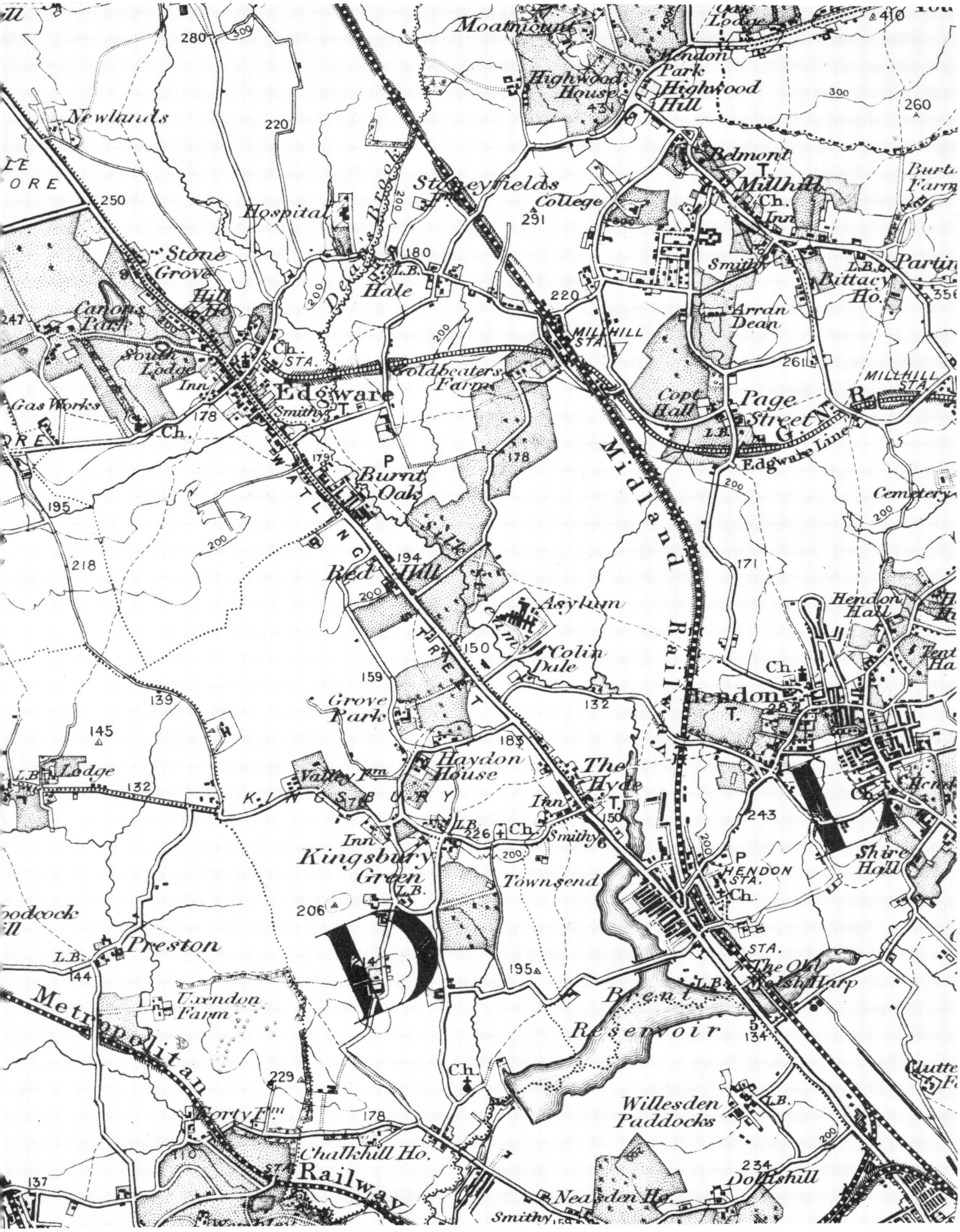

74 ▷

99 ▽

Surveyed 1862-1871. Revised 1902. Published 1904.

40

65

Burton Hole
Frith Manor
Moss Hall
Colney Hatch
Wood Ho
Beaver Hall
Nether Street
Dollis
Finchley
Finchley Common
Brown's Wells
Tottenham Wood F.
Coppets F.
Finchley
Holders Hill
Manor House
East End
Hog Market
Muswell Hill
Dirt House
Abbots F.
Bishops Wood
Caen Wood
Highgate
Golders Green
North End
Hampstead Heath
Clutterhouse F.
Childs Hill
Millfield F.
Mains F.
Hampstead
The Slade
Pond Street
Toll bar
Kentish
Hornsey Lane

100

1 2

1 mile approx.

△
41

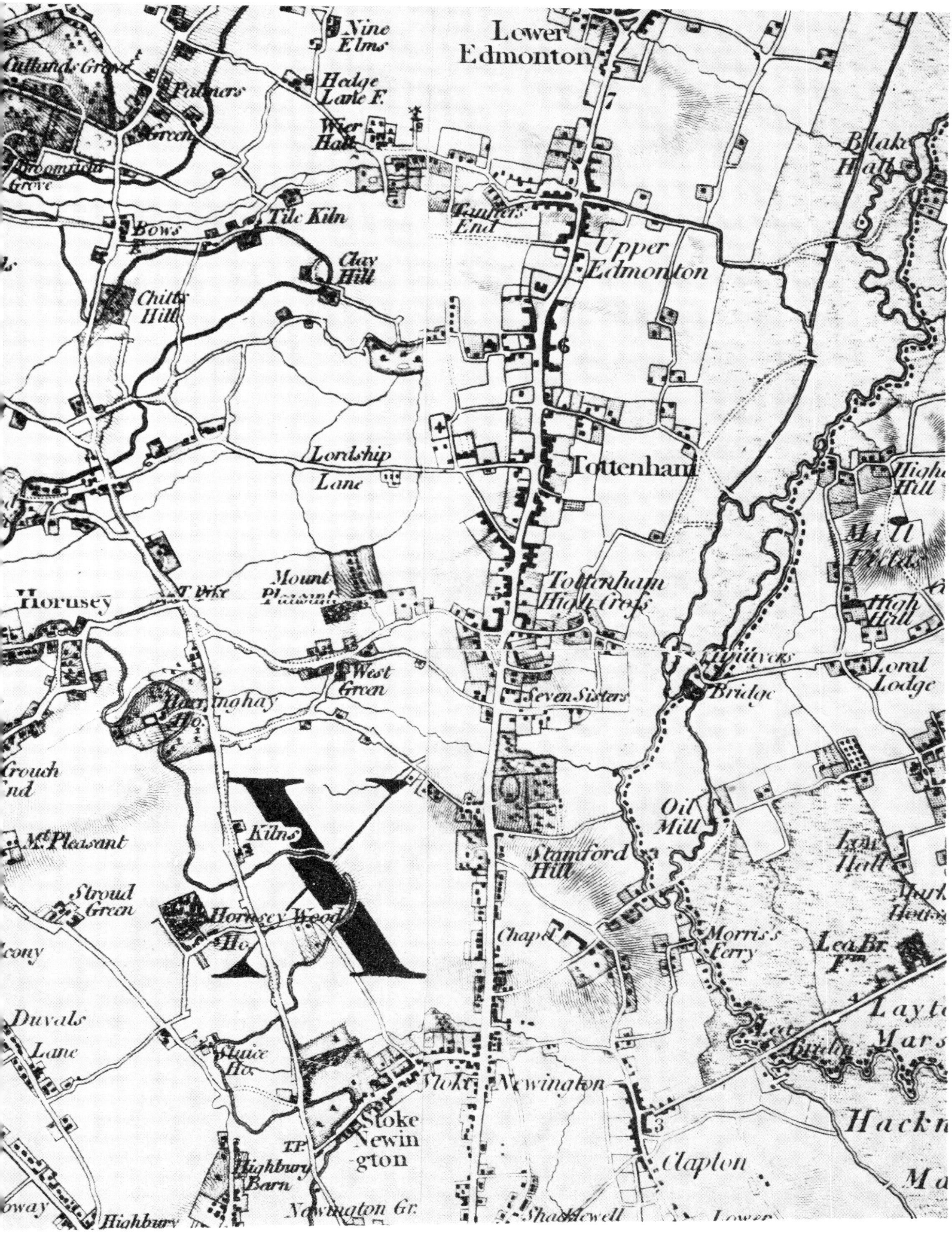
Nine Elms
Lower Edmonton
Palmers
Hedge Lane F.
Wier Hall
Green
Grove
Tile Kiln
Bows
Tanners End
Upper Edmonton
Clay Hill
Chitts Hill
7
6
Lordship Lane
Tottenham
High Hill
Mill Fields
Mount Pleasant
T. Pike
Horusey
Tottenham High Cross
High Hill
Bridge
Lord Lodge
West Green
Seven Sisters
5
Crouch End
X
Oil Mill
Kilns
Mt. Pleasant
Stamford Hill
Stroud Green
Hornsey Wood Ho.
Chapel
Morris's Ferry
Lea Br. F.
Duvals Lane
Sluice Ho.
Stoke Newington
Stoke Newin-gton
T.P.
3
Clapton
Highbury Barn
Newington Gr.
Shacklewell
Highbury
Lower

76 ▷

Published 1822.

101
▽

42

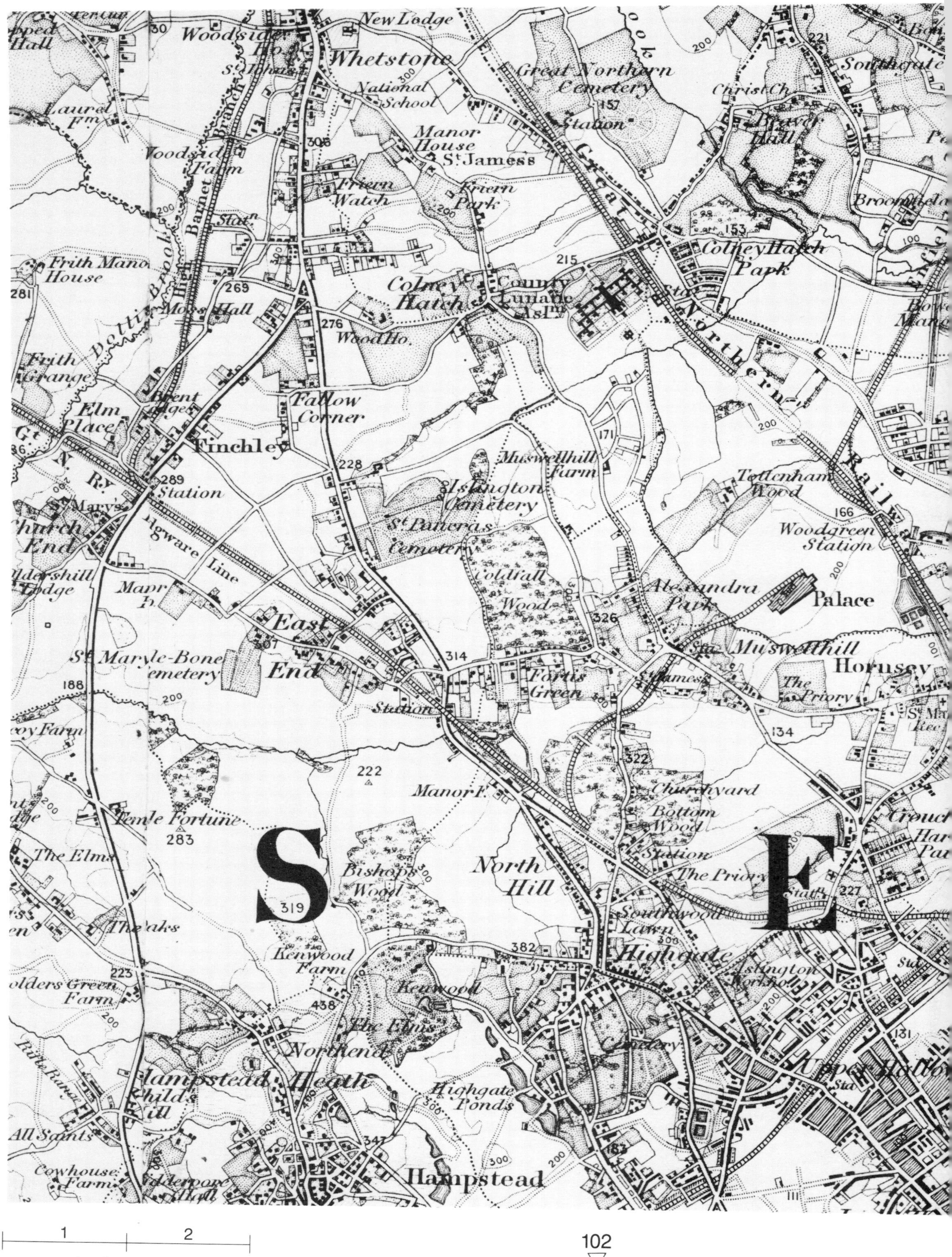

Whetstone
New Lodge
Woodside Ho.
St. Johns
National School
Great Northern Cemetery
Station
Christ Ch.
Southgate
Laurel Fm.
Woodside Farm
Barnet Branch
Manor House
St. James
Friern Watch
Friern Park
Bowes Park
Broomfield
Barnet Stat.
Colney Hatch Park
Frith Manor House
Colney Hatch
County Lunatic Asl.m
Moss Hall
Dollis Brook
Wood Ho.
Frith Grange
Fallow Corner
Great Northern
Elm Place
Finchley
Station
Gt. N. Ry.
St. Mary's
Church End
Muswellhill Farm
Tottenham Wood
Islington Cemetery
St. Pancras Cemetery
Edgware Line
Woodgreen Station
Coldfall Wood
Alexandra Park
Palace
East End
St. Marylebone Cemetery
Muswellhill
Hornsey
Fortis Green
St. James
The Priory
Station
Manor F.
Churchyard Bottom Wood
Temple Fortune
The Elms
S
E
Bishops Wood
North Hill
Station
The Priory
Southwood Lawn
Highgate
Islington Workho.
Kenwood Farm
Kenwood
Golders Green Farm
The Elms
Northend
Hampstead Heath
Childs Hill
Highgate Ponds
All Saints
Cowhouse Farm
Hampstead
Upper Holloway

1 2

1 mile approx.

◁ 67

102

△
43

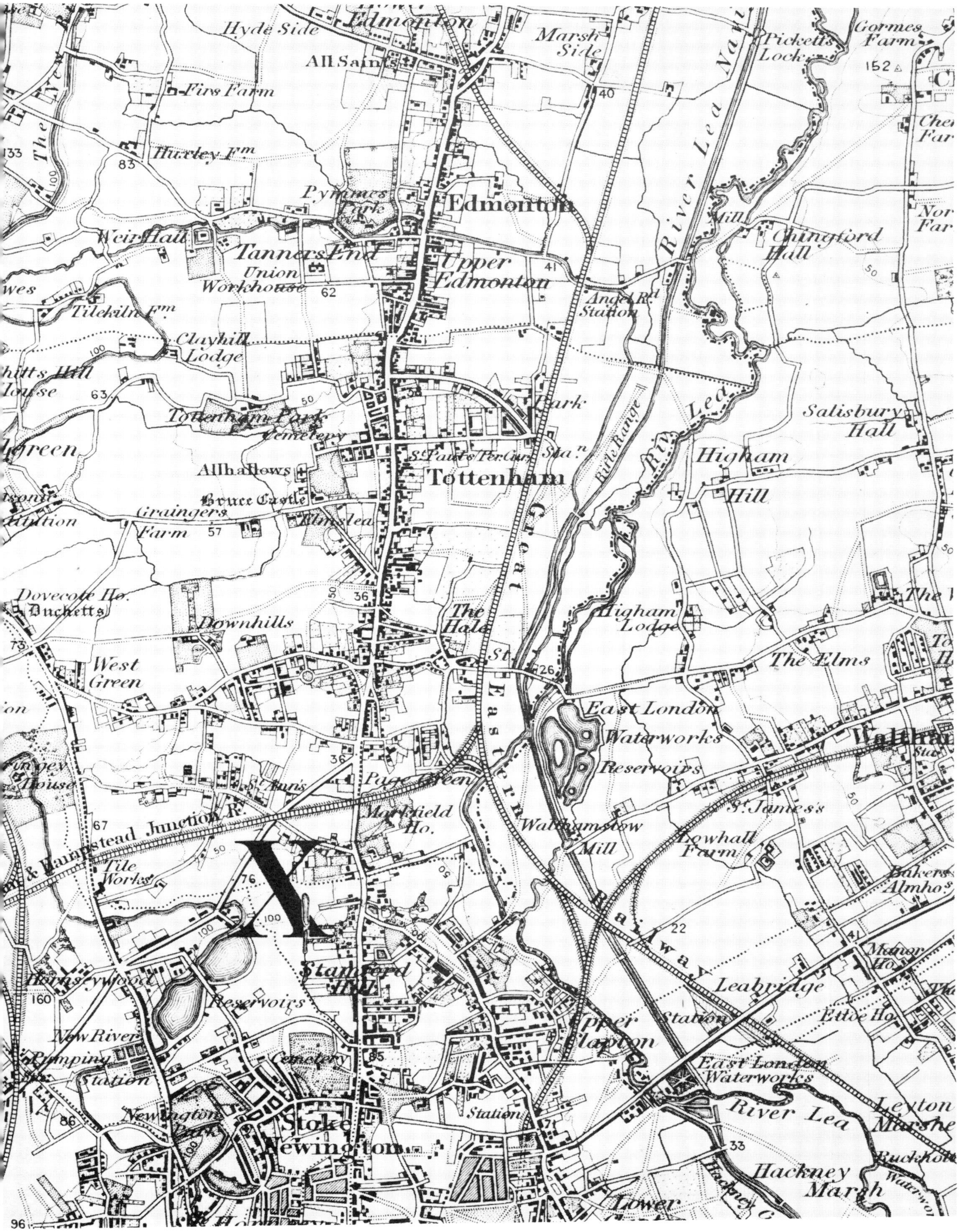
Edmonton
Hyde Side
Marsh Side
All Saints
Pickett's Lock
Gormes Farm
Firs Farm
Huxley Fm
Pymmes Park
Edmonton
Weir Hall
Tanners End
Union Workhouse
Upper Edmonton
Chingford Hall
River Lea Navigation
Tilekiln Fm
Angel Rd Station
Clayhill Lodge
Tottenham Park Cemetery
Park
Rifle Range
Salisbury Hall
St. Paul's Ter. Cur. Stan.
Allhallows
Tottenham
Higham Hill
Bruce Castle
Graingers Farm
Elmslea
Great Eastern
Dovecote Ho.
Duckett's
Downhills
The Hale
Higham Lodge
West Green
The Elms
East London Waterworks Reservoirs
St. Ann's
Page Green
Markfield Ho.
Walthamstow Mill
St. James's
Lowhall Farm
Hampstead Junction R.
Tile Works
X
Railway
Bakers Almhs
Stamford Hill
Reservoirs
Leabridge
Station
Manor Ho.
Ettoe Ho.
New River Pumping Station
Cemetery
Upper Clapton
East London Waterworks
River Lea
Newington Park
Station
Stoke Newington
Leyton Marshes
Hackney Marsh
Lower

78▷

103
▽

Surveyed 1862-1871. Published 1877.

△ 44

◁ 69

Whetstone
Manor House
Friern Watch
Friary Park
Friern Barnet
Cemeteries
New Southgate
Frith Manor House
Nether Court
Colney Hatch
Asylum
Wood Ho.
Fallow Corner
Finchley
Dollis Brook
Church End
Islington Cemetery
St. Pancras Cemetery
Hospital
Coldfall Wood
Mawr Ho.
St. Mary-le-Bone Cemetery
East Finchley
Fortis Green
Muswell Hill
Alexandra Palace
HORNSEY
Manor Fm.
Churchyard Bottom Wood
Brent Bridge
Temple Fortune
The Elms
North Hill
Bishops Wood
Golders Green
The Oaks
Highgate
Kenwood
Northend
Hampstead Heath
Highgate Ponds
Child's Hill
Parliament Hill
Hampstead

1 mile approx.

104 ▽

45

80

105

Surveyed 1863-1876. Revised 1902. Published 1904.

△ 46

◁71

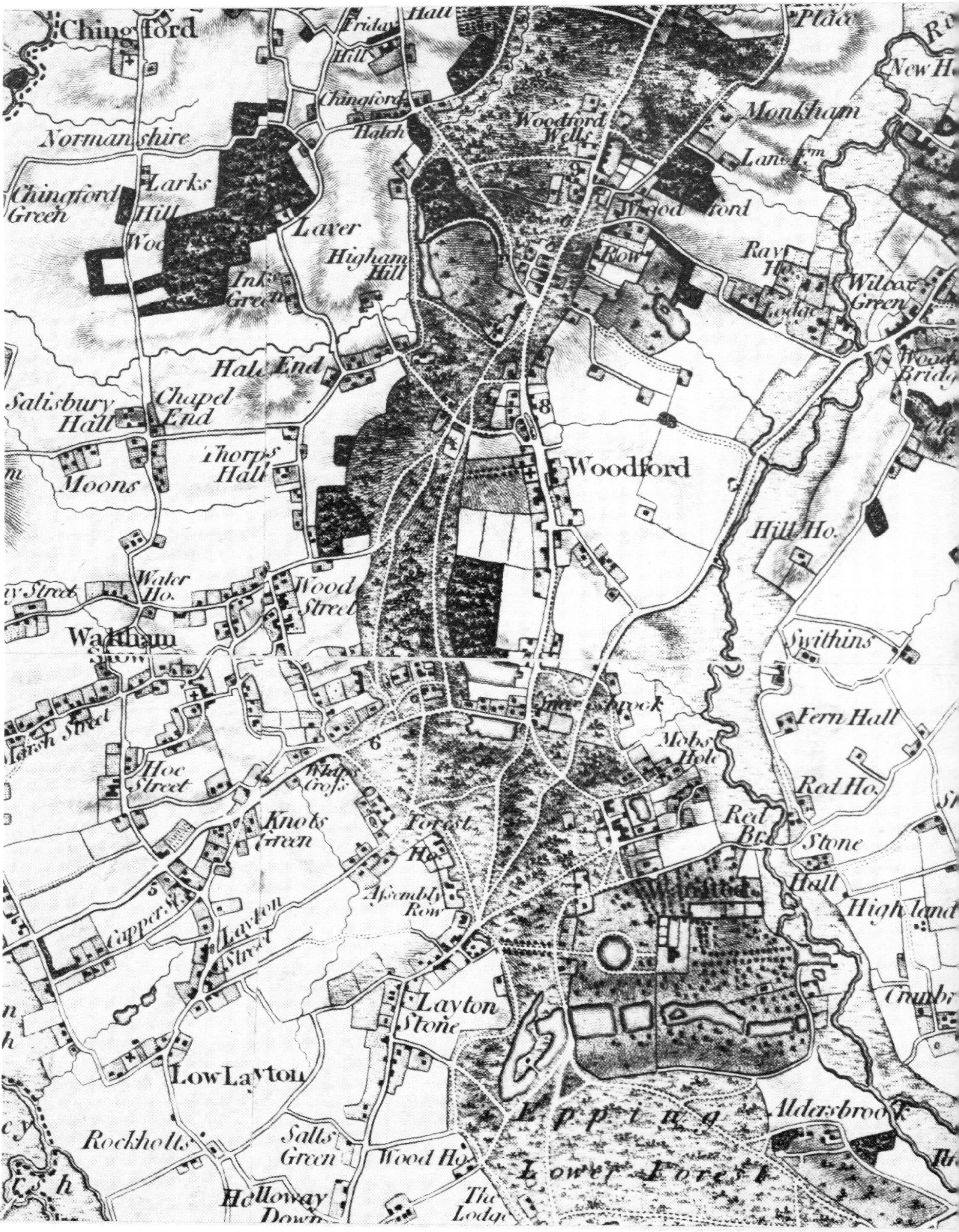
Chingford
Friday Hill
Hall
Place
Chingford Hatch
Normanshire
Woodford Wells
Monkham
Lane Fm
Larks Hill Wood
Chingford Green
Laver
Higham Hill
Ink Green
Woodford Row
Ray Ho.
Wilcox Green
Lodge
Hale End
Salisbury Hall
Chapel End
Thorps Hall
Moons
Woodford
Hill Ho.
Water Ho.
Wood Street
Walthamstow
Swithins
Marsh Street
Fern Hall
Mobs Hole
Hoe Street
Whip Cross
Red Ho.
Knots Green
Forest Ho.
Red Br.
Stone Hall
Assembly Row
Capper St.
Layton Street
Highland
Layton Stone
Low Layton
Aldersbrook
Epping Lower Forest
Rockholts
Salts Green
Wood Ho.
Holloway Down
The Lodge

1 2

1 mile approx.

106 ▽

47

82

107

Published 1805.

△ 48

◁73

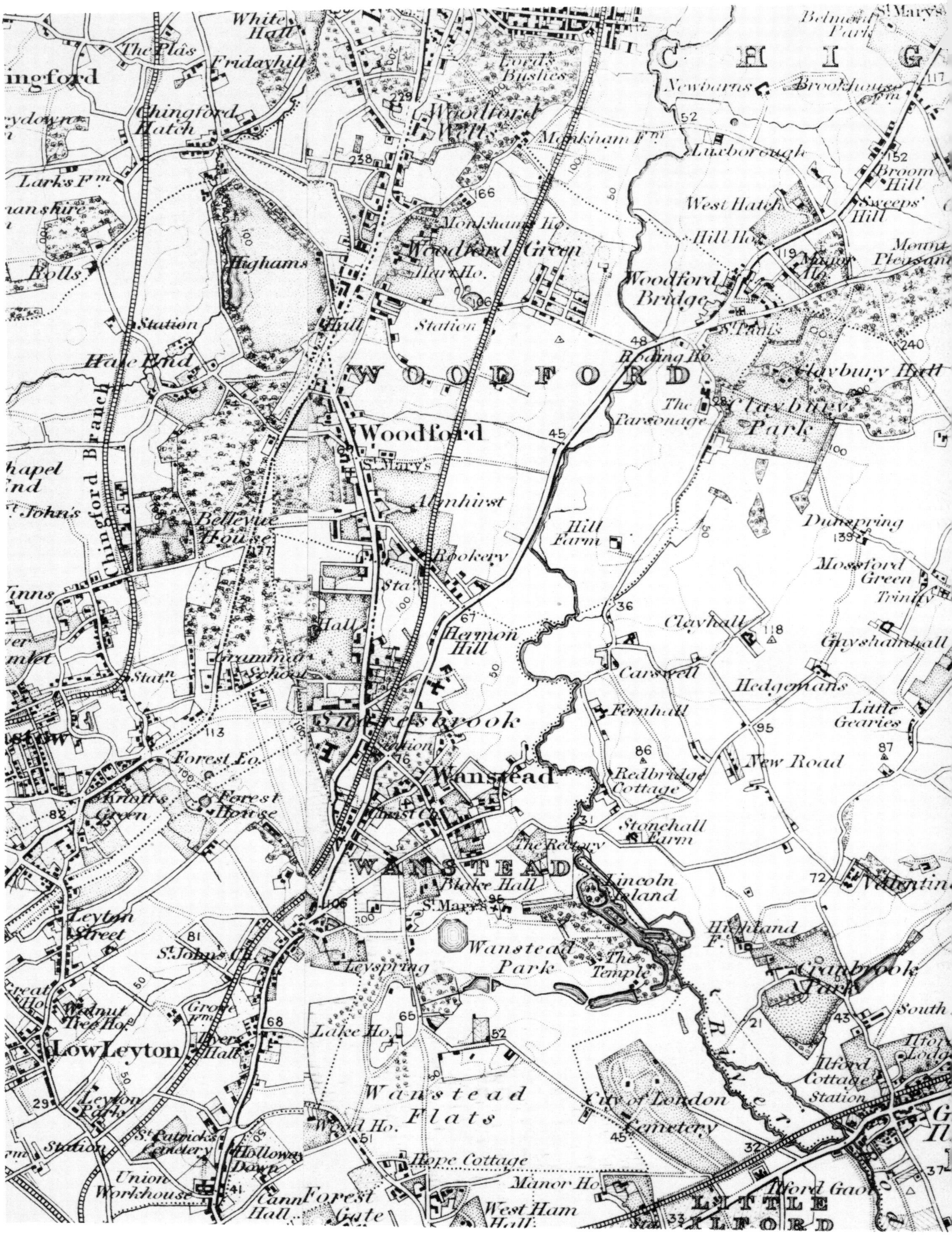
White Hall
The Plâs
Fridayhill
Lords Bushes
Chingford Hatch
Woodford Wells
Monkham Fm
Larks Fm
Highams
Monkhams Ho.
Woodford Green
Hart Ho.
Rolls
Station
Hale End
Chingford Branch
WOODFORD
Woodford
St. Mary's
Bellevue House
Rookery
Hermon Hill
Grammar School
Snaresbrook
Station
Wanstead
Forest Ho.
Forest House
Christ Ch.
WANSTEAD
Blake Hall
St. Mary's
Wanstead Park
The Temple
Leyspring
Lake Ho.
Leyton Street
St. John's Ch.
Grove Fm.
Low Leyton
Leyton Park
St. Patrick's Cemetery
Hollow Down
Union Workhouse
Cann Hall
Forest Gate
Wanstead Flats
Wood Ho.
Hope Cottage
Manor Ho.
West Ham Hall
City of London Cemetery
LITTLE ILFORD
Ilford Gaol
Ilford Cottage
Station
River
Newbarns
Brookhouse Fm.
Luxborough
West Hatch
Hill Ho.
Woodford Bridge
St. Paul's
Roding Ho.
The Parsonage
Claybury Hall
Claybury Park
Hill Farm
Dunspring
Mossford Green
Clayhall
Gayshamhall
Carswell
Hedgemans
Fernhall
Little Gearies
Redbridge Cottage
New Road
Stonehall Farm
The Rectory
Lincoln Island
Highland F.
Cranbrook Park
Broom Hill
Sweeps' Hill
Mount Pleasant
Manor Ho.
Belmont Park
CHIG
Hale End

108 ▽

1 2

1 mile approx.

49

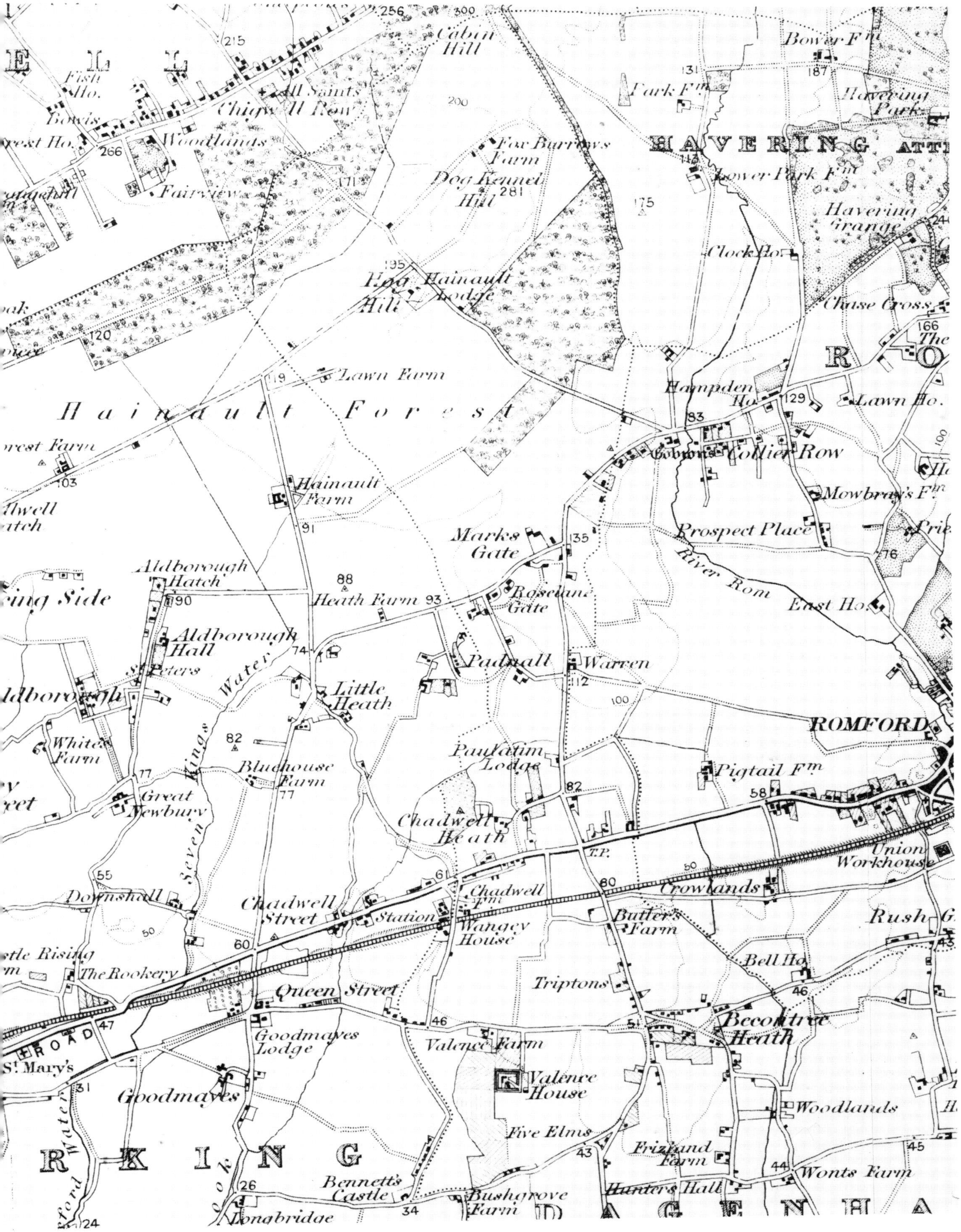
Cabin Hill
Fish Ho.
All Saints
Chigwell Row
Woodlands
Fairview
Fox Burrows Farm
Dog Kennel Hill
Bower Fm
Park Fm
Havering Park
HAVERING
Lower Park Fm
Havering Grange
Clock Ho.
Hog Hill
Hainault Lodge
Chase Cross
Lawn Farm
Hainault Forest
Hampden Ho.
Lawn Ho.
Collier Row
Hainault Farm
Mowbray's Fm
Prospect Place
Marks Gate
River Rom
Aldborough Hatch
Heath Farm
Roselane Gate
East Ho.
Aldborough Hall
St Peters
Padnall
Warren
Little Heath
Seven Kings Water
White Farm
ROMFORD
Pigtail Fm
Bluehouse Farm
Great Newbury
Chadwell Heath
Union Workhouse
Downshall
Crowlands
Chadwell Fm
Chadwell Street
Station
Wangey House
Butler's Farm
The Rookery
Bell Ho.
Queen Street
Triptons
Becontree Heath
ROAD
Goodmayes Lodge
Valence Farm
St Mary's
Valence House
Goodmayes
Woodlands
Five Elms
Frizland Farm
Wonts Farm
Bennett's Castle
Bushgrove Farm
Hunters Hall
Longbridge

84

109

Surveyed 1862-1873. Published 1883.

△ 50

◁75

Chingford
Smithy
Inn
Ch.
Cem.y
Chingford Hatch
White Hall
Fridayhill
Normanshire Farm
Rolls
Highams
Hale End
Chingford Branch G.E.R.
Woodford Wells
Lord's Bushes
Woodford Green
Hart Ho.
Woodford
Luxborough
West Hatch
Hill Ho.
Woodford Bridge
Parsonage
Claybury Fm.
Hill Farm
Hermon Hill
Snaresbrook
Fernhall
Clayhall
Hedgemans
Smithy
Wanstead
Stonehall Farm
Infirmary
Blake Hall
Lincoln Island
The Castle
Wanstead Park
Golf Course
Leytonstone
Lake Ho.
River Roding
Wanstead Flats
City of London Cemetery
Forest Gate
Manor Park
Chigwell S

110 ▽

1 2

1 mile approx.

△ 51

86 ▷

111 ▽

Surveyed 1862-1873. Revised 1903. Published 1904.

△
52

◁77

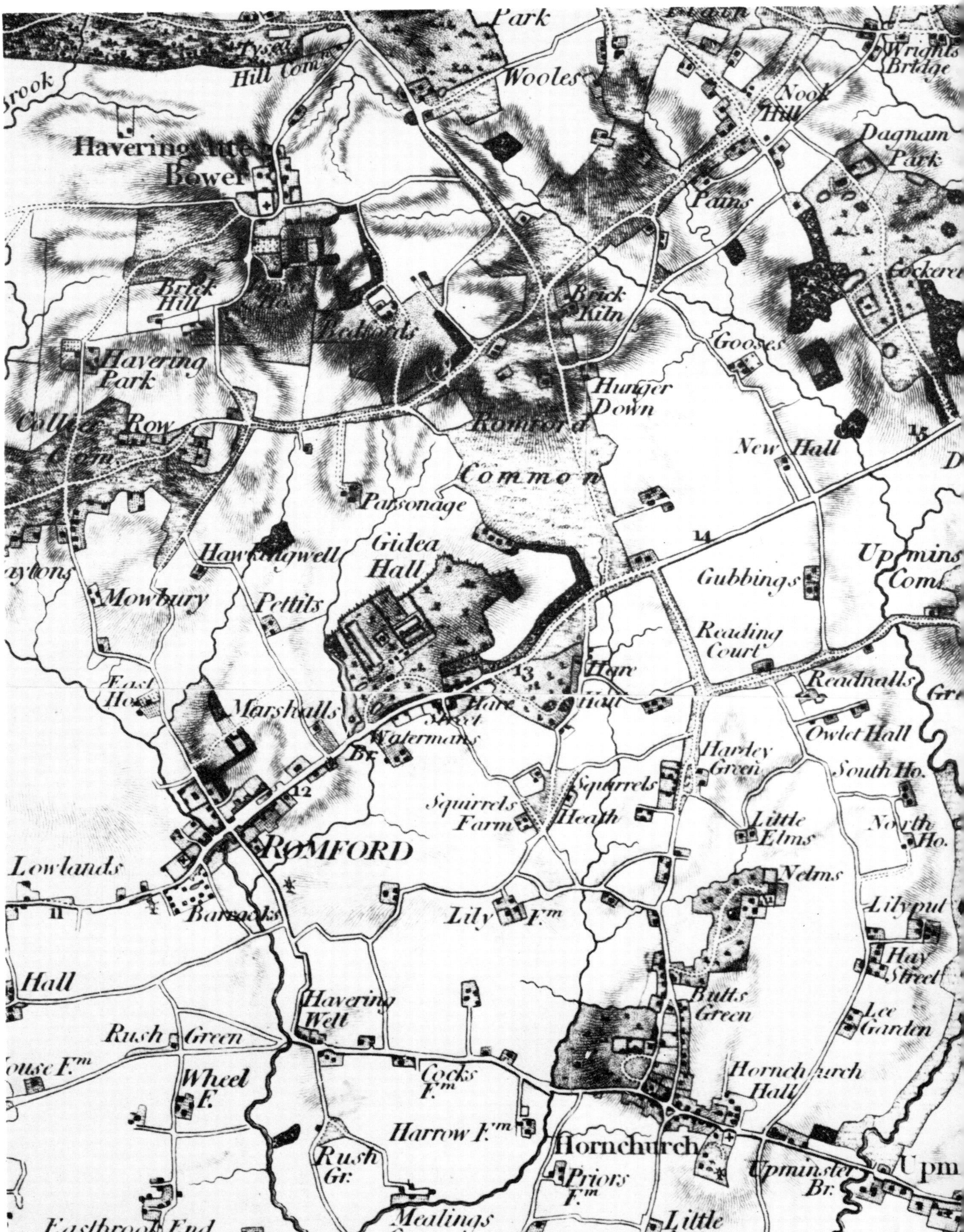

Park
Hill Com.
Wooles
Wrights Bridge
Nook Hill
Havering Atte Bower
Dagnam Park
Pains
Brick Hill
Brick Kiln
Havering Park
Gooses
Hunger Down
Collier Row
Com.
Romford
Common
New Hall
Parsonage
Hawkingwell
Gidea Hall
Upminster Com.
Mowbury
Pettits
Gubbings
Reading Court
Readnalls
Hare Hall
Hare Street
Marshalls
Watermans Br.
Owlet Hall
Hardey Green
South Ho.
Squirrels Heath
Squirrels Farm
Little Elms
North Ho.
ROMFORD
Lowlands
Nelms
Barracks
Lily Fm
Lilyput
Hall
Hay Street
Butts Green
Lee Garden
Havering Well
Rush Green
Wheel F.
Cocks Fm
Hornchurch Hall
Harrow Fm
Hornchurch
Rush Gr.
Priors Fm
Upminster Br.
Upm
Mealings Green
Little Sulton
Eastbrook End

112
▽

1 2
1 mile approx.

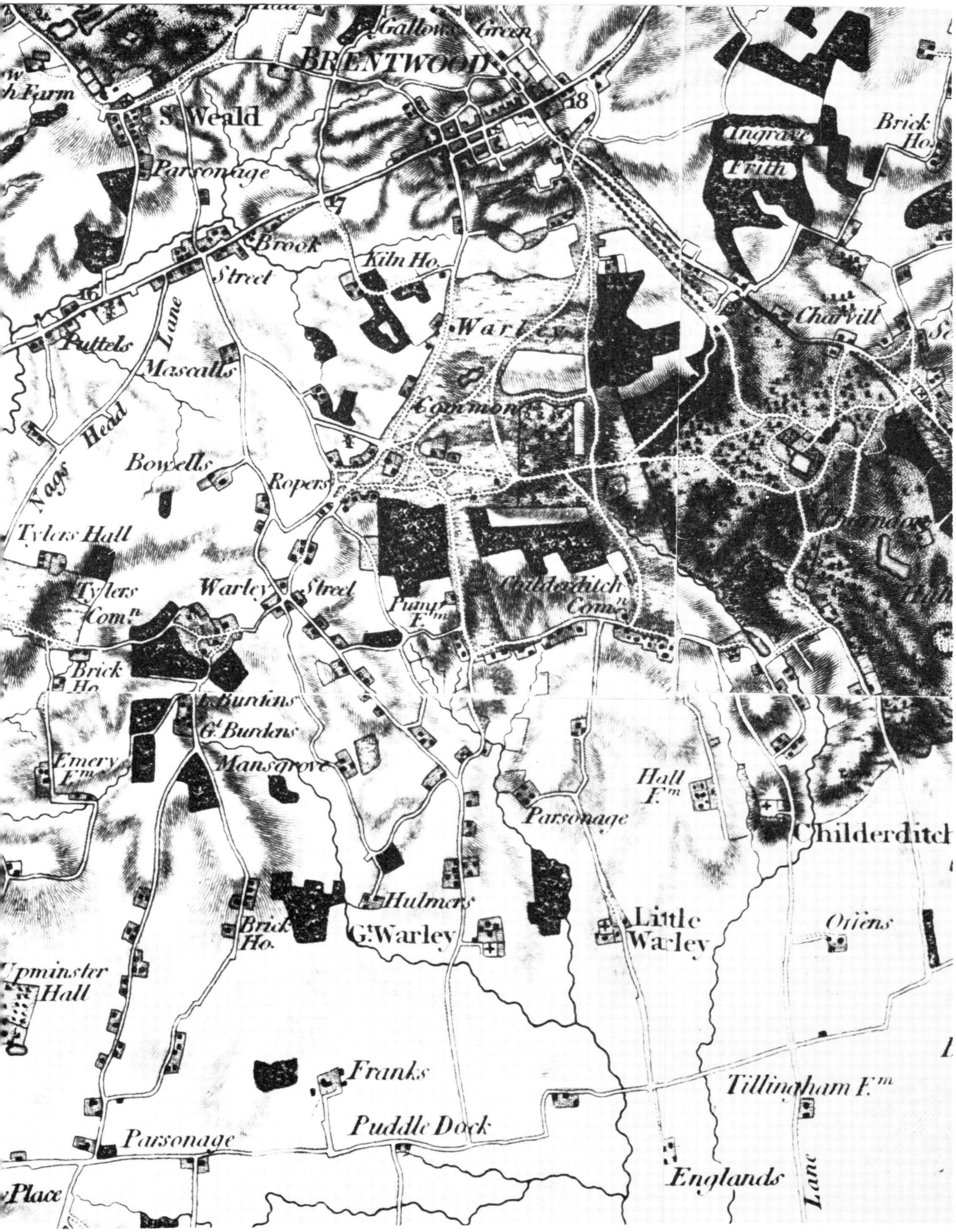
Gallows Green
BRENTWOOD
18
S. Weald
Parsonage
17
Brook
Street
Kiln Ho.
Ingrave
Frith
Brick
Ho.
Charvill
Puttels
Lane
Warley
Mascalls
Common
Nags Head
Bowells
Ropers
Tylers Hall
Tylers
Com.n
Warley Street
Pump F.m
Childerditch
Com.n
Brick
Ho.
L. Burdens
G.t Burdens
Emery
F.m
Mansgrove
Hall
F.m
Parsonage
Childerditch
Hulmers
Brick
Ho.
G.t Warley
Little
Warley
Offens
Upminster
Hall
Franks
Tillingham F.m
Parsonage
Puddle Dock
Englands
Lane
Place

Published 1805.

△ 54

◁79

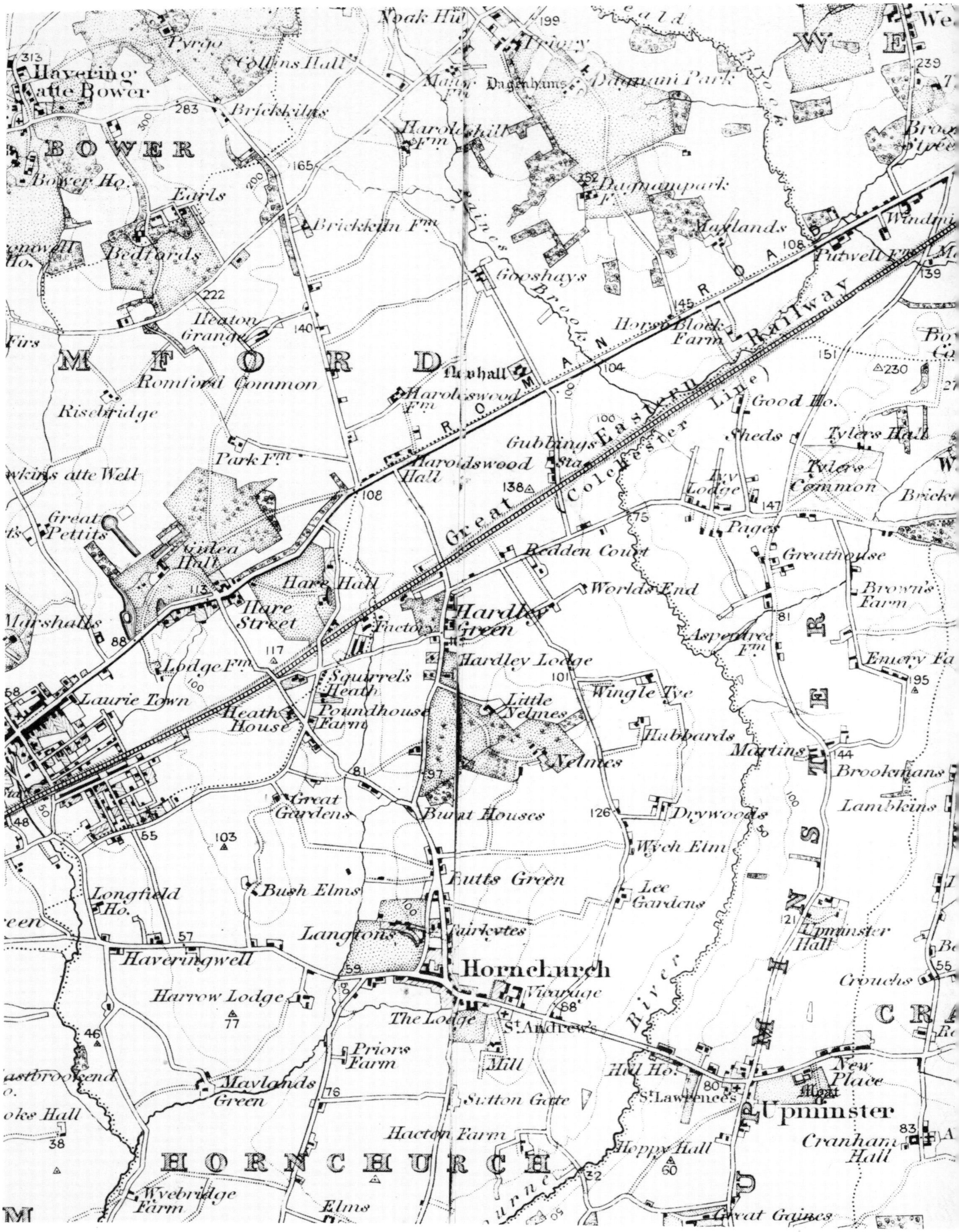
Noak Hill
Priory
Pyrgo
Collins Hall
Havering atte Bower
Dagenhams
Dagnam Park
Brickkilns
BOWER
Bower Ho.
Harold Hill Fm.
Earls
Bedfords
Brickkiln Fm.
Dagnampark F.
Maylands
Gooshays
Brook
Heaton Grange
Horse Block Farm
Putwell Fm.
Railway
ROMAN ROAD
M
F
O
R
D
Newhall
Romford Common
Haroldswood Fm.
Risebridge
Good Ho.
Sheds
Tylers Hall
Park Fm.
Gubbings
Haroldswood Sta.
Haroldswood Hall
Great Eastern
Colchester Line
Tylers Common
Ivy Lodge
Pages
Great Pettits
Guidea Hall
Redden Court
Greathouse
Hare Hall
Worlds End
Brown's Farm
Hare Street
Hardley Green
Factory
Marshalls
Aspentree Fm.
Lodge Fm.
Hardley Lodge
Emery Farm
Squirrel's Heath
Wingle Tye
Laurie Town
Heath House
Poundhouse Farm
Little Nelmes
Hubbards
Nelmes
Martins
Brookmans
Lambkins
Great Gardens
Burnt Houses
Drywoods
Wych Elm
Bush Elms
Butts Green
Lee Gardens
Longfield Ho.
Langtons
Fairkytes
Upminster Hall
Haveringwell
Hornchurch
Vicarage
Crouchs
Harrow Lodge
The Lodge
St. Andrew's
River
Priors Farm
Mill
Hill Ho.
St. Lawrence's
New Place
Moat
Upminster
Maylands Green
Sutton Gate
Cranham Hall
Hacton Farm
Hoppy Hall
HORNCHURCH
Wyebridge Farm
Elms
Great Gaines

1 2

1 mile approx.

114 ▽

△
55

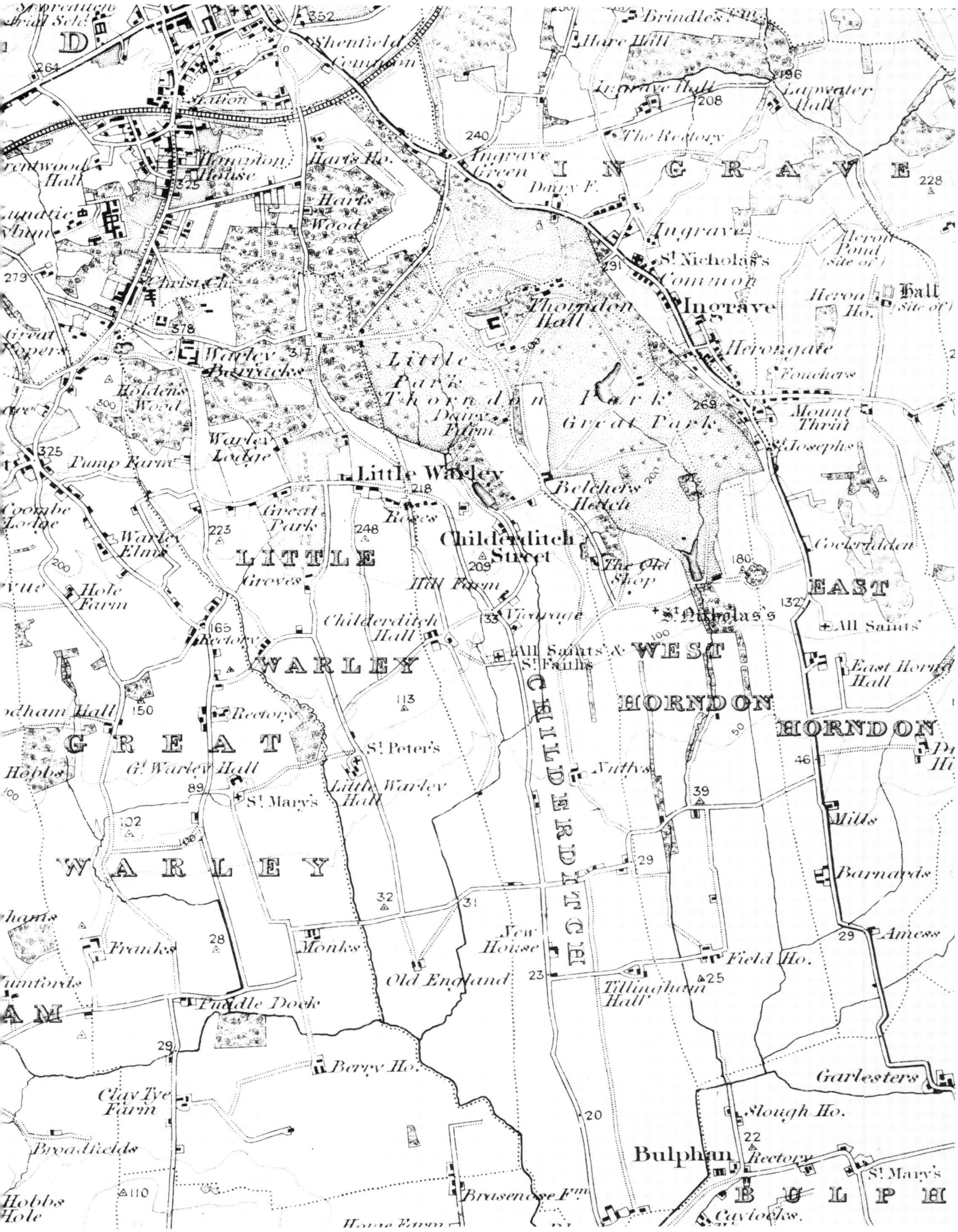

115
▽

Surveyed 1862-1873. Published 1883.

56

81

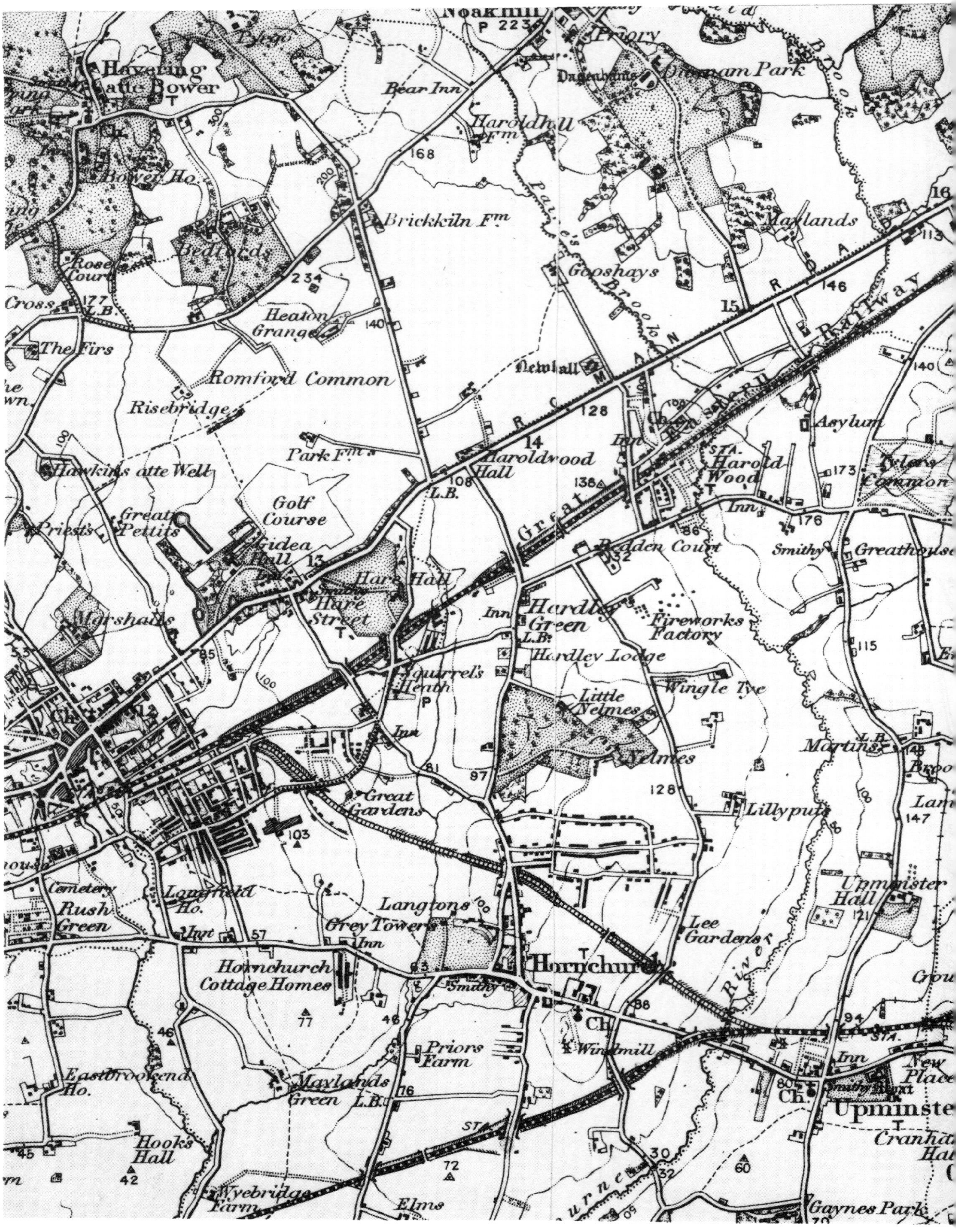
Noakhill
Havering atte Bower
Bear Inn
Priory
Dagenhams
Haroldhill Fm
Bower Ho.
Brickkiln Fm
Marlands
Bedfords
Rose Court
Gooshays
Heaton Grange
Cross
The Firs
Newhall
Romford Common
Risebridge
Park Fm
Asylum
Haroldwood Hall
Harold Wood
Hawkins atte Well
Golf Course
Great Pettits
Priests
Gidea Hall
Hare Hall
Hare Street
Redden Court
Smithy
Greathouse
Marshalls
Hardley Green
Fireworks Factory
Hardley Lodge
Squirrel's Heath
Wingle Tye
Little Nelmes
Nelmes
Martins
Great Gardens
Lillyputs
Cemetery
Longfield Ho.
Rush Green
Langtons
Grey Towers
Lee Gardens
Upminster Hall
Hornchurch Cottage Homes
Hornchurch
Ch.
Windmill
Priors Farm
New Place
Eastbrookend Ho.
Maylands Green
Upminster
Hook's Hall
Wyebridge Farm
Elms
Gaynes Park
Railway
Great Eastern
River

1 2

1 mile approx.

116

△
57

Surveyed 1862-1873. Revised 1903. Published 1904.

△ 58

◁ 119

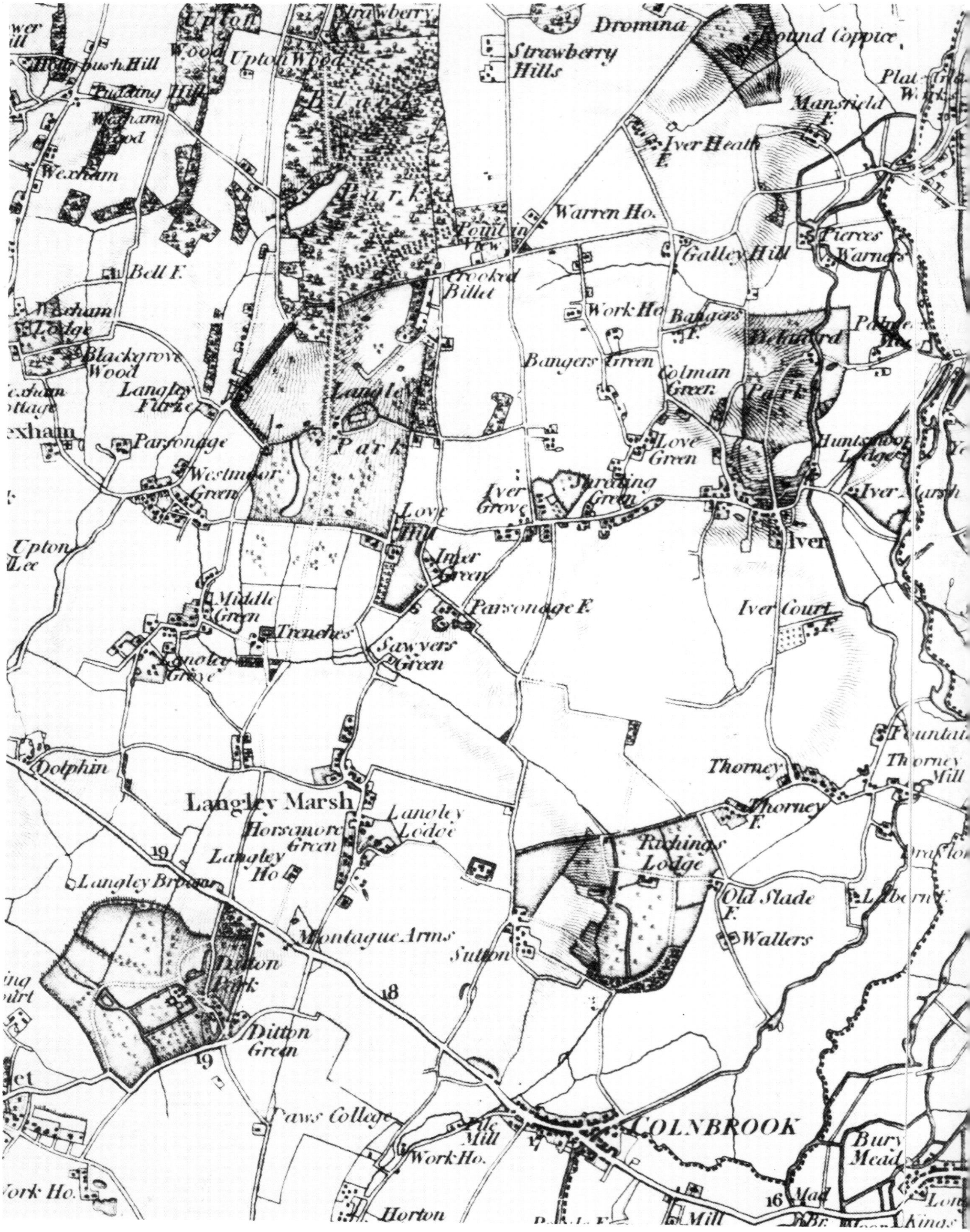
Upton
Strawberry
Dromina
Round Coppice
Strawberry Hills
Upton Wood
Hollybush Hill
Pudding Hill
Wexham Wood
Wexham
Black Park
Mansfield F.
Iver Heath F.
Warren Ho.
Fountain View
Crooked Billet
Galley Hill
Pierces Warners
Bell F.
Wexham Lodge
Blackgrove Wood
Work Ho.
Bangers F.
Delaford Park
Bangers Green
Colman Green
Langley Furze
Langley Park
Parsonage
Love Green
Huntsmoor Lodge
Westmoor Green
Iver Grove
Shreding Green
Iver Marsh
Love Hill
Iver
Upton Lee
Iver Green
Middle Green
Parsonage F.
Iver Court
Trenches
Sawyers Green
Langley Grove
Dolphin
Thorney
Thorney Mill
Langley Marsh
Thorney F.
Horsemore Green
Langley Lodge
Richings Lodge
Langley Ho
Langley Broom
Old Slade F.
Montague Arms
Wallers
Sutton
Ditton Park
Ditton Green
Paws College
Mill
Work Ho.
COLNBROOK
Bury Mead
Horton
Mill
19
18
17
16

1 2

1 mile approx.

124 ▽

△ 59

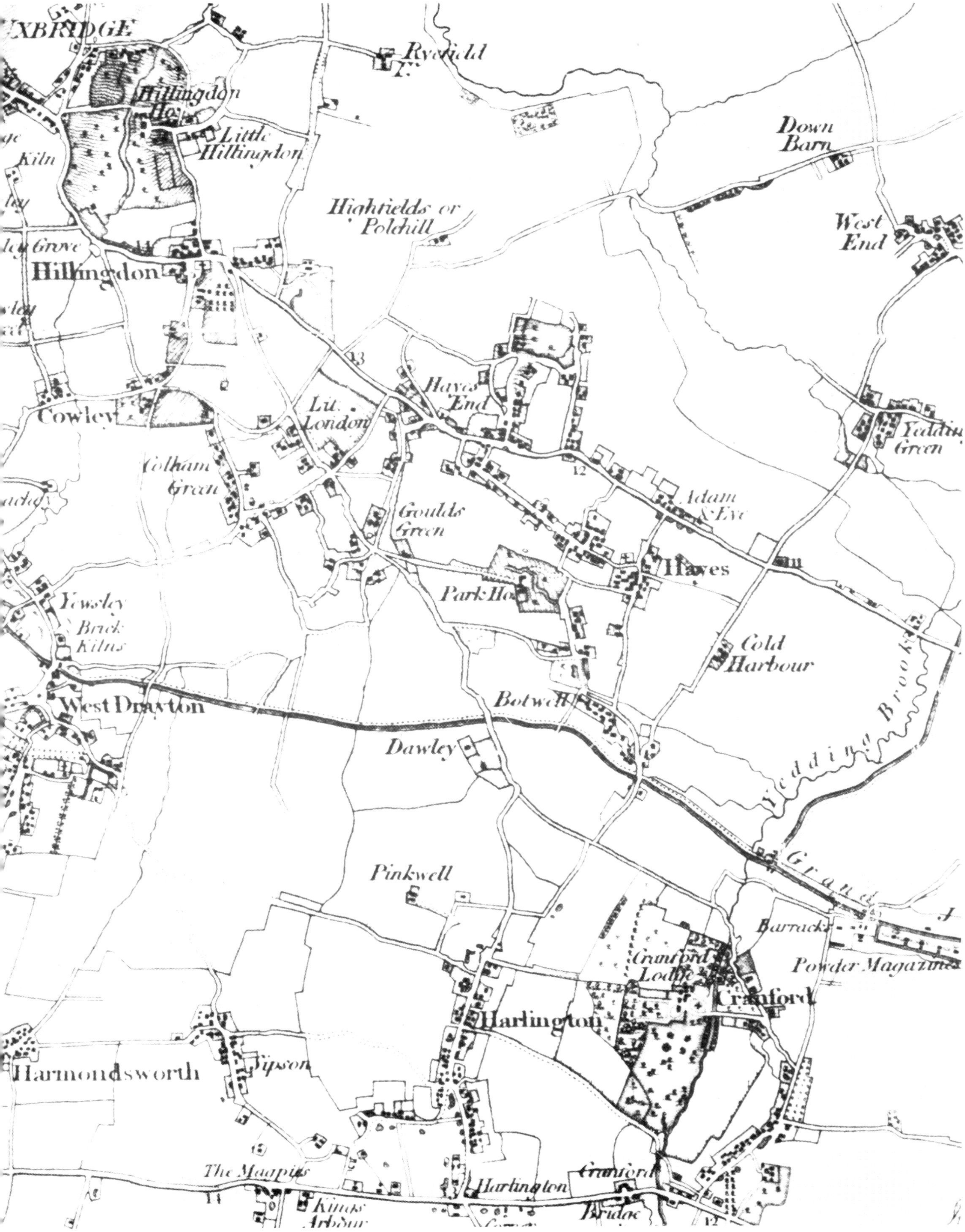
UXBRIDGE
Rycfield
Hillingdon Ho.
Little Hillingdon
Kiln
Highfields or Polehill
Down Barn
West End
Hillingdon
Cowley
Lit. London
Hayes End
Yedding Green
Colham Green
Goulds Green
Adam & Eve
Hayes
Park Ho.
Yewsley
Brick Kilns
Cold Harbour
Botwell
West Drayton
Dawley
Yedding Brook
Pinkwell
Grand
Barracks
Cranford Lodge
Powder Magazine
Cranford
Harlington
Sipson
Harmondsworth
The Magpies
Harlington
Cranford
Kings Arbour
Bridge

94 ▷

125 ▽

Published 1816-1822.

△
60

◁121

Fulmer Ho.
St. James
Wood
Rush Green
132
Queen's Head
114
Alder Bourne
Lower Fm.
Fernacre
Alderbourne Fm.
Ivyhouse Fm.
226
222
Dromenagh
Denham Newtown
Southlands
Fernacre Cott.
241
Langley Corner
Round Coppice
Heatherden
Upton Fm.
Mill
Mansfield Ho.
158
Black Park
School
Iver Heath
Park Lodge
185
Warren Ho.
St. Margaret's
Gallow Hill
107
Iver Moor
187
Southey Lodge
Warner's Fm.
Rowley Fm.
191
Lodge
Westend Ho.
Gibbs's Fm.
Banger's
Palmer's Moor Fm.
125
Cowley
148
Norwood Fm.
107
St. John's Wood
Swallow Street
Delaford Park
Cowley Hall
Langley Furze
156
Love Green
Huntsmoor Park
Langley Park
George Green
Heath Lodge
Shreding Green
Iver Grove
92
St. Peter's
96
Frays R.
101
Parkside Fm.
Love Hill
145
Iver
Delaford Ho.
Ch.
Parsonage Fm.
Trenches
Sawyer's Green
School
Great Western Railway
Station
118
Station
85
115
Fountains Farm
100
Langley Marish
St. Mary's
98
113
Thorney
Paper Mill
Thorney Ho.
Mill
82
Horsemoor Green
Langley Ho.
Parlaunt Park Fm.
Richings Park
74
Lambourne Farm
Langley Broom
87
Sutton
79

126
▽

1 2
1 mile approx.

61

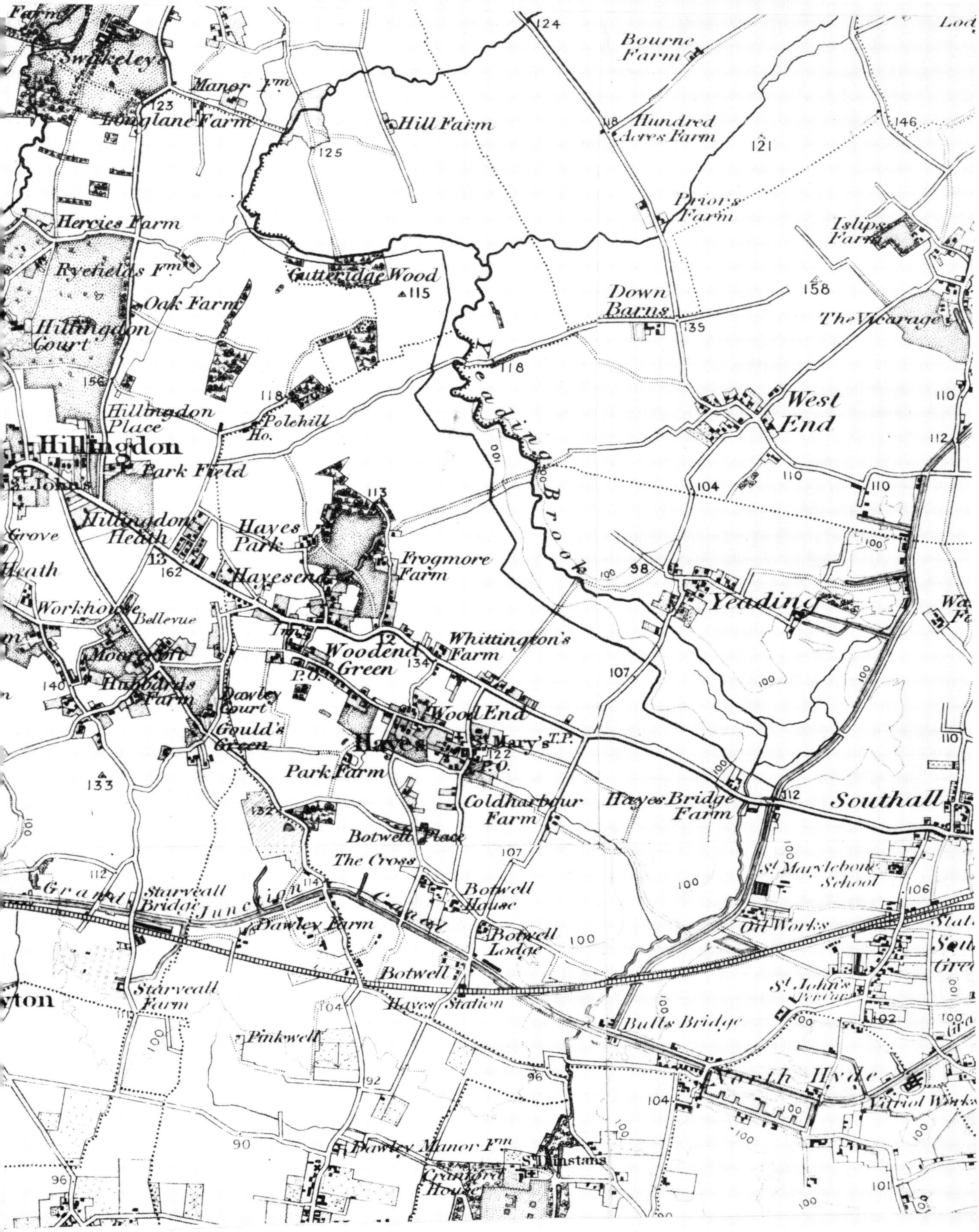
Swakeley
Manor Fm
Longlane Farm
Hill Farm
Bourne Farm
Hundred Acres Farm
Priors Farm
Islips Farm
Hercies Farm
Ryefields Fm
Gutteridge Wood
Oak Farm
Hillingdon Court
Down Barns
The Vicarage
West End
Hillingdon Place
Polehill Ho.
Hillingdon
Park Field
St. John's
Yeading Brook
Hillingdon Heath
Hayes Park
Frogmore Farm
Hayesend
Yeading
Workhouse
Bellevue
Moorcroft
Hubbards Farm
Woodend Green
Whittington's Farm
Dawley Court
Gould's Green
Wood End
Hayes
St. Mary's
P.O.
Park Farm
Coldharbour Farm
Hayes Bridge Farm
Southall
Botwell Place
The Cross
Botwell House
St. Marylebone School
Grand Junction Canal
Starveall Bridge
Dawley Farm
Oil Works
Botwell Lodge
Botwell
Hayes Station
Starveall Farm
St. John's
Bulls Bridge
Pinkwell
North Hyde
Vitriol Works
Dawley Manor Fm
St. Dunstans
Cranford House

96

127

Surveyed 1863-1876. Published 1880.

△ 62

◁123

Rush Green
Smithy
Lower Fm
Ivyhouse Fm
Fernacres
Alderbourne Fm
Inn
16
Shire Ditch
113
New Denham
UXBRIDGE
107
Mill
222
Langley Corner
240
Heatherden
Round Coppice
176
Mansfield Ho.
Mill
103
Ch.
Inn
Iver Heath
Park Lodge
Warren Ho.
Ch.
188
Ford
Smithy
Ivy Lodge
Warner's Fm
Rowley
L.B.
202
The Brambles
Smithy
Inn
141
Bangors Park
97
Cowley
174
Swallow Street
Manor Ho.
St John's
Delaford Park
G.W.R.
Uxbridge
George Green
Langley Park
Heath Lodge
Love Green
Smithy
Inn
150
Shreding Green
Inn
Ch.
89
Inn
145
Iver
Delaford Ho.
Ford
L.B.
121
80
Parsonage Fm
Canal
Trenches
Grand
Junction
Railway
Great Western
Mill
Ford
Inn
L.B.
95
STA.
Inn
115
Langley Marish
Inn
Ch.
100
Thorney
Paper Mill
92
Thorney Ho.
84
Mill
82
Horsemoor Green
Langley Ho.
Smithy
Parlaunt Park Fm
Richings Park
Larbourne Farm
Sutton
72
Inn
85
Ford
Ch.

1 2

1 mile approx.

128 ▽

△ 63

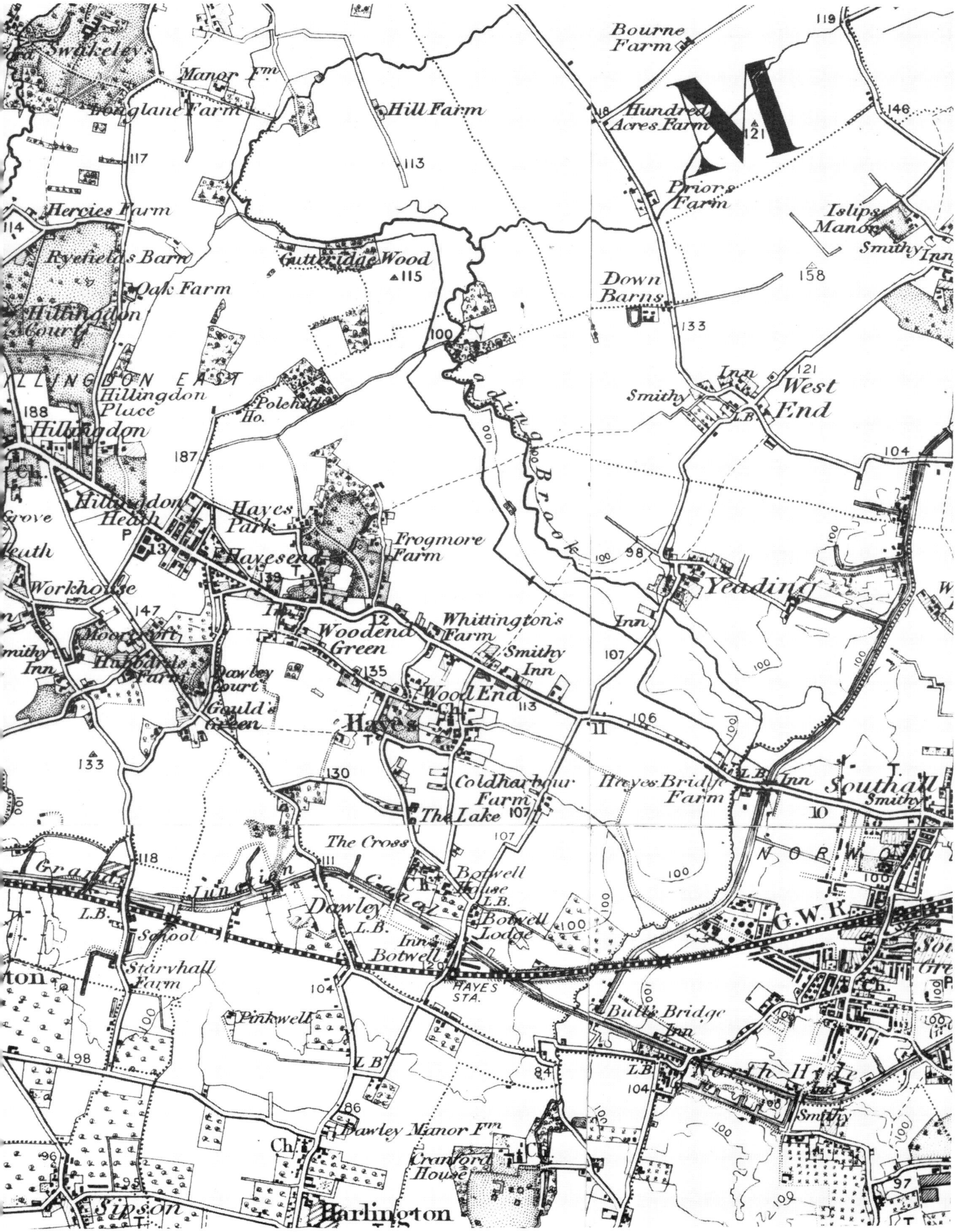

98 ▷

129 ▽

Surveyed 1863-1876. Revised 1902. Published 1904.

△ 64

◁ 89

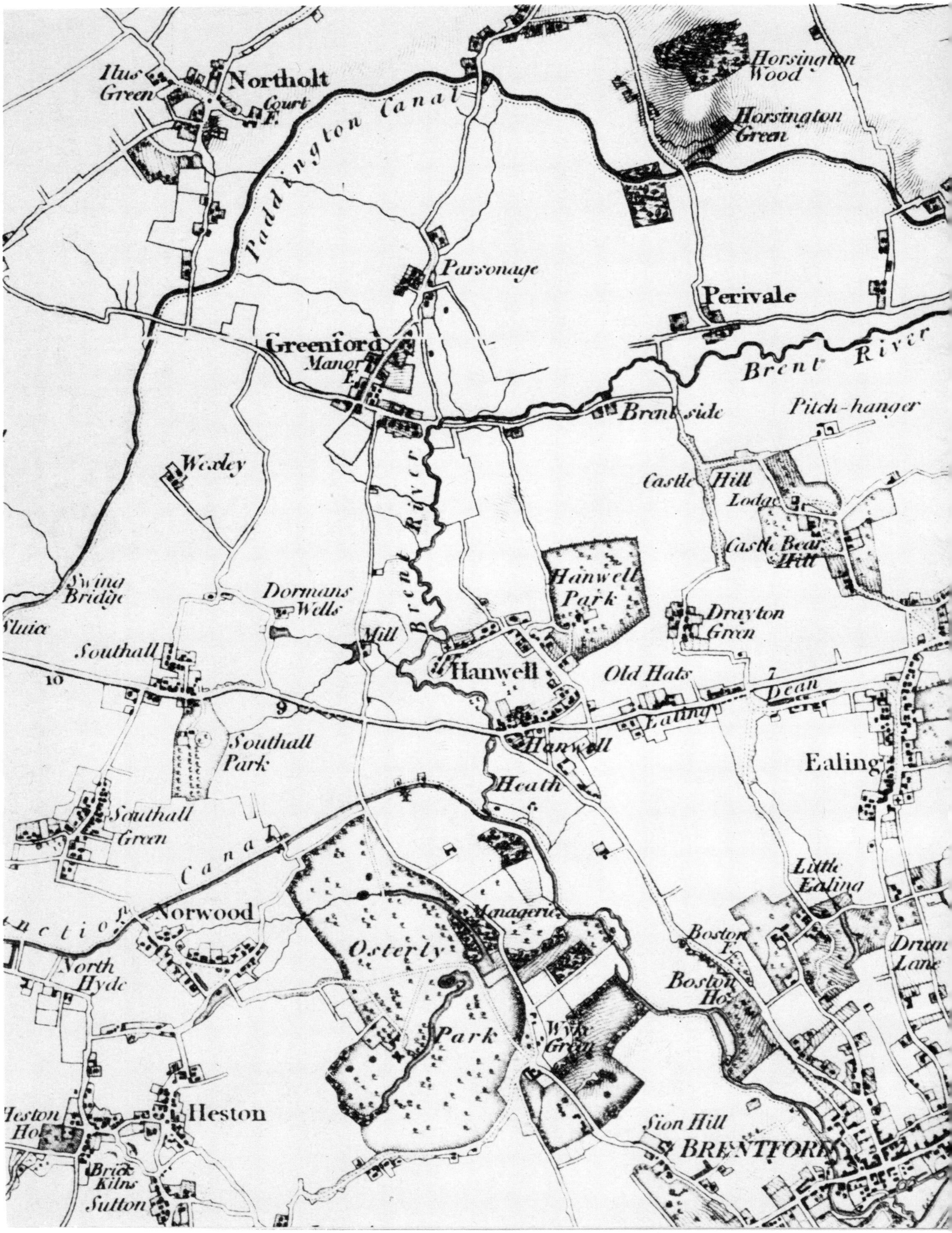

Ilus Green
Northolt
Court F.
Paddington Canal
Horsington Wood
Horsington Green
Parsonage
Perivale
Greenford
Manor F.
Brent River
Brent side
Pitch-hanger
Wexley
Brent River
Castle Hill Lodge
Castle Bear Hill
Hanwell Park
Swing Bridge
Sluice
Dormans Wells
Mill
Drayton Green
Southall
10
9
Hanwell
Old Hats
7
Ealing Dean
Southall Park
Hanwell Heath
Ealing
Southall Green
Canal
Little Ealing
Norwood
Menagerie
Osterly
North Hyde
Boston F.
Boston Ho.
Drum Lane
Park
Heston Ho.
Heston
Sion Hill
BRENTFORD
Brick Kilns
Sutton

1 2
1 mile approx.

130 ▽

△ 65

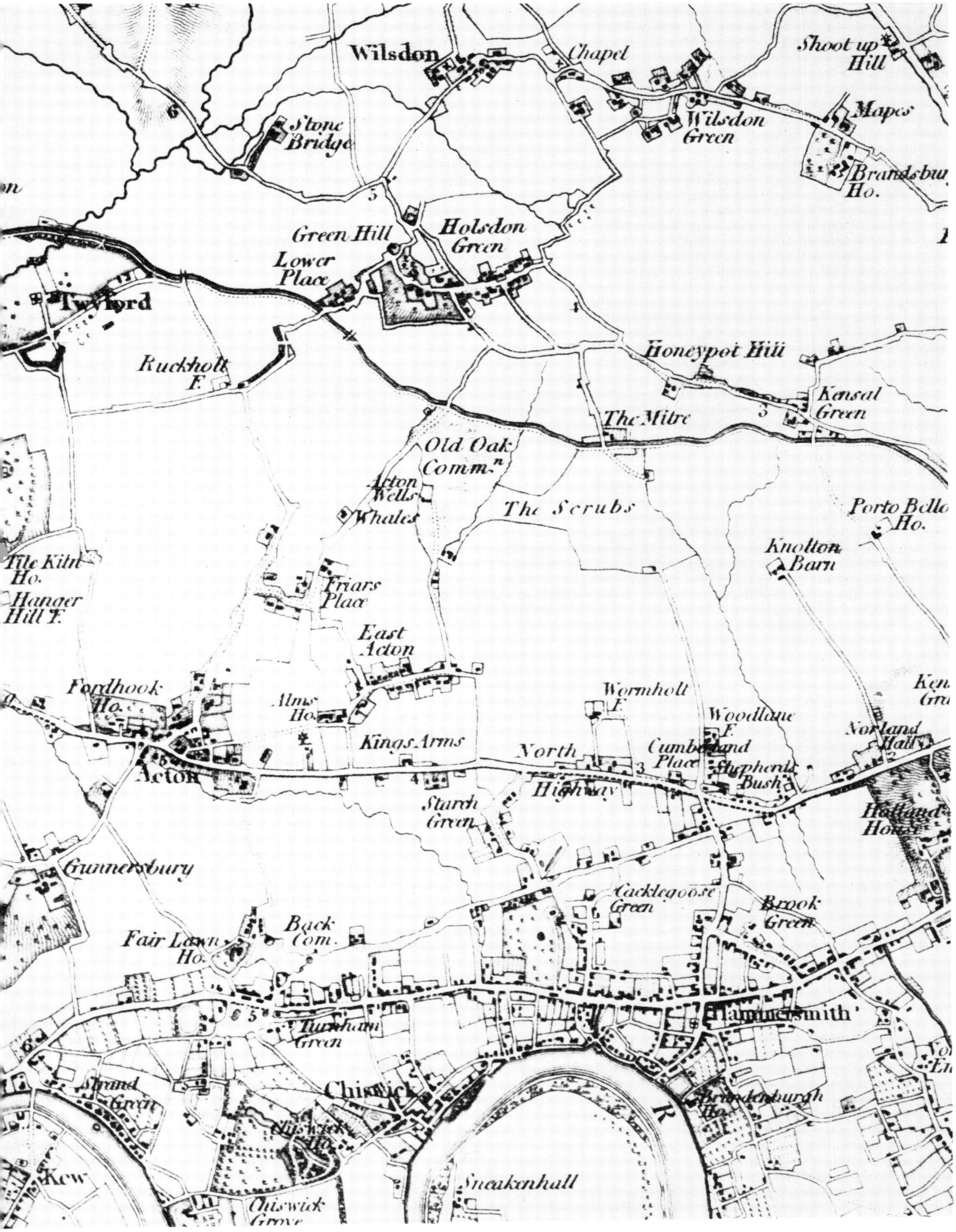
Wilsdon
Chapel
Shoot up Hill
Mapes
Stone Bridge
Wilsdon Green
Brandsbu
Ho.
Green Hill
Holsdon Green
Lower Place
Twyford
Ruckholt F.
Honeypot Hill
Kensal Green
The Mitre
Old Oak Comm.n
Acton Wells
Whales
The Scrubs
Porto Bello Ho.
Knolton Barn
Tile Kiln Ho.
Friars Place
Hanger Hill F.
East Acton
Fordhook Ho.
Alms Ho.
Wormholt F.
Woodlane F.
Norland Hall
Kings Arms
North
Cumberland Place
Shepherds Bush
Acton
Highway
Starch Green
Holland House
Gunnersbury
Cacklegoose Green
Brook Green
Back Com.
Fair Lawn Ho.
Hammersmith
Turnham Green
Chiswick
Brandenburgh Ho.
R
Kew
Sneakenhall
Chiswick Grove

100 ▷

Published 1822.

131 ▽

△ 66

◁ 91

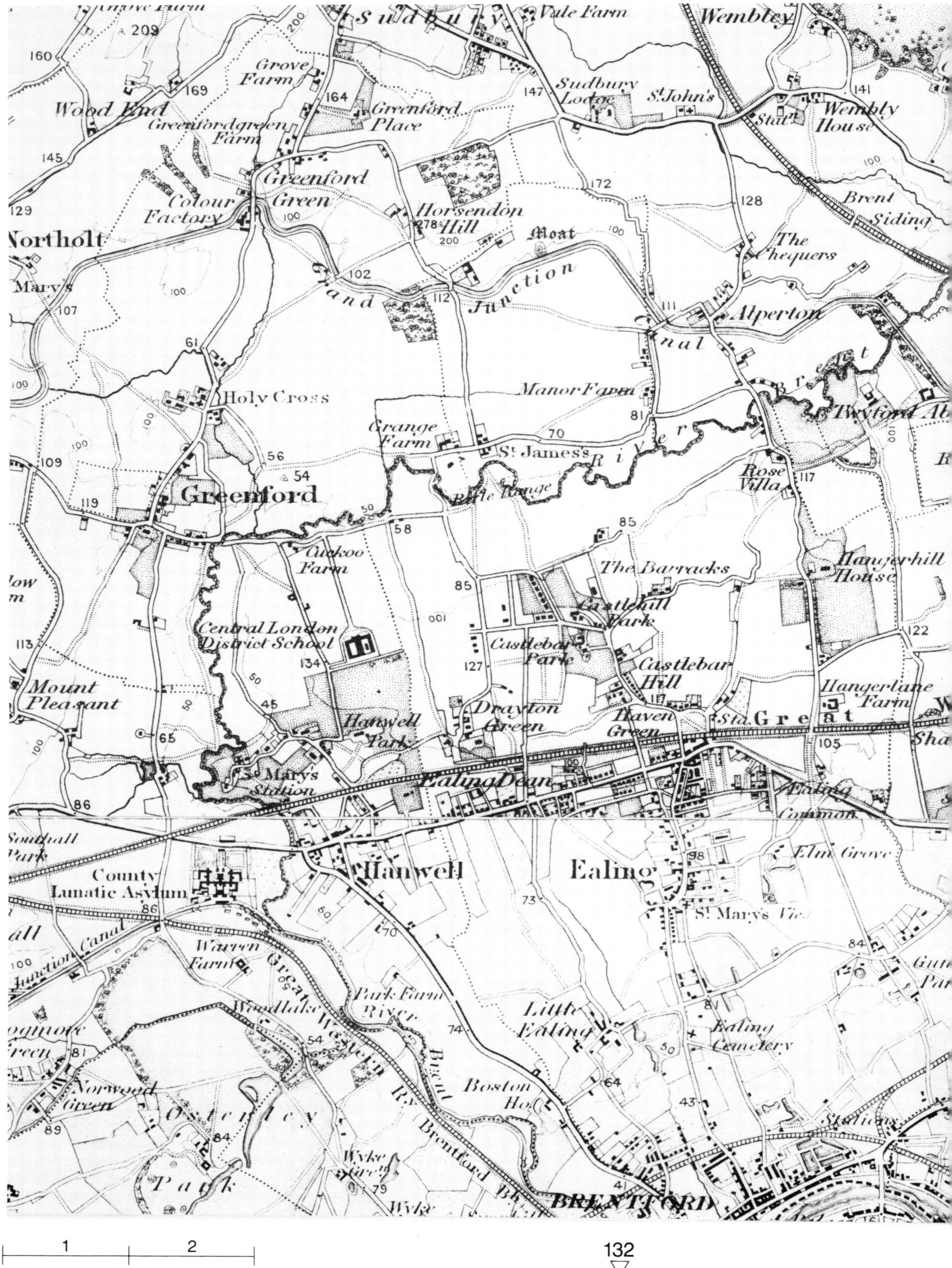

Sudbury
Vale Farm
Wembley
Grove Farm
Sudbury Lodge
St. John's
Wood End
Greenford Place
Greenfordgreen Farm
Wembly House
Greenford Green
Colour Factory
Horsendon Hill
Brent Siding
Northolt
Moat
The Chequers
Grand Junction Canal
Alperton
Holy Cross
Manor Farm
Grange Farm
St. James's
River Brent
Greenford
Rifle Range
Rose Villa
Cuckoo Farm
The Barracks
Hangerhill House
Castlehill Park
Central London District School
Castlebar Park
Castlebar Hill
Mount Pleasant
Hangerlane Farm
Drayton Green
Haven Green
Hanwell Park
Great
St. Mary's Station
Ealing Dean
Ealing Common
Southall Park
County Lunatic Asylum
Hanwell
Ealing
Elm Grove
St. Marys Vic.
Warren Farm
Park Farm
River Brent
Woodlake
Great Western Ry.
Little Ealing
Ealing Cemetery
Norwood Green
Boston Ho.
Osterley Park
Brentford
Wyke Green
Stations
BRENTFORD

1 2

1 mile approx.

132 ▽

△
67

Neasden
The Grove
Cricklewood
Model Farm
The Slade
Station
135
Junction Ry.
98
West End
Rosslyn Park
Pheasant Lodge
174
Chapel End
St. Marys
Willesden
The Elms
180
Willesden Green
Mapesbury House
Oaklands Hall
Brandesbury Park
Rifle Range
Glynfield Ho.
Kilburn
Midland & Sth. Wn.
200
Roundwood Ho.
182
Paddington Cemetery
139
Harlesden Green
Hampstead Junction
St. Johns
Willesden Station
Junction
148
108
Naphtha Works
Kensal Green
Cemetery
100
Old Oak
Wesbourne Green
109
Kensal New Town
Common
Wormwood Scrubs
50
119
Portobello Fm.
Notting Barn
Friars Place
38
East Acton
N. & S. W. Junc. Ry.
23
Old Oak Farm
Manor Ho.
Thorpebanks
Kensington Gardens
Acton Vale
27
24
Palace
Acton
Shepherds Bush
Holland Park
Kensington
Starch Green
34
Hammersmith Branch
Stamford Brook
18
Brook Green
32
Acton Green
Kensington & Richmond Line
St. Judes
Earls Court
22
19
28
Hammersmith
North End
Fulham Un. Work Ho.
27
24
22
Stations
Cemetery
Chiswick
16
Castlenau
Fulham

102 ▷

133
▽

Surveyed 1861-1871. Published 1876-77.

68

93

Vale Farm
Wembley
SUDBURY HILL STA.
Inn
Smithy
Sudbury Lock
Wood End
Greenford Place
SUDBURY TOWN STA.
Wembley House
Metro. Dist. Ry.
Greenford Green
Horsendon Hill
Moat
Grand Junction Canal
Acton & High Wycombe
G.W.R.
Alperton
Manor Farm
Perivale
Ch.
West Ealing Loop
Greenford
Rifle Range
River
PARK ROYAL STA.
Mount Pleasant
School
Drayton Green
Hanwell Lock
Mills
HANWELL STA.
Ealing Dean
NORTH EALING STA.
Ealing Common
Southall Park
Asylum
Hanwell
EALING
Locks
Warren Farm
Junction Canal
Gunnersbury
Gunnersbury Park
Woodlake
Little Ealing
Norwood Green
Boston
Brent Ho.
Weir
Lock
BRENTFORD
Kew Br.

134

1 2

1 mile approx.

△ 69

104 ▷

135 ▽

Surveyed 1861-1871. Revised 1901-1902. Published 1904.

70

95

West End
Rosslyn Ho.
Haverstock Hill
Belsize Ho.
Chalcott
Town
Spring Place
Chapel
Copenhagen Ho.
Primrose Hill
Chalk F.
Camden Town
Kilburn Wells
Portland Town
REGENTS PARK
Regents Canal
St. Pancras
Pentonville
Barracks
Somers Town
Maida
Paddington
Westbourn Green
Grd Junction Water Works
Reservoir
Craven Place
Bayswater
HYDE PARK
Palace
Kensington
GREEN PARK
St. JAMES'S PARK
Westminster Br.
Waterloo Bridge
Gore
Brompton
Knights Bridge
Work Ho.
Earls Terrace
Pavilion
Pimlico
Earls Court
Old Brompton
Penitentiary
Queens Elm
Little Chelsea
Hospital
Mill Bank
Vauxhall Bridge
Lambeth
Vauxhall Gardens
Chelsea
Red Ho.

136

1 2

1 mile approx.

△
71

Clapton
Highbury Place
Balls Pond
Datston
Hommerton
Hackney
Hackney Wick
Canonbury Ho.
Kingsland
Festing Pl.
White Lead Works
Regents Canal
Regents Canal
Grove Street
Old Ford Road
Old Ford
Haggerstone
Bonners Hall
Basin
Stratford le Bow
Bancrofts Hosp.
Bethnal Green
Mile End Road
Bow Com
Maritime Alms Houses
London Hosp.
Stepney
Limehouse Cut
Lime house
Basin
London Dock
Shadwell Dock
POOL
LIMEHOUSE REACH
West India Docks
Canal
Rotherhithe
ISLE OF DOGS
St. Helena
T.P.
Kings Dock Yard
GREENWICH
Grand Surrey Canal
Canal
Walworth
Halfway House

106▷

137
▽

Published 1822.

△
72

◁ 97

Station
City Prison
Highbury
145
121
188
216
Primrose Hill
Camden Town
138
Regents Park
117
St Pancras Station
Kings Cross Station
Euston Station
76
63
St Pauls
Waterloo Br.
Southwark Br.
Hyde Park
Infantry Barracks
50
68
Serpentine
60
Green Park
St James Park
Buckingham Palace
Waterloo Station
Westminster Br.
Lambeth Pal.
20
Victoria Station
Millbank Prison
Lambeth
Walworth
Kennington
Royal Hospital
Victoria Br.
Chelsea Br.
Station
Chelsea
32

138
▽

1 2

1 mile approx.

73

Homerton
Temple Mills
Stratford New Town
High Meads
Stratford
Channel
Gas Works
West Ham
Victoria Park
Bethnal Green
Mill Mead
Three Mills
West Marsh
Rocket Works
Bromley
Stepney
Limehouse
E. India
Dock
Poplar
Blackwall
Lower Pool
W. India
Dock
Surrey Commercial Docks
Rotherhithe
Limehouse Reach
Isle of Dogs
Cubitt Town
Millwall
Blackwall Reach
Greenwich Marshes
Greenwich Reach
Grand Surrey Canal
DEPTFORD
Royal Hospital
GREENWICH

108

139

Surveyed 1861-1868. Published 1876.

△ 74

◁ 99

Lower Holloway
Primrose Hill
Camden Town
Regents Park
Hyde Park
Serpentine
Albert Mem.
Green Park
St James's Park
Palace
Buckingham Palace
Westminster
Westminster Br.
Houses of Parliament
Lambeth Pal.
Blackfriars Br.
Waterloo Br.
Southwark Br.
Lambeth
Vauxhall Br.
Nine Elms
Kennington
Chelsea
Royal Hospital Chelsea
Chelsea Br.
Victoria Br.

140 ▽

1 2

1 mile approx.

△
75

110▷

141
▽

Surveyed 1861-1871. Revised 1902. Published 1904.

76

101

Wood Grange
Eagle & Child
Moulsey
Little Ilford
Maryland Pt
Potatoe Hall
Stratford Com.
North End
Upton
Plashett
Ham Ho.
West Ham
East Ham
Barking
Green Street House
W. Ham Abbey
Wall End
High Br.
Plaistow
South End
WESTHAM
ABBEY
MARSH
East Ham
Lea River
EAST HA
E. India
Docks
PLAISTOW
LEVEL
LEVEL
Devall House
BUGSBYS REACH
WOOLWICH REACH
BLACKWALL REACH
Over Brickfield
Royal Dock Yard
Coomb Fm
Woolwich
Barrack Field

142

1 2
1 mile approx.

△
77

Long bridge F.m
Castle
Gibralter
Fox F.m
Fair Cross
Manor F.m
G.t Porters
Lit. Porters
Halbull Street
Dagenham
Upney
G.t Mays Brook
Lodge F.m
Church Elm
Whites F.m
Broad Street
Westbury F.m
Eastbury F.m
Ripple Side
Pound Ho.
BARKING LEVEL
DAGENHAM MARSH
Horseshoe Corner
Creeks Mouth
Magazine
Breach House
BARKING REACH
Halfway House
HALFWAY REACH
Plumsted Magazine
Tripcock Trees
Practice Butt
PLUMSTED MARSHES
Erith Magazine
ERITH MARSHES
Abbey F.m
Plumsted
Boston F.m
Boston
Picardy
Erith Ch
Abbey Wood
Lesness Heath
Holly Hill

112▷

143
▽

Published 1805.

△ 78

◁103

ILFORD
Greenhill Grove
Manor Ho.
Little Ilford
Uphall
Place
Loxford Hall
Fair Cross
Woodgrange
Plashet Hall
Upton
Barking New Town
Station
Mayes
Upney
North End
BARKING
Ham Ho.
Plashet
Station
St. Margarets
Eastbury House
Manor Ho.
Station
Ivy Ho.
Bifrons
London
St. Johns
Walland
Westbury Level
Movers Ho.
Greenstreet
St. Mary's
Anne Boleyn's Tower
EAST HAM
Barking
Plaistow
East Ham
The Vicarage
Eastbury
Northern Outfall Sewer
St. Mary's
Cumberland Ho.
HAM
Plaistow Marsh
East Ham Level
Northern Outfall Reservoir
Cherry Island
Sta.
School
Victoria Dock Cut
Royal Albert Dock
Victoria Dock
Gallions Reach
Silvertown Station
St. Mark's
North Woolwich
Station
Plumstead
Woolwich Reach
WOOLWICH
ROMAN CAMP
Station
Plumstead
Charlton
Plumstead Common
Charlton Ho.
Woolwich Common
Cemetery

144 ▽

1 2

1 mile approx.

79

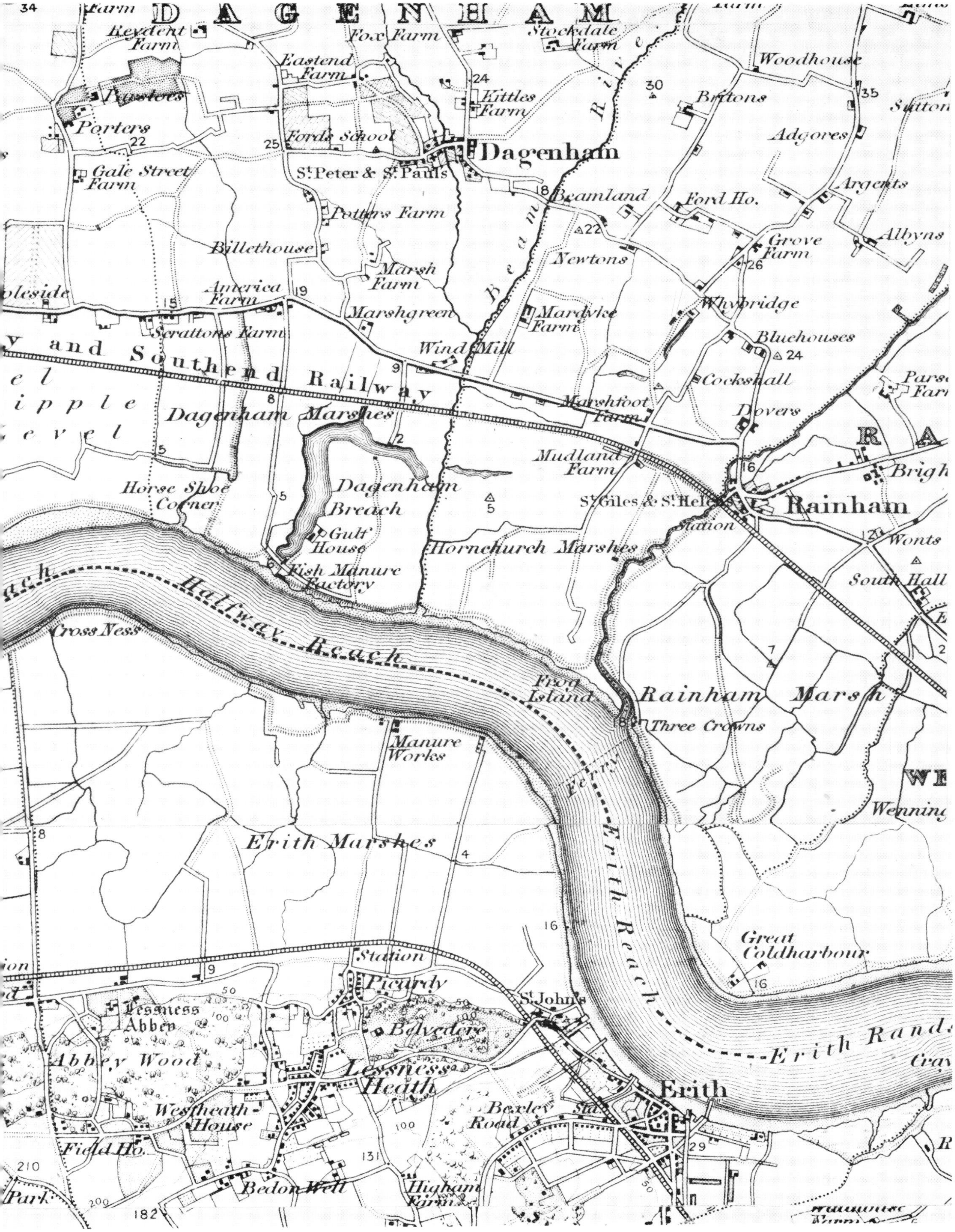
DAGENHAM
Reydent Farm
Fox Farm
Stockdale Farm
Woodhouse
Eastend Farm
Kittles Farm
Britons
Sutton
Porters
Fords School
Dagenham
Adgores
Gale Street Farm
St. Peter & St. Pauls
Beamland
Ford Ho.
Argents
Potters Farm
Grove Farm
Albyns
Billethouse
Newtons
Marsh Farm
America Farm
Whybridge
Marshgreen
Mardyke Farm
Scrattons Farm
Bluehouses
Wind Mill
and Southend Railway
Cockshall
Marshfoot Farm
Dovers
Dagenham Marshes
Mudland Farm
Horse Shoe Corner
Dagenham Breach
St. Giles & St. Hel
Rainham
Station
Gulf House
Hornchurch Marshes
Wonts
Fish Manure Factory
South Hall
Halfway Reach
Cross Ness
Frog Island
Rainham Marsh
Three Crowns
Manure Works
Ferry
Wenning
Erith Marshes
Erith Reach
Great Coldharbour
Station
Picardy
St. John's
Lessness Abbey
Belvedere
Erith Rands
Abbey Wood
Lessness Heath
Erith
Westheath House
Bexley Road
Field Ho.
Belon Well
Higham Farm
Park

114

145

Surveyed 1862-1873. Published 1888.

△ 80

◁105

Little Ilford
Loxford
Fair Cross
EAST HAM
BARKING
Wallend
Plaistow
Electric Ry.
Northern Outfall Sewer
WEST HAM
Plaistow East Ham Level
Marsh
Canning Town
Beckton
Victoria Dock Cut
Royal Albert Dock
Victoria Dock
Locks
North Woolwich
Silvertown
Steam Ferries
Woolwich Reach
Bugsby's Reach
Gallions Reach
WOOLWICH
ROMAN CAMP
Charlton
Cemetery
Charlton Ho.
Woolwich Common
Plumstead Common

146 ▽

1 2

1 mile approx.

△ 81

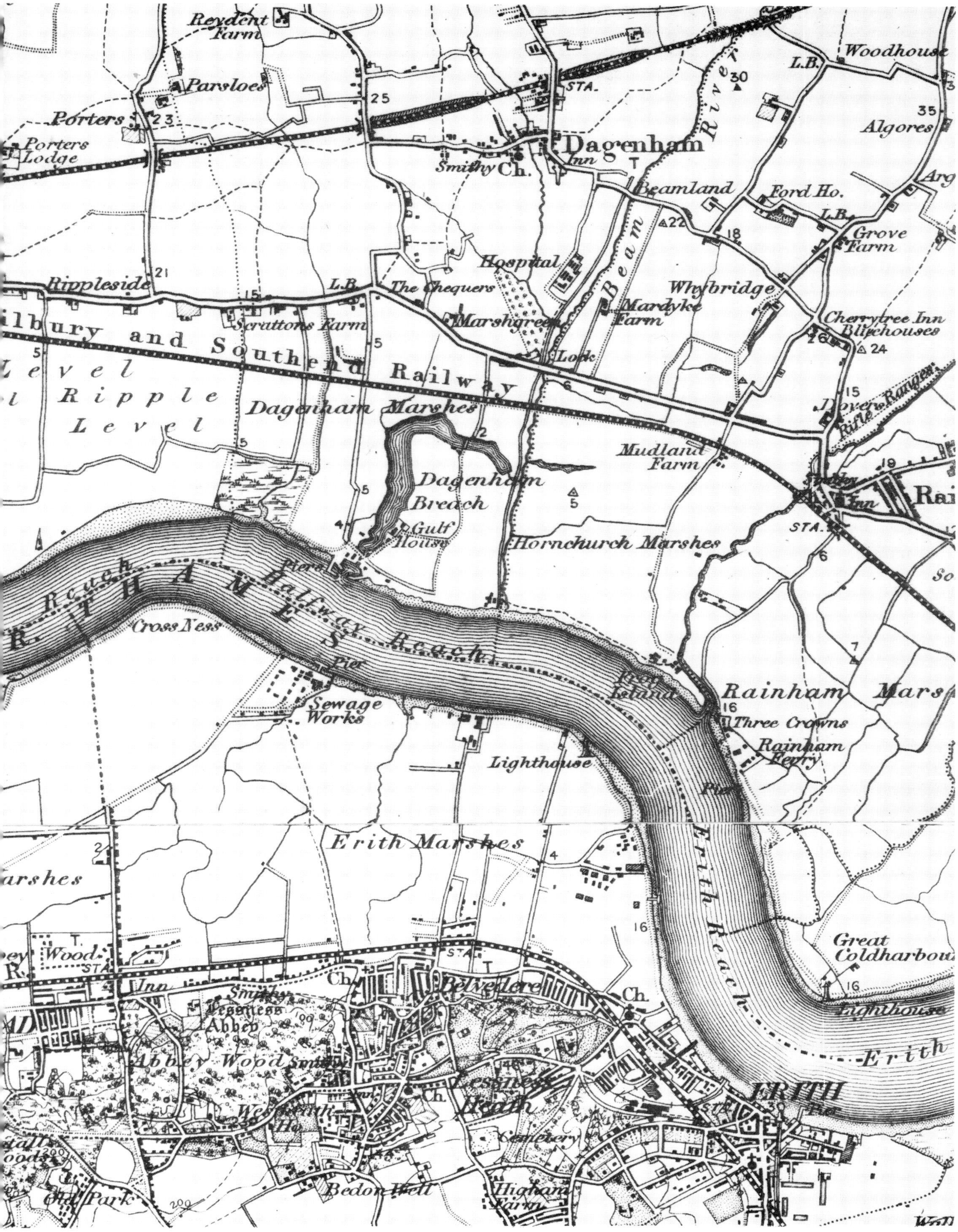

116 ▷

147 ▽

Surveyed 1862-1873. Revised 1903. Published 1904.

△ 82

◁107

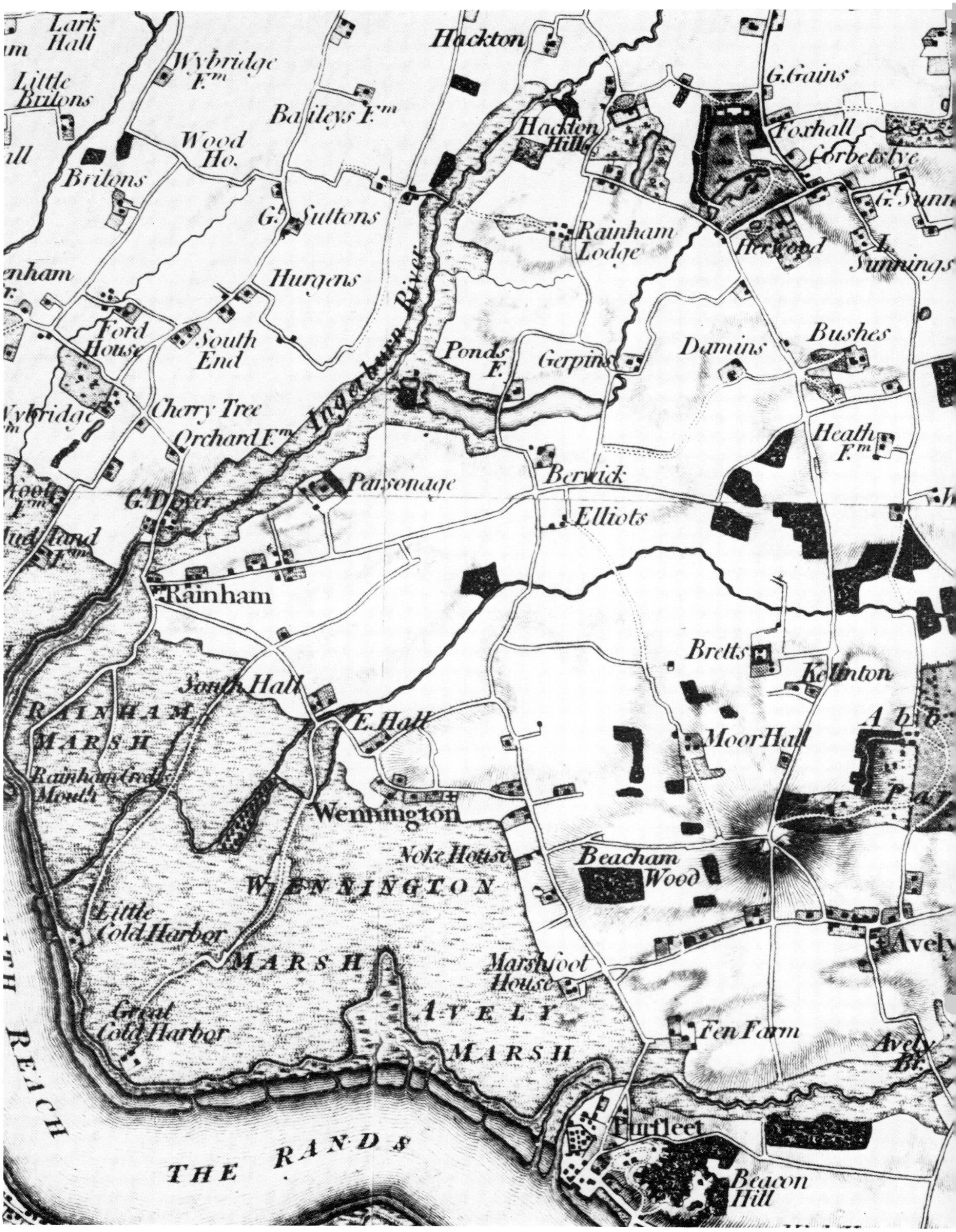

Lark Hall
Wybridge Fm
Little Britons
Baileys Fm
Hackton
G. Gains
Hackton Hill
Foxhall
Corbetslye
Wood Ho.
Britons
Gt. Suttons
Rainham Lodge
Herwood
Sunnings
Hurgens
Ingerburn River
Ford House
South End
Ponds F.
Gerpins
Damins
Bushes
Cherry Tree Orchard Fm
Heath Fm
Berwick
Parsonage
Gt. Dovar
Elliots
Rainham
Bretts
Kelinton
South Hall
RAINHAM MARSH
E. Hall
MoorHall
Rainham Creek Mouth
Wennington
Noke House
Beacham Wood
WENNINGTON
Little Cold Harbor
MARSH
Marshfoot House
Avely
Great Cold Harbor
AVELY
Fen Farm
MARSH
Avely Br.
Purfleet
THE RANDS
REACH
Beacon Hill

1 2
1 mile approx.

148 ▽

△
83

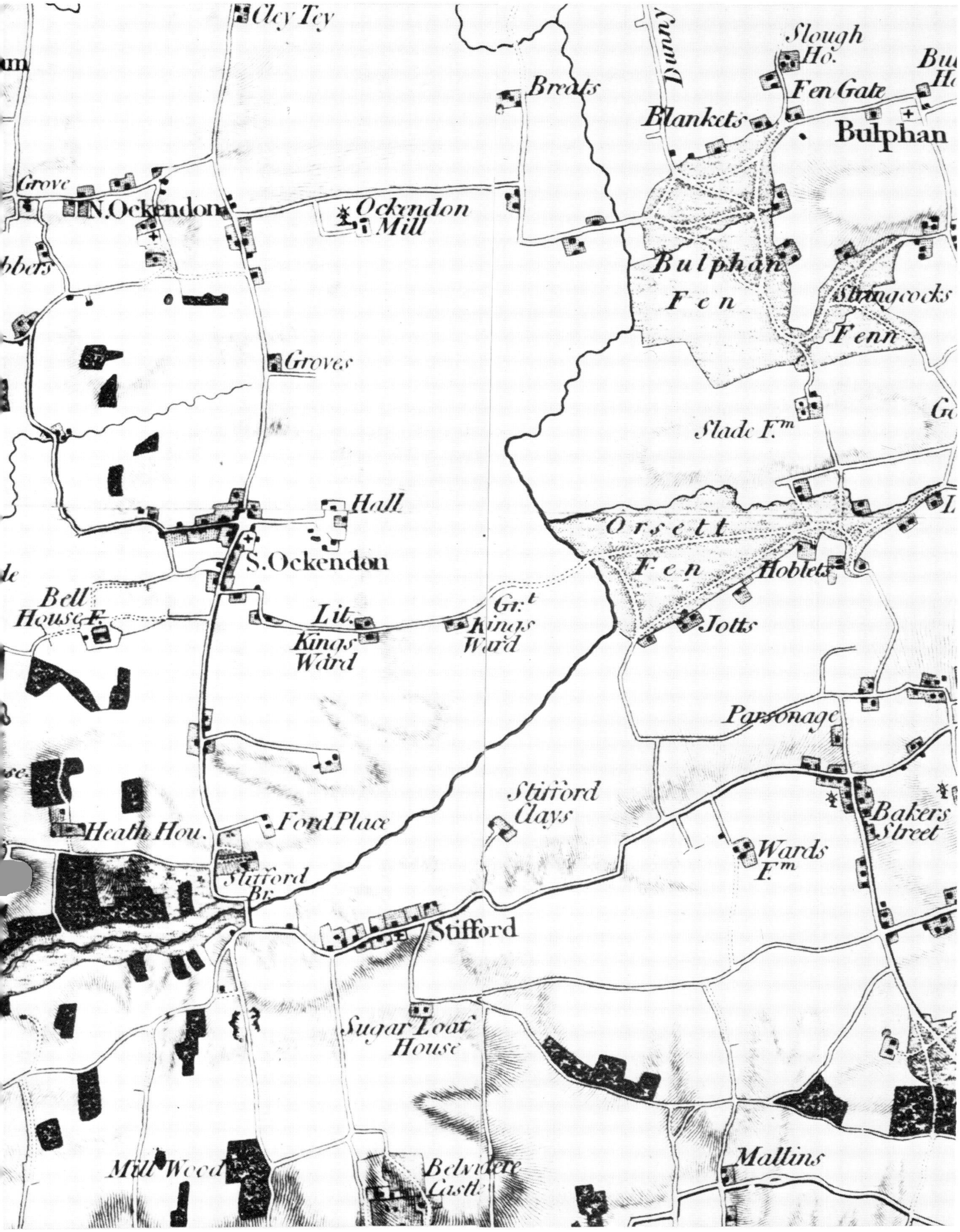
Cley Tey
Slough Ho.
Breats
Fen Gate
Blankets
Bulphan
Grove
N.Ockendon
Ockendon Mill
Bulphan Fen
Stangcocks Fenn
Groves
Slade F.m
Hall
Orsett Fen
S.Ockendon
Hoblets
Bell House F.
Lit. Kings Ward
Gr.t Kings Ward
Jolts
Parsonage
Stifford Clays
Bakers Street
Heath Hou.
Ford Place
Wards F.m
Stifford Br.
Stifford
Sugar Loaf House
Mallins
Mill Wood
Belvidere Castle

149
▽

Published 1805.

△ 84

◁109

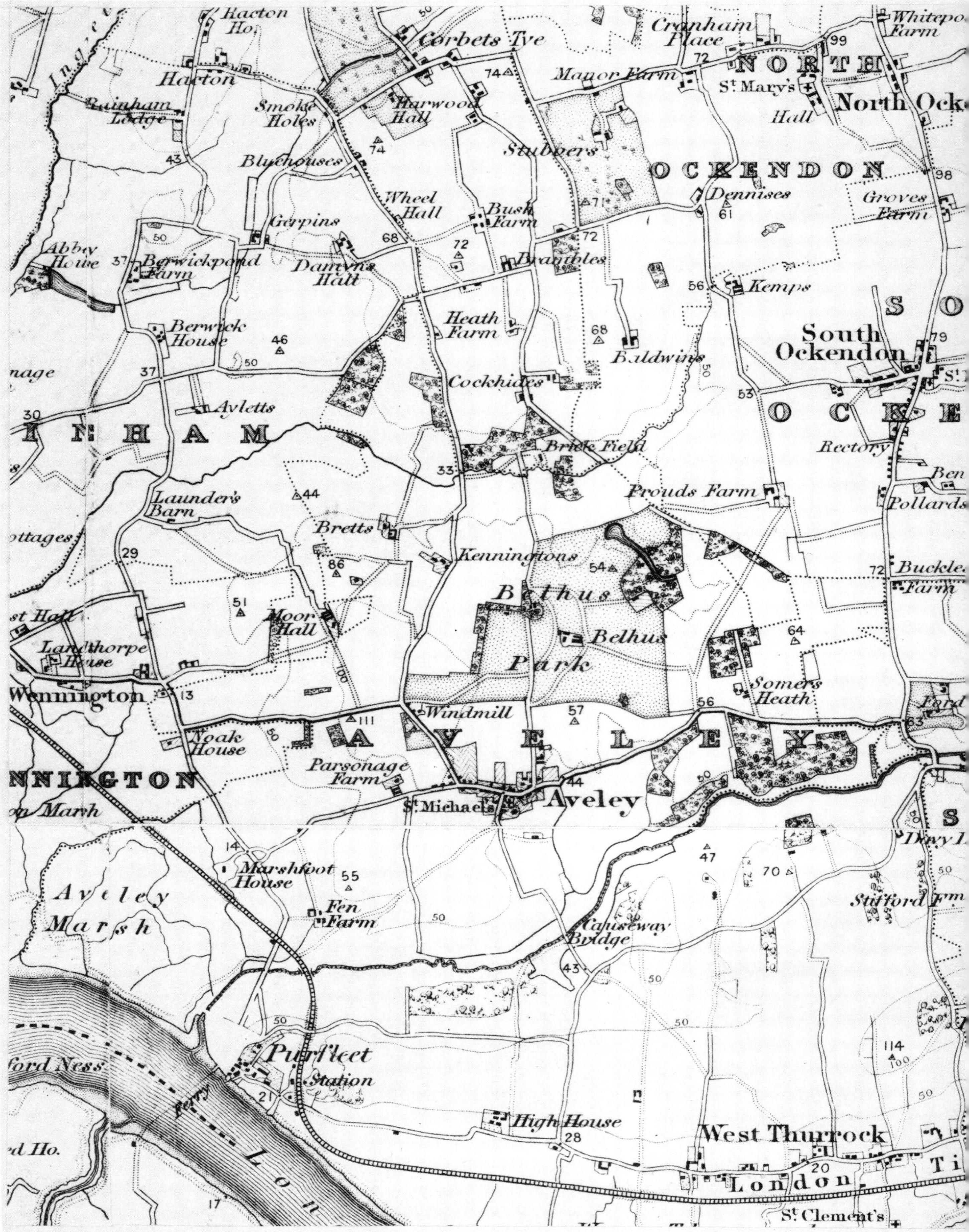
Hacton Ho.
Corbets Tye
Cranham Place
Whitepo
Farm
Harton
Manor Farm
NORTH
St Mary's
Hall
North Ock
Rainham Lodge
Smoke Holes
Harwood Hall
Stubbers
Bluehouses
OCKENDON
Dennises
Groves Farm
Wheel Hall
Bush Farm
Garpins
Abbey House
Berwickpond Farm
Damyns Hall
Brambles
Kemps
Heath Farm
Berwick House
Baldwins
South Ockendon
Cockhides
Aveletts
Bride Field
Rectory
Prouds Farm
Pollards
Launder's Barn
Bretts
Kenningtons
Buckles Farm
Bethus
Moor Hall
Belhus
Landthorpe House
Park
Somers Heath
Wennington
Windmill
Ford
Noak House
AVELEY
Parsonage Farm
NNINGTON
St Michael's
Aveley
Marshfoot House
Aveley Marsh
Fen Farm
Stifford Frm
Causeway Bridge
Purfleet
Station
ford Ness
Ferry
High House
West Thurrock
London
St Clement's

150 ▽

1 2
1 mile approx.

△
85

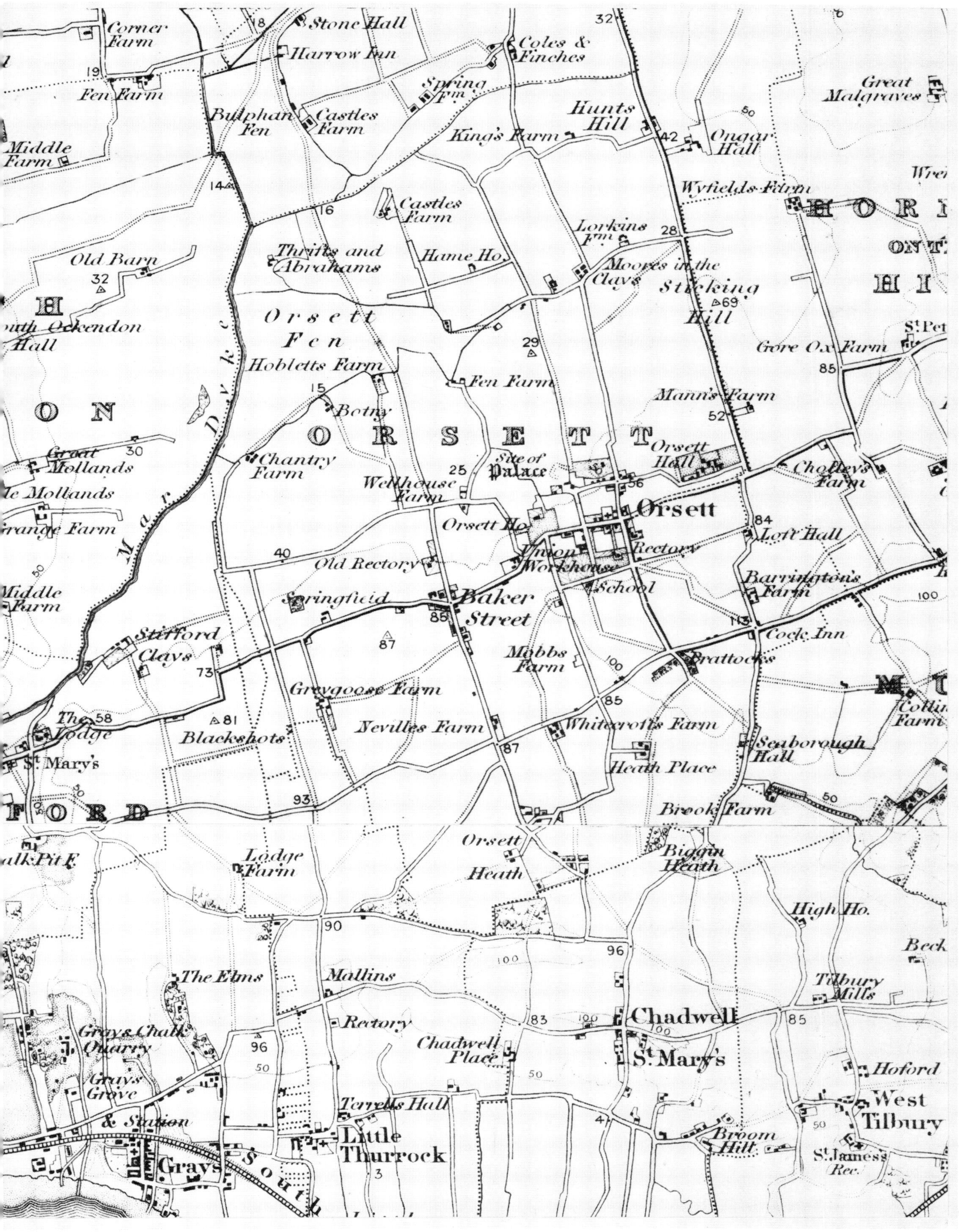

151
▽

Surveyed 1862-1873. Publised 1883.

△ 86

◁ 111

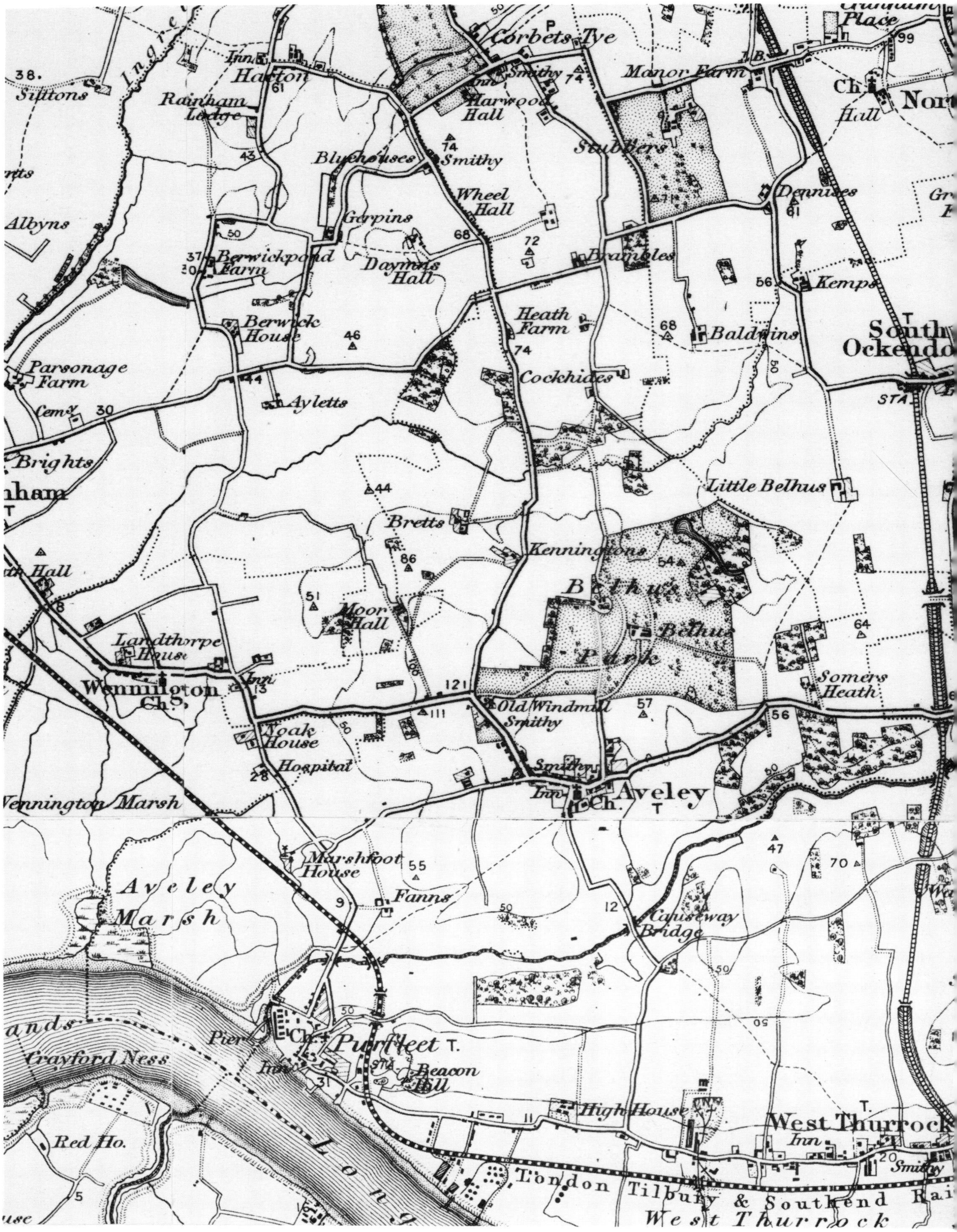

Corbets Tye
Grangham Place
Inn
Harton
Suttons
Ingrebourne
Rainham Lodge
Smithy
Harwood Hall
Manor Farm
Ch.
Hall
North
Stubbers
Bluehouses
Smithy
Wheel Hall
Dennises
Albyns
Gerpins
Daymns Hall
Brambles
Berwickpond Farm
Kemps
Berwick House
Heath Farm
Baldwins
South Ockendon
STA.
Parsonage Farm
Cockhides
Ayletts
Cemy
Brights
Little Belhus
Bretts
Kenningtons
Belhus
Belhus
Park
Moor Hall
Landthorpe House
Wennington Ch.
Inn
Old Windmill
Smithy
Somers Heath
Noak House
Hospital
Smithy
Inn
Ch.
Aveley
Wennington Marsh
Marshfoot House
Fanns
Aveley Marsh
Causeway Bridge
Pier
Ch.
Purfleet
Crayford Ness
Inn
Beacon Hill
High House
West Thurrock
Inn
Smithy
Red Ho.
London Tilbury & Southend Rai
West Thurrock

1 2

1 mile approx.

152 ▽

△
87

153
▽

Surveyed 1862-1873. Revised 1903. Published 1904.

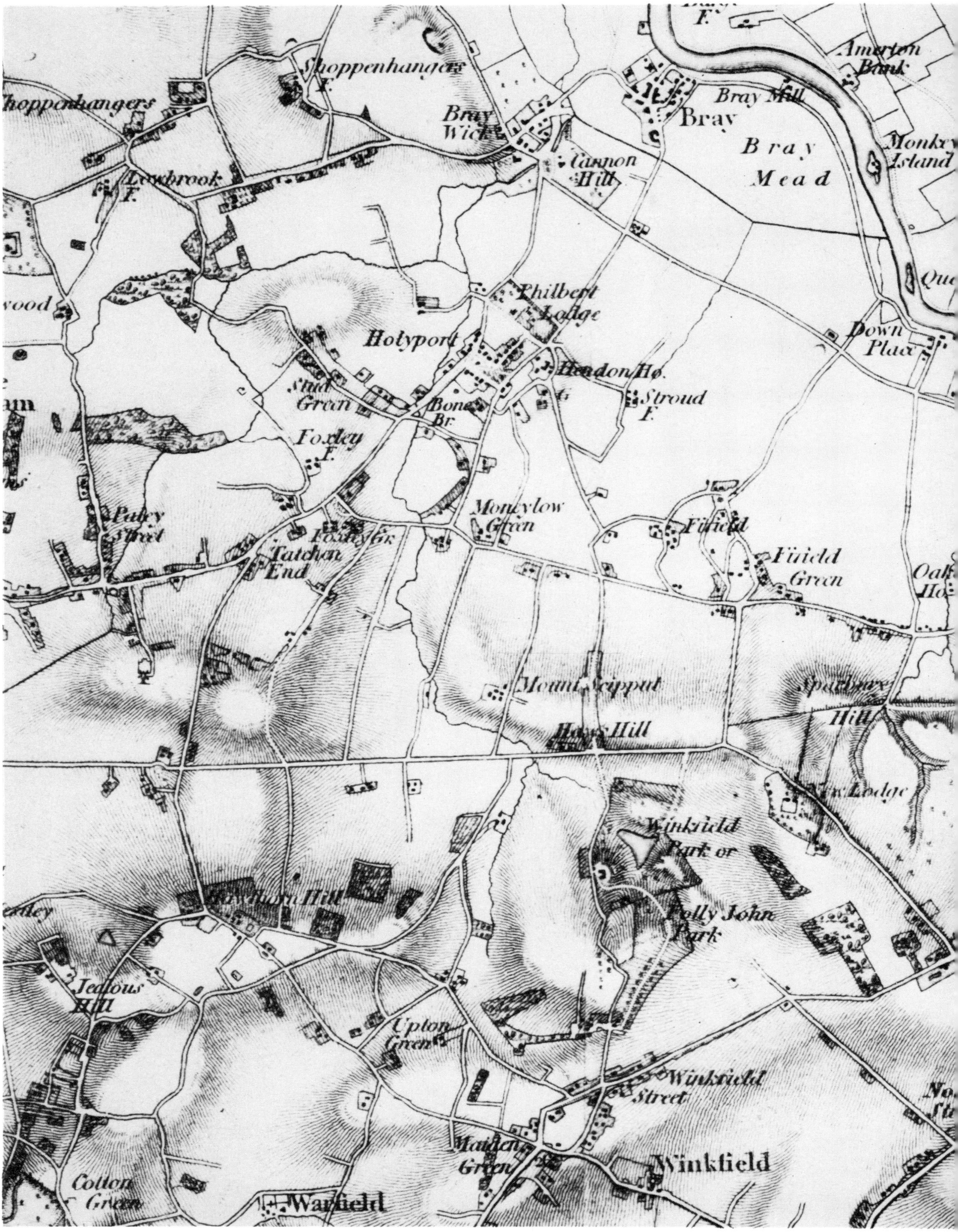
Shoppenhangers F.
Shoppenhangers
Bray Wick
Bray
Bray Mill
Amerton Bank
Bray Mead
Monkey Island
Cannon Hill
Philbert Lodge
Holyport
Down Place
Hendon Ho.
Stroud F.
Bone Br.
Foxley F.
Paley Street
Moneylow Green
Fifield
Fifield Green
Tatchen End
Mount Scippat
Hawe Hill
Winkfield Park or Folly John Park
Jealous Hill
Upton Green
Winkfield Street
Maiden Green
Winkfield
Cotton Green
Warfield
1
2
1 mile approx.

Cippenham
Farnham End
Salt Hill
Slough
Lake End
North Field
Chalvey Grove
Chalvey Green
Herschels Telescope
Upton
Little Common
Court F.
Dorney Green
Eton Wick
Willowbrook Place
Dutchmans Garden
Oakley
Boveney
Boveney Court
Fishery
Black Potts
Eton
Mill
Willows
Surly Hall
Lodge
Clewer
Bullocks Hatch
Kiln
Parsonage
WINDSOR
Delworth
Littleworth
Windmill Field
Spencers F.
Clewer Cottage
Clewer Green
Lodge
Shaws F.
Swans Br
Nelson
Leonards Hill
Leonards Dale
Hospital
Long Walk
Clayhall
Double Ga.
Old Windsor
Old Wind Green
Lodge
Poor Ho.
Queens Walk
Hill
Park Place
Battle Bourn Pond

88/124 ▷

Published 1816.

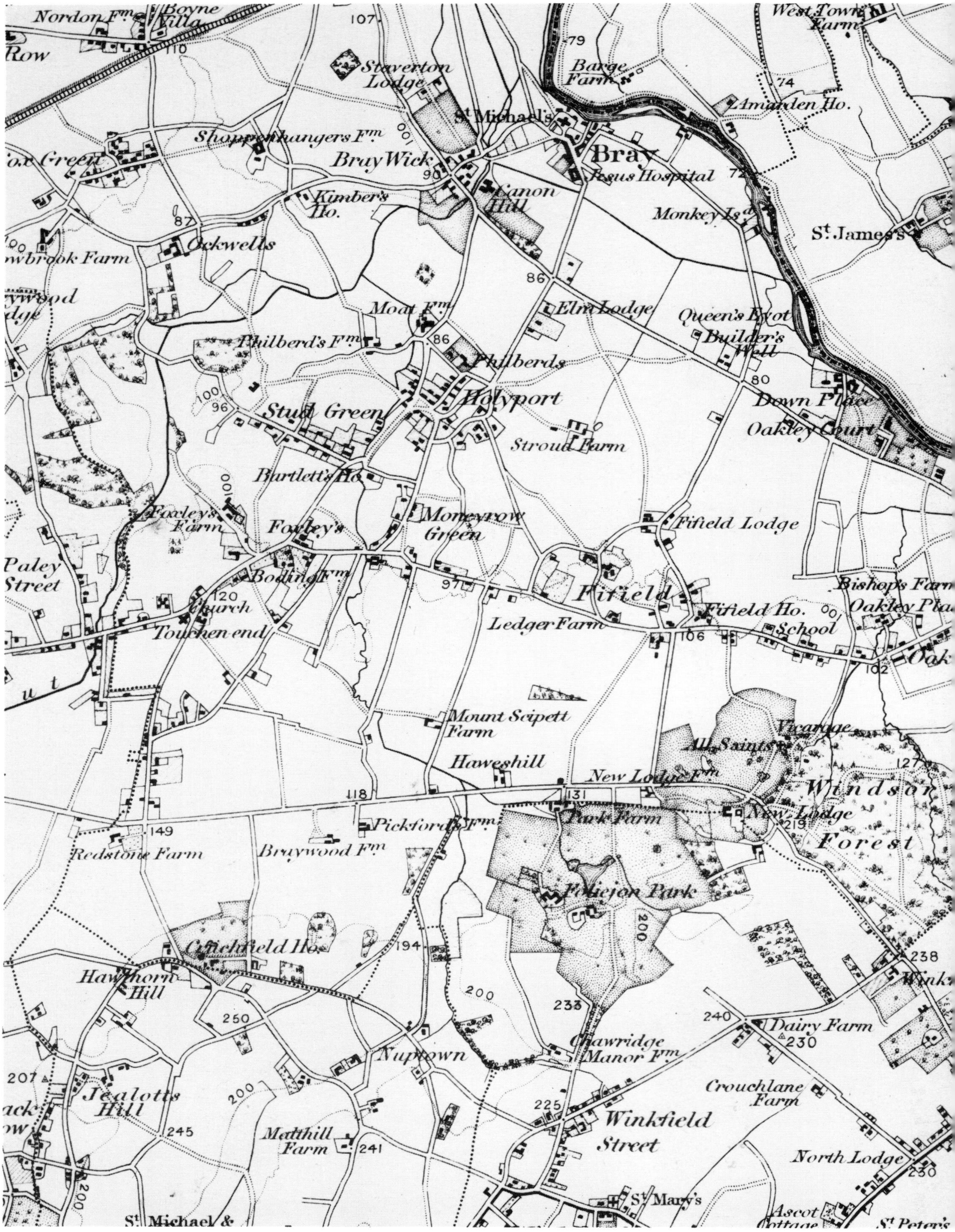
Nordon Fm.
Boyne Villa
Row
Staverton Lodge
St. Michael's
Bray
Barge Farm
West Town Farm
Amarden Ho.
Shoppenhangers Fm.
Bray Wick
Jesus Hospital
Canon Hill
Kimber's Ho.
Ockwells
Monkey Isd.
St. James's
Moat Fm.
Elm Lodge
Queen's Eyot
Builder's Well
Philberd's Fm.
Philberds
Holyport
Down Place
Oakley Court
Stud Green
Stroud Farm
Bartlett's Ho.
Foxley's Farm
Foxley's
Moneyrow Green
Fifield Lodge
Paley Street
Bodine Fm.
Fifield
Bishop's Farm
Church
Touchen end
Ledger Farm
Fifield Ho.
School
Oakley Place
Mount Scipett Farm
Haweshill
Vicarage
All Saints
New Lodge Fm.
Windsor
Park Farm
New Lodge
Forest
Redstone Farm
Pickford's Fm.
Braywood Fm.
Foliejon Park
Critchfield Ho.
Hawthorn Hill
Dairy Farm
Nuptown
Chawridge Manor Fm.
Crouchlane Farm
Jealotts Hill
Winkfield Street
Matthill Farm
North Lodge
St. Michael &
St. Mary's
Ascot Cottage
St. Peter's

1 2

1 mile approx.

Salt Hill
Plough Lees
Cippenham
Cippenham School
Cippenham Lodge
Court
Station
SLOUGH
Chalvey
Chalvey Grove
Aldin Ho.
Springfield Ho.
St. Lawrence's
Upton
Dorney
Dorney Common
North Field
Eton Wick
Dutchman's Farm
St. John the Baptist's
South Field
Boveney
St. Mary's
Race Course
Grand Stand
ETON
St. John's
Black Potts
Riding Court
Churchmead House
Datchet
Clewer Park
Clewer
The Willows
Terminus
Windsor Castle
The Home Park
Station
The Rectory
Dedworth Green
WINDSOR
Holy Trinity
Adelaide Lodge
All Saints
Clewer New Town
Barracks
Southlea
Southlea Ho.
Frogmore
Royal Mausoleum
Clewer Green
Clewer Lodge
Albert Br.
Ham Fields
Cemetery
Spital
Shaw Farm
Royal Gardens
St. Leonardshill
St. Leonards Dale
Queen Anne's Gate
Manor Ho.
The Elms
St. Peters
Tileplace Farm
St. Lukes
Flemish Farm
Old Windsor
National Schools
WINDSOR
The Long Walk
Queen Anne's Ride
Burfield Lodge
Union Workhouse
Cranbourne Park
Bullirts Lodge
Woodside
Beaumont R.C. School
Cranbourne Tower
Holly Grove
Snow Hill
Statue
Upper Farm
Prince Consort's Workshops
Bishops Gate
Windsor

Surveyed 1874. Published 1880.

90/126▷

Fishery Estate
Shoppenhangers Fm
Golf Course
Bray Wick
Kimber's Ho.
Ockwells
Bray
Jesus Hospital
Cannon Hill
Monkey Is.
Amerden Ho.
Lock
Mill
West Town Farm
Bray Court
Elm Lodge
Queen's Eyot
Builder's Well
Moor Fm
Philberd's Fm
Philberds
Thrift Woods
Holyport
Stud Green
Smithy
Stroud Farm
Down Place
Oakley Court
Moneyrow Green
Foxleighs
Hare & Hounds
Fifield
Bishop's Farm
Ledger Farm
Touchen-end
Oakley
Mount Scipett Farm
Haweshill
Newlodge Fm
Royal Forester
Park Farm
Windsor Forest
Redstone Farm
Race Course
Cruchfield Ho.
Hawthorn Hill
Hawthorndale
Nuptown
Chawridge Manor Fm
Dairy Farm
Crouchlane Farm
Winkfield Street
Jealotts Hill
Moss End
Maidens Green
North Street
Winkfield

1 2

1 mile approx.

Surveyed 1863-1874. Revised 1901-1902. Published 1904.

92/128▷

△ 88

◁ 119

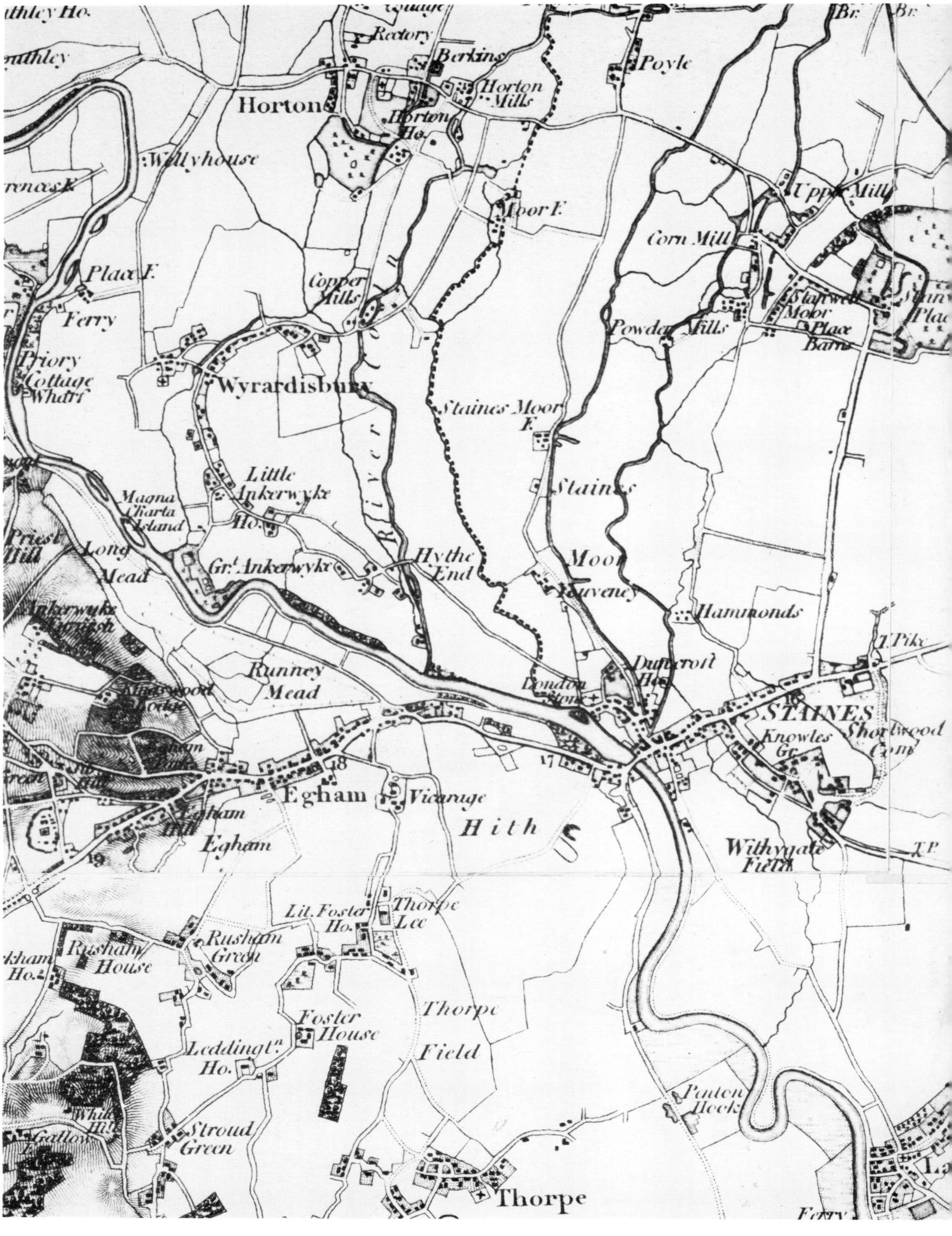
Rectory
Berkins
Poyle
Horton
Horton Mills
Horton Ho.
Wellyhouse
Moor F.
Upper Mill
Corn Mill
Place F.
Copper Mills
Ferry
Stanwell Moor
Place Barn
Powder Mills
Priory Cottage Wharf
Wyrardisbury
River
Staines Moor F.
Little Ankerwyke
Magna Charta Island
Ankerwyke Ho.
Staines
Long Mead
Gr.t Ankerwyke
Hythe End
Moor
Yeoveney
Hammonds
Runney Mead
Duncroft Ho.
London Stone
STAINES
Knowles Gr.
Shortwood Com.
Egham
Vicarage
Egham Hill
Egham
Hith
Withygate Field
Lit. Foster Ho.
Thorpe Lee
Rusham Green
Rusham House
Foster House
Thorpe
Field
Leddingt.n Ho.
Penton Hook
Stroud Green
Thorpe
Ferry

154 ▽

1 2
1 mile approx.

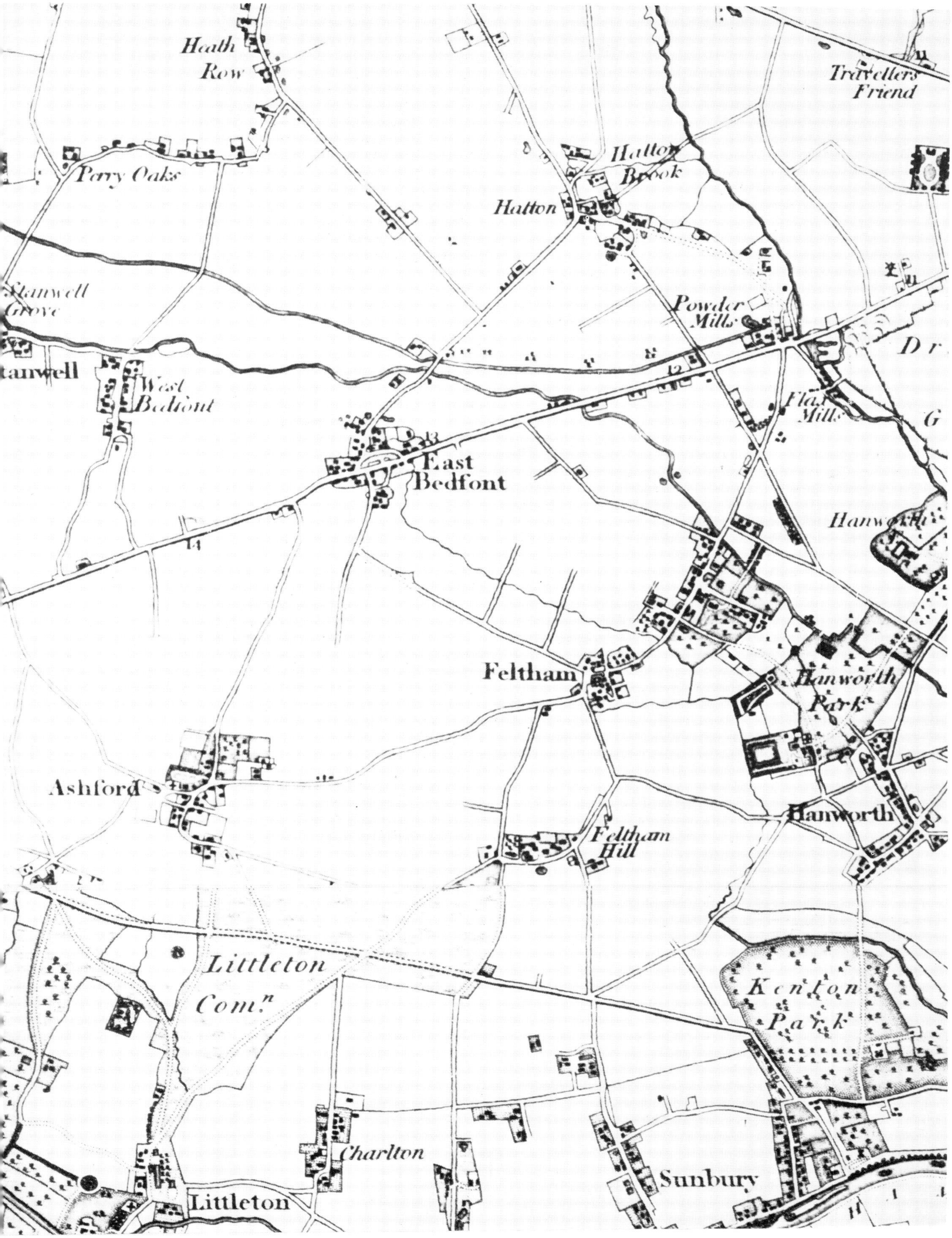
Heath
Row
Travellers
Friend
Perry Oaks
Hatton
Brook
Hatton
Stanwell
Grove
Powder
Mills
tanwell
West
Bedfont
Flat
Mills
East
Bedfont
Hanworth
Feltham
Hanworth
Park
Ashford
Hanworth
Feltham
Hill
Littleton
Com.n
Kenton
Park
Charlton
Sunbury
Littleton

130 ▷

155
▽

Published 1822.

△ 90

◁121

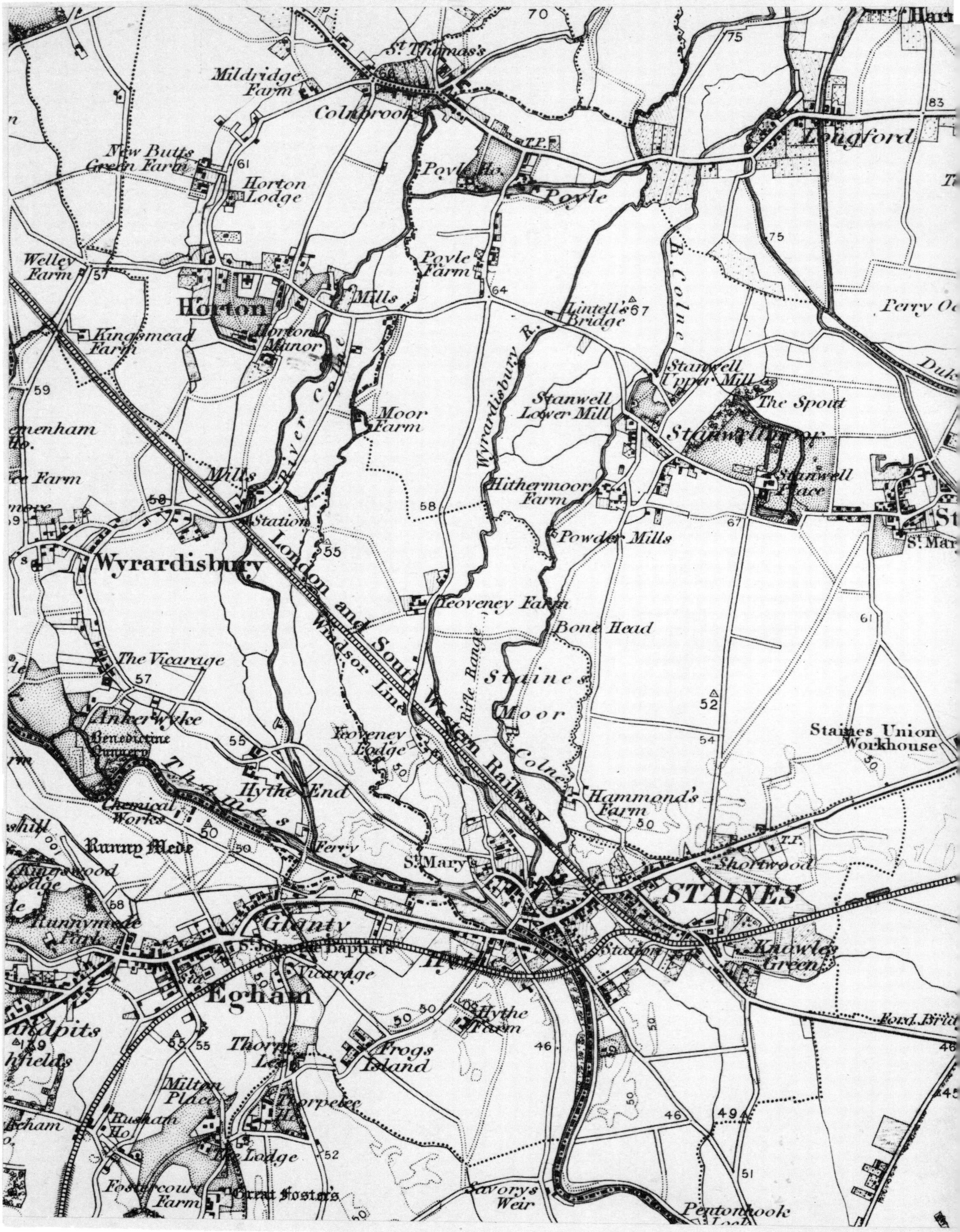
St. Thomas's
Mildridge Farm
Colnbrook
New Butts Green Farm
Horton Lodge
Poyle Ho.
Poyle
Longford
Welley Farm
Poyle Farm
Horton
Mills
Lintell's Bridge
Kingsmead Farm
Horton Manor
River Colne
R. Colne
Stanwell Upper Mill
Moor Farm
Wyrardisbury R.
Stanwell Lower Mill
The Spout
Stanwell Place
Hithermoor Farm
Station
Powder Mills
Wyrardisbury
London and South Western Railway
Windsor Line
Yeoveney Farm
Bone Head
The Vicarage
Rifle Range
Staines Moor
Ankerwyke
Benedictine Nunnery
Yeoveney Lodge
Staines Union Workhouse
Thames
Hythe End
Hammond's Farm
Chemical Works
Runny Mede
Ferry
St. Mary's
Shortwood
STAINES
Kingswood Lodge
Runnymede Park
Glanty
St. John the Baptist's
Vicarage
Hythe
Station
Knowles Green
Egham
Hythe Farm
Thorpe Lee
Frogs Island
Milton Place
Thorpelee Ho.
Rusham Ho.
The Lodge
Fostercourt Farm
Great Fosters
Savorys Weir
Pentonhook Lock

156 ▽

1 2
1 mile approx.

91

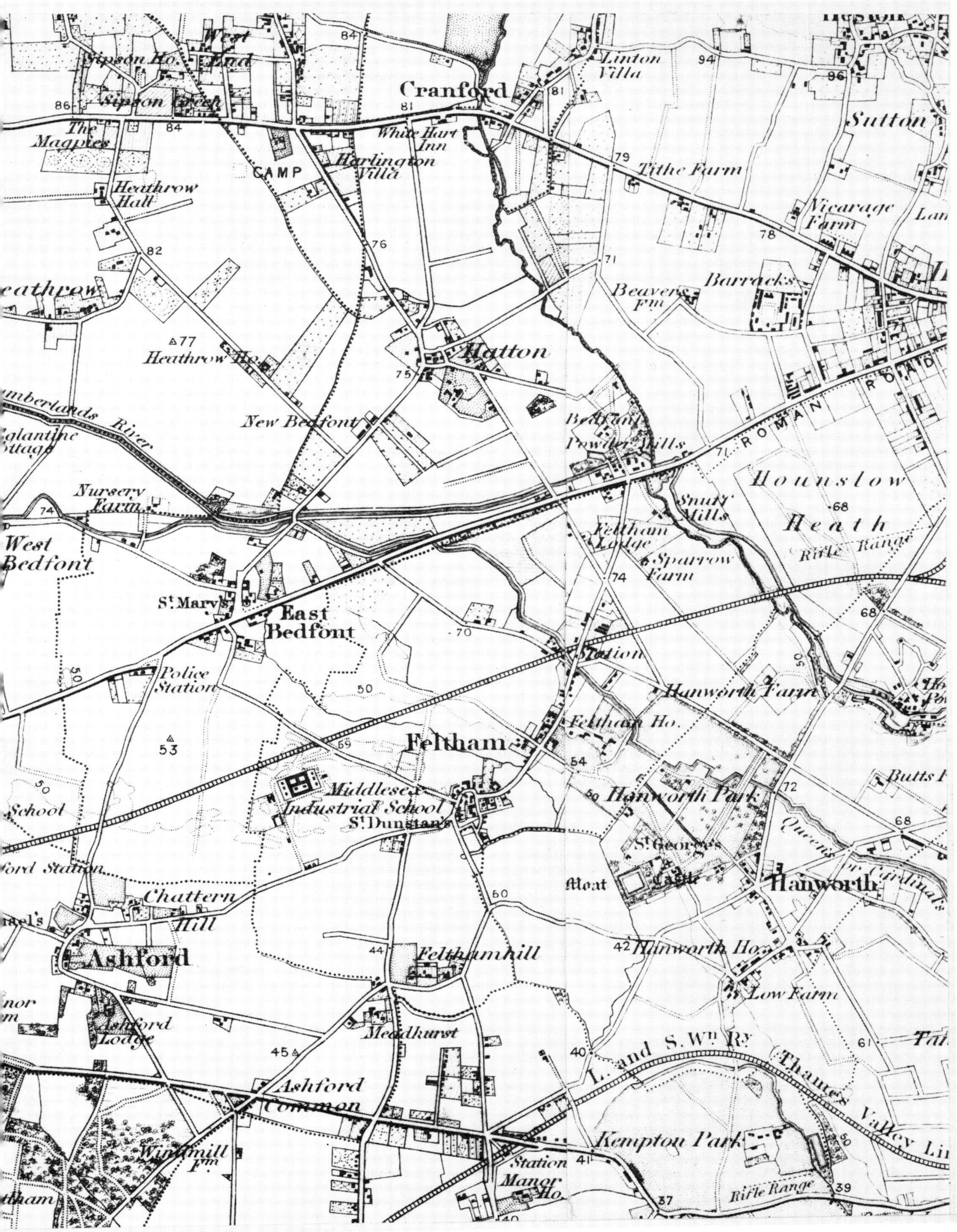
West End
Sipson Ho.
Sipson Green
Cranford
White Hart Inn
Harlington Villa
The Magpies
CAMP
Heathrow Hall
Linton Villa
Sutton
Tithe Farm
Vicarage Farm
Barracks
Beavers Fm
Heathrow
Heathrow Ho.
Hatton
New Bedfont
ROMAN ROAD
Bedfont Powder Mills
Hounslow Heath
Snuff Mills
Feltham Lodge
Sparrow Farm
Rifle Range
Eglantine Cottage
Nursery Farm
West Bedfont
St. Mary's
East Bedfont
Station
Police Station
Hanworth Farm
Feltham Ho.
Feltham
Middlesex Industrial School
St. Dunstan's
Hanworth Park
St. George's
Moat
Hanworth
Butts F
School
Chattern Hill
Ashford
Felthamhill
Hanworth Ho.
Low Farm
Ashford Lodge
Meadhurst
L. and S. Wn. Ry.
Thames Valley Line
Ashford Common
Kempton Park
Windmill Fm.
Station
Manor Ho.
Rifle Range

132

157

Surveyed 1874. Published 1880.

△ 92

◁123

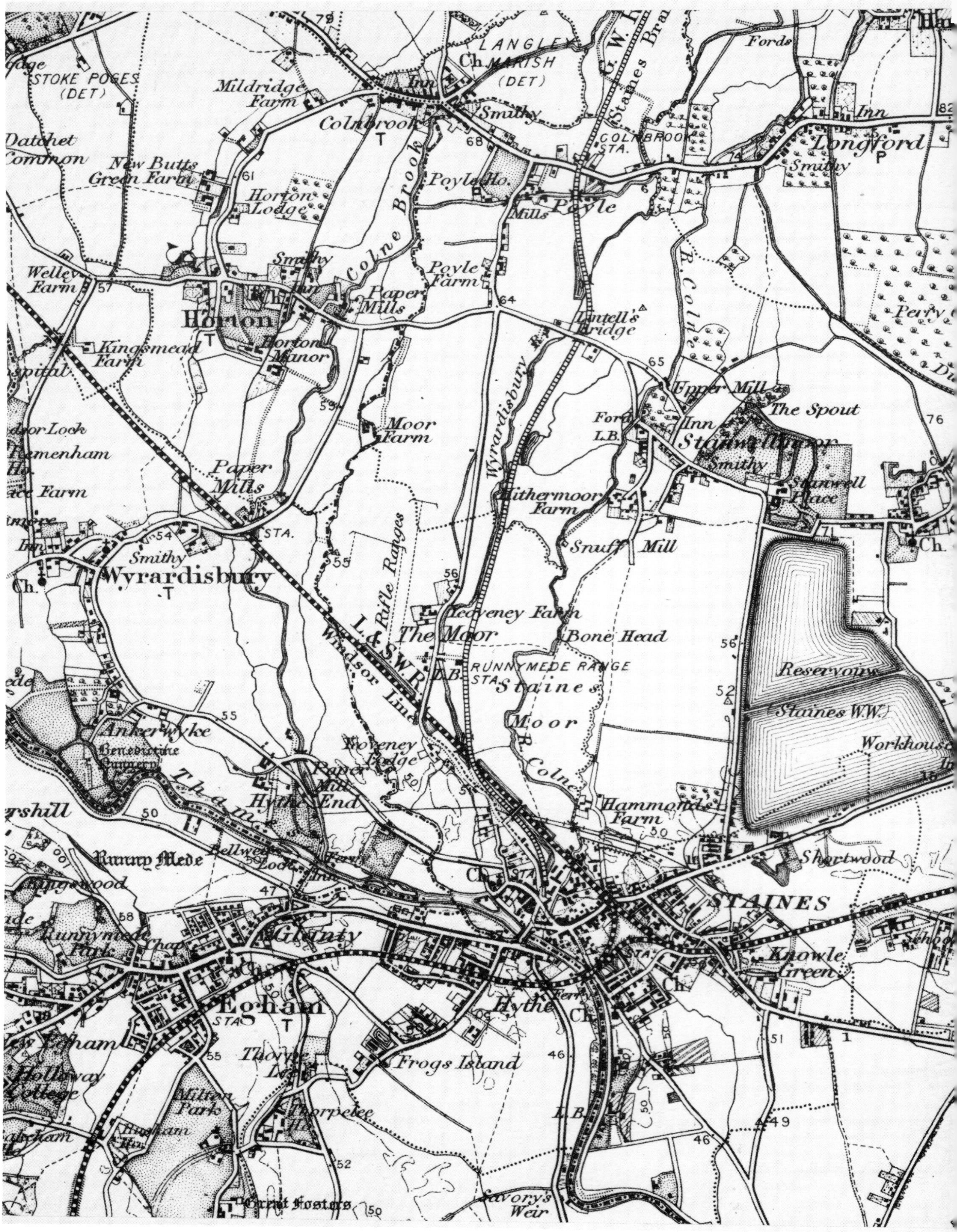

STOKE POGES (DET)
Mildridge Farm
LANGLEY MARISH (DET)
Inn
Smithy
Colnbrook
G. W. R.
Staines Branch
COLNBROOK STA.
Fords
Inn
Longford
Smithy
Datchet Common
New Butts Green Farm
Horton Lodge
Poyle Ho.
Poyle
Mills
Colne Brook
R. Colne
Welley Farm
Smithy
Inn
Paper Mills
Poyle Farm
Horton
Horton Manor
Kingsmead Farm
Lintell's Bridge
Perry
Upper Mill
The Spout
Moor Farm
Wyrardisbury
Ford
L.B.
Inn
Stanwell Moor
Smithy
Stanwell Place
Paper Mills
Hithermoor Farm
STA.
Snuff Mill
Ch.
Smithy
Wyrardisbury
Rifle Ranges
Yeoveney Farm
The Moor
Bone Head
L.&S.W.R.
Windsor Line
RUNNYMEDE RANGE
L.B. STA.
Staines Moor
Reservoirs
Staines W.W.
Workhouse
Ankerwyke
Benedictine Nunnery
Yeoveney Lodge
Paper Mill
Hythe End
R. Colne
Hammonds Farm
Thames
Runny Mede
Bellweir Lock
Inn
Shortwood
STAINES
STA.
Ch.
Runnymede Park
Glanty
Knowle Green
Egham
STA.
Hythe
Ferry
Ch.
Thorpe Lea
Frogs Island
Holloway College
Milton Park
Thorpelee Ho.
L.B.
Great Fosters
Savory's Weir

1 2

1 mile approx.

158 ▽

△ 93

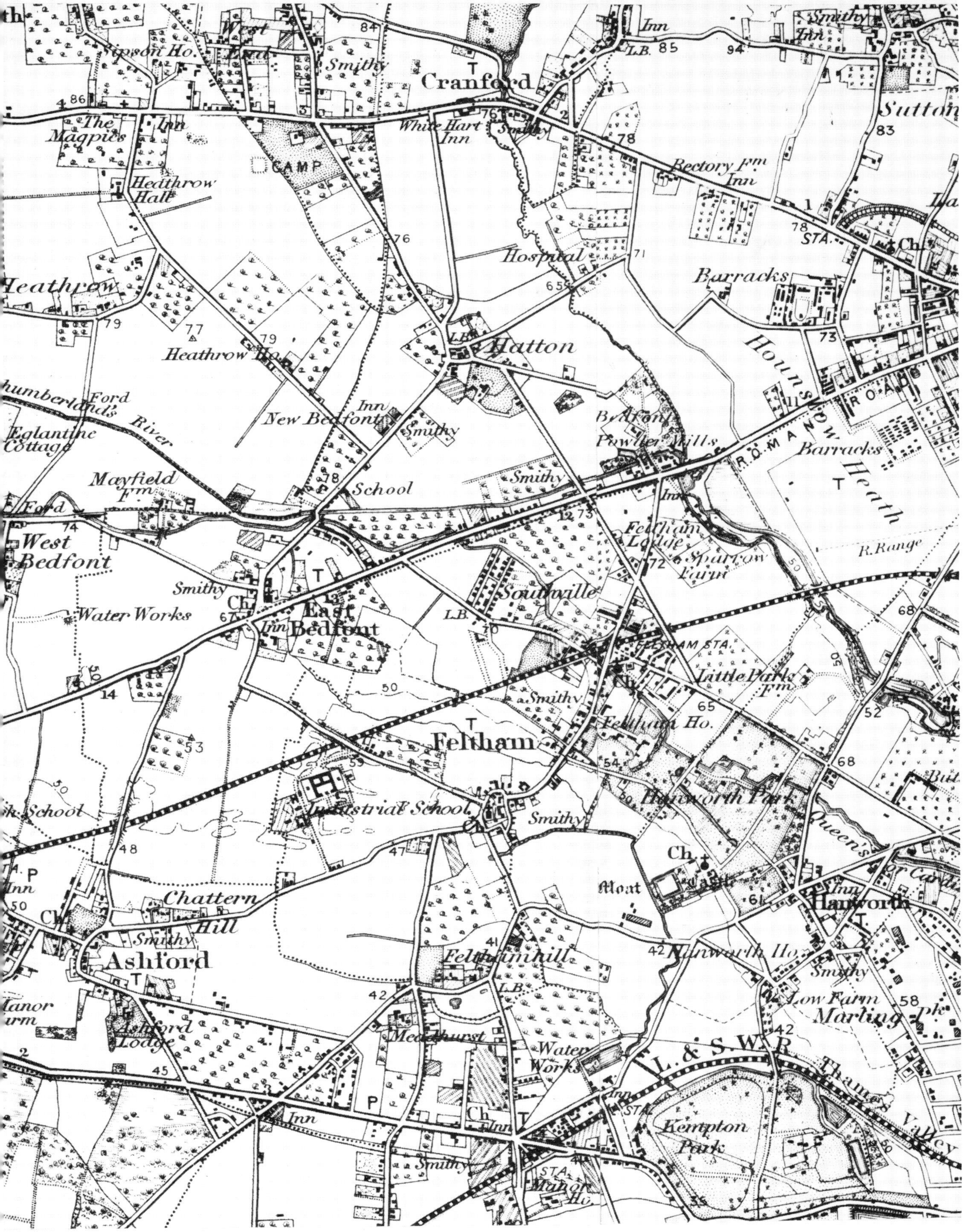

134 ▷

159 ▽

Surveyed 1863-1874. Revised 1901-1902. Published 1904.

△ 94

◁ 125

Lampton
Springrove
Smallbury Green
Lampton Hills
Poor Ho.
Hounslow
Barracks
Isleworth
Observatory
Worton
Whitton Dean
Queens Br.
Mother Ives Br.
Twickenham Park
Whitton Ho.
Whitton Park
Chase Br.
Ivy Cottage
Chatham Lodge
Marble Hill
Little Marble Hill
Twickenham
Sluice
Powder Mills
Oil Mill
Petersham
Hospital Bridge
Fulwell Lodge
Strawberry Hill
Ham
Ham Field
Toll Ho
Mill
Maude Cottage
Teddington
Broom Hall
Poor Ho.
Upper Lodge
Holly Bush Lane
Lower Lodge
Broad Lane
BUSHY PARK
Keepers Lodge
Old Field Lane
Pheasantry
Hampton Wick
Brick Yard
Hampton
Ferry
Moulsey Hurst

1 2
1 mile approx.

160 ▽

95

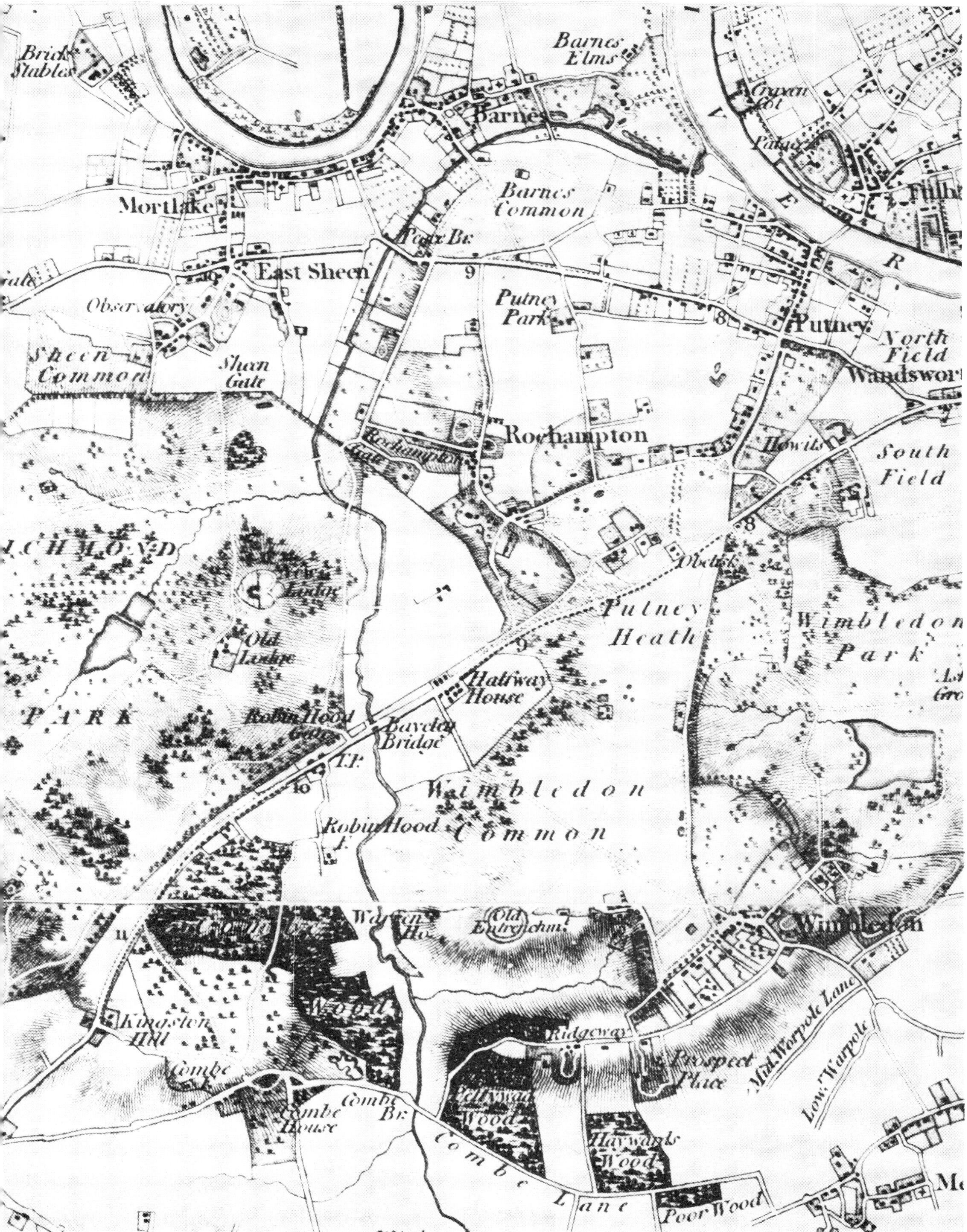
Brick Stables
Barnes Elms
Craven Cot
Barnes
Palace
Mortlake
Barnes Common
Pale Br.
East Sheen
Observatory
Putney Park
Putney
North Field
Sheen Common
Sheen Gate
Roehampton
Roehampton Gate
South Field
Obelisk
New Lodge
Old Lodge
Putney Heath
Wimbledon Park
Halfway House
PARK
Robin Hood Gate
Bridge
T.P.
Wimbledon Common
Robin Hood
Warren Ho.
Old Entrenchmt.
Wimbledon
Wood
Kingston Hill
Ridgeway
Prospect Place
Mid. Warpole Lane
Low. Warpole
Combe
Combe Br.
Combe House
Combe Lane
Haywards Wood
Poor Wood

136

161

Published 1816.

△
96

◁127

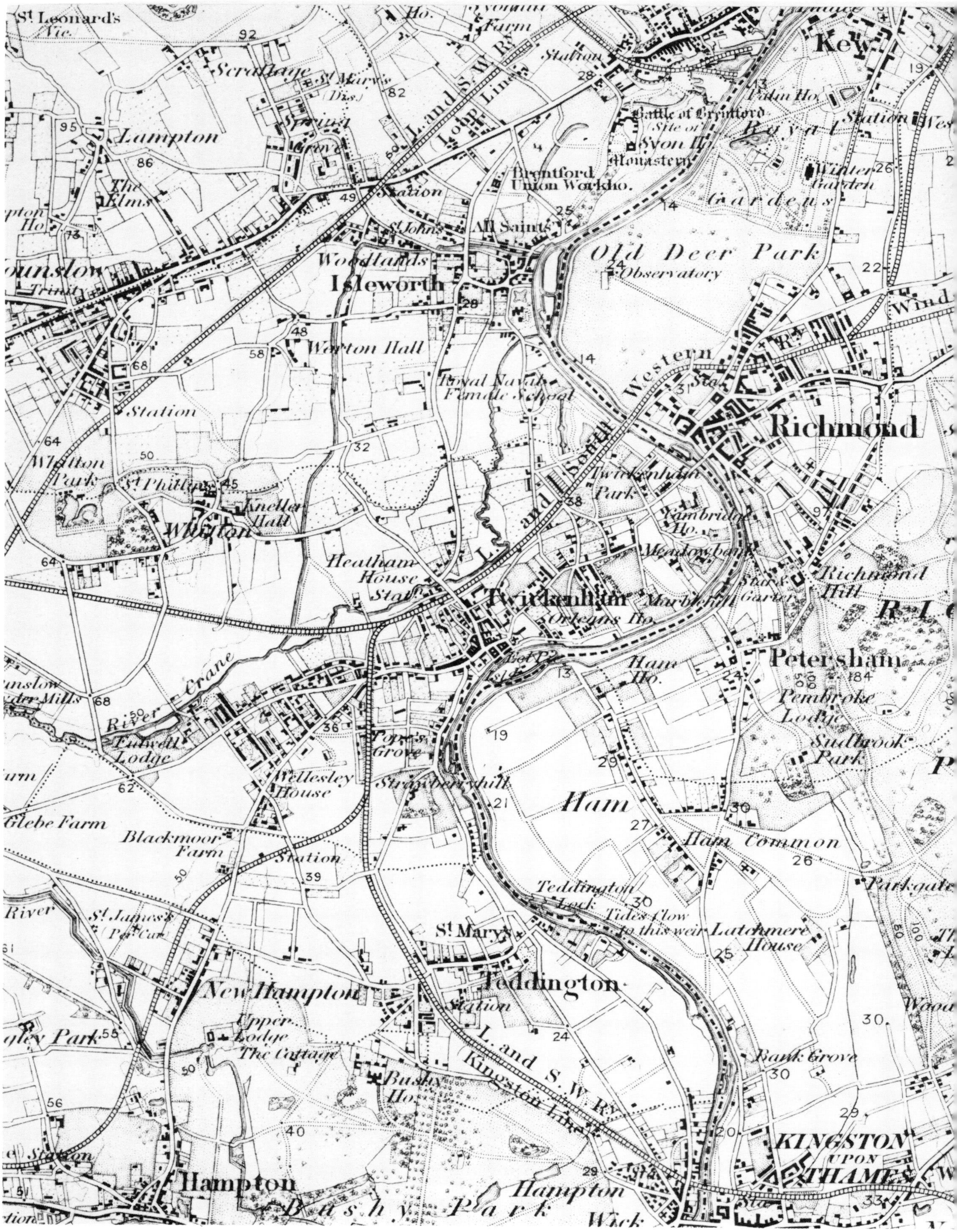
St. Leonard's
Scrattage
St. Mary's (Dis.)
Lampton
Spring Grove
The Elms
Station
L and S. W. Ry.
Loop Line
Farm
Station
Battle of Brentford (Site of)
Syon Ho.
Monastery
Brentford Union Workho.
Key
Palm Ho.
Station
Royal
Winter Garden
Gardens
Hounslow
Trinity
St. John's
All Saints
Woodlands
Isleworth
Old Deer Park
Observatory
Worton Hall
Royal Naval Female School
Western
Richmond
Station
Whitton Park
St. Philip's
Kneller Hall
Whitton
Twickenham Park
South
Cambridge Ho.
Meadowbank
Heatham House
Station
Twickenham
Orleans Ho.
Marble Hill
Star & Garter
Richmond Hill
Petersham
Pembroke Lodge
Sudbrook Park
Ham Ho.
River Crane
Fulwell Lodge
Pope's Grove
Strawberry hill
Wellesley House
Ham
Ham Common
Glebe Farm
Blackmoor Farm
Station
Parkgate
Teddington Lock
Tides flow to this weir
Latchmere House
River
St. James's
St. Mary's
Teddington
New Hampton
Station
Upper Lodge
The Cottage
L. and S. W. Ry.
Kingston Line
Bushy Ho.
Bank Grove
Station
Hampton
Bushy Park
Hampton Wick
KINGSTON UPON THAMES

162
▽

1 2

1 mile approx.

97

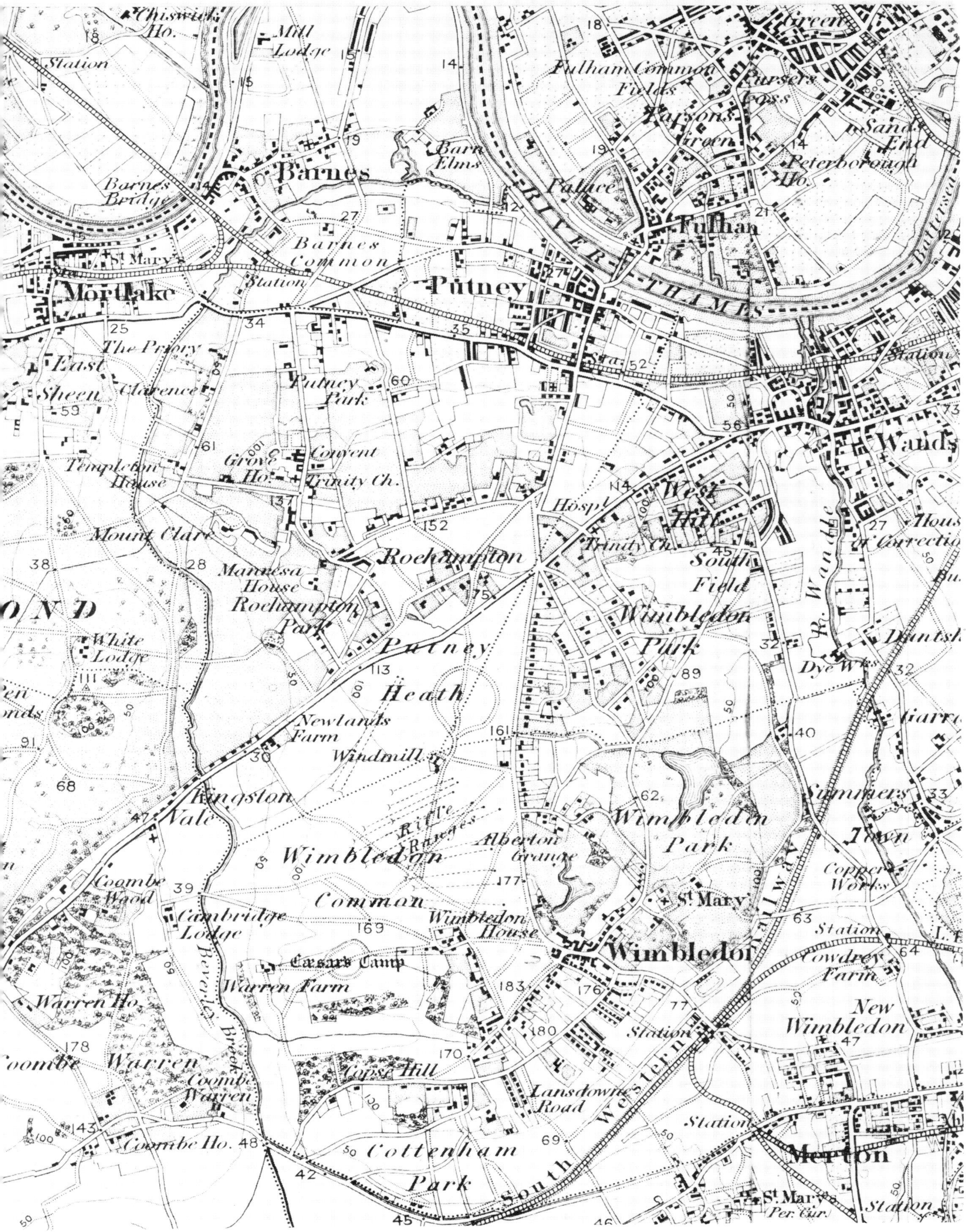

138

163

Surveyed 1861-1871. Published 1876.

98

129

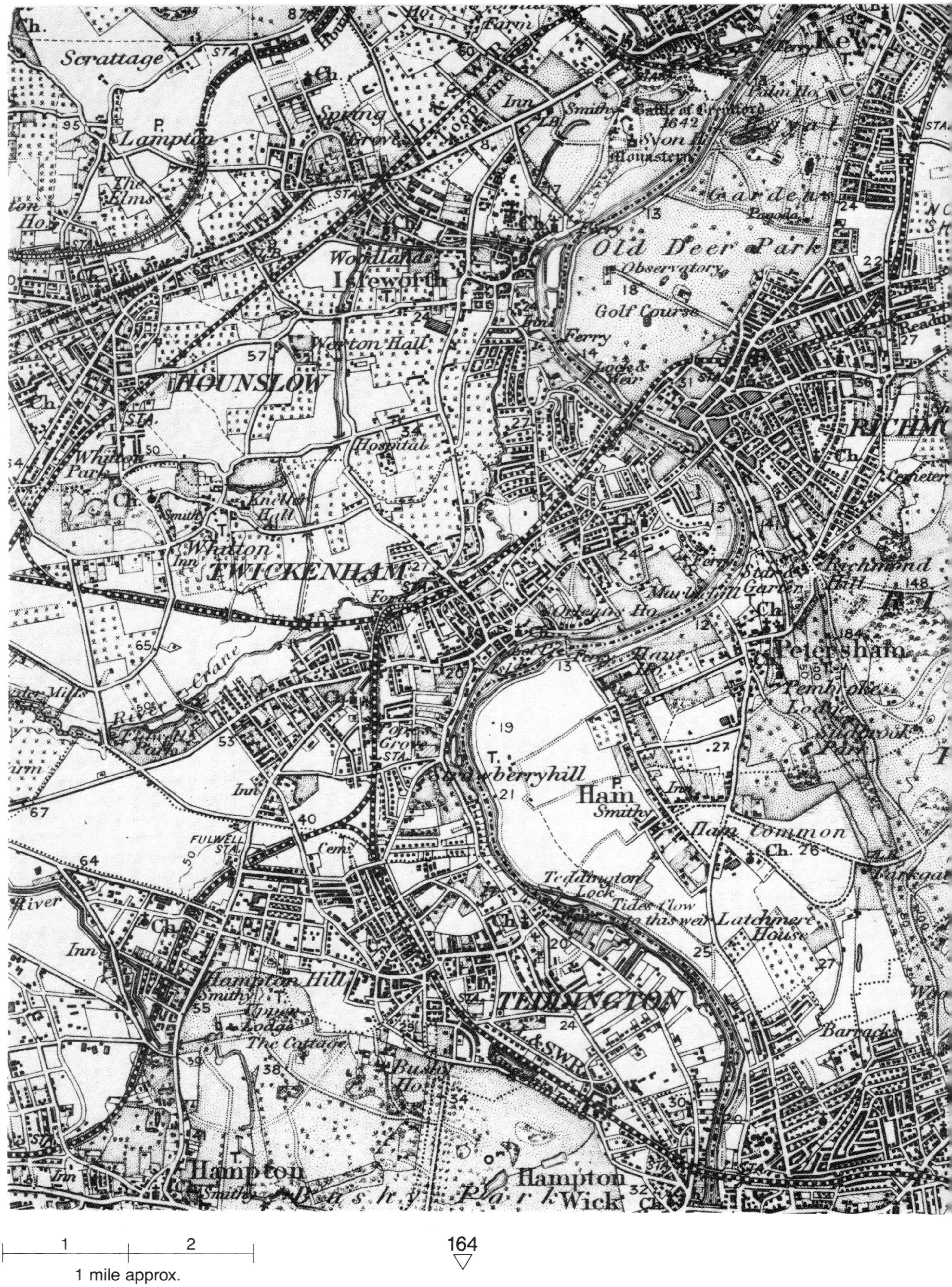
Scrattage
Lampton
The Elms
Kew
Palm Ho.
Battle of Brentford 1642
Syon Ho.
Monastery
Spring Grove
Inn
Smithy
Gardens
Pagoda
Old Deer Park
Observatory
Golf Course
Woodlands
Isleworth
Ferry
Lock & Weir
Worton Hall
HOUNSLOW
Hospital
RICHMOND
Whitton Park
Kneller Hall
Whitton
TWICKENHAM
Richmond Hill
Marble Hill
Orleans Ho.
Petersham
Ham Ho.
Pembroke Lodge
River Crane
Fulwell Park
Strawberryhill
Ham
Ham Common
FULWELL STA.
Teddington Lock
Tide flows up to this weir
Latchmere House
Hampton Hill
TEDDINGTON
Barracks
The Cottage
Bushy Ho.
Hampton
Bushy Park
Hampton Wick

1 2

1 mile approx.

164

140▷

165-6
▽

Surveyed 1861-1871. Revised 1901-1902. Published 1904.

△ 100

◁131

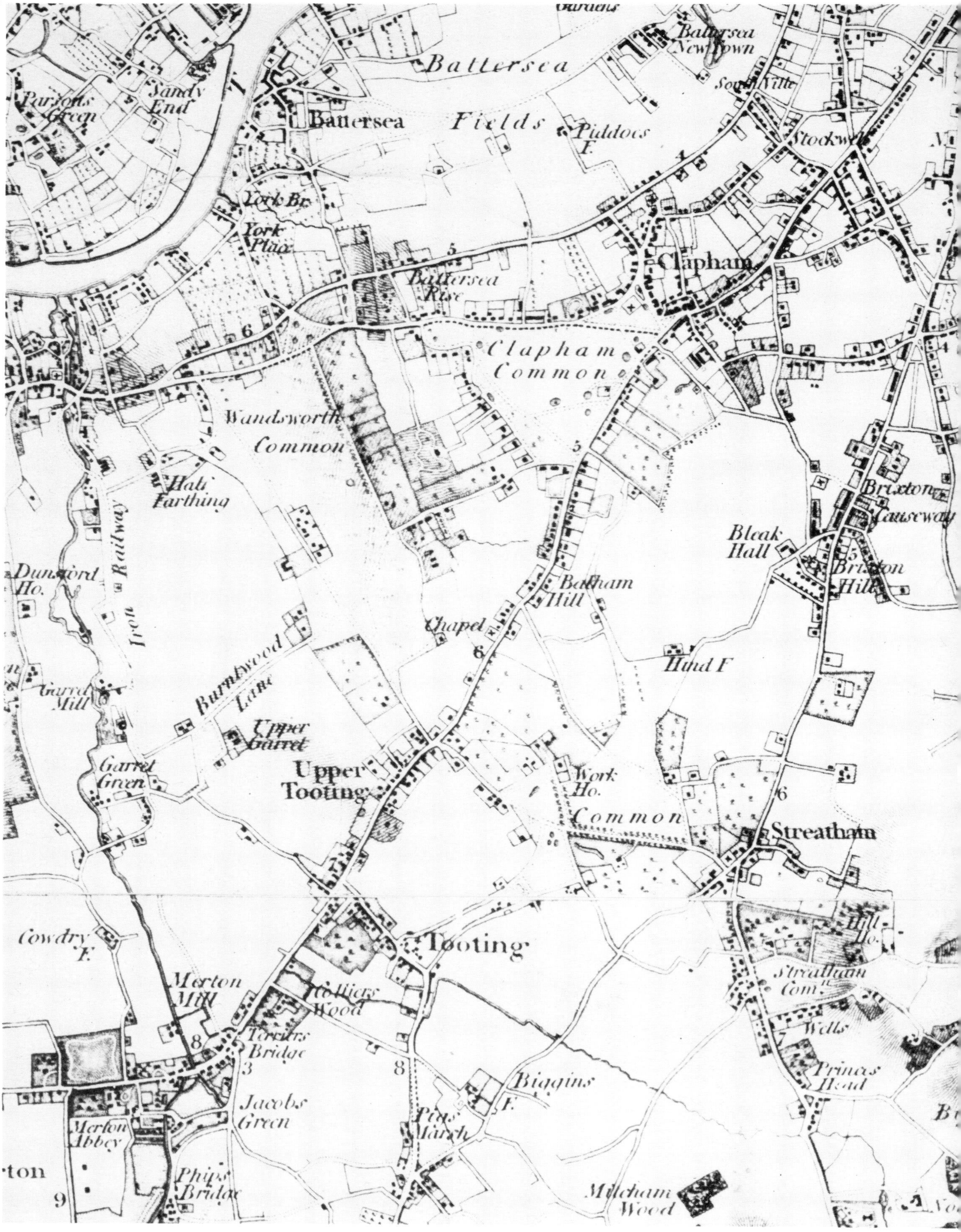
Battersea
Battersea New Town
South Ville
Parsons Green
Sandy End
Battersea
Fields
Piddocs F.
Stockwell
York Br.
York Place
Clapham
Battersea Rise
Clapham Common
Wandsworth Common
Half Farthing
Brixton Causeway
Bleak Hall
Brixton Hill
Dunsford Ho.
Iron Railway
Balham Hill
Chapel
Hind F
Burntwood Lane
Garrat Mill
Upper Garrat
Garret Green
Upper Tooting
Work Ho.
Common
Streatham
Cowdry F.
Tooting
Hill Ho.
Streatham Com.
Merton Mill
Colliers Wood
Wells
Princes Head
Biggins F.
Jacobs Green
Merton Abbey
Pigs March
Phips Bridge
Mitcham Wood

166 ▽

1 2

1 mile approx.

101

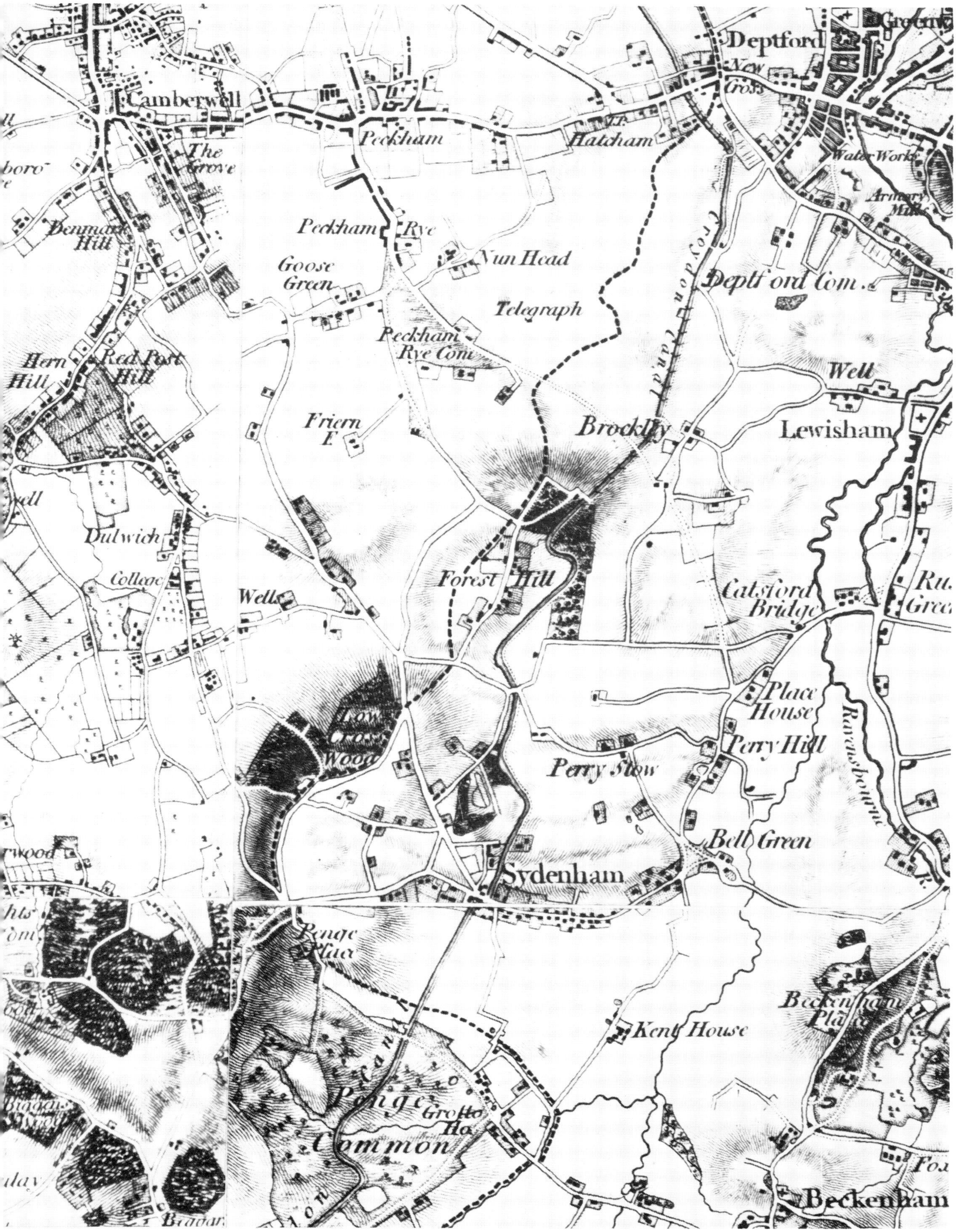
Deptford
New Cross
Camberwell
Peckham
T.P.
Hatcham
The Grove
Water Works
Armoury Mills
Peckham Rye
Nun Head
Goose Green
Croydon Canal
Deptford Com.
Telegraph
Peckham Rye Com
Hern Hill
Red Post Hill
Well
Friern F
Brockley
Lewisham
Dulwich
College
Wells
Forest Hill
Catsford Bridge
Place House
Perry Hill
Ravensbourne
Wood
Perry Slow
Bell Green
Sydenham
Penge Place
Kent House
Beckenham Place
Penge
Grotto Ho
Common
Beckenham

142

167

Published 1816.

△
102

◁ 133

Battersea Park
Lr. Wandsworth Rd.
Battersea
Clapham
Clapham Junc.n
Holy Trinity
Clapham Common
Clapham Park
St. James
St. Saviour's
Brixton
Herne Hill
St. Paul's
London Chatham
Brockwell Hall
All Saints
Wandsworth Common
Balham Station
Crystal Palace Line
Streatham Hill Station
Knights Hill
Station
School
County Lunatic Asylum
Bedford Hill Ho.
Priory
Park Hill
Park Ho.
Upper Tooting
Tooting Bec Com.n
Brighton
Almshouses
Tooting Lodge
Streatham
Hospital
Lower Norwood
Lambeth Cemetery
Lower Tooting
Station
Furze Down
Lower Streatham
Coast Ry.
R. Graveney
Colliers Wood Station
Norwood Grove
Station
Coast
Peckham and Sutton
Merton Branch
Biggin Farm
Figges Marsh
Beulah Hill
Lonesome Chemical W.ks
Norbury Farm
Balham
St. George's Schools
Upper
Norbury

1 2

1 mile approx.

168
▽

103

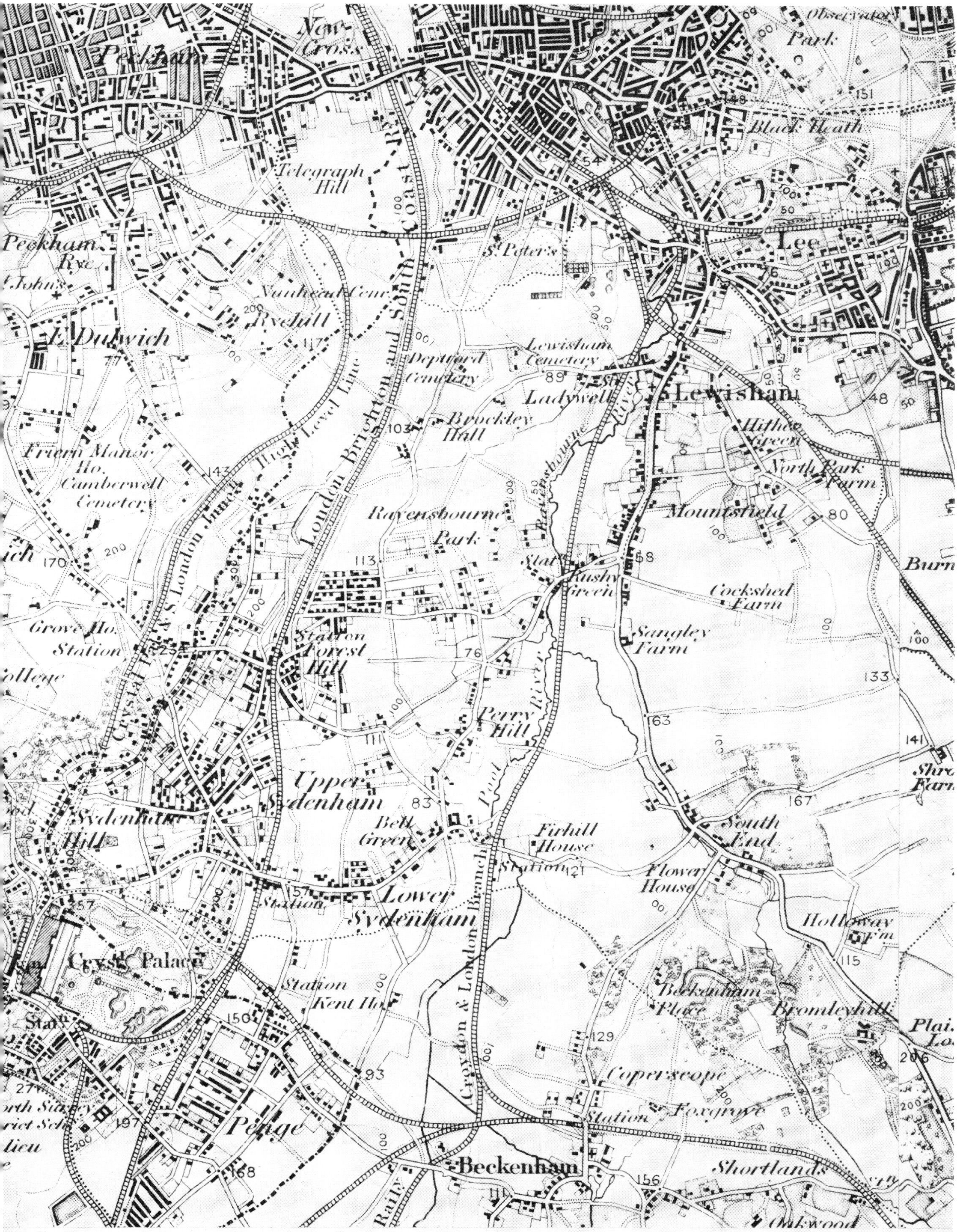
New Cross
Peckham
Park
Black Heath
Telegraph Hill
Peckham Rye
St. Peter's
Lee
Nunhead Cem.
Ryehill
E. Dulwich
Lewisham Cemetery
Deptford Cemetery
Ladywell
Lewisham
Brockley Hall
Hither Green
Friern Manor Ho.
Camberwell Cemetery
North Park Farm
High Level Line
London Brighton and South Coast Ry.
Ravensbourne Park
Mountsfield
Ravensbourne River
Rushy Green
Cockshed Farm
Sangley Farm
Grove Ho. Station
Station Forest Hill
Crystal P. & S. London Junct.
Perry Hill
Pool River
Upper Sydenham
Sydenham Hill
Bell Green
Firhill House
South End
Flower House
Lower Sydenham
Croydon & London Branch
Holloway Fm
Station
Crys. Palace
Station Kent Ho.
Beckenham Place
Bromleyhill
Coperscope
Foxgrove
Penge
Beckenham
Shortlands
Railway
Oakwood

144 ▷

169

104

135

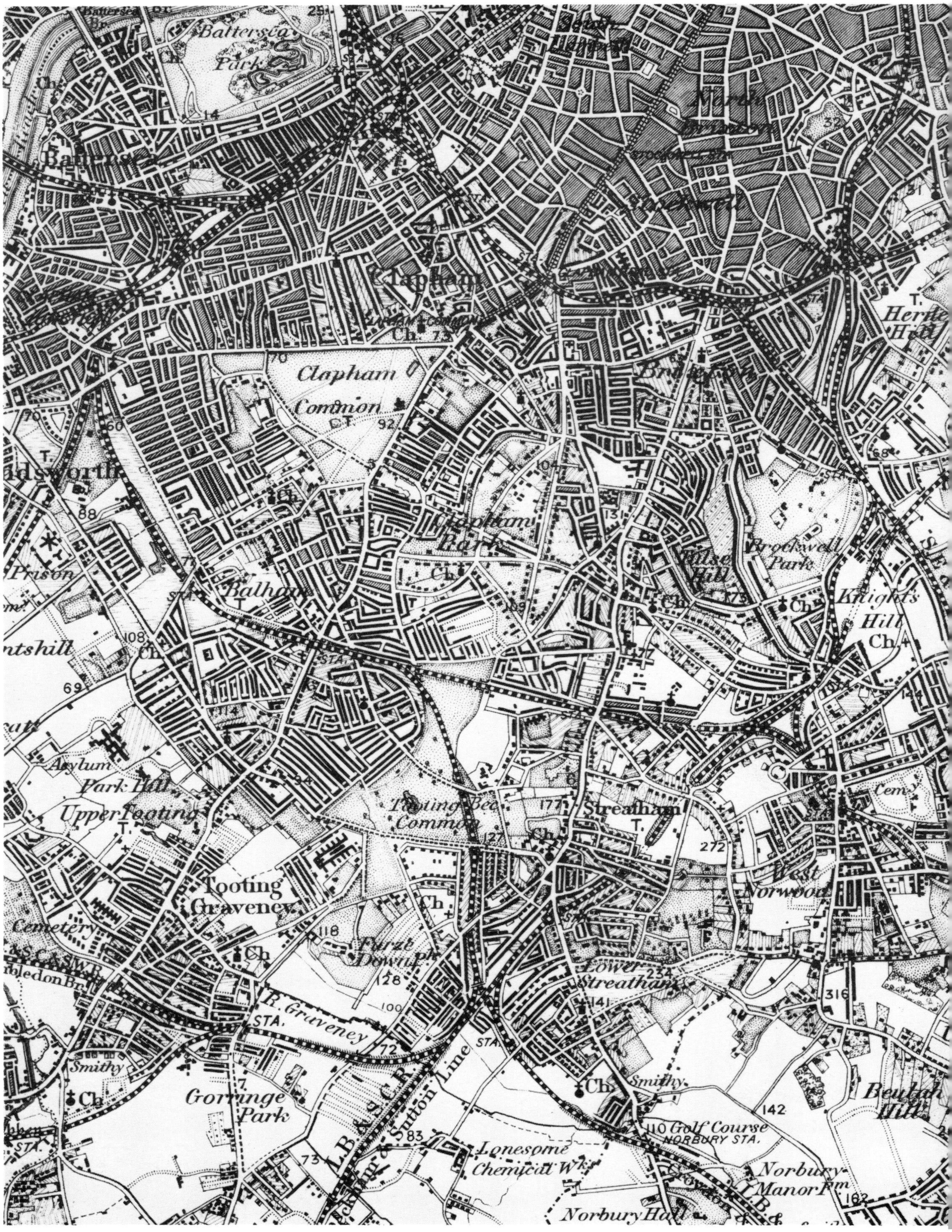
Battersea Park
Battersea
Clapham
Clapham Common
Clapham Park
Brixton
Balham
Brockwell Park
Knight's Hill
Herne Hill
Prison
Asylum
Park Hill
Upper Tooting
Tooting Bec Common
Streatham
West Norwood
Tooting Graveney
Cemetery
Furze Down
Lower Streatham
R. Graveney
Smithy
Gorringe Park
Sutton Line
Lonesome Chemical Wks
Golf Course
NORBURY STA.
Norbury Manor Fm
Norbury Hall
Beulah Hill

170

1 2
1 mile approx.

105

New Cross
Telegraph Hill
Peckham Rye
Ryehill Pk.
Cem'y
S.E.&C.R.
High Level Line
L.B.&S.C.R.
Golf Course
Cemeteries
Lewisham
Workho
Black Heath
Golf Course
Hither Green
Rushey Green
Sangley Farm
Grove Ho.
Forest Hill
Perry Hill
Bellingham Sta.
Smithy
Upper Sydenham
Firhill Lodge
Inn
Mill
South End
Beckenham Hill Sta.
Rifle Range
Holloway
Lower Sydenham
Crystal Palace
Beckenham Place
Croydon Br.
Ravensbourne Sta.
Golf Course
Penge
Anerley
STA.

146

171

△ 106

◁137

Myrtle Place
Woolwich Comn
Black Heath
Sun in Sands
Lower Kidbrook
Shooters Hill
Mordant College
Black Heath
Upper Kidbrook
Wricklesmarsh
Lee Church
Lee
Well Hall
Park Fm
Eltham
Hither Green
Horn Park
Middle Park
Burnt Ash Gr.
Southend
Eltham Place
Burnt Ash
Mottingham
Pope St
Whitechaple Farm
Clay Farm
Shrofield
Southend
Cold Harbor
Sundridge
Elmsted
Warren Ho.
Plaistow
Camden Place
Grove
BROMLEY

1 2
1 mile approx.

172 ▽

△
107

148 ▷

173
▽

Published April 18th 1805.

108

139

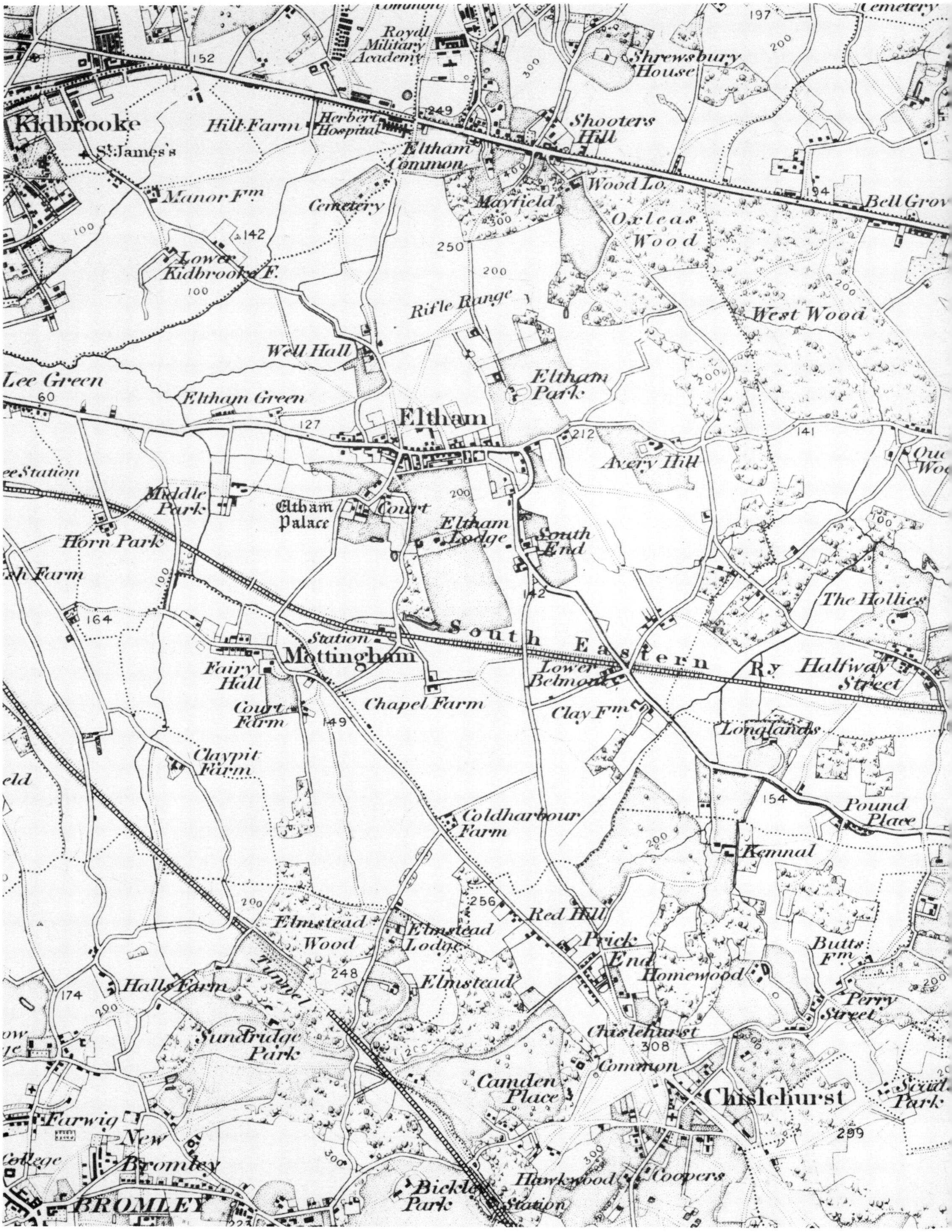
Royal Military Academy
Shrewsbury House
Kidbrooke
Hill Farm
Herbert Hospital
Shooters Hill
St. James's
Eltham Common
Wood Lo.
Manor Fm.
Cemetery
Mayfield
Bell Grove
Oxleas Wood
Lower Kidbrooke F.
Rifle Range
West Wood
Well Hall
Lee Green
Eltham Park
Eltham Green
Eltham
Avery Hill
Middle Park
Eltham Palace
Court
Eltham Lodge
South End
Horn Park
The Hollies
Station
South Eastern Ry
Mottingham
Fairy Hall
Lower Belmont
Halfway Street
Chapel Farm
Court Farm
Clay Fm.
Longlands
Claypit Farm
Pound Place
Coldharbour Farm
Kemnal
Red Hill
Elmstead Wood
Elmstead Lodge
Prick End
Butts Fm.
Tunnel
Homewood
Elmstead
Halls Farm
Perry Street
Sundridge Park
Chislehurst Common
Camden Place
Chislehurst
Farwig
New Bromley
College
Hawkwood
Coopers
Bickley Park
Station
BROMLEY

1 2

1 mile approx.

174

△
109

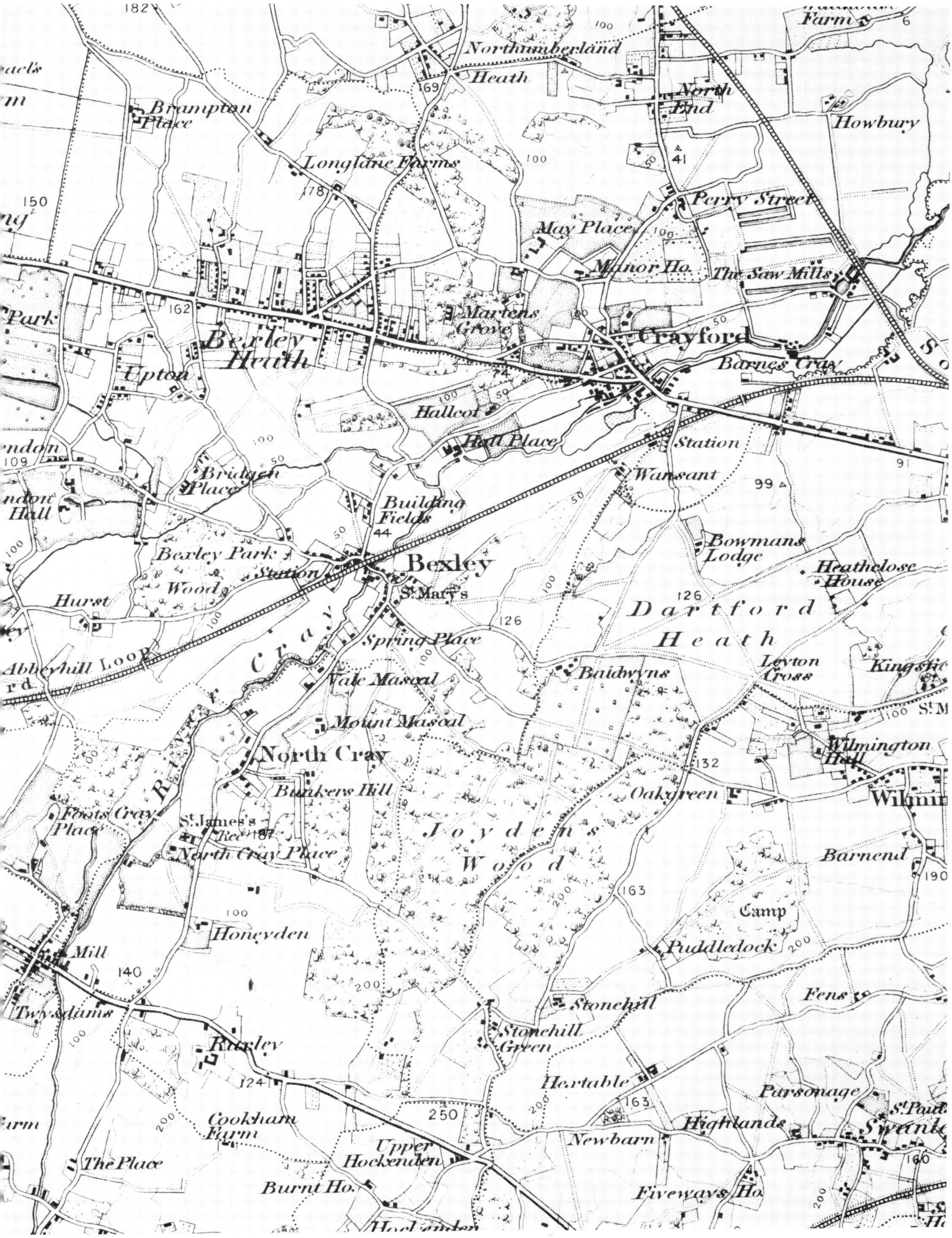

150 ▷

175
▽

Surveyed 1861-1868. Published 1876.

△ 110

◁ 141

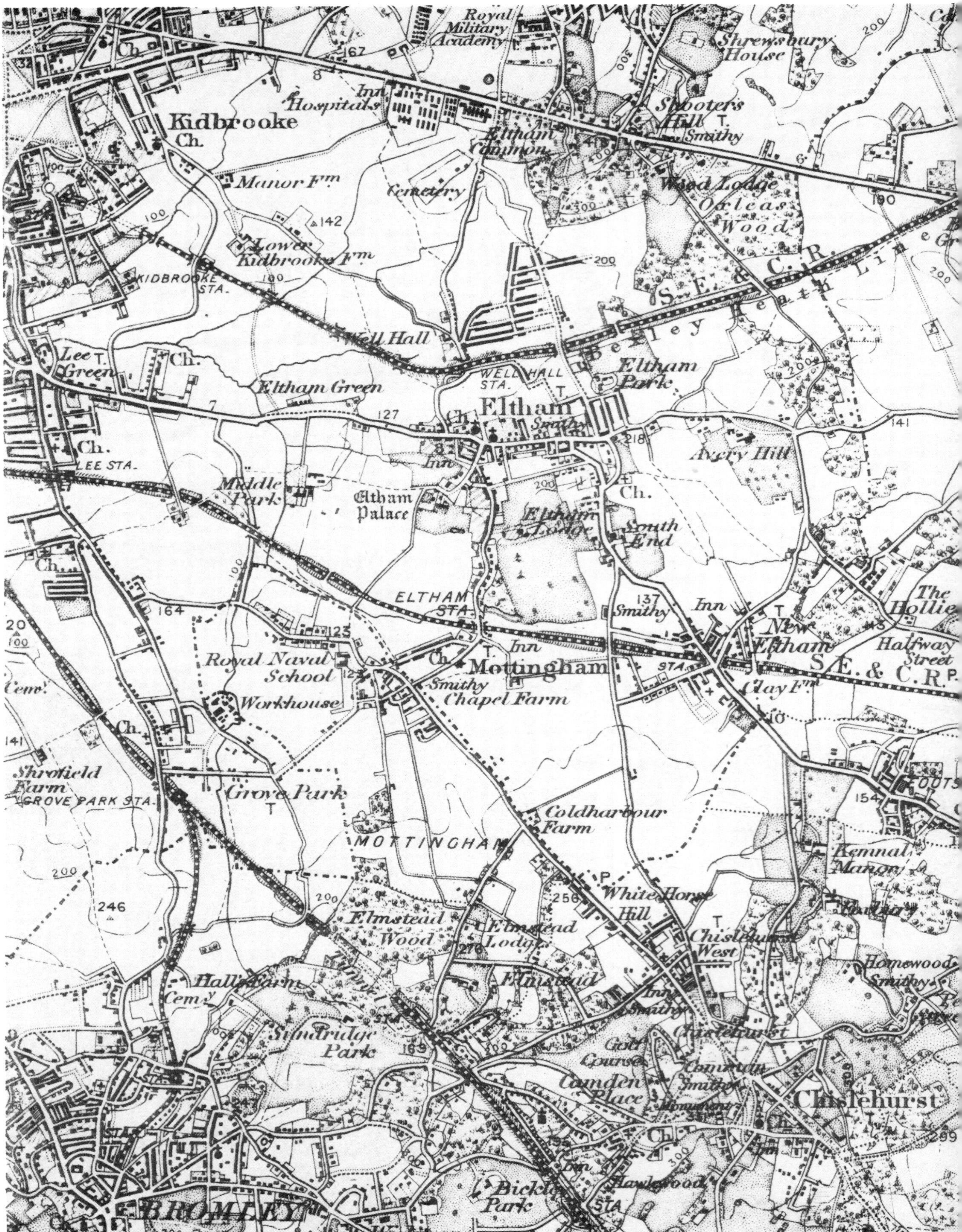
Royal Military Academy
Shrewsbury House
Kidbrooke
Ch.
Hospitals
Inn
167
Shooters Hill
Smithy
Eltham Common
Manor Fm.
Cemetery
Wood Lodge
Oxleas Wood
Lower Kidbrooke Fm.
142
KIDBROOKE STA.
S. E. & C. R.
Bexley Heath Line
Well Hall
WELL HALL STA.
Lee Green
Eltham Green
Eltham
Eltham Park
127
Smithy
218
141
Avery Hill
LEE STA.
Middle Park
Eltham Palace
Eltham Lodge
South End
ELTHAM STA.
164
137
The Hollies
New Eltham
Halfway Street
Royal Naval School
Mottingham
Chapel Farm
Clay Fm.
S. E. & C. R.
Workhouse
Shroffield Farm
GROVE PARK STA.
Grove Park
Coldharbour Farm
MOTTINGHAM
154
Kemnal Manor
White Horse Hill
246
256
Elmstead Wood
Elmstead Lodge
Chislehurst West
Elmstead
Homewood
Halls Farm
Cemy.
Sundridge Park
183
Golf Course
Chislehurst
Camden Place
Common
Chislehurst
Bickley Park
Hawkwood
BROMLEY
Widmore
200
300

176 ▽

1 2
1 mile approx.

△
111

Cemetery
Ch.
Wickham
Inn
Brampton Place
Longlane Farms
Northumberland
Heath
Smithy
North End
STA.
Slade Green
BEXLEY HEATH STA
BARNEHURST STA
Smithy
Perry Street
May Place
Manor Ho.
Welling
Smithy
Inn
Ch.
Danson Park
Martens Grove
Crayford
Barns Cray
Smithy
Upton
Bexleyheath
Hallcot
Hall Place
Inn
STA.
Blendon
A106
Bridgen Place
Mill
Wansunt
Blendon Hall
Smithy
Bowmans Lodge
Bexley Park Wood
Ch.
Inn
Bexley
STA.
Hurst
Lamorbey
Coldblow
Dartford
Heath
Spring Place
Cray
Abbeyhill Loop
Dartford
Vale Mascal
Leyton Cross
Mount Mascal
Asylum
North Cray
Bunkers Hill
Hookgreen
Smithy
Foots Cray Place
North Cray Place
Joydens
Well
Wood
Smithy
Ch.
Honeyden
Smithy
Twysdens
Stonehill
Ruxley
Stonehill Green
Hextable
Spring
Gray's Farm
Cookham Farm
Highlands
Rectory
Home Fm
Upper Hockenden
Smithy
Inn
Inn
Paper Mill
Inn
Fiveways Ho.
Smithy
Hockenden

152 ▷

177
▽

Surveyed 1861-1868. Revised 1903. Published 1905.

△ 112

◁143

Erith
Crayford
Marshes
New Inn
Dartford Creek
Wall House
Dartford
Slads Green
Marshes
North End
West Thurrock
Long Reach
Stone Ho.
May Place
Perry Street
Marsh Street
Joyces F.m
Parsonage
Iron Mills
Barns Cray
Crayford
Little Brook
Cotton F.m
Stoneham
14
Fullege
DARTFORD
T. Pike
16
Bowmans Lodge
Roman
Dartford Heath
Dartford Brent
Paper Mills
Powder Mills
Black Dale
Baldwins
Lower Dale
Wilmington Common
Wilmington
Gore F.m
Mount Pleasant
Shere Hall
Burnt Ho.
Rowhill Wood
Darent
Sutton Place
Gots Hill
Clement Street
Sutton at Hone
Malthouse F.
St. Johns
Hackstable
Gilton Hill

1 2

1 mile approx.

Grays Hall
Chadwell
West Thurrock
Mill
Grays Thurrock
Little Thurrock
MARSH
St. CLEMENTS REACH
NORTHFLEET HOPE
WEST TIL
MARSH
Greenhithe
Ingress
18
19
Stone Br.
Galley Hill
GRA
Knockholt
Milton Street
Stone Castle
North Fleet
Northfleet Hithe
Hockenden
Swanscomb
GRAVESE
Pell Street
21
Parsonage
Swanscomb Park W.
Windfield Bank
Wombwell Hall
Perry Street
Stone Wood
Telegraph
Bean
South Fleet
Green Street Green
Hook Place
Hook Gr.
Westwood
Red Street
Broad ditch
Northfleet Green
Hazle
Scadbury

Published 1805.

150 △ 114

◁ 145

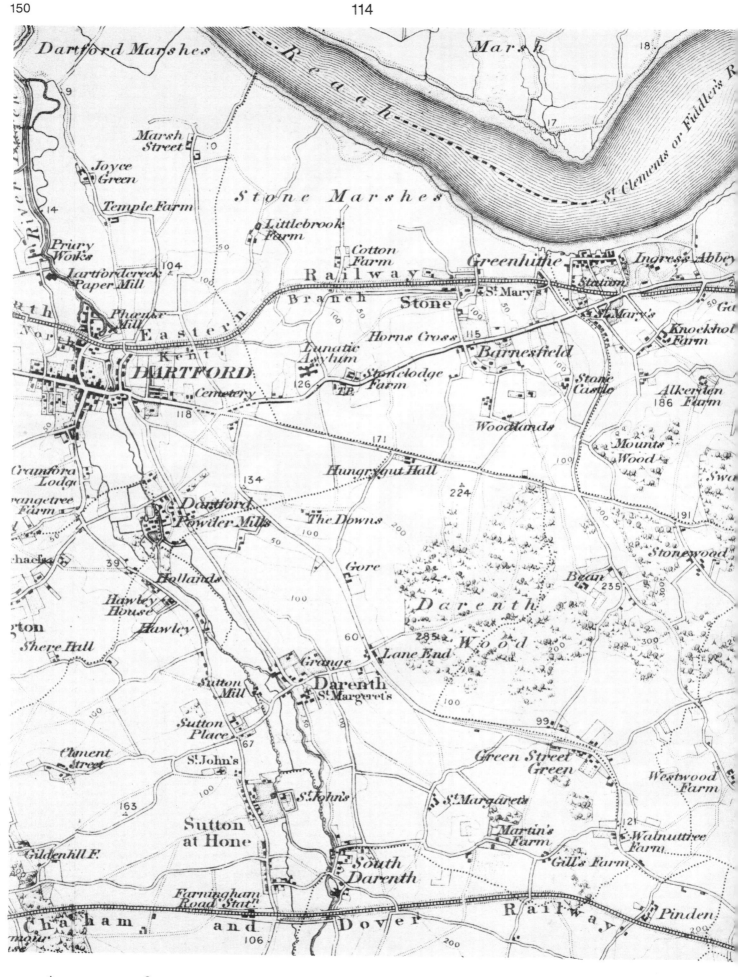

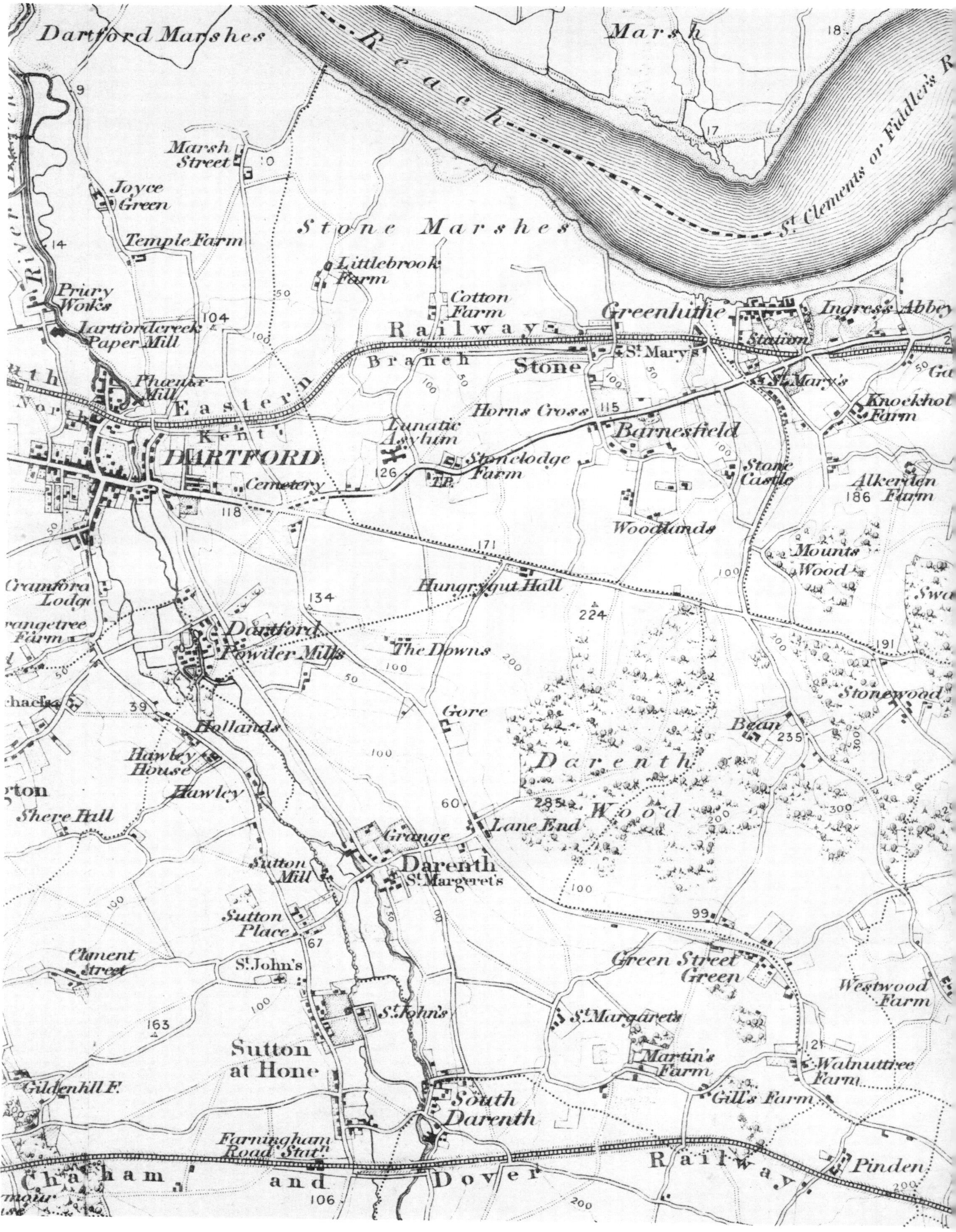
Dartford Marshes
Reach
Marsh
St. Clements or Fiddler's R
River
Marsh Street
Joyce Green
Temple Farm
Stone Marshes
Littlebrook Farm
Cotton Farm
Priory Works
Dartford Creek Paper Mill
Railway
Greenhithe
Ingress Abbey
Station
St. Mary's
Branch
Stone
Phœnix Mill
North
Eastern
Kent
Horns Cross
Barnesfield
Knockhol Farm
Lunatic Asylum
DARTFORD
Stonelodge Farm
Stone Castle
Cemetery
Alkerden Farm
Woodlands
Mounts Wood
Hungryhut Hall
Cranford Lodge
Orangetree Farm
Dartford Powder Mills
The Downs
Stonewood
Gore
Bean
Hollands
Hawley House
Hawley
Darenth
Wood
Shere Hall
Lane End
Grange
Darenth
St. Margaret's
Sutton Mill
Sutton Place
Clement Street
St. John's
Green Street Green
Westwood Farm
St. Margarets
St. John's
Sutton at Hone
Martin's Farm
Walnuttree Farm
Gildenhill F.
South Darenth
Gill's Farm
Farningham Road Statn
Railway
Pinden
Chatham
and
Dover

1 2

1 mile approx.

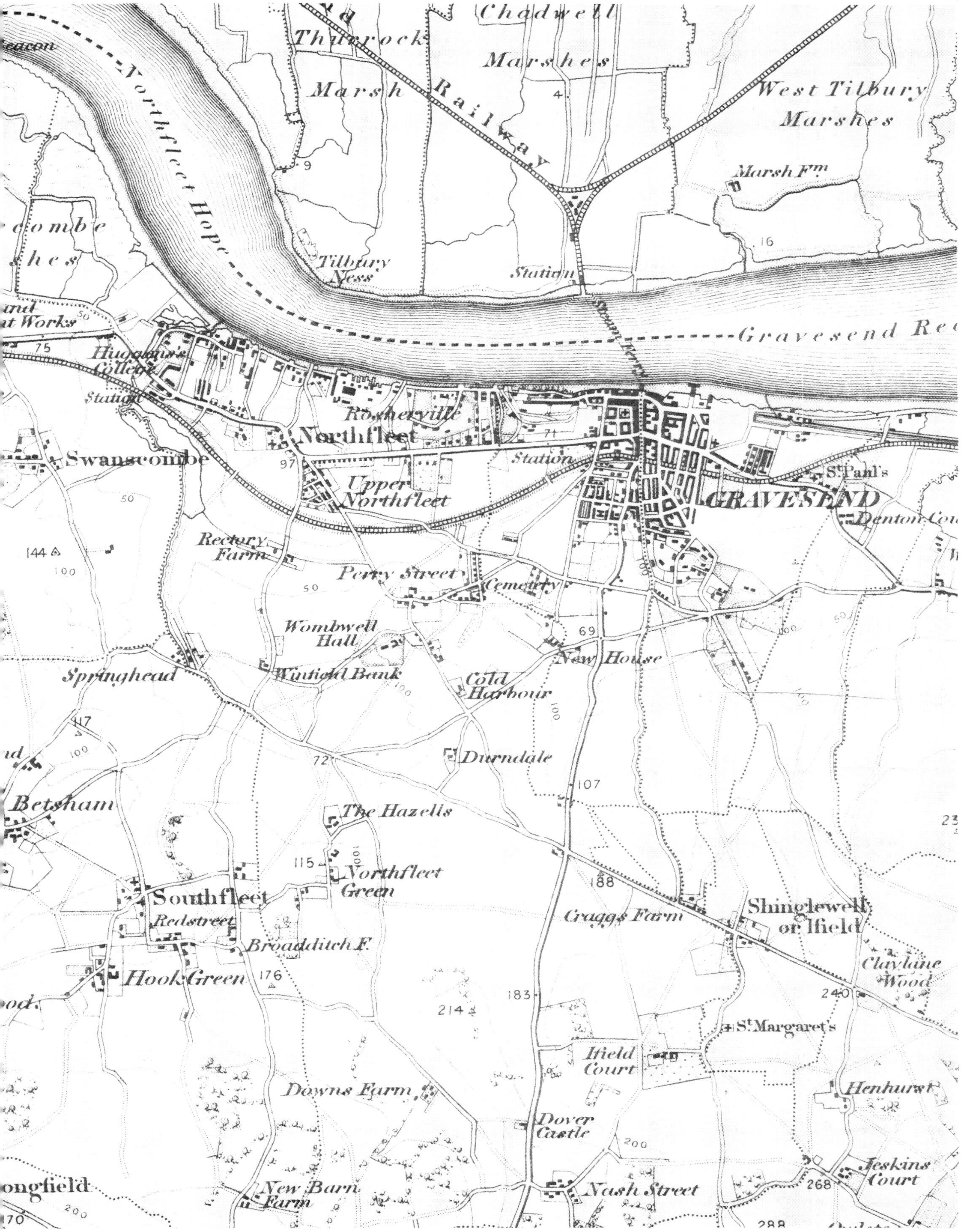
115
Chadwell
Thurrock
Marshes
Marsh
Railway
West Tilbury
Marshes
Marsh Fm.
Northfleet Hope
Tilbury Ness
Station
Gravesend Reach
Huggens's College
Station
Rosherville
Northfleet
Swanscombe
Station
Upper Northfleet
St. Paul's
GRAVESEND
Denton Court
Rectory Farm
Perry Street
Cemetery
Wombwell Hall
New House
Springhead
Wingfield Bank
Cold Harbour
Durndale
Betsham
The Hazells
Northfleet Green
Southfleet
Redstreet
Broadditch F.
Hook Green
Craggs Farm
Shinglewell or Ifield
Claylane Wood
St. Margaret's
Ifield Court
Downs Farm
Henhurst
Dover Castle
Jeskins Court
New Barn Farm
Nash Street

Surveyed 1866-1868. Published 1876

116

147

Dartford Marshes
Reach
RIVER
Marsh
Hospital
River Darent
Joyce Green
Temple Fm
Stone Marshes
Stone Ness
Lighthouse
Pier
Littlebrook Farm
Cotton Fm
Priory Works
Paper Mill
Greenhithe
Branch
Stone
S. E. & C. R.
DARTFORD
Horns Cross
Inn
Barnesfield
Lunatic Asylum
Smithy
Stone Castle
Cem.
Female Penitentiary
Woodlands
WATLING STREET
Cranford Lodge
Imbecile Asylum & Schools
The Downs
Powder Mills
Kingsfield
Gore Fm
Darenth Wood
Gore Fm Hospital
Bean
Wilmington
Shire Hall
Hawley
Mill
Grange
Lane End
Lord's Wood
Darenth
Ch.
Sutton Place
Remains of ROMAN VILLA
Green Street Green
Clement Street
St Johns
St Margarets
Sutton at Hone
South Darenth
Gill's Farm
Swanley
Smithy
FARNINGHAM ROAD STA.
Eastern
Chatham
Boy's Home
Tweed Hill

1 2

1 mile approx.

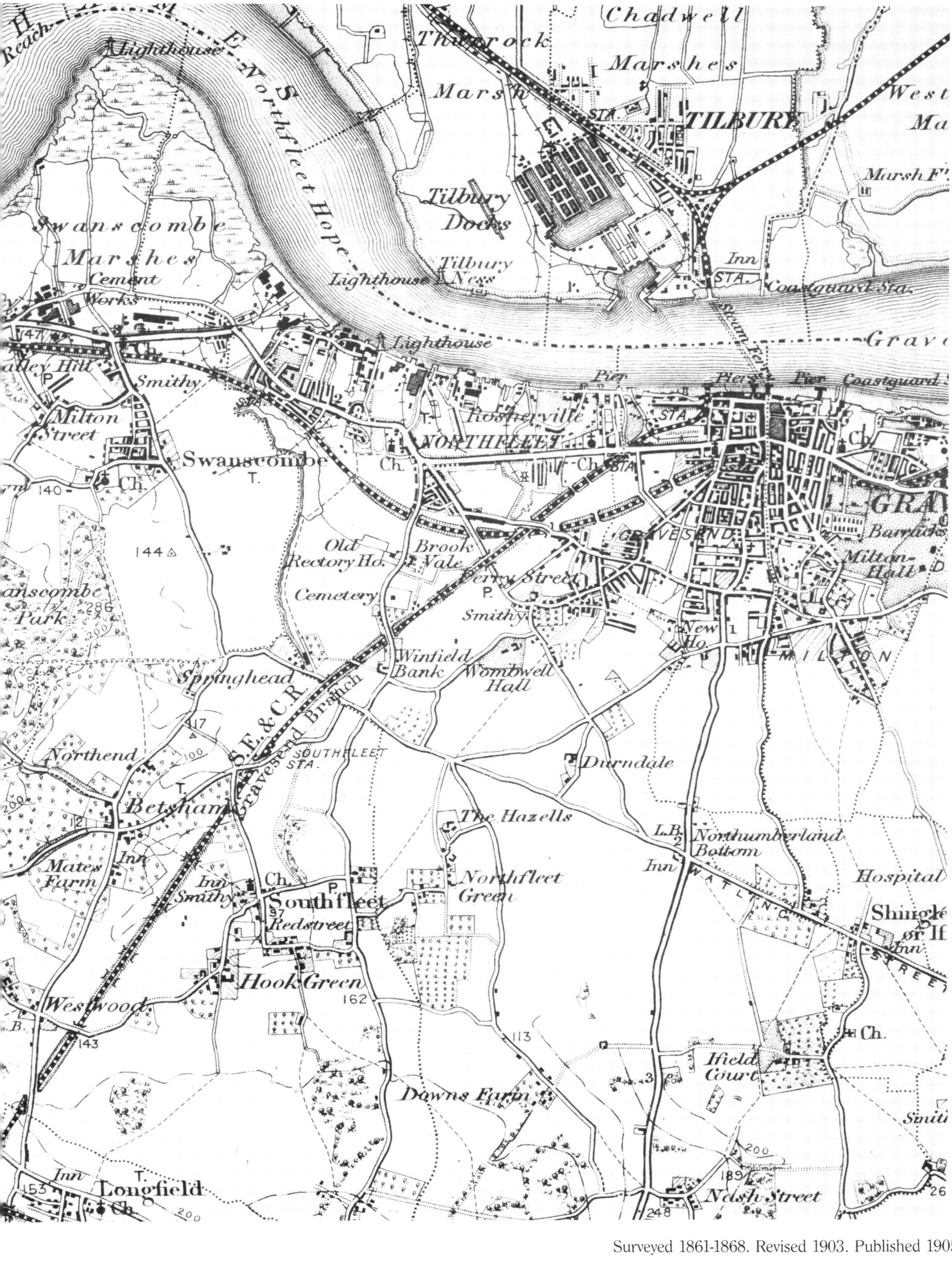

Surveyed 1861-1868. Revised 1903. Published 1905.

△
124

Trottsworth
Sunton Heath
Thorpe Gr.
Mill
Wentworth
Worlds End
Trumps Mill
Potnall
Trumps Green
Potnall Warren
Crayford Fm
Bullock Grove
Lyne Green
Knowle Hill
Knowle Grove
Trumps' F.
Lyne Grove
Golden Grove
Stony
Fan Grove
Harwich Court F.
Three Barrow Hills
Try Lodge
Sedge Pond
Flutters Hill
Andrew New Gr.
Long Cross
Pond
Flutters Hill
Chitdown
Fox Hills
Botleys
Botley's Park
White Beech Hill
Staples Hill
Glovers Ponds
Gracious Pond
Potters Park
Otter
Marlake
Honish
Brooks F.
Burrow Hill
Timber Hill
New House F.
Fernhill
Stanners Hill
Otershaw
Chobham Park
Park
Stanners Grove
Fowlers Well
Dolleys F.
Chobham
Emmets Mill
Mill
Durnford Br.
Annensley F.
Sandpit Hill
Brook
Bourn
Pond F.
Milford Green
Coxhill Ho.
Straught
Castle Grove
Millbrook
Youngs F.
Coxhill Green
Woodham
Heath
Deeppool
Homebush

1 2

1 mile approx.

△
125

160▷

Published 1816.

△
126

1 2

1 mile approx.

△
127

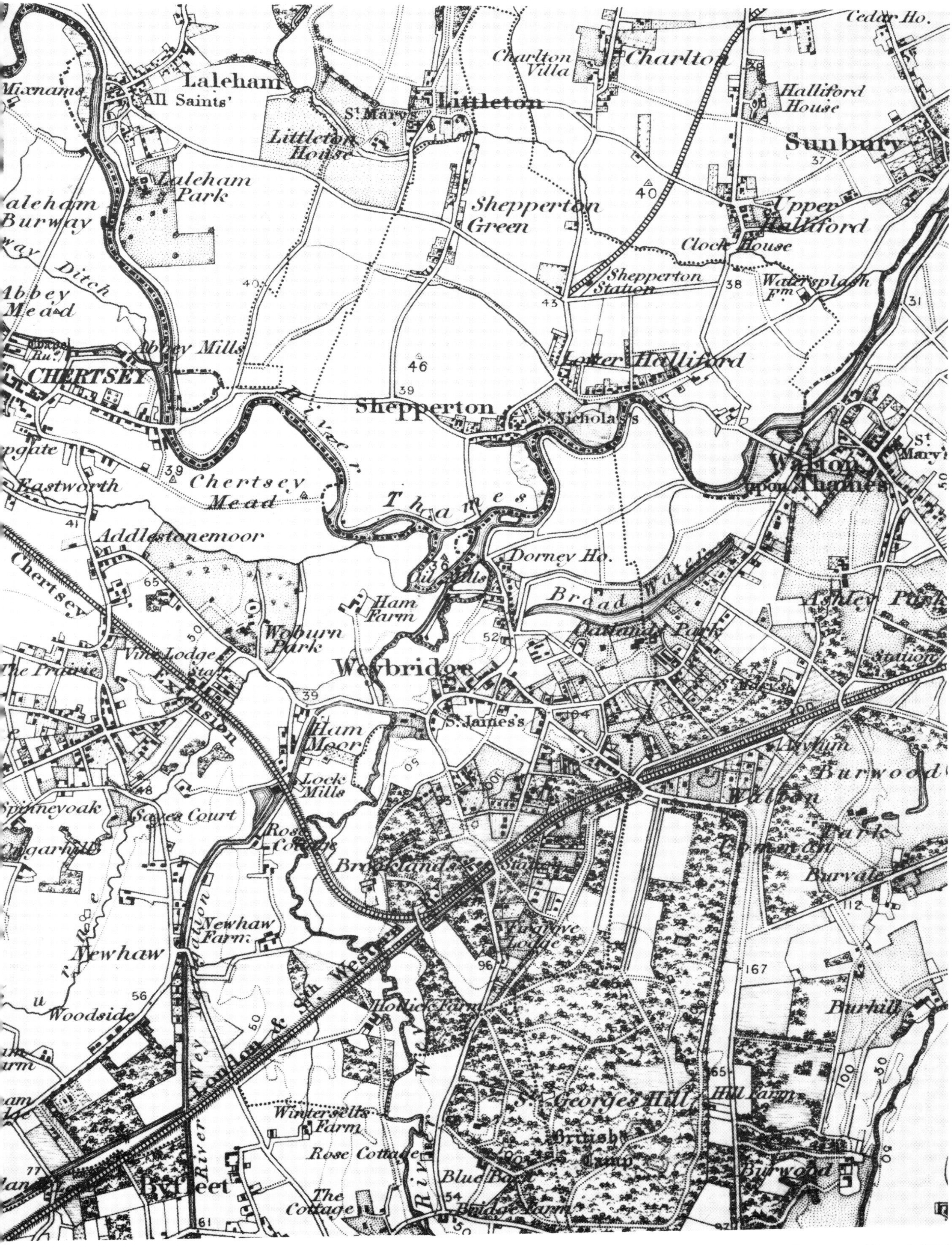

Surveyed 1874. Published 1880.

162 ▷

△
128

Thorpe
Stroude
St. Ann's Heath Sanatorium
VIRGINIA WATER STA.
Wentworth
Knowlehill
Trumpsgreen
Trumps Farm
Lyne
Chertsey Common
Hersham Farm
Barrowhills
The Vicarage
Flutters Hill
The Homestead
Foxhills
Albury Bottom
Chobham
Ottershaw
Queenwood
Stonehill
Stanners Hill
Stannershill Farm
Otershaw Park
Brox
Rodwell's Farm
Chobham Park
Stanyards Farm
Dolley's Farm
Brooklands
Dunford Br.
Mill
Bonsey's Farm
Scotchers Farm
Dunford Farm
Botleys
Botleys Park
Church Farm
Sandgates
Lyne
The Hollies
Pyrcroft
Smithy
Inn
Mill
St. Ann's Hill
Gallowhill
Glenridge
Childown Hall
Burrishot
Lukingshaw Farm
Gracious Pond Farm
Butts Hill
North Bourne
France Farm
Langcross Ho.
Home Farm
Portnall Park
Warren F.

1 2
1 mile approx.

△ 129

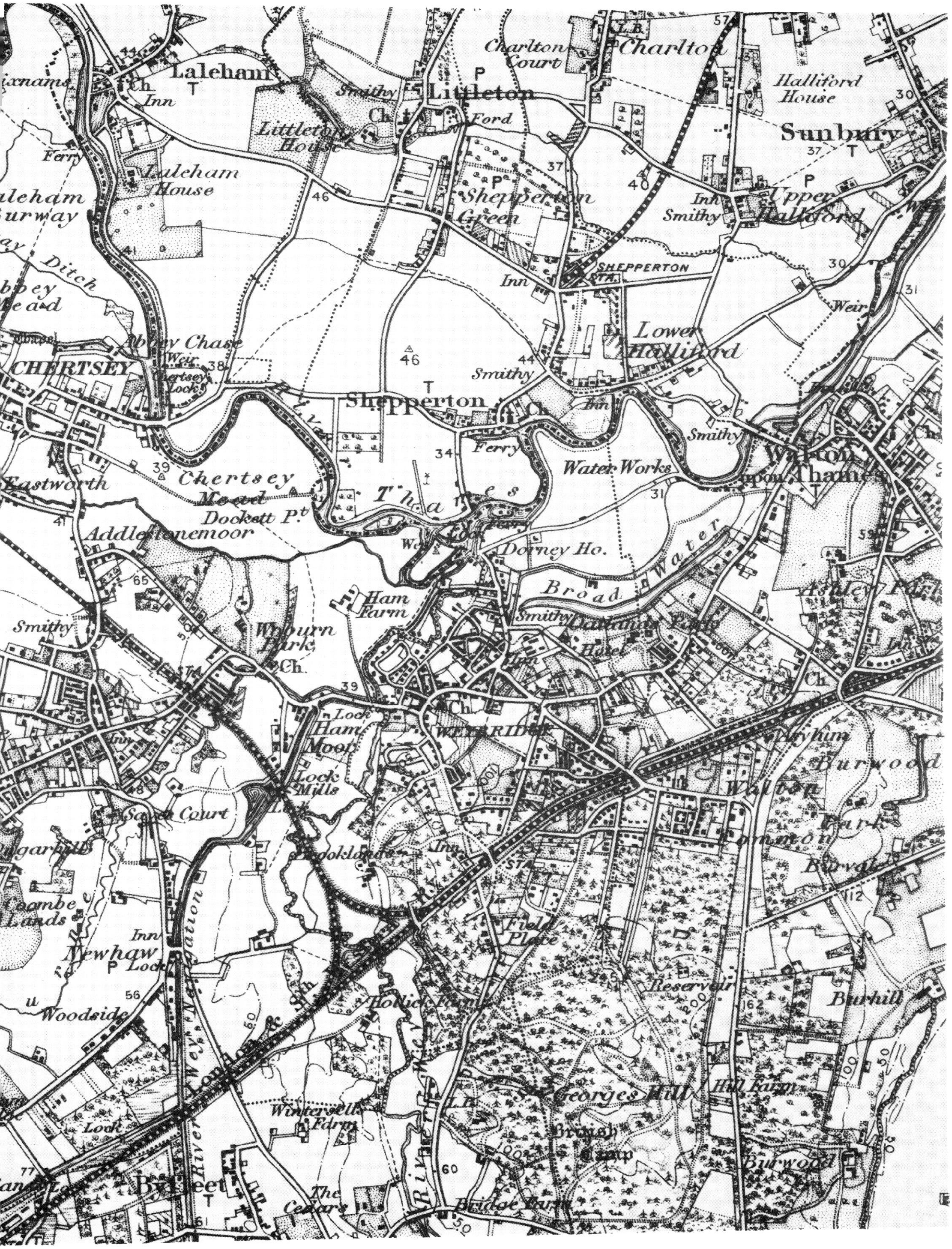

164 ▷

Surveyed 1863-1874. Revised 1901-1902. Published 1904.

△
130

◁155

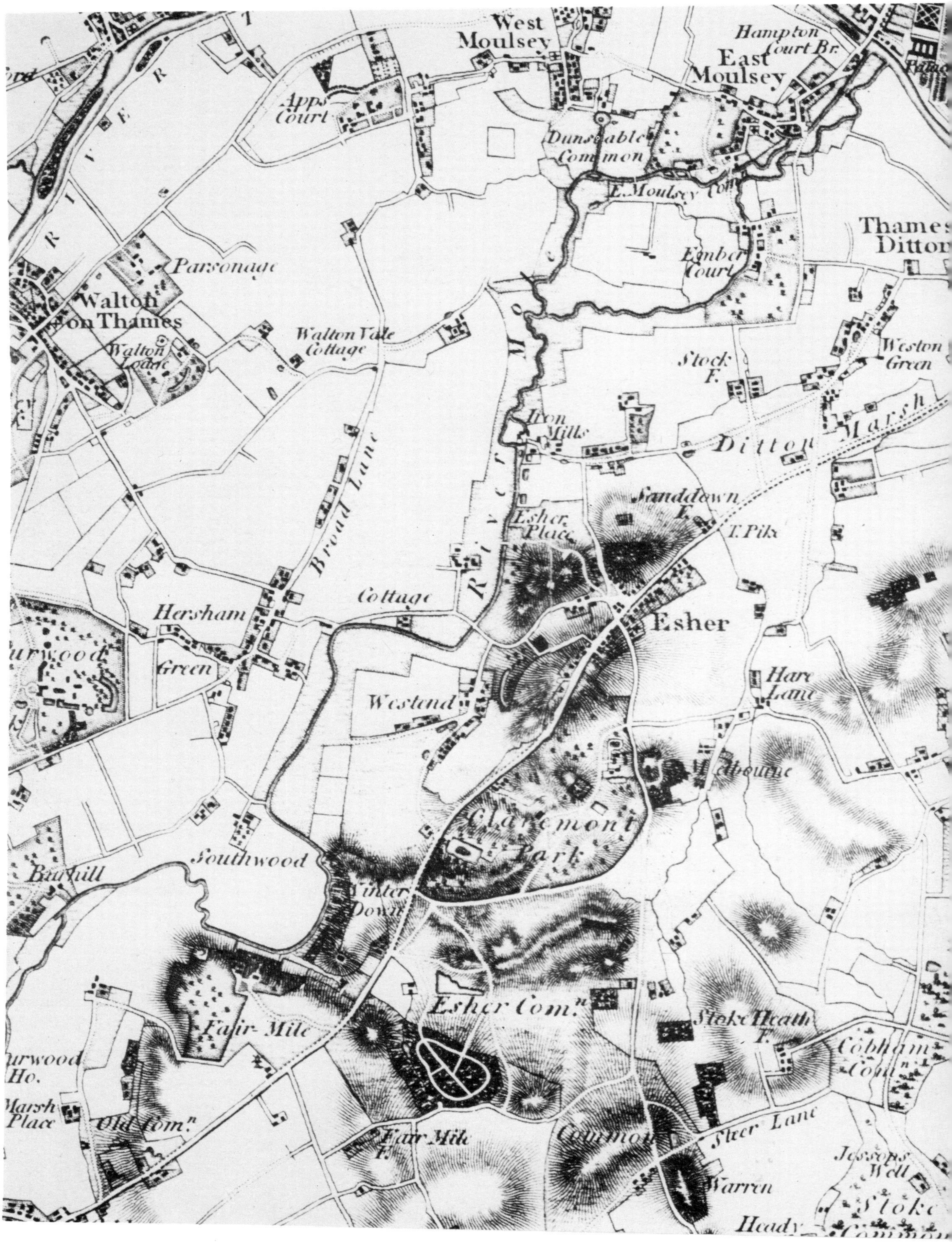
West Moulsey
East Moulsey
Hampton Court Br.
Apps Court
Dunseable Common
E. Moulsey Com.
Ember Court
Thames Ditton
River
Parsonage
Walton on Thames
Walton Lodge
Walton Vale Cottage
Weston Green
Stock F.
Iron Mills
Ditton Marsh
Broad Lane
Sanddown F.
T. Pike
Esher Place
River Mole
Cottage
Hersham
Esher
Green
Hare Lane
Westend
Claremont Park
Southwood
Burhill
Winter Down
Esher Com.n
Stoke Heath F.
Fair-Mile
Cobham Com.n
Marsh Place
Old Com.n
Fair Mile F.
Common
Slcer Lane
Jessops Well
Warren
Heady
Stoke

1 2
1 mile approx.

178
▽

△
131

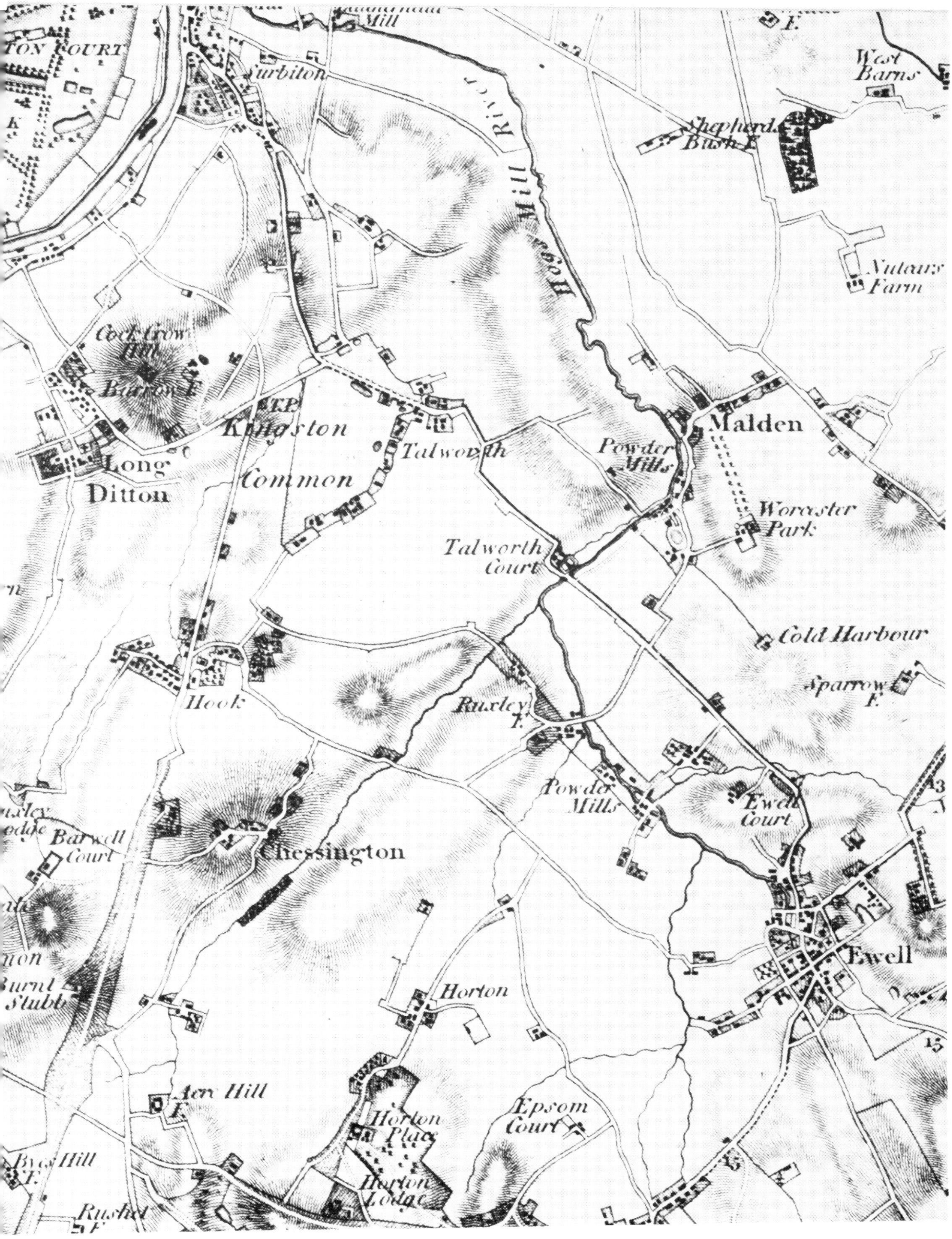

166 ▷

179
▽

Published 1819.

Mill
Surbiton
West
Barns
River
Hogs Mill
Shepherds
Bush F.
Nutcurs
Farm
Cock Crow
Hill
Barrow F.
T.P.
Kingston
Common
Malden
Talworth
Long
Ditton
Powder
Mills
Worcester
Park
Talworth
Court
Cold Harbour
Sparrow
F.
Hook
Ruxley
F.
Powder
Mills
Ewell
Court
Barwell
Court
Chessington
Ewell
Burnt
Stubb
Horton
Acr Hill
F.
Epsom
Court
Horton
Place
Horton
Lodge

△ 132

◁157

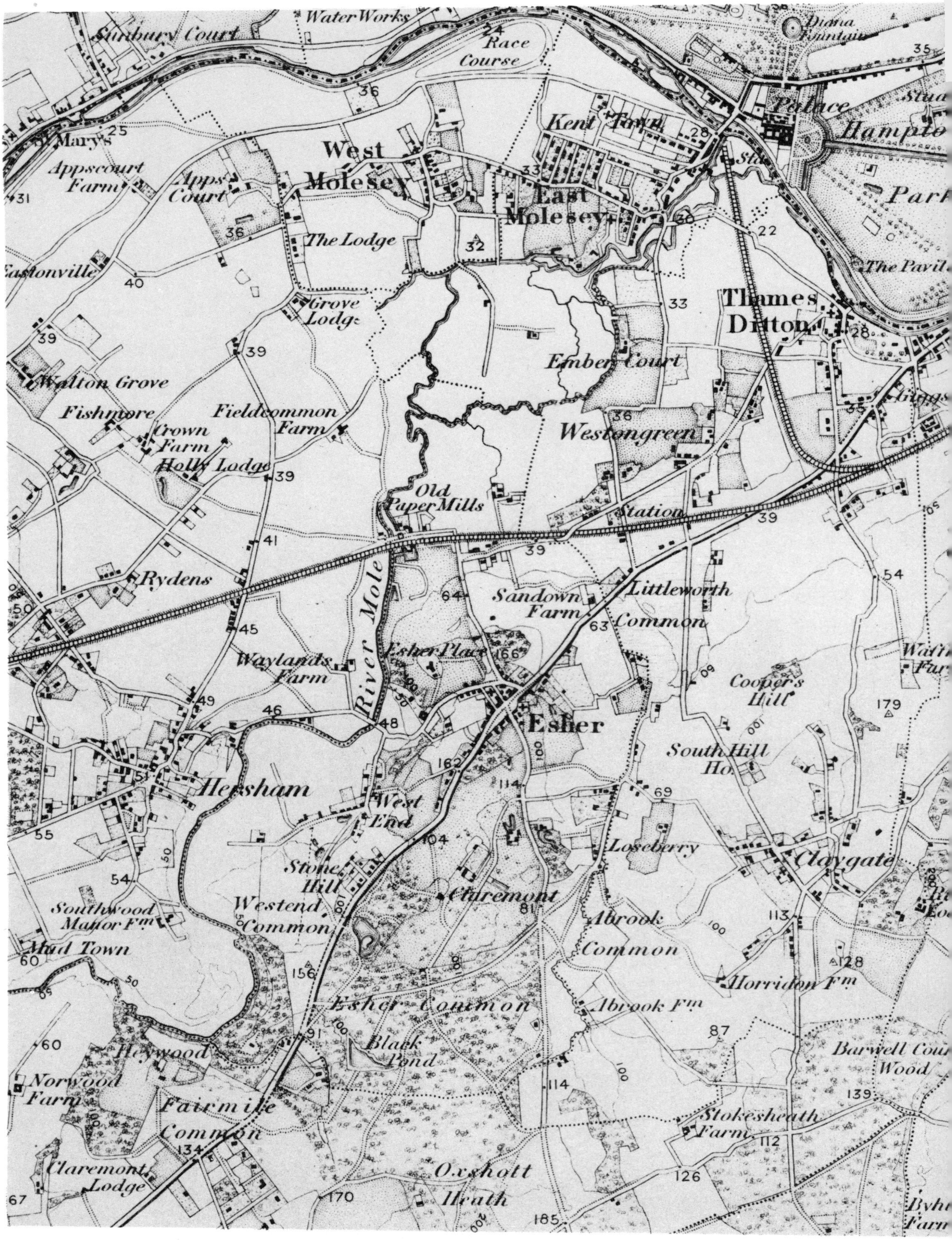
Water Works
Sunbury Court
Race Course
Diana Fountain
St. Mary's
Appscourt Farm
Apps Court
West Molesey
Kent Town
East Molesey
Palace
Hampton
Park
The Lodge
The Pavilion
Eastonville
Grove Lodge
Thames Ditton
Walton Grove
Ember Court
Fishmore
Fieldcommon Farm
Crown Farm
Holly Lodge
Westongreen
Old Paper Mills
Station
Rydens
Sandown Farm
Littleworth Common
River Mole
Esher Place
Waylands Farm
Cooper's Hill
Esher
South Hill Ho
Hersham
West End
Loseberry
Claygate
Stone Hill
Claremont
Westend Common
Southwood Manor Fm
Abrook Common
Mud Town
Horridon Fm
Esher Common
Abrook Fm
Black Pond
Heywood
Barwell Court Wood
Norwood Farm
Fairmile Common
Stokesheath Farm
Claremont Lodge
Oxshott Heath

1 2

1 mile approx.

180 ▽

△ 133

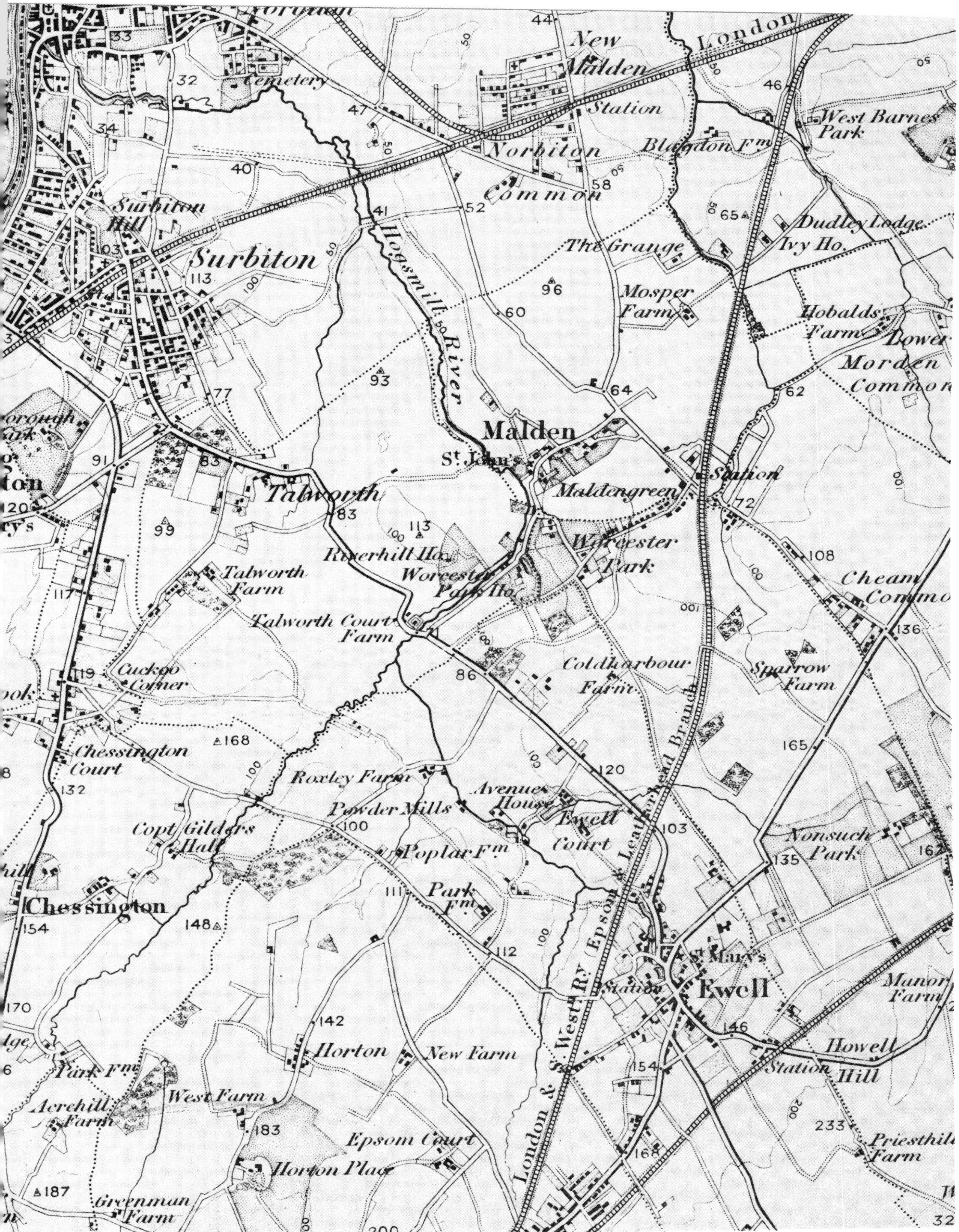
New Malden
London
Station
West Barnes Park
Norbiton
Blagdon Fm
Common
Cemetery
Surbiton Hill
Surbiton
Dudley Lodge
Ivy Ho.
The Grange
Mosper Farm
Hogsmill River
Hobalds Farm
Lower Morden Common
Malden
St John's
Station
Maldengreen
Talworth
Riverhill Ho.
Worcester Park
Worcester Park Ho.
Talworth Farm
Talworth Court Farm
Cheam Common
Cuckoo Corner
Coldharbour Farm
Sparrow Farm
Chessington Court
Roxley Farm
Avenue House
Powder Mills
Ewell Court
Copt Gilders Hall
Poplar Fm
Nonsuch Park
Chessington
Park Fm
Epsom & Leatherhead Branch
St Mary's
Station
Ewell
Manor Farm
Horton
New Farm
Howell Hill
Station
Park Fm
West Farm
Acrehill Farm
Epsom Court
Priesthill Farm
Horton Place
Greenman Farm
London & S. West Ry

168 ▷

181 ▽

Surveyed 1861-1868. Published 1876.

129/134

159

Sunbury Court
Water Works
Hurst Park
Ferry
Barracks
Diana Fountain
Smithy
Palace
Reservoirs
Kent Town
Molesey Lock
Sunbury Lock
West Molesey
East Molesey
The Lodge
Grove Lodge
Thames Ditton
Ember Court
River Ember
Walton Grove
Fieldcommon Farm
Holly Lodge
Weston Green
Old Paper Mills
Lowergreen
Rydens
Sandown Park
Littleworth Common
Palace
River Mole
Waylands Farm
Cooper's Hill
Golf Course
Esher
South Hill Ho
Hersham
West End
Claremont
Westend Common
Arbrook Common
Mud Town
Esher Common
Black Pond
Heywood
Fairmile Common
Stokesheath Farm
Prince's Coverts
Claremont Lodge
Oxshott Heath
Fairmile
Claygate
1 2
1 mile approx.

182

△ 135

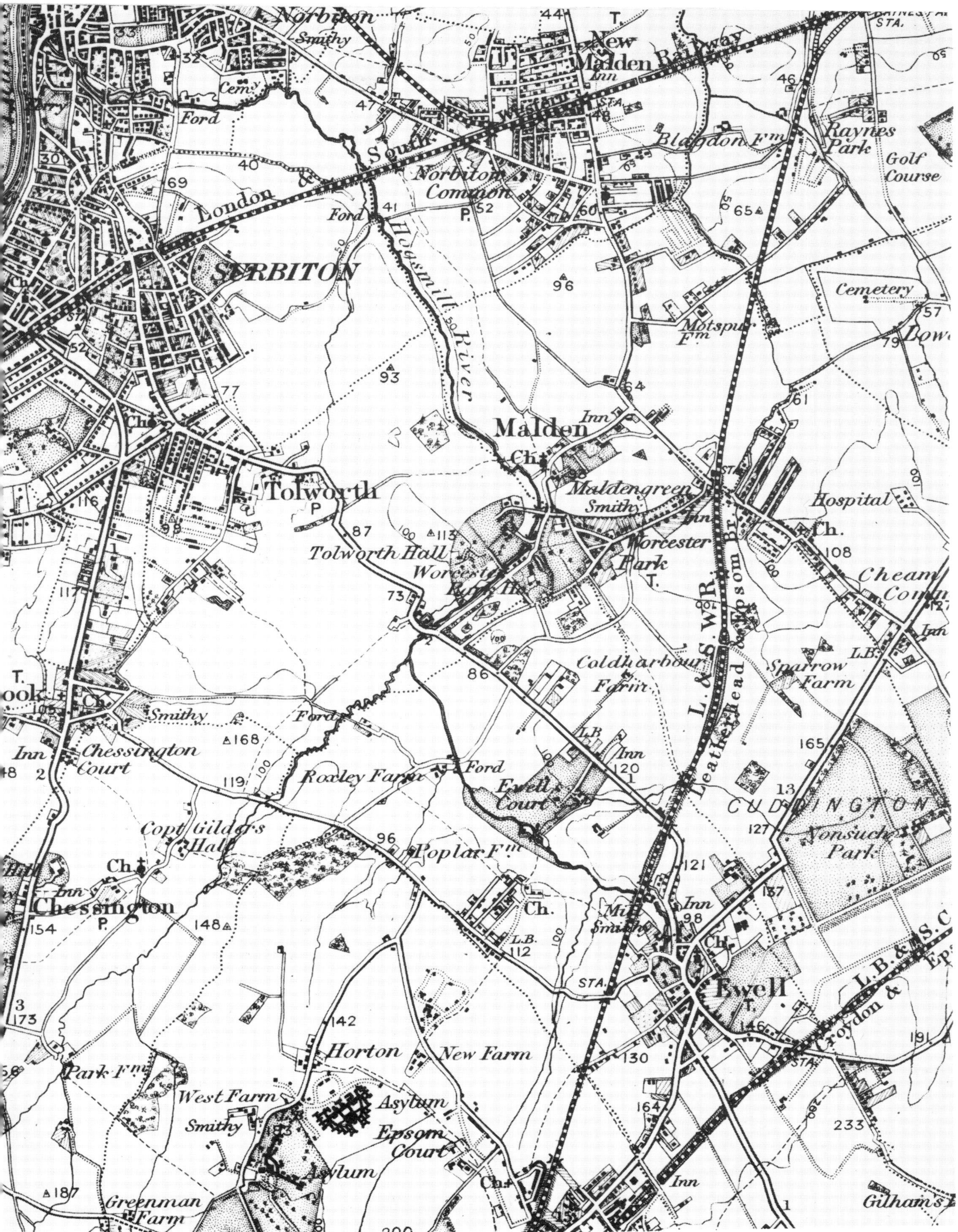

170 ▷

183 ▽

Surveyed 1861-1868. Revised 1903. Published 1905.

△
135/136

◁161

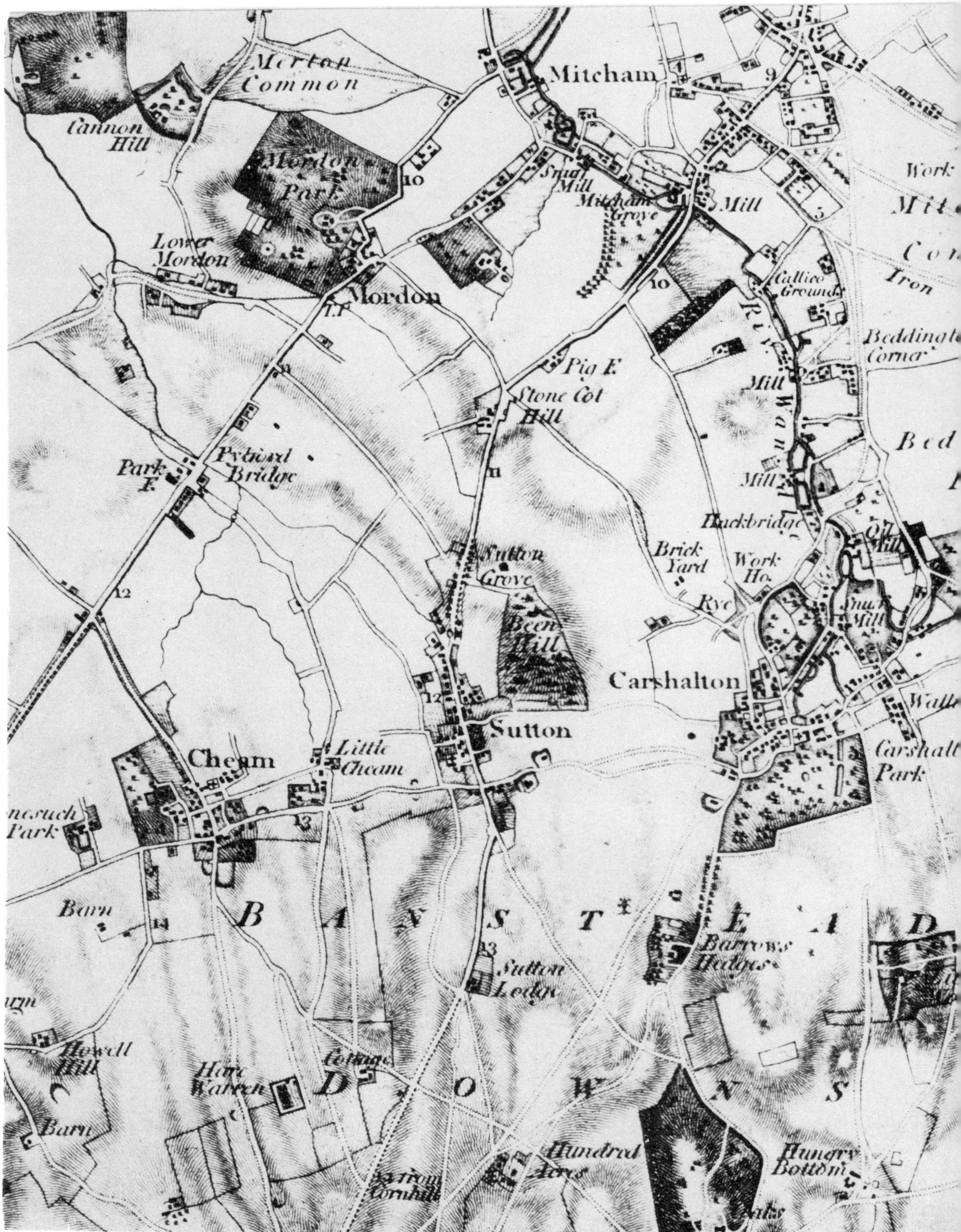
Merton Common
Mitcham
Cannon Hill
Mordon Park
Snuff Mill
Mitcham Grove
Mill
Work
Lower Mordon
Mordon
Callico Ground
Iron
Bedding Corner
Pig F.
Stone Cot Hill
Mill
Mill
Park F.
Pybird Bridge
Hackbridge
Brick Yard
Work Ho.
Sutton Grove
Ryc
Snuff Mill
Been Hill
Carshalton
Sutton
Cheam
Little Cheam
Carshalt Park
Park
Barn
B A N S T E A D
Barrows Hedges
Sutton Lodge
Howell Hill
Hare Warren
Cottage
D O W N S
Barn
Hundred Acres
Hungry Bottom

184
▽

1 2
1 mile approx.

△ 137

Bottom
Fernham Wood
Parch moor
Whitehouse Wood
Colliers Water
White Ho. F.
Gilpens F.
Thornton Heath
Selhurst
Selhurst Wood
Goat Ho.
Blind Corner
Clay Lane
9 Acre Wood
Woodside
18 Acre Wood
Croydon Common
Broad Green
Common Place
Barracks
Addiscombe House
Shirley
Bleaching M.
Flour M.
Snuff M.
CROYDON
Park Hill
Waddon Court
Waddon
Dubber Hill
Combe F.
Combe Lane
Combe House
Cold Harbour
Havling House
Crome F.
Ballards
Combe Hill
Beggars Bush
Purley F.
Purley Ho.
Bottom to Reed Way
Selsdon
T.P.
Sanderstead

172 ▷

185 ▽

Published 1819.

△ 133/138

◁ 163

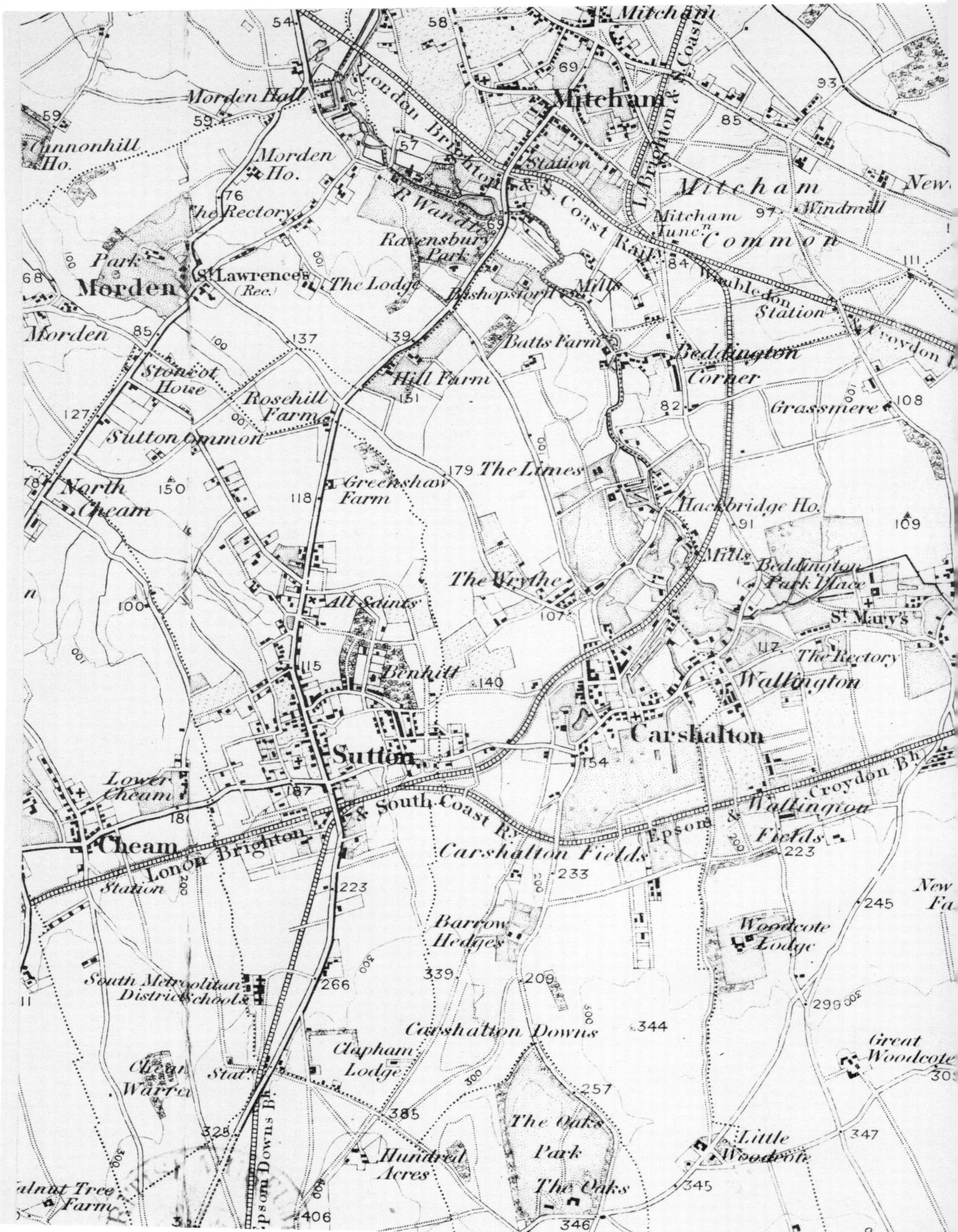
Mitcham
Mitcham
London Brighton
L. Brighton & S. Coast
Morden Hall
Morden Ho.
The Rectory
Park
Morden
St Lawrence
(Rec.)
The Lodge
Ravensbury Park
R. Wandle
Station
Mitcham Common
Mitcham Junc.n
Windmill
Wimbledon Station
Croydon
Mills
Bishopsford
Batts Farm
Beddington Corner
Grassmere
Hill Farm
Stoncot House
Rosehill Farm
Sutton Common
North Cheam
Greenshaw Farm
The Limes
Hackbridge Ho.
Mills
Beddington Park Place
The Wrythe
All Saints
St Mary's
The Rectory
Wallington
Benhill
Carshalton
Sutton
Lower Cheam
Cheam
& South Coast Ry.
London Brighton
Station
Carshalton Fields
Epsom & Wallington
Croydon
Fields
Barrow Hedges
Woodcote Lodge
South Metropolitan District Schools
Carshalton Downs
Great Woodcote
Clapham Lodge
Stat.
Cheam Warren
The Oaks Park
The Oaks
Hundred Acres
Little Woodcote
Walnut Tree Farm
Epsom Downs

186 ▽

1 mile approx.

139

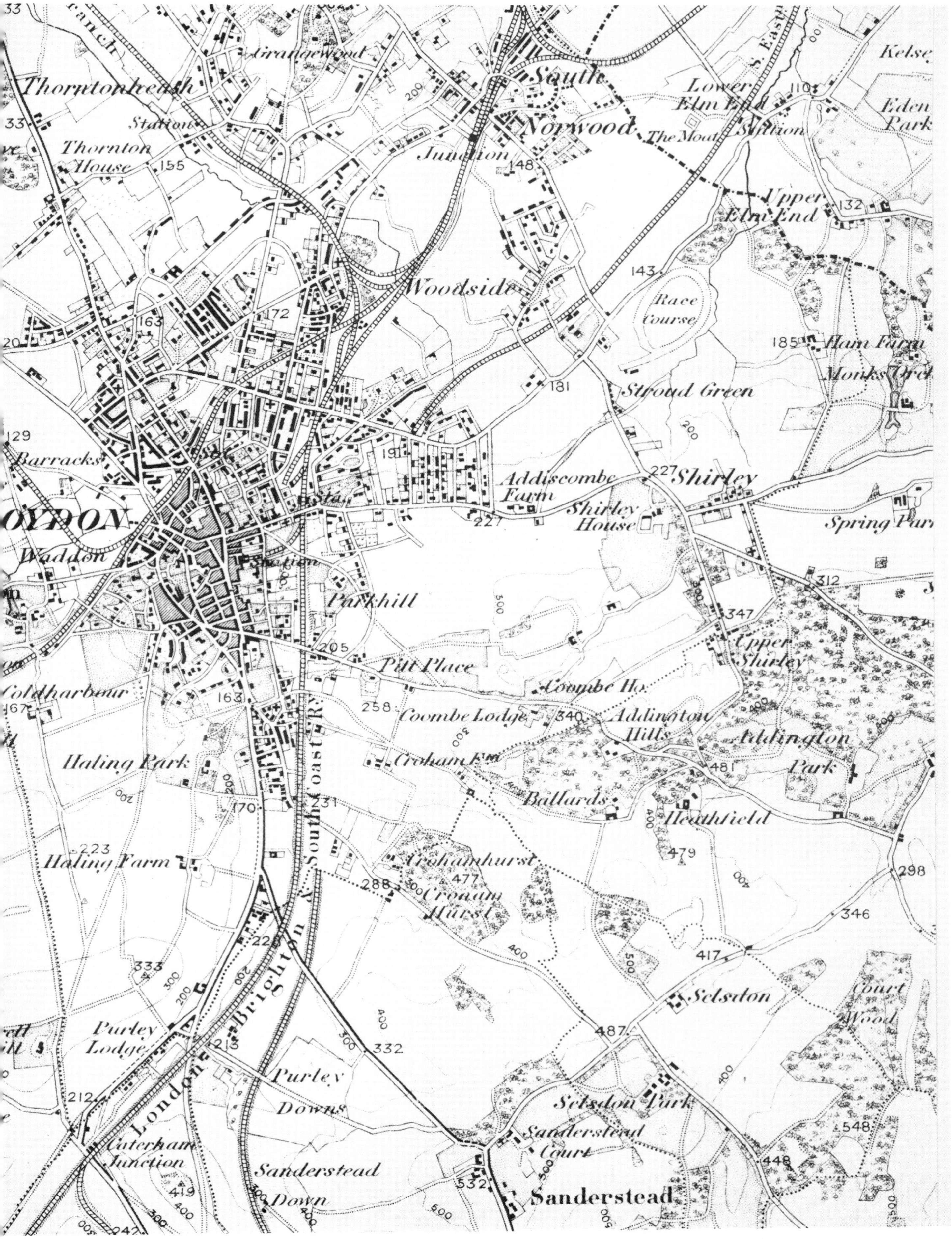
Thorntonheath
Station
Thornton House
South Norwood
Junction
Lower Elm End
Station
The Moat
Kelsey
Eden Park
Upper Elm End
Woodside
Race Course
Ham Farm
Monks Orch
Stroud Green
Barracks
Addiscombe Farm
Shirley
Shirley House
Spring Park
Waddon
Station
Parkhill
Upper Shirley
Pitt Place
Coombe Ho.
Coldharbour
Coombe Lodge
Addington Hills
Addington Park
Haling Park
Croham Fm
Ballards
Heathfield
South Coast Ry
Haling Farm
Crohamhurst
Croham Hurst
Brighton
London
Selsdon
Court Wood
Purley Lodge
Purley Downs
Selsdon Park
Caterham Junction
Sanderstead Court
Sanderstead
Sanderstead Down

174

187

Surveyed 1861-1868. Published 1876.

135/140

165

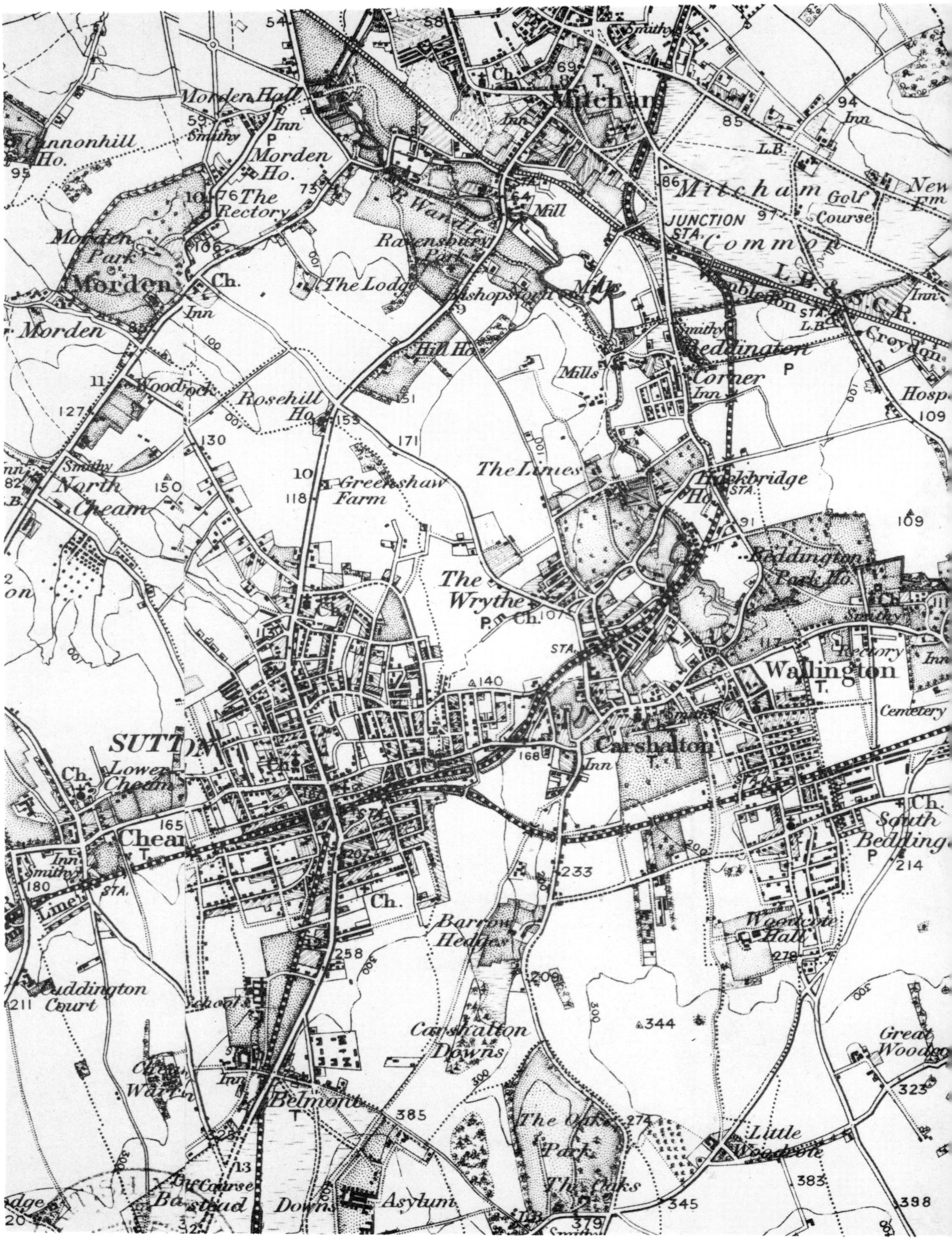

Morden Hall
Cannonhill Ho.
Morden Ho.
The Rectory
Morden Park
Morden
Mitcham
Mitcham Common
Mitcham Golf Course
Junction Sta.
R. Wandle
Ravensbury Park
The Lodge
Bishopsford
Mills
Hill Ho.
Beddington Corner
Croydon
Woodcock
Rosehill Ho.
North Cheam
Greenshaw Farm
The Limes
Hackbridge Ho.
Beddington Park Ho.
The Wrythe
Wallington
Rectory
Cemetery
SUTTON
Lower Cheam
Cheam
Carshalton
South Beddington
Barrow Hedges
Woodcote Hall
Cuddington Court
Carshalton Downs
Great Woodcote
Belmont
Little Woodcote
The Oaks Park
The Oaks
Banstead Downs
Asylum
Race Course

188

1 2
1 mile approx.

Thorntonh

Kelse
Elmers End
Eden Park

South Norwood

Cemetery
STA.

131

158

Ch. Cemy.

164

SELHURST STA.

168

L.B.

Ch.

Woodside

133

STA.

135

Ch.

162

Golf Course

Inn
178

Stroud Green

218

Monks

STA.

Shirley
216

240

Shirley House
242

Inn

Ch.

Spring Par

300

Tunnel

Old Windmill

330

Spath

347

Upper Shirle

243

342

Combe

326

Coombe Lodge

Addington Hills

Addington Park

Inn

Haddon

Coldharbour

177

Haling Park

Ballards

Heathfield

179

200

223

Croham hurst
471

Croham Hurst

346

400

417

Selsdon

Court Wood

SANDERSTEAD STA.

PURLEY OAKS STA.

300

400

187
L.B.

Purley Lodge

Schools

224

249

Purley Downs
366

Selsdon Park

372

495

518

Sanderstead Court

STA.

Purley
T

Sanderstead Down

532

Sanderstead
P.O.

419

300

400

500

Surveyed 1861-1868. Revised 1903. Published 1905.

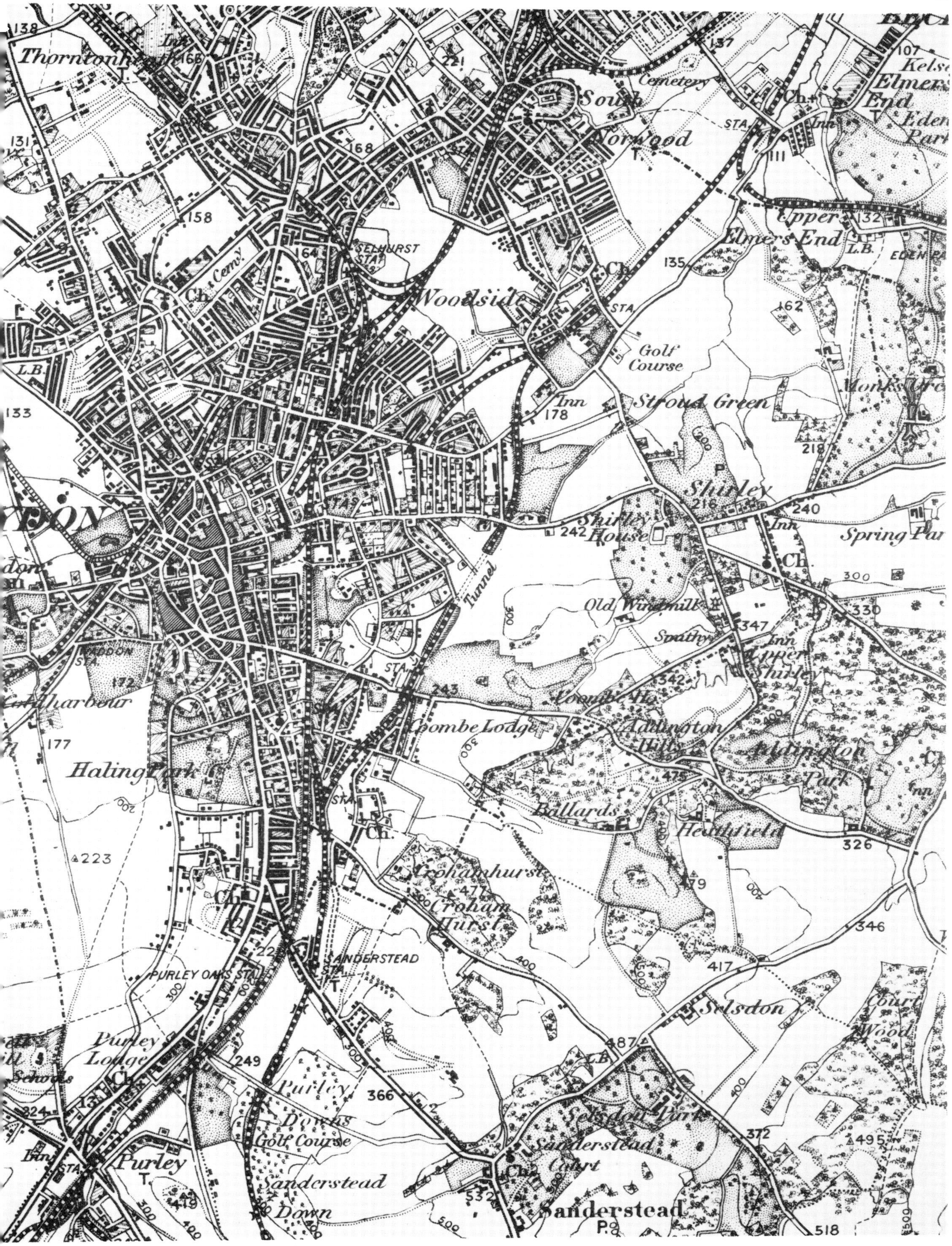

△
142

◁167

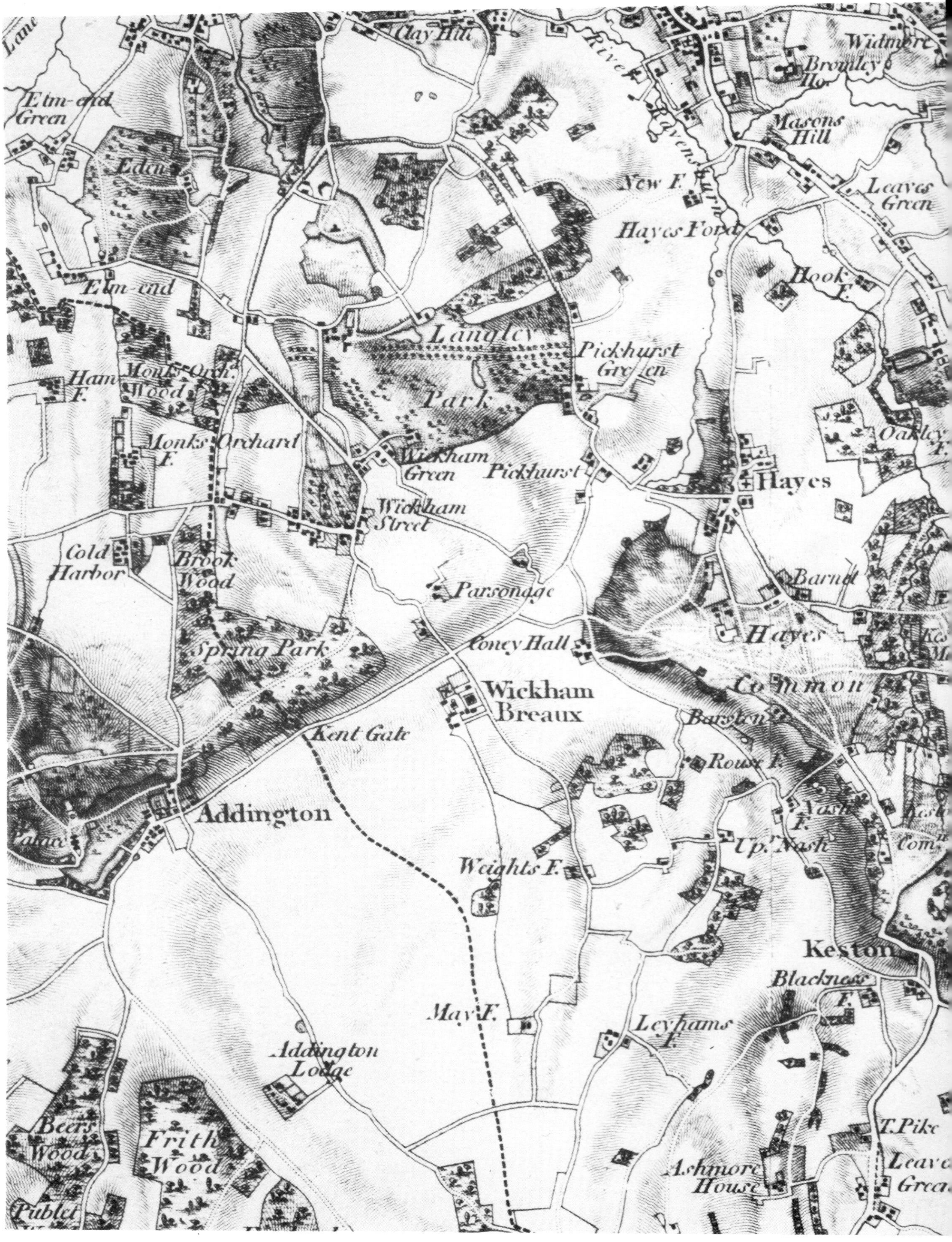
Clay Hill
River Ravensburn
Widmore
Bromley Ho.
Elm-end Green
Eden
Masons Hill
New F.
Leaves Green
Hayes Ford
Hook F.
Elm-end
Langley
Pickhurst Green
Ham F.
Monks Orch. Wood
Park
Oakley F.
Monks Orchard F.
Wickham Green
Pickhurst
Hayes
Wickham Street
Cold Harbor
Brook Wood
Barnet
Parsonage
Hayes
Spring Park
Coney Hall
Wickham Breaux
Common
Kent Gate
Barston
Rouse F.
Addington
Nash F.
Up.r Nash
Com.
Weights F.
Keston
Blackness F.
May F.
Leyhams F.
Addington Lodge
T. Pike
Beers Wood
Frith Wood
Ashmore House
Publet

1 2

1 mile approx.

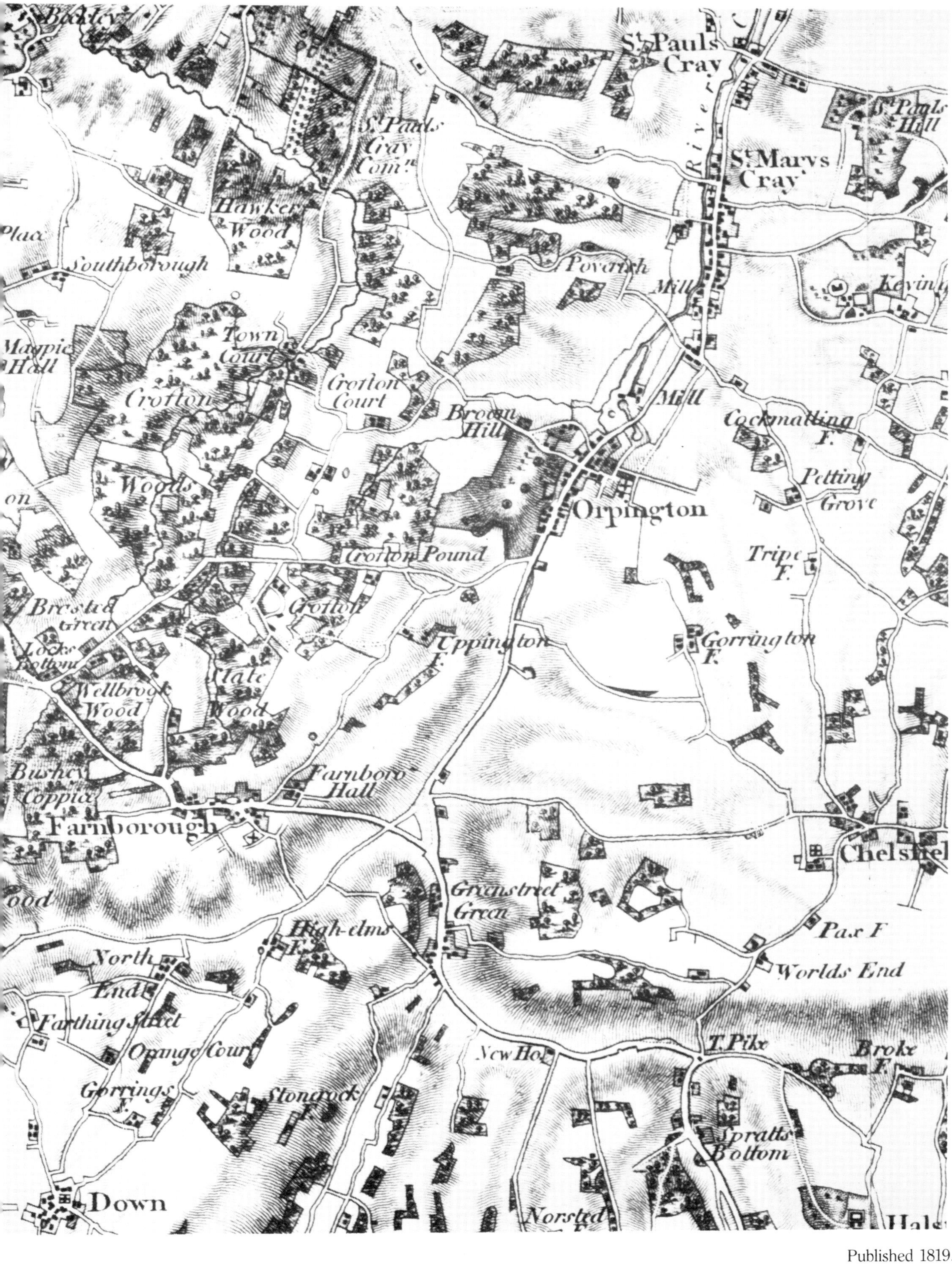
St. Pauls Cray
St. Pauls Hill
River
St. Marys Cray
St. Pauls Cray Com.n
Hawker Wood
Southborough
Poverish
Mill
Town Court
Magpie Hall
Crofton Court
Crofton
Broom Hill
Mill
Cockmalling F.
Petting Grove
Woods
Orpington
Crofton Pound
Tripe F.
Brasted Green
Crofton
Uppington F.
Gorrington F.
Locks Bottom
Wellbrook Wood
Tate Wood
Bushey Coppice
Farnboro' Hall
Farnborough
Greenstreet Green
High-elms
Pax F
North End
Worlds End
Farthing Street
Orange Court
New Ho
T. Pike
Broke F.
Gorrings F.
Stonerock F.
Spratts Bottom
Down
Norsted

Published 1819.

△ 139/144

◁169

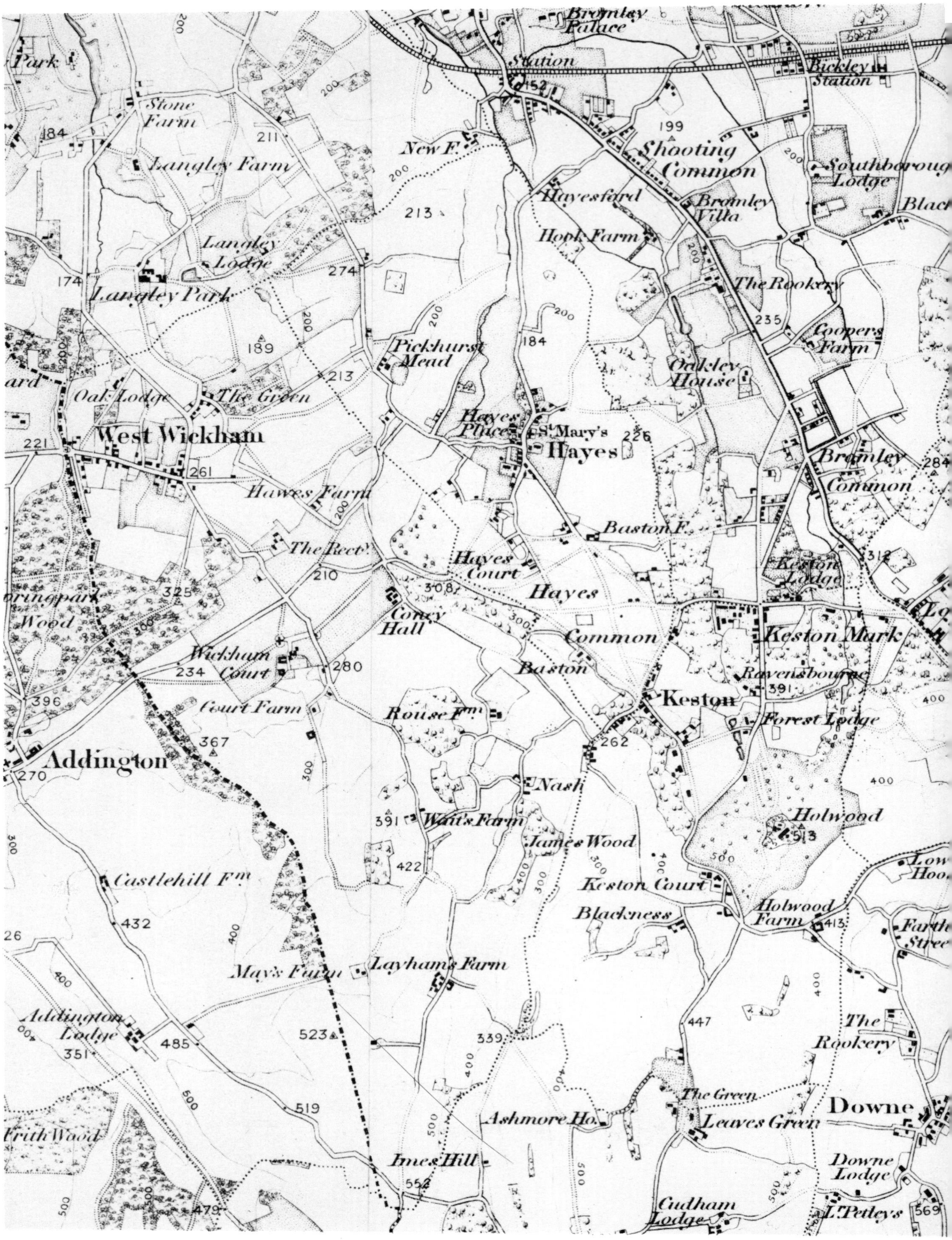

Bromley Palace
Station
Bickley Station
Stone Farm
Langley Farm
New F.
Shooting Common
Southborough Lodge
Hayesford
Bromley Villa
Hook Farm
Langley Lodge
Langley Park
The Rookery
Coopers Farm
Pickhurst Mead
Oakley House
Oak Lodge
The Green
Hayes Place
St. Mary's
Hayes
West Wickham
Bromley Common
Hawes Farm
Baston F.
The Rect.
Hayes Court
Keston Lodge
Springpark Wood
Coney Hall
Hayes Common
Keston Mark
Wickham Court
Baston
Ravensbourne
Keston
Court Farm
Rouse Fm.
Forest Lodge
Addington
Nash
Holwood
Watt's Farm
James Wood
Castlehill Fm.
Keston Court
Blackness
Holwood Farm
May's Farm
Layham's Farm
Addington Lodge
The Rookery
Downe
Ashmore Ho.
The Green
Leaves Green
Frith Wood
Imes Hill
Downe Lodge
Cudham Lodge
L. Petleys

1 2

1 mile approx.

△
145

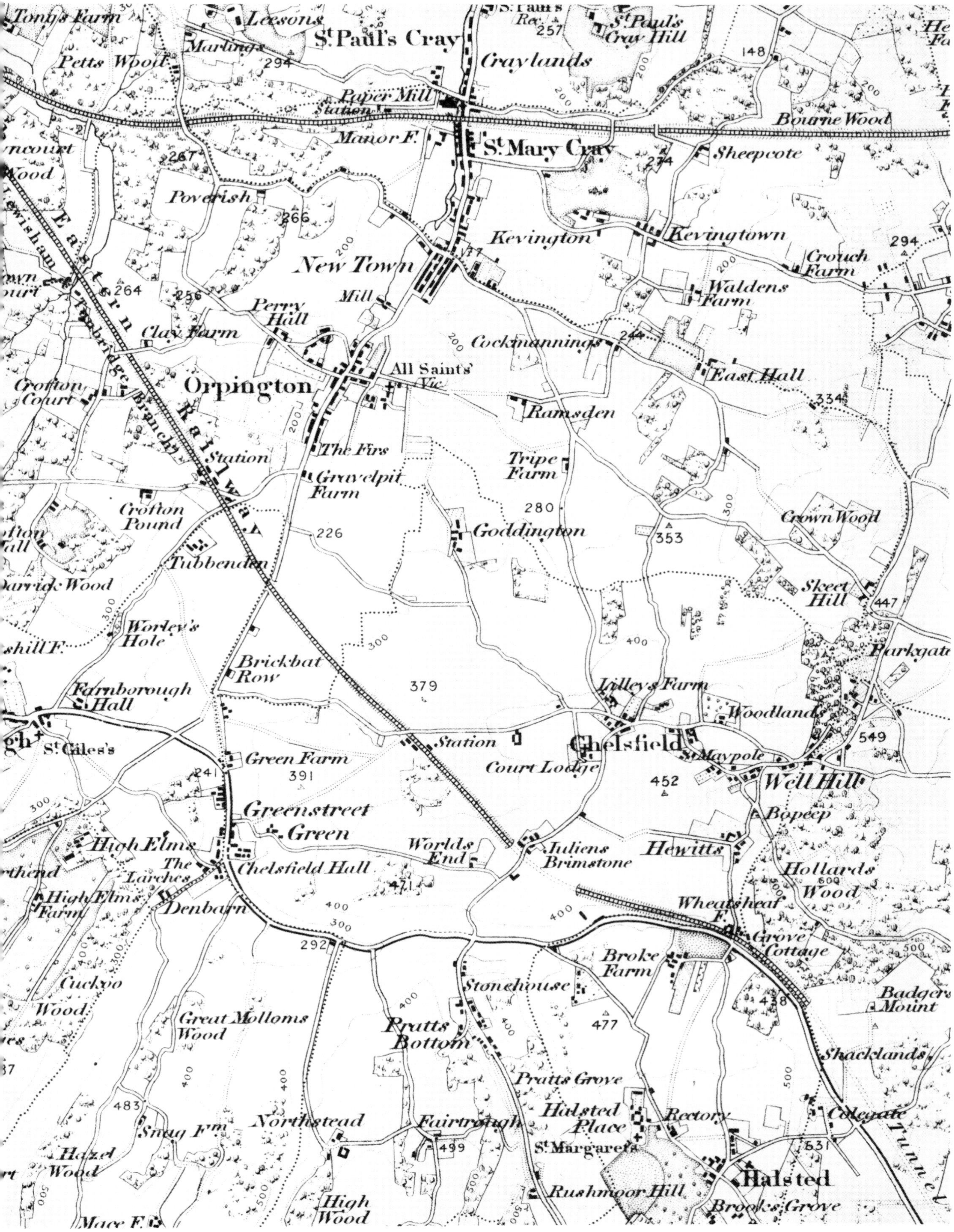
Tong's Farm
Leesons
St. Paul's Cray
St. Paul's Rec.
257
St. Paul's Cray Hill
Marlings
294
Petts Wood
Craylands
148
200
Paper Mill
Station
Bourne Wood
Manor F.
St. Mary Cray
Sheepcote
267
274
Wood
Poverish
266
Kevington
Kevingtown
294
Crouch Farm
New Town
Mill
264
256
Waldens Farm
Perry Hall
Clay Farm
Cockmannings
244
Eastern Railway
Tonbridge Branch
Crofton Court
Orpington
All Saints' Vic.
East Hall
334
Ramsden
The Firs
Station
Tripe Farm
Gravelpit Farm
280
Crofton Pound
Crown Wood
226
Goddington
353
Tubbenden
Skeet Hill
447
Worley's Hole
300
400
Brickbat Row
379
Farnborough Hall
Lilley's Farm
Woodlands
St. Giles's
Station
Chelsfield
Maypole
549
Green Farm
391
Court Lodge
452
Well Hill
241
Greenstreet Green
Bopeep
High Elms
The Larches
Chelsfield Hall
Worlds End
Juliens Brimstone
Hewitts
Hollards Wood
High Elms Farm
471
Denbarn
Wheatsheaf F.
292
Grove Cottage
Broke Farm
Cuckoo Wood
Stonehouse
438
Badgers Mount
Great Molloms Wood
Pratts Bottom
477
Shacklands
Pratts Grove
483
Halsted Place
Rectory
Colegate
Northstead
Fairtrough
Snag Fm.
499
St. Margarets
531
Tunnel
Hazel Wood
Halsted
Rushmoor Hill
High Wood
Brooks Grove
Mace F.
500

Surveyed 1861-1868. Published 1876.

△ 141/146

◁171

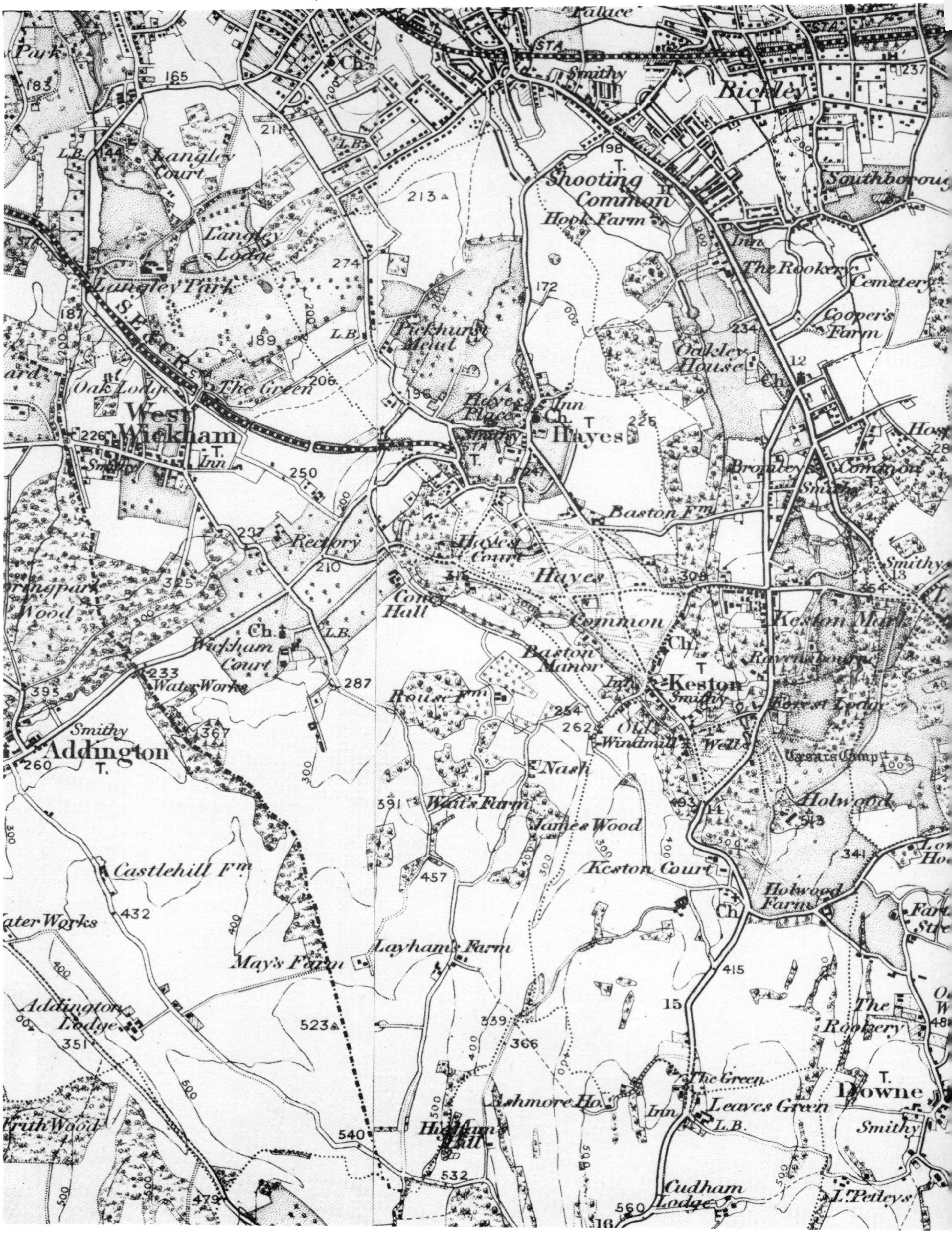

Palace
Smithy
Bickley
Southborough
Langley Court
Langley Lodge
Langley Park
Shooting Common
Hook Farm
The Rookery
Cemetery
Cooper's Farm
Pickhurst Mead
Oakley House
Oak Lodge
The Green
West Wickham
Hayes Place
Hayes
Bromley Common
Baston Fm.
Rectory
Hayes Court
Hayes Common
Keston Mark
Springpark Wood
Coney Hall
Wickham Court
Baston Manor
Keston
Water Works
Rouse Fm.
Forest Lodge
Addington
Old Windmill
Nash
Cæsars Camp
Holwood
Watt's Farm
James Wood
Castlehill Fm.
Keston Court
Holwood Farm
Water Works
Layhams Farm
May's Farm
Addington Lodge
The Rookery
The Green
Downe
Ashmore Ho.
Leaves Green
Smithy
Frith Wood
Cudham Lodge
L. Petleys

1 2

1 mile approx.

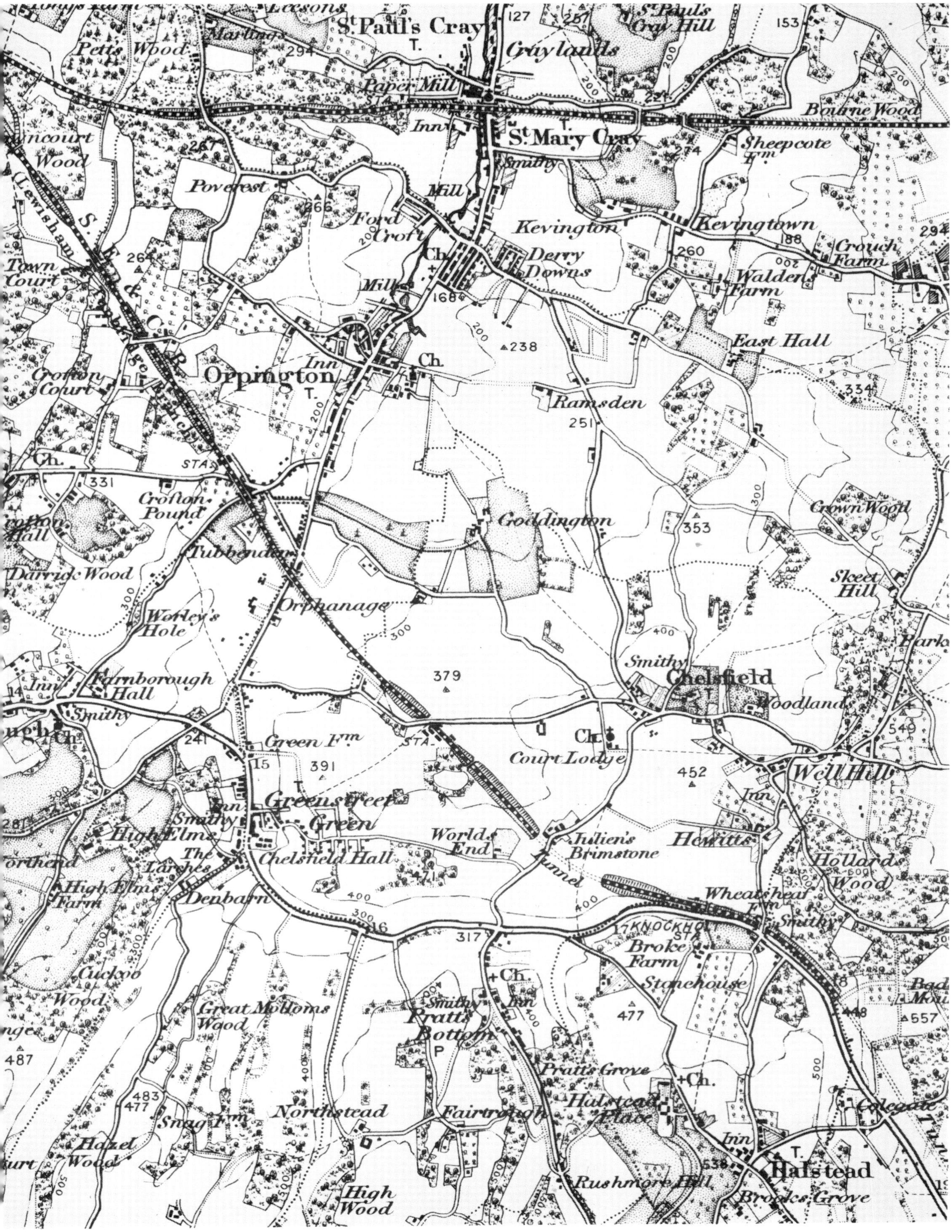

Surveyed 1861-1871. Revised 1901-2. Published 1904.

△
160

Cobham Street
Brooks Place
Little Heath
Ockshot Street
Cobham Till
Cobham Park
Leatherhead Common
Bullocks F.
Stoke D'Abernon
Down Mill
Downside
Well Ho.
Platsome Green
Slyfield F.
Sheep Bill F.
Randall Ho.
Fetcham Common
Isle of Wight
Farm
Mill
Bookham Common
The Rough
Fetcham
Effingham Com.
Eastwick Park
Barn
Lee Wood
Great Bookham
Little Bookham
Fetcham
Roring Ho.
Downs
Effingham
Barn
Common Fields
R

1 2
1 mile approx.

190
▽

△
161

Epsom
Common
Horton
Wood
Epsom
Epsom
Wells
Dukes
Hall
Haunch of
Venison
Woodcot
Park
Rubbing
Ho.
Ashtead
Park
Course
Chapel
Grove
Warren
Walton Downs
Pitt
Wood
from Cornhill
Leatherhead
Common
Little Hurst
Wood
Highlands
F.
Hurst
F.
Parsonage
Fields
from W. Bridge
Headley Court
Headley
Walton
Park
Walton on
the Hill
Gibbons
Grove
Truckler
Wood
Down
Lodge
Mickleham
Ashhurst
Headley
Headley Grove
House
Piblane
Barn
Heath
Bush
Wood

184 ▷

191
▽

162

Brewery
Kniphill Farm
Stoke Wood
Telegraph Hill
Leighill Farm
Little Heath
Oxshott
Oak Shade
Church Cobham
St. Andrew's
Brook Farm
Knowlehill
Charlwood Farm
Newpond Ho.
Cobham Till
Stoke Lodge
Pachesham Park
Leatherhead Common
Cobham Park
Stoke D'Abernon
Woodlands Park
Oak Lawn
Cobham Lodge
Bowhurst Fm.
St. Mary's
Manor Ho.
Brickfield
Sawmill
Downside
Downside Farm
Pachesham
Slyfield House
New Barn Farm
Millfield
Bookham Lodge
Randalls Park
Randalls Farm
Sheepbell Fm.
Dudwick Farm
Bryant's Fm.
Barracks Farm
Station
Monksgreen Farm
Cannoncourt Farm
Newmarsh Farm
Great Bookham Common
Bank's Common
Fetcham Mill
Little Bookham Common
Fetcham Lodge
Fetcham
Thorncroft
Norwood Farm
Church
Fetcham Park
Lonesome Farm
Petty's Farm
The Kennels
River Mole
Lower Farm
Park Farm
Eastwick Park
Eastwick
Indian Farm
Bocketts Farm
St. Nicholas
Great Bookham
Little Bookham
Roaringhouse Farm
The Grange
Church
Fetcham Downs
The Priory
The Rectory
Orestan Farm
St. Lawrence's
Common Fields
Norbury Park
Effingham
The Villa
Effingham Ho.
Goldstone Farm
Lodge Farm
London
Phœnice Farm

192

1 2
1 mile approx.

△
163

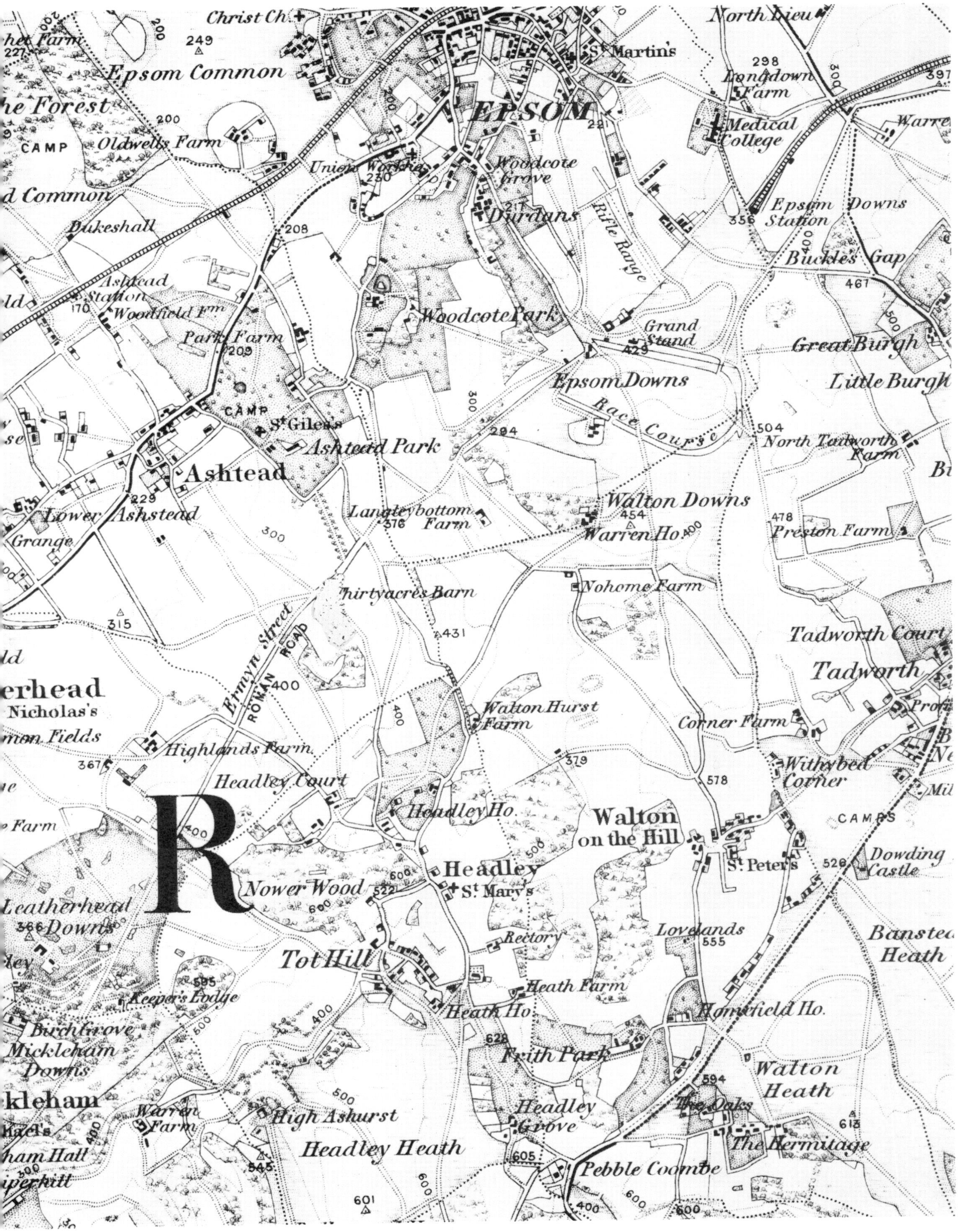

186▷

193
▽

Surveyed 1866-1871. Published 1878.

△
164

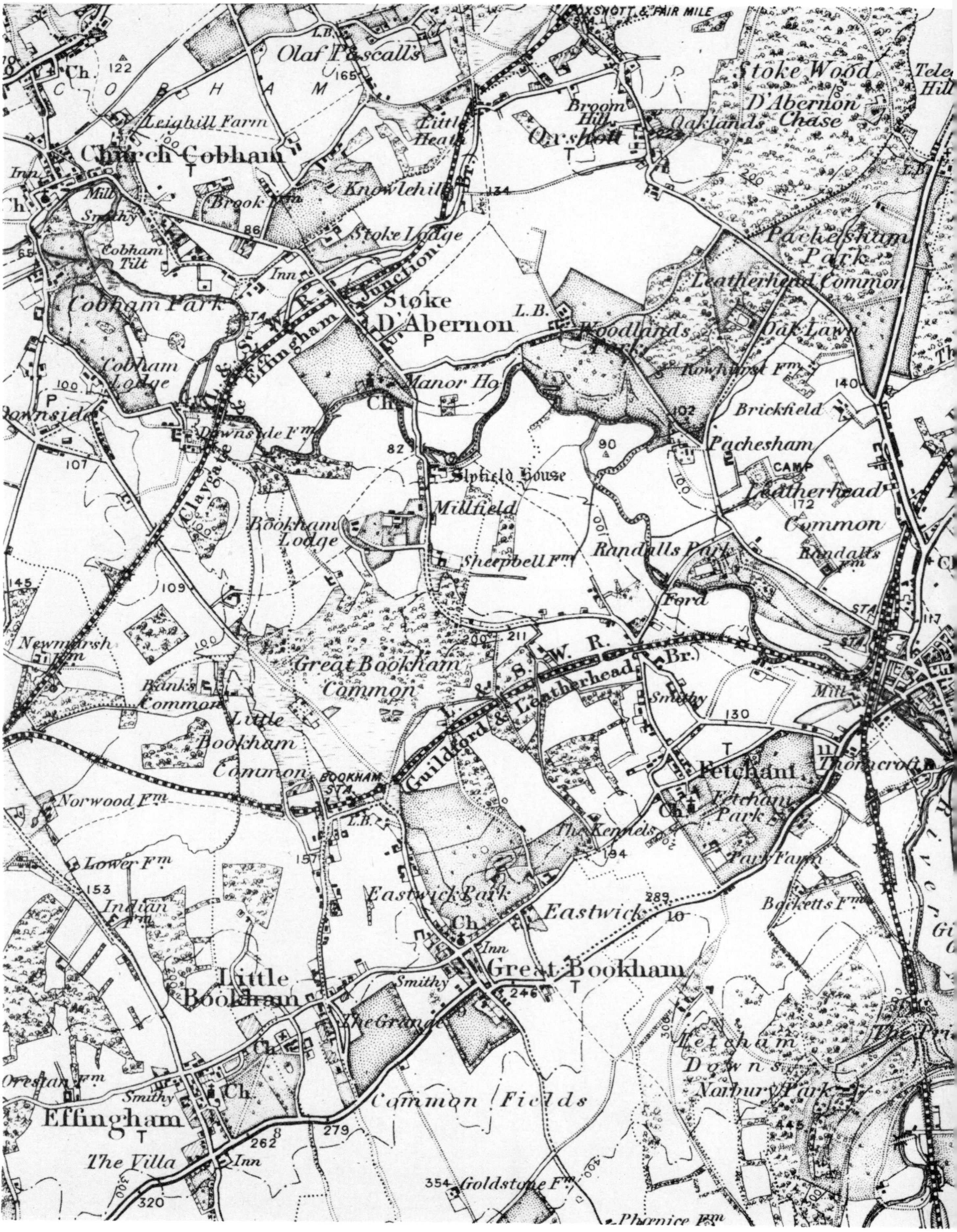
OXSHOTT & FAIR MILE
Olaf Pascall's
Stoke Wood
D'Abernon Chase
Ch.
C O B H A M
Leighill Farm
Church Cobham
Little Heath
Broom Hill
Oakland's
Oxshott
Inn
Mill
Smithy
Brook Fm
Knowlehill
Stoke Lodge
Cobham Tilt
Inn
Junction
Pachesham Park
Leatherhead Common
Cobham Park
Stoke D'Abernon
L. B.
Woodlands
Oak Lawn
Cobham Lodge
Manor Ho.
Rowhurst Fm
Downside
Downside Fm
Brickfield
Pachesham
Slyfield House
CAMP
Leatherhead Common
Millfield
Bookham Lodge
Sheepbell Fm
Randalls Park
Randalls
Claygate
Newmarsh Fm
Ford
S. W. R.
Great Bookham Common
Guildford & Leatherhead
Smithy
Bank's Common
Little Bookham Common
Mill
Fetcham
Thorncroft
BOOKHAM STA.
Norwood Fm
Fetcham Park
The Kennels
Lower Fm
Park Farm
Indian Fm
Eastwick Park
Eastwick
Bocketts Fm
Ch.
Inn
Little Bookham
Smithy
Great Bookham
The Grange
Fetcham Downs
Ch.
Norbury Park
Orestan Fm
Smithy
Effingham
Common Fields
The Villa
Inn
Goldstone Fm
Phenice Fm

194
▽

1 2
1 mile approx.

165

188

195

Surveyed 1866-1871. Revised 1901. Published 1904.

△
166

◁179

Barn
Warren F.
From W. Bridge
Barn
Woodmanstone
Banstead
Parsonage
Banstead Court F.
Borough Street
North Preston
Banstead Heath
South Preston
Reads Rest
Banstead Ho.
Perrots F.
Tadworth Court
Kingswood F.
Chiphouse Wood
Yew Tree Pond F.
Outwood
Great Shabden
The Warren
Old Warren
Old Pigeon Ho. F.
Parsons Green
Rauses
Mugs
Marshall
Hole
Heath
T.Pike
Kingswood
Lodge
Gatton

1 2

1 mile approx.

196
▽

△
167

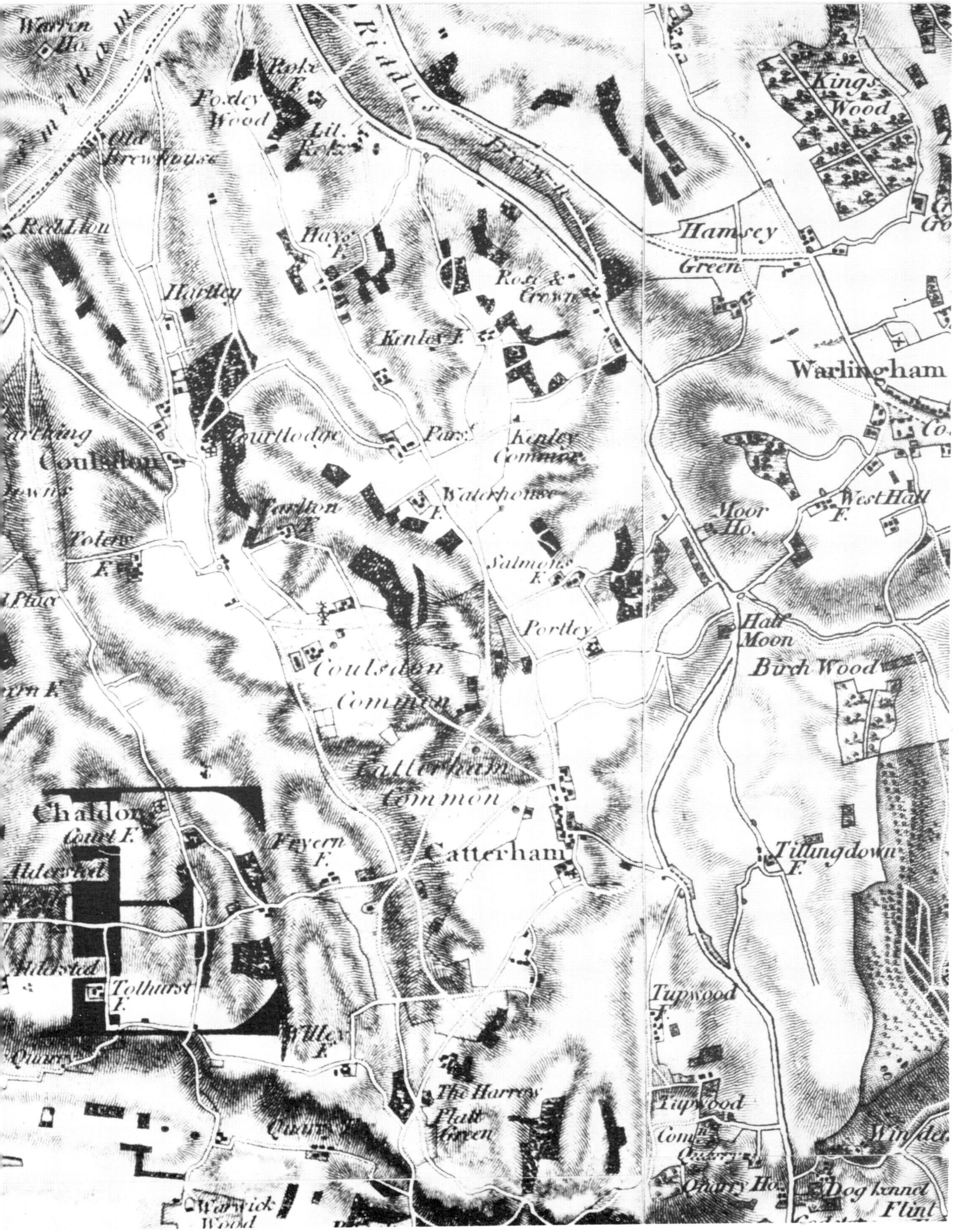

197
▽

Published 1816.

△ 168

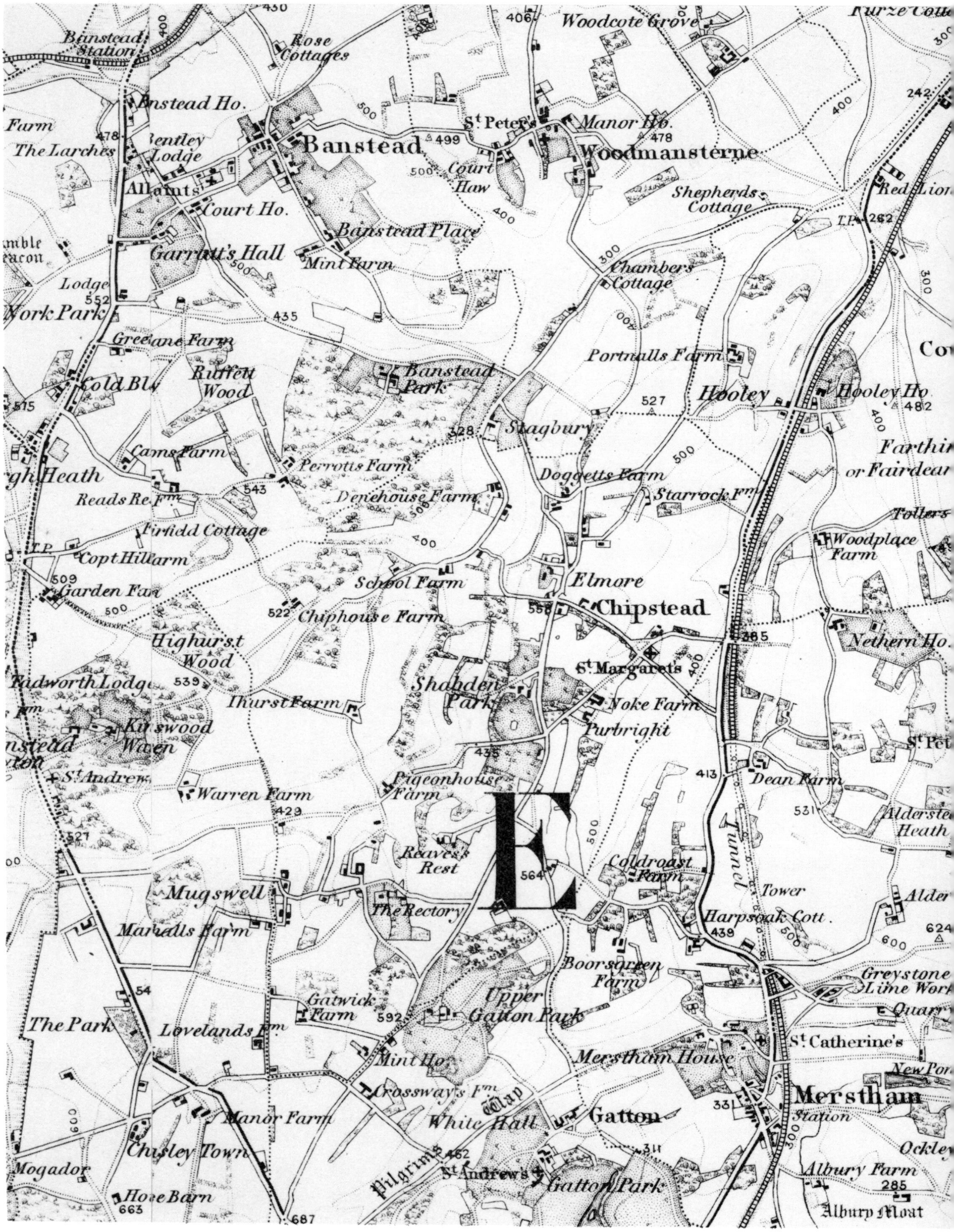
Banstead Station
Rose Cottages
Woodcote Grove
Banstead Ho.
Farm
The Larches
Bentley Lodge
Banstead
St. Peter's
Manor Ho.
Woodmansterne
Court Haw
Court Ho.
Shepherds Cottage
Red Lion
Banstead Place
Garratt's Hall
Mint Farm
Chambers Cottage
Lodge
Portnalls Farm
Banstead Park
Ruffett Wood
Hooley
Hooley Ho.
Stagbury
Cams Farm
Perrotts Farm
Doggetts Farm
Starrock Fm.
Denehouse Farm
Firfield Cottage
Woodplace Farm
School Farm
Elmore
Chipstead
Garden Farm
Chiphouse Farm
Nethern Ho.
Highurst Wood
St. Margarets
Tadworth Lodge
Shabden Park
Ihurst Farm
Noke Farm
Purbright
Kingswood Warren
St. Andrews
Warren Farm
Pigeonhouse Farm
Dean Farm
Reaves's Rest
Coldroast Farm
Tunnel
Tower
Mugswell
The Rectory
Harpsoak Cott.
Marnalls Farm
Boorsgreen Farm
Greystone Lime Works
Upper Gatton Park
Gatwick Farm
The Park
Lovelands Fm.
St. Catherine's
Mint Ho.
Merstham House
Crossways Fm.
Merstham
Station
Manor Farm
White Hall
Gatton
Chussley Town
Mogador
St. Andrew's
Gatton Park
Albury Farm
Hoe Barn
Albury Moat
E

◁ 181

1 2
1 mile approx.

198 ▽

△
169

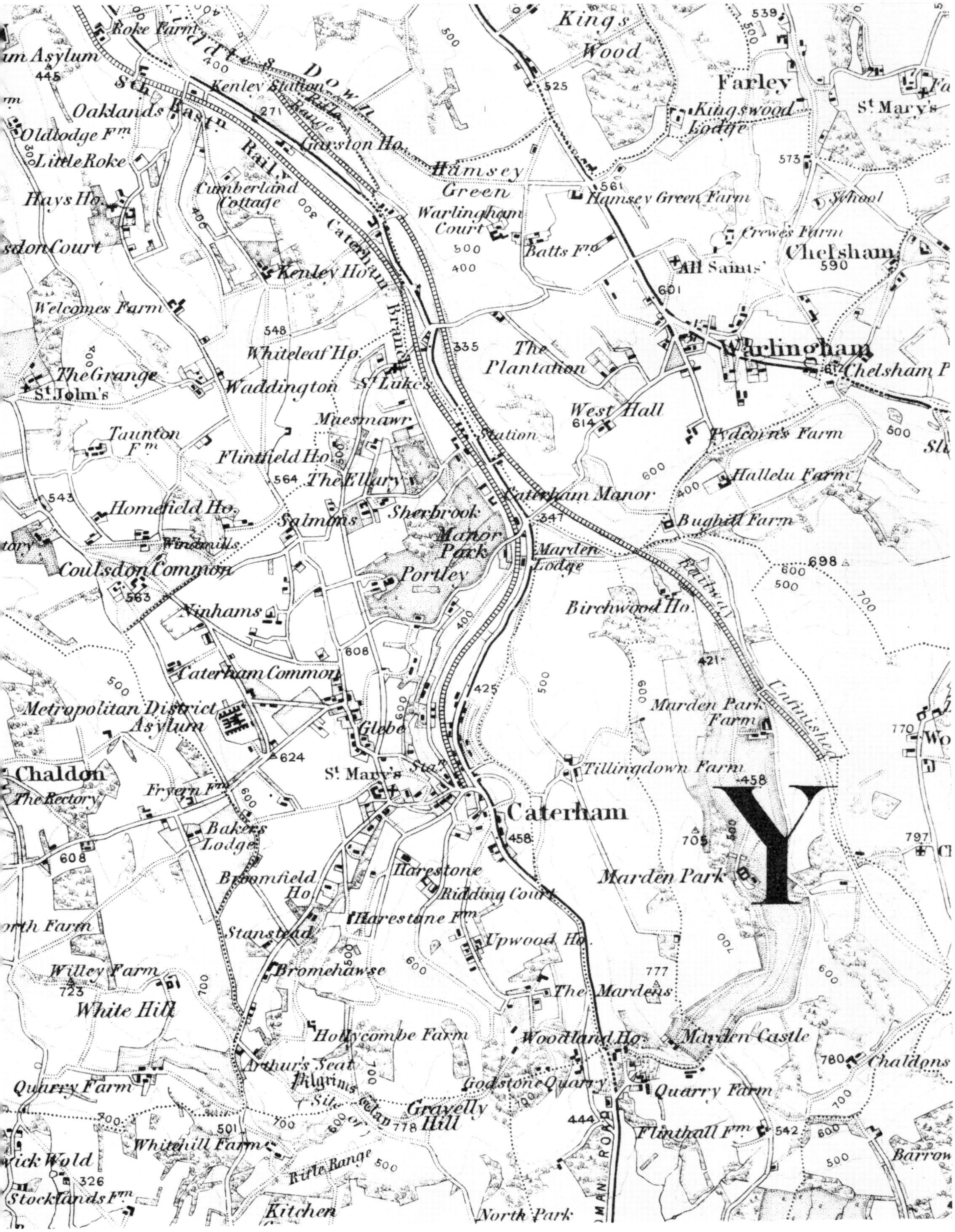

199
▽
Surveyed 1866-1871. Published 1878.

△ 170

◁183

Woodcote Grove
Banstead Sta.
L.B.
Banstead Ho.
Smithy
Banstead
Manor Ho.
Inn
Woodmansterne
Smithambottom
Smithy
The Larches
Ch
Court Haw
Court Ho.
Shepherd's Cottage
Tumble Beacon
Banstead Place
Garratts Hall
Mint Fm
Court Hill
York Park
Asylum
Park Downs
Cold Blow
Ruffett Wood
Chipstead Sta.
Chipstead Valley Rd.
S.E. & C.R.
Hooley
Banstead Wood
Stagbury
Canons Fm
Doghurst Fm
Burgh Heath
Smithy
Copt Hill Ho.
Garden Fm
Elmore
Chipstead
Chipshouse Fm
Kingswood & Burgh Heath Sta.
Highhurst Wood
Shabden
Noke Fm
Tunnel
Kingswood Warren
Smithy
Purbright
Banstead Newton
Kingswood
Old Windmill
Warren Fm
Pigeonhouse Fm
Dean Fm
E
The Reeve
Coldroast Fm
Tunnel
Tower
Mugswell
Rectory
Harpsoak Cott.
Boorsgreen Fm
Gatwick Fm
Upper Gatton Park
Lovelands Fm
Lower Kingswood
Smithy
Mint Ho.
Merstham House
Merstham
Crossways Fm
Manor Fm
White Hall Fm
Gatton
Mogador
Pilgrims
Gatton Park
Albury

200 ▽

1 2

1 mile approx.

△
171

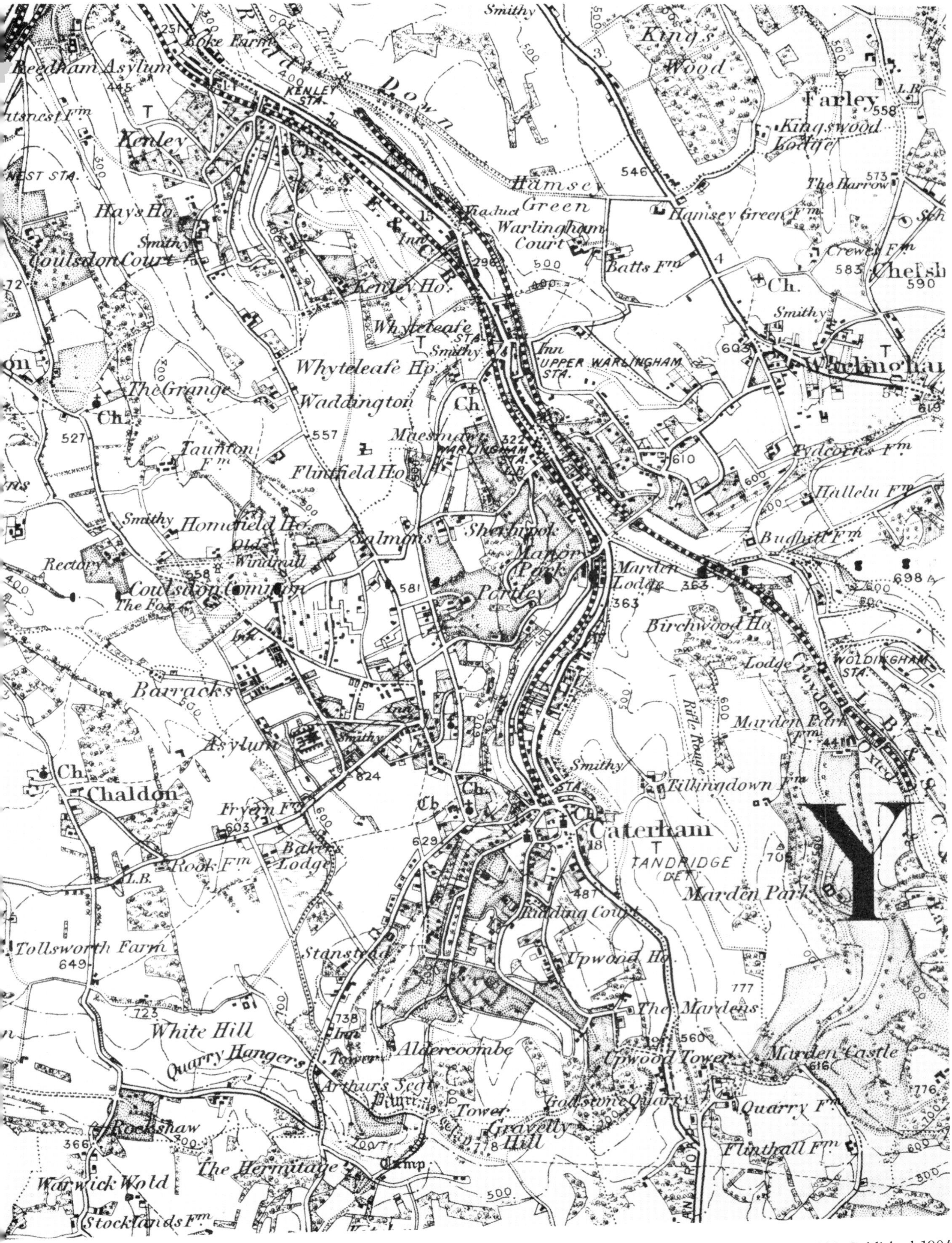

Surveyed 1866-1871. Revised 1901. Published 1904.

201
▽

△
178

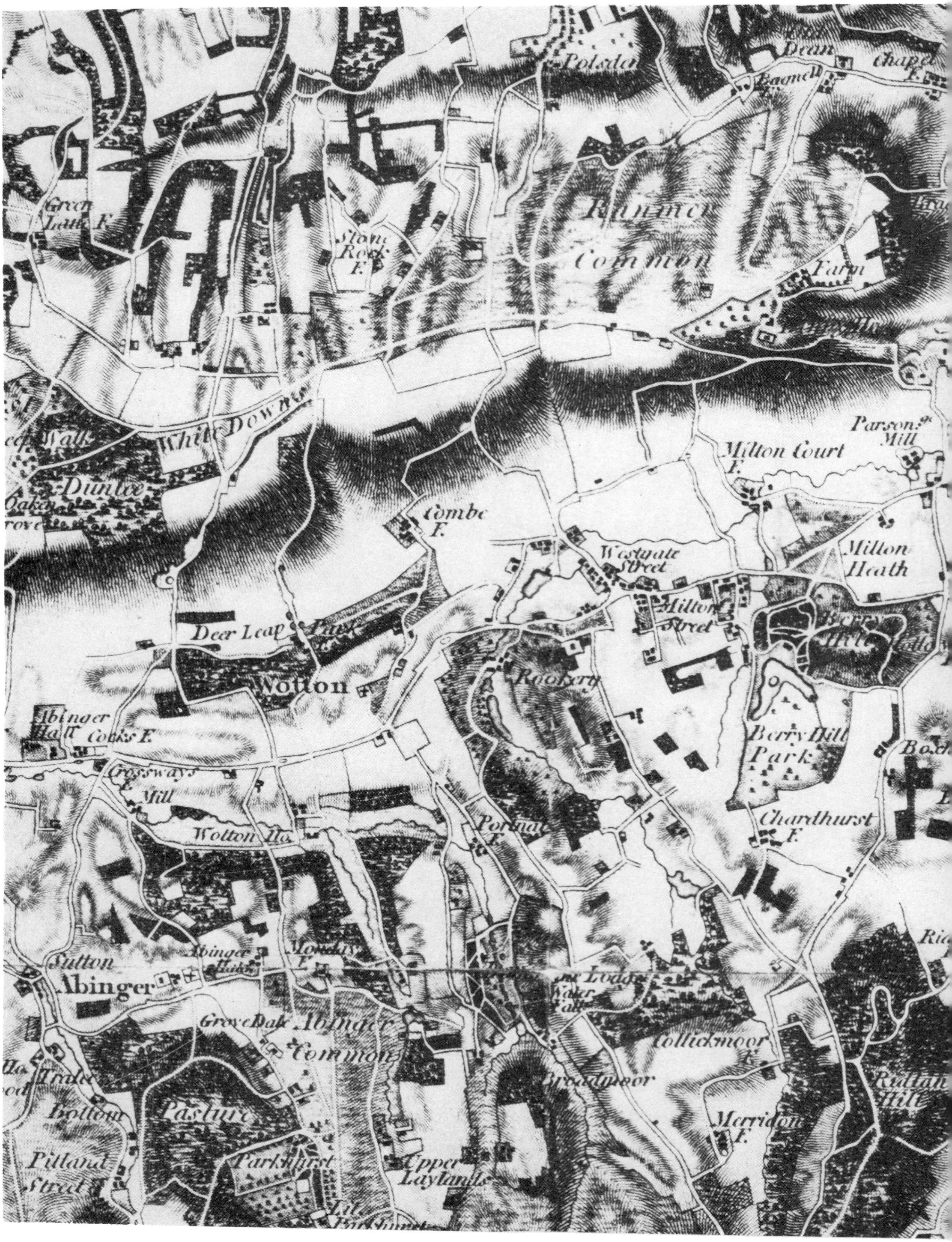
Polsden
Dean
Bagnell
Chapel F.
Green Lane F.
Stone Rock F.
Ranmer
Common
Farm
White Downs
Parson's Mill
Milton Court F.
Dunlee
Oaken Grove
Combe F.
Westgate Street
Milton Heath
Milton Street
Berry Hill
Deer Leap Park
Wotton
Rookery
Abinger Hall
Cooks F.
Berry Hill Park
Crossways F.
Mill
Chardhurst F.
Wotton Ho.
Portnal F.
Sutton
Abinger
Abinger Hall
Monday F.
Grove Dale
Abinger Common
Collickmoor F.
Broadmoor
Bottom
Pasture
Merridon F.
Pitland Street
Parkhurst
Upper Laylands

1 2

1 mile approx.

△
179

DORKING
Box Hill
Mill
Punch Bowl
Betchworth Castle
Betchworth
Brockham Green
Park F.
Chart Park
Parkpale F.
Stove Br.
Scammels F.
Stumblehole F.
Brockham Common
Farnells Com.
Holmwood Common
Peters F.
Ewood F.
Ewood
Shelwood F.
Shelwood Com.
Dun Common
Dawes Green
Leigh
Leigh Place
Leigh Br.
Hill Ho
Gadbrook Com.
Providence
Snower Hill
Moor Place
Wonum Ho
Tranquil Dale
Buckland
Hill F.
Hoppers
Parsonage
Mill
Rice Br.

196▷

Published 1816.

△
180

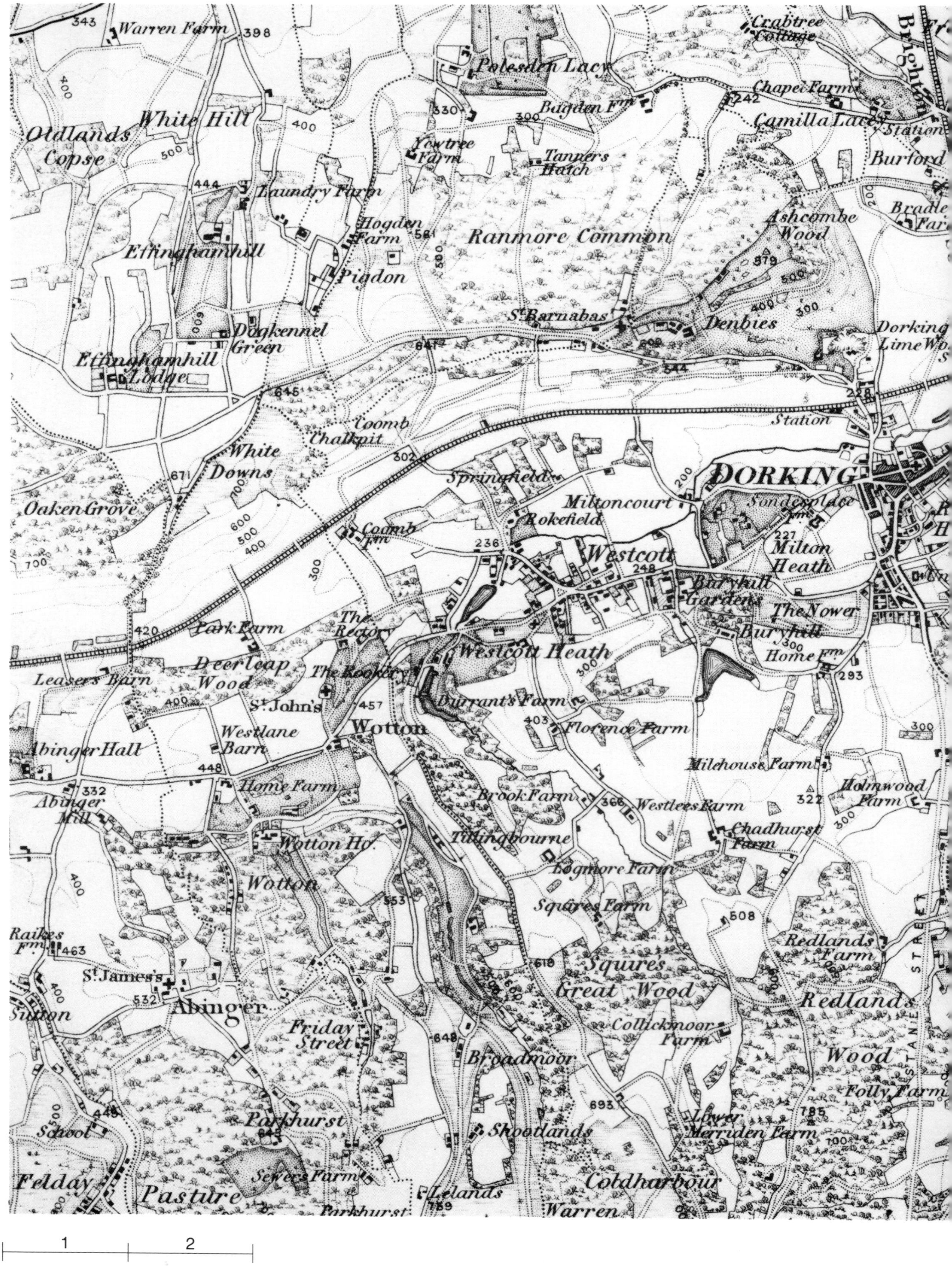
Warren Farm
Polesden Lacy
Crabtree Cottage
Chapel Farm
Bagden Fm
Camilla Lacey
Station
Burford
White Hill
Oldlands Copse
Yewtree Farm
Tanners Hatch
Laundry Farm
Hogden Farm
Ranmore Common
Ashcombe Wood
Effinghamhill
Pigdon
St. Barnabas
Denbies
Dorking Lime Wo
Dogkennel Green
Effinghamhill Lodge
Coomb Chalkpit
Station
White Downs
DORKING
Springfield
Miltoncourt
Sondesplace Fm
Oaken Grove
Rokefield
Coomb Fm
Westcott
Milton Heath
Buryhill Gardens
The Nower
Park Farm
The Rectory
Buryhill
Home Fm
Westcott Heath
Deerleap Wood
The Rookery
Leasers Barn
Durrant's Farm
St. John's
Florence Farm
Westlane Barn
Wotton
Abinger Hall
Milehouse Farm
Home Farm
Holmwood Farm
Abinger Mill
Brook Farm
Westlees Farm
Chadhurst Farm
Tillingbourne
Wotton Ho.
Bogmore Farm
Wotton
Squires Farm
Raikes Fm
Redlands Farm
St. James's
Squires Great Wood
Abinger
Redlands Wood
Sutton
Collickmoor Farm
Friday Street
Broadmoor
Folly Farm
Lower Merriden Farm
Parkhurst
School
Shootlands
Felday
Sewers Farm
Pasture
Coldharbour Warren
Lelands
Parkhurst
STANE STREET

1 2

1 mile approx.

△
181

198▷

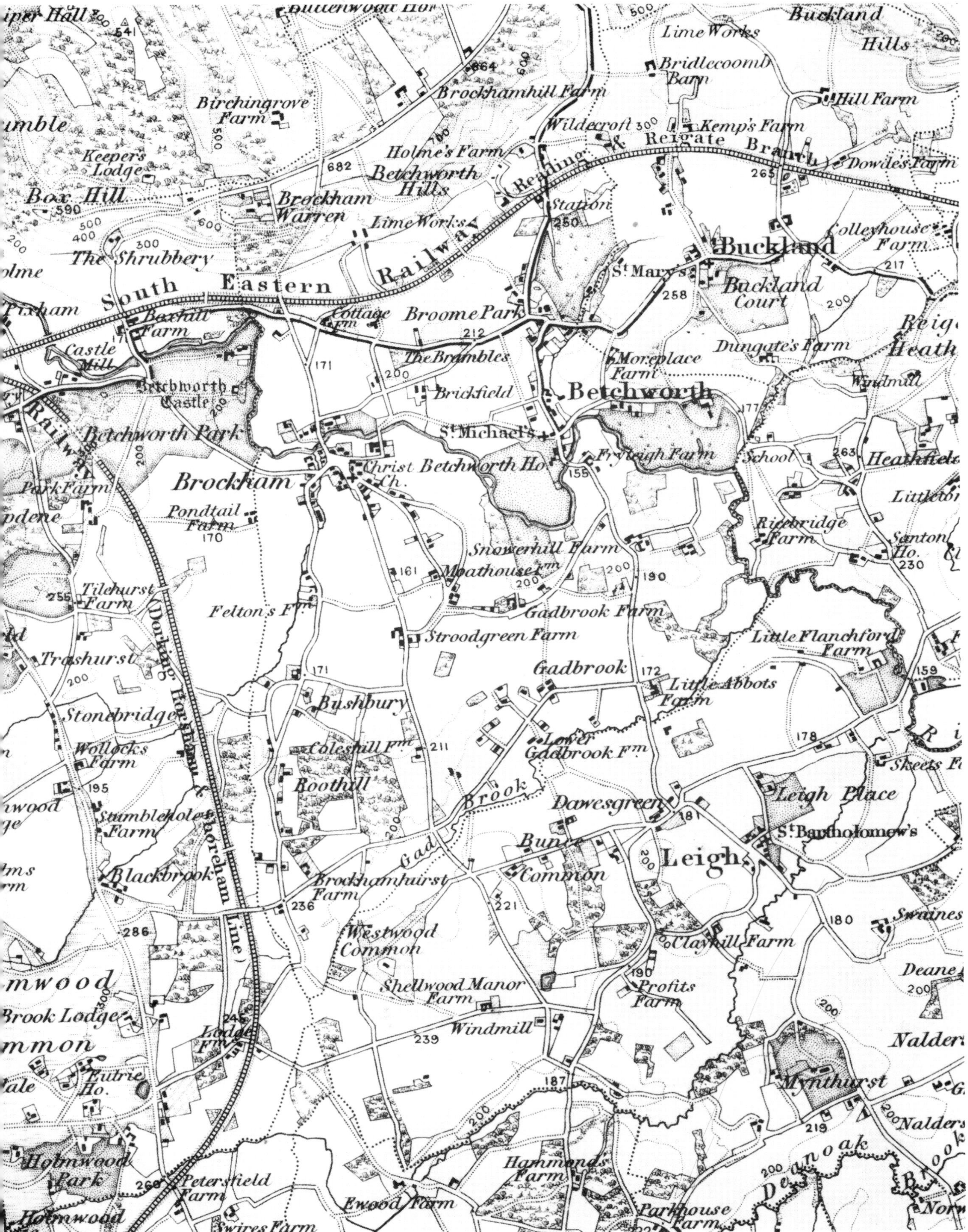
Box Hill
Keeper's Lodge
Birchingrove Farm
Brockhamhill Farm
Holme's Farm
Betchworth Hills
Brockham Warren
Lime Works
The Shrubbery
South Eastern Railway
Reading & Reigate Branch
Station
Buckland
Buckland Hills
Lime Works
Bridlecoomb Barn
Hill Farm
Wildecroft
Kemp's Farm
Dowdes Farm
Collyhouse Farm
St. Mary's
Buckland Court
Broome Park
Cottage Fm.
Pixham
Baxhill Farm
Castle Mill
Betchworth Castle
Betchworth Park
The Brambles
Brickfield
Moreplace Farm
Betchworth
Dungate's Farm
Windmill
St. Michael's
Christ Ch.
Betchworth Ho.
Fryleigh Farm
School
Brockham
Park Farm
Pondtail Farm
Snowerhill Farm
Ricebridge Farm
Santon Ho.
Moathouse Fm.
Gadbrook Farm
Tilehurst Farm
Felton's Fm.
Stroodgreen Farm
Little Flanchford Farm
Trashurst
Gadbrook
Little Abbots Farm
Bushbury
Stonebridge
Wollocks Farm
Coleshill Fm.
Lower Gadbrook Fm.
Roothill
Gad Brook
Skeets Fm.
Leigh Place
Dawesgreen
St. Bartholomew's
Stumblehole Farm
Bunce Common
Leigh
Blackbrook
Brockhamhurst Farm
Westwood Common
Clayhill Farm
Swaines
Deane
Shellwood Manor Farm
Profits Farm
Brook Lodge
Windmill
Lodge Fm.
Nalders
Eutrie Ho.
Mynthurst
Nalders
Holmwood Park
Petersfield Farm
Hammonds Farm
Deanoak Brook
Ewood Farm
Holmwood Corner
Swires Farm
Parkhouse Farm
(Dorking Horsham & Shoreham Line)

Surveyed 1866-1871. Published 1878.

△
182

Warren Farm
Polesden Lacey
Bagden Fm
Chapel Fm
Camilla Lacey
White Hill
Oldlands Copse
Yewtree Fm
Timbers Hatch
Laundry Fm
Hogden Fm
Ranmore Common
Effinghamhill
Pigdon
Ranmore Common
Ch
Denbies
Dogkennel Green
Dunley Hill
S.E. & C.R.
Inn
Reading & Reigate Br.
STA.
DORKING
White Downs
Springfield
Milton Court
Mill
Rokefield
Oaken Grove
Coomb Fm
Westcott
Milton Heath
Mill
Ch
Milton Street
The Nower
Park Fm
Westcott Heath
Home Fm
Deerleap Wood
The Rookery
Tumulus
Ch
Wotton
Florence Fm
Westlane Barn
Inn
Abinger Hall
L.B.
Manor Fm
Westlees Fm
Holmwood
Wotton Ho
Tillingbourne
Chadhurst Fm
Wotton
Logmore Fm
Squires Fm
Raikes Fm
Redlands Fm
Smithy
Tumulus
Ch
Abinger
Squires Great Wood
Redlands Wood
Friday Street
Broadmoor
School
Parkhurst
Abinger Bottom
Shootlands
Lower Merriden Fm
Felday
Coldharbour

1 2

1 mile approx.

△
183

200 ▷

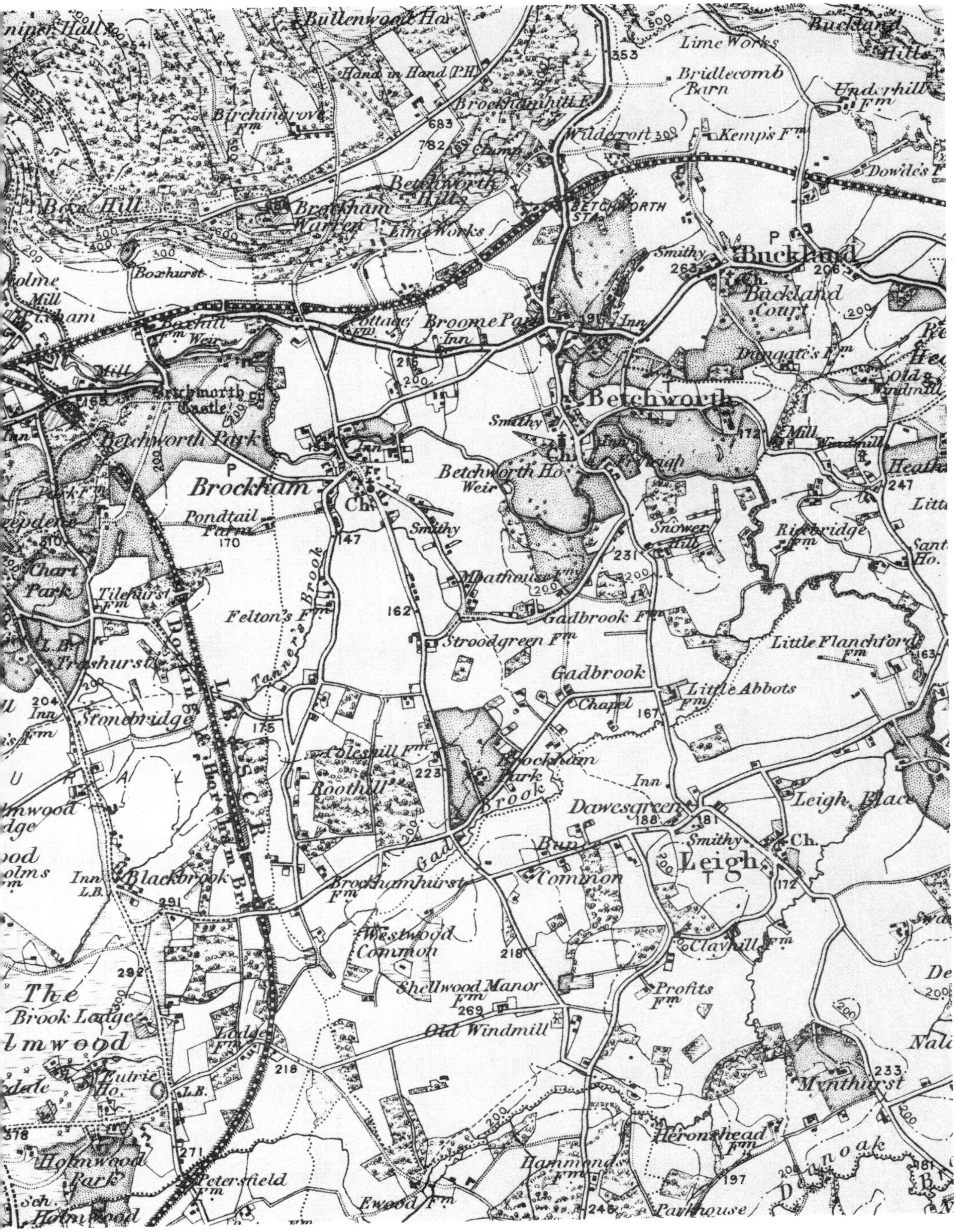

Surveyed 1866-71. Revised 1901. Published 1904.

△
184

◁191

Gatton Park
Kew Lodge
Frenches
Wiggy F.
East Green
Colley F.
Reigate Heath
REIGATE
Linkfield Street
Loose
Ridgley
Oak
Redstone Hill
Copyhold F.
High Trees F.
Red Hill Common
Tan Yard
Cockham Mills
Park Hill
Little London
Roberts Hole
Tan Yard
Work Ho.
Clay Hall
Gander Hole
White Hall
Wood Hatch
Earls Wood Common
Samuel Ho.
Flanchford Place
Hartswood
Hartsw. Lane
River Mole
Kennersley Bridge
Earls Wood
Petridge Wood Common
Petridge Wood
Bears F.
Bell Coppice
T.P.
Kennersley F.
Stumblehole F.
Lodge
Heavywood F.
Lady F.
Wolvers F.
Lodgers F.
Benchurst
20
22
23
24
25

1 2

1 mile approx.

Spins
Barn
Bushes
Wellars
Corner
Tylers Green
Flower Ho.
Place F.
Pendhill
Mercers F.
Nutfield Marsh
Brewer Street
Town F.
Cross Ways
Godstone
Godstone Green
Ivy Ho.
Parson
Courtlodge
Nutfield
Bletchingley
Mill
Gasson Ho.
Stratton Ho.
Chevington Brew Ho.
Woolpits
Brick Kiln
Fox Hole
Lucas
Onions in Hole
Mitchener
Cold Harbor
Porters F.
Kentwin F.
Mill Street
Lit. Hale
Hill F.
Pricklove F.
Stansted Borough
Nashes F.
Nobright F.
Peartree Ho.
Cooks
South Park F.
Henhaw F.
Doghurst F.
Pound Hill
Pound Hill Wood
Grabhill F.
Water F.
Perrys F.
Burstow Park
South Hall F.
Park
Lodge F.
Roughet
Shepherds F.
Brownshill F.
High Stile
Hook House
Stockwood F.
Hook Stile
Woolborough F.
Outwood Comm.
Gay house F.
Anchor F.
Bye Lane
Tedhams
Puckmire F.
Lostland F.
Horne Court F.
Jolly Farmer
Rookery F.
Harrisons
Pagefield

198
186
193

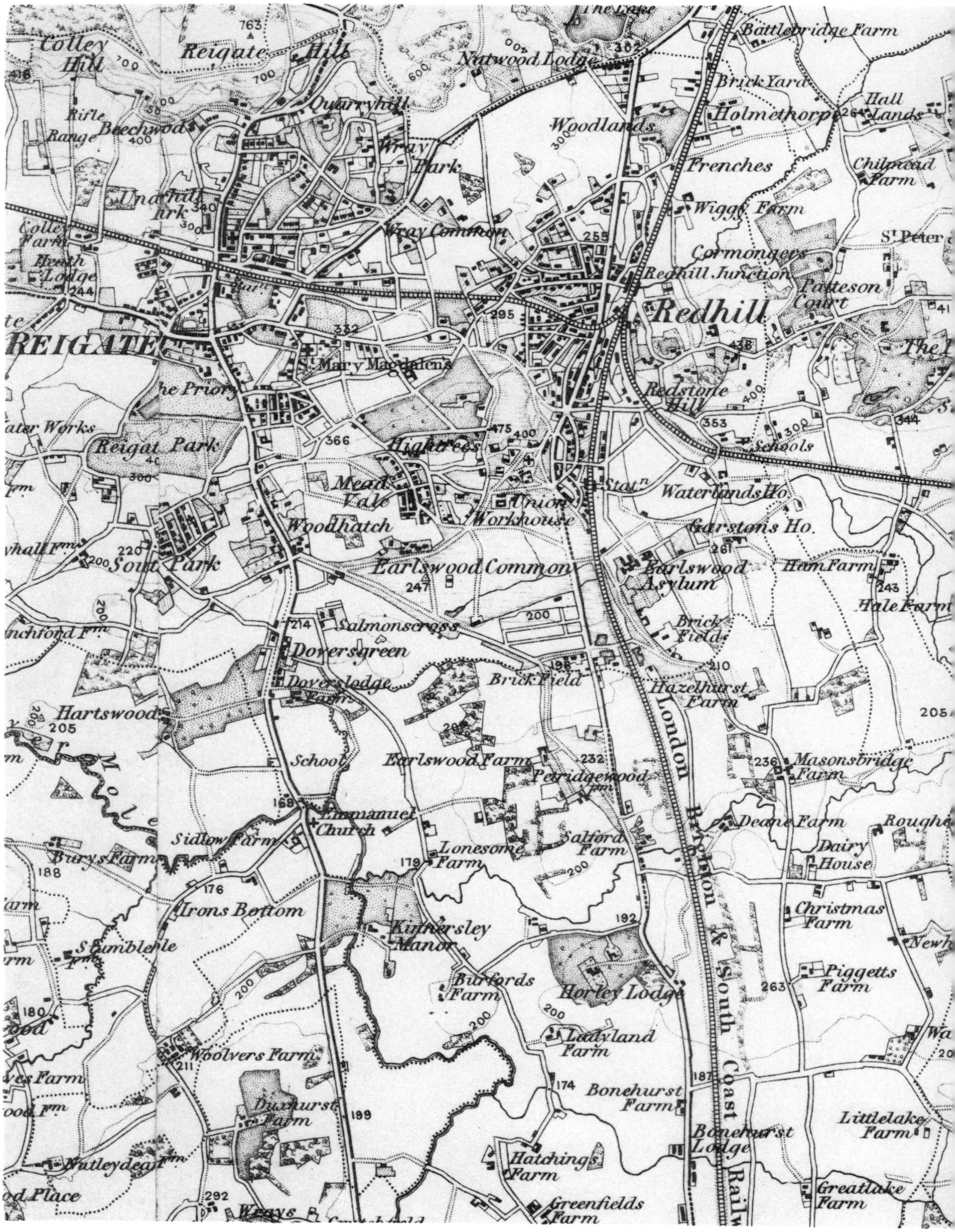
Colley Hill
Reigate Hill
Natwood Lodge
Battlebridge Farm
Brick Yard
Holmethorpe
Hall Lands
Rifle Range
Beechwood
Quarryhill
Woodlands
Wray Park
Frenches
Chilmead Farm
Wiggey Farm
Wray Common
Colley Farm
Heath Lodge
Cormongers
Redhill Junction
Patteson Court
Redhill
REIGATE
St. Mary Magdalen's
Redstone Hill
Water Works
Reigat Park
Hightrees
Schools
Mead Vale
Union Workhouse
Waterlands Ho.
Woodhatch
Garstons Ho.
South Park
Earlswood Common
Earlswood Asylum
Ham Farm
Hale Farm
Salmonscross
Brick Field
Doversgreen
Doverslodge
Hazelhurst Farm
Hartswood
London
Brighton & South Coast Railway
School
Earlswood Farm
Petridgewood Fm.
Masonsbridge Farm
Mole
Emmanuel Church
Deane Farm
Sidlow Farm
Salford Farm
Dairy House
Burys Farm
Lonesome Farm
Irons Bottom
Christmas Farm
Kinnersley Manor
Burfords Farm
Piggetts Farm
Horley Lodge
Ladyland Farm
Woolvers Farm
Bonehurst Farm
Duxhurst Farm
Littlelake Farm
Bonehurst Lodge
Hatchings Farm
Nutleydean Fm.
Greatlake Farm
Greenfields Farm

1 2

1 mile approx.

Place Farm
Lower Barn
Tyler's Green
Rooks Nest
Nagshall Fm
Godstone
The Rectory
Pendhill
Ivyhouse Farm
St Nicholas's
The Vicarage
Waterhouse Farm
Leigh Place
Mill
Union Workhouse
Chevington Farm
Stratton
St Mary's
Garston Ho.
Blechingley
Tilburstowhill
Common
Nutfield
Castle Hill
Sandhills
Coldharbour Fm
Wonham
Oak Cottages
Tilburstow Lodge
Lyttel Hall
Tilburstowhill
Underhills Farm
Posterngate Farm
Nash's Farm
Stansted Ho.
The Shaw
Cucksey's Farm
South Park Farm
Sunnyside
Lagham Wood
South Eastern Railway
Station
Poundhill
Doghurst Farm
Water Farm
Lagham Park
Sunnyside Farm
Lagham
Yewtree Farm
Burstow Park
Lagham Lodge
Old Park Farm
The Mount
Hale Farm
Tower Ho.
Lodge Farm
Woodside
The Grange
Harewood Ho.
Springfield
High Stile
The Poplars
St John the Baptist's Ch
Oaklands
St John's
Outwood
Malt House
Norris's Farm
Blindley
Windmills
Tedham Farm
Road
Hornecourt Manor Farm
Whitewood
Rookery Farm
Whitewood Ho
Oldhall Farm
St Mary's
Horne
Jenkinsland Fm
Burstow

Surveyed 1866-1871. Published July 1878.

△ 188

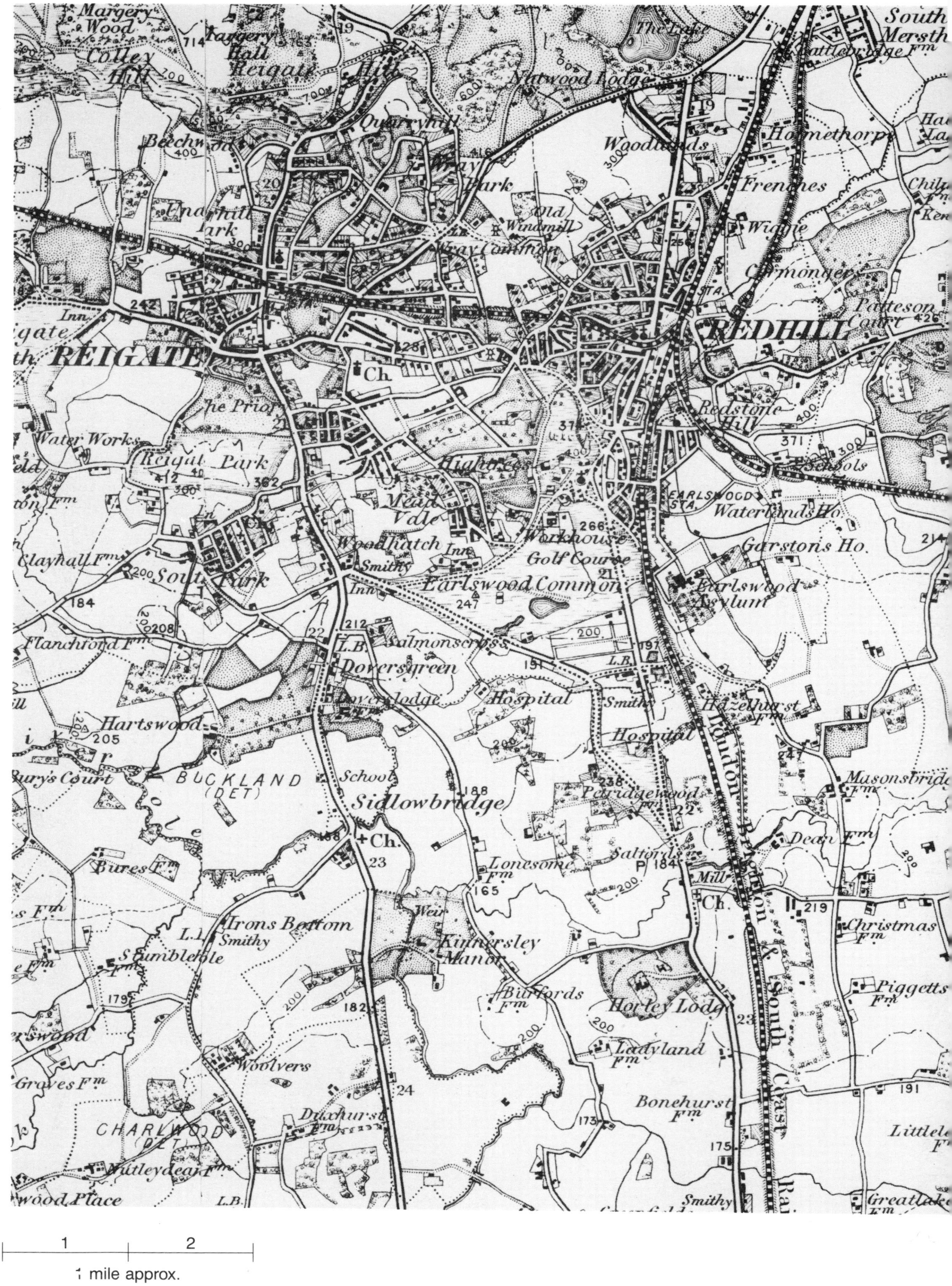
Margery Wood
Colley Hill
Margery Hall
Reigate Hill
Quarryhill
The Lake
Natwood Lodge
South Merstham
Battlebridge Fm
Holmethorpe
Woodlands
Wray Park
Frenches
Underhill Park
Old Windmill
Wray Common
Wiggie
Patteson Court
REDHILL
REIGATE
Ch.
The Priory
Redstone Hill
Water Works
Reigate Park
Schools
Earlswood Sta.
Waterlands Ho.
Mead Vale
Woodhatch
Inn
Smithy
Workhouse
Golf Course
Garstons Ho.
Clayhall Fm
South Park
Earlswood Common
Earlswood Asylum
Flanchford Fm
Salmonscross
L.B.
Doversgreen
Dovers Lodge
Hospital
Hartswood
Hazelhurst Fm
BUCKLAND (DET)
School
Sidlowbridge
Petridgewood
Masonsbridge Fm
Dean Fm
Bures Fm
Lonesome Fm
Mill
Christmas Fm
Weir
Irons Bottom
Kinnersley Manor
Burfords Fm
Horley Lodge
Piggetts Fm
Ladyland Fm
Woolvers
Graves Fm
Bonehurst Fm
CHARLWOOD (DET)
Duxhurst Fm
Nutleydean Fm
Greatlake Fm
London Brighton & South Coast

◁195

1 2

1 mile approx.

△
189

201

Surveyed 1866-71. Revised 1901. Published 1904.

BIBLIOGRAPHY

Greater London: Edited by J.T. Coppock & Hugh C. Price. Published by Faber & Faber Ltd.

London Recollected: Walter Thornbury & Edward Walford. Published by The Alderman Press

The Historian's Guide to Ordnance Survey Maps: J.B. Harley B.A., PH.D. Published by The National Council of Social Service.

Victoria's London – The Suburbs: Percy Fitzgerald. Published by The Alderman Press.

Village London: Edward Walford. Published by The Alderman Press

Index

Map references are indicated by Roman numerals. e.g. Acton 95 97 99. Places refered to in text by italics e.g. Manor House *6*.